Creating Place in Early Modern European Architecture

Creating Place in Early Modern European Architecture

Edited by
Elizabeth Merrill

Routledge
Taylor & Francis Group
LONDON AND NEW YORK

This volume originated as a conference and workshop hosted by the Max Planck Institute for the History of Science in Berlin, on 17-18 May 2018. I would like to thank each of the contributors whose enthusiasm in joining the project and working to shape its aims yielded ten remarkably original and insightful articles. Thanks also to Alina Aggujaro, Susan Klaiber and Anthony Gerbino, who participated in the workshop. I am indebted to Matteo Valleriani, my mentor and champion during my postdoctoral research at the Max Planck, who first encouraged me to undertake this research initiative. Wolfgang Lefèvre deserves special thanks for his kindness and constant encouragement. His research remains a model and inspiration. Finally, I am immensely grateful to Jürgen Renn, the Institute's librarians, and the staff of Department I, who supported this project throughout its many stages. This volume is the result of the generosity and benevolence of the Max Planck Institute for the History of Science.

First published in 2022 by Amsterdam University Press Ltd.

Published 2025 by Routledge
4 Park Square, Milton Park, Abingdon, Oxon OX14 4RN
605 Third Avenue, New York, NY 10158

Routledge is an imprint of the Taylor & Francis Group, an informa business

ISBN: 9789463728027 (hbk)
ISBN: 9781041177692 (pbk)
ISBN: 9781003693383 (ebk)

NUR 654

Cover illustration: Antonio Tempesta, Plan of the city of Rome (detail). Rome: Giovanni Domenico de Rossi, 1645. The Metropolitan Museum of Art, Accession Number: 1983.1027(1-12). Edward Pearce Casey Fund, 1983.

Cover design: Coördesign, Leiden

DOI 10.5117/9789463728027

Table of Contents

Part III Excavating Place

List of Illustrations

Abbreviations

ADN	Archives départementales du Nord, Lille
ANTT	Arquivo Nacional Torre do Tombo, Lisbon
ASPVe	Archivio Storico del Patriarcato di Venezia
ASR	Archivio di Stato di Roma
ASSi.	Archivio di Stato di Siena
ASVe	Archivio di Stato di Venezia
BAV	Biblioteca Apostolica Vaticana
BMCVe	Biblioteca del Museo Correr
BNCF	Biblioteca Nazionale Centrale Firenze
BnF	Bibliothèque nationale de France
BSB	Bayerische Staatsbibliothek, Munich
MET	The Metropolitan Museum of Art, New York City
MLUB	Universitätsbibliothek Kassel, Landesbibliothek und Murhardsche Bibliothek
NA	Nationaal Archief, The Hague
OAR	Oud Archief van Rijnland, Leiden
ONB	Österreichisches Nationalbibliothek
SLUB	Sächsische Landesbibliothek, Staats- und Universitätsbibliothek, Dresden
SUB	Niedersächsische Staats- und Universitätsbibliothek, Göttingen

Introduction: Embracing Specificity, Embracing Place

Elizabeth Merrill

A place is defined both by geographical location and human experience. Place is space, occupying real physical form, which has been arrogated for a given social use. The Roman concept *genius loci* recognizes the spirit of place as independent and unique to each location. Architecture, in turn, can be understood as an activity that both signals and responds to place in the recognition, delimitation and establishment of confines. Distinguishing between the site and the structures erected on it, Aristotle defined place as the immobile surface of the containing body in direct contact with the contained body. There is place that is physically marked, as well as place that is more nebulously defined by institutional factors, political borders and sensorial elements. Yet places are by no means passive, objects to the actors of human ingenuity. They contain the capacity for generation and are inherently generative, their innate qualities – in the sense of a landscape, climatic zone or geographical environment – being formative in the creation of architecture. A place can serve as a locus of a project, directing architecture's discovery of what already exists, and illuminating roots, outlines and unvarying constants.[1]

This book explores the construction of place in architecture in early modern Europe (1400-1750).[2] Each of the book's ten essays takes a distinct historical subject and examines the wider relationships between environmental categories (place, site and context), different stages in the design process, the interaction between project and construction, and the contextual use of tools and materials. 'Architecture', as explored here, corresponds to that of the period considered, and encompasses the built environment in its entirety, as well as the tools and machines applied

1 This definition of place draws upon Casey, 'How to Get from Space to Place in a Fairly Short Stretch of Time'; de Sola-Morales, 'Place'; Lefebvre, *The Production of Space*; Norberg-Schulz, *Genius Loci*; Summers, *Real Spaces*; and Cosgrove and della Dora, 'Introduction'.

2 The decision to characterize this period as 'early modern', as opposed to 'medieval' or 'Renaissance', is deliberate. Whereas the latter terms carry distinct historiographic connotations, 'early modern' is more inclusive.

Merrill, E. (ed.), *Creating Place in Early Modern European Architecture*.
Taylor & Francis Group 2022
DOI: 10.5117/9789463728027_INTRO

in its production. The objects of examination include mills and machines, dams, sluices and scaffolding, foundations and fortifications, as well as church balconies, imposing palaces and canonical theories. Archival evidence takes the form of patent records, workaday drawings and graphic models, maps, musical scores, workshop inventories and legal texts. Collectively, the essays show how the making of early modern architecture was inseparable from context, and from the social relations, institutional supports and strategic processes upon which it was founded.

The contributions to this book were originally developed as part of a workshop dedicated to 'The Spaces of Early Modern Architectural Production', hosted in May 2017 at the Max Planck Institute for the History of Science in Berlin. Our common interest lay in the manifold practices, materials and social structures that contributed to the production of architecture in the early modern period. The aim was to combine approaches of the history of science and the history of architecture, moving away from the inordinate focus typically placed on the individual – whether this be the singular architect or the unparalleled construction – and instead to call attention to systems of knowledge and more quantifiable practices. Assembling a group of scholars expert in different epochs of European architecture and building, the meeting also presented an opportunity to look beyond modern political boundaries and national historiographies. The coherence of the contributions was in part due to planning, and in part by chance. While all of the meeting's participants came prepared to speak on space and architectural production, as we proceeded it became increasingly clear that the collective concern was not generic, homogenous and isometric 'spaces'. Rather, we were interested in more distinct *places*, and the architectural practices that were enacted on or derived from a given site and culture.

As the product of this collective research endeavour, this volume investigates topics that are highly site (and place) specific, concerning Amsterdam, Ulm, Rome and Venice, a given workshop, a singular church, a specific drawing. The fact that nearly all of the essays are heavily based on primary source materials is telling. To study place is to study in detail. Individually, each of the ten essays enriches a more specific subfield to which it belongs, whether this be geographically, thematically or temporally defined. But united in their investigation of common questions about the structures of architecture – whether these be intellectual, creative or physical – the contributions join a common dialogue.

Between Space and Place in Early Modern Architecture

As an examination of place, this volume joins an expansive body of literature. The philosophies of Gaston Bachelard and Henri Lefebvre are definitive, along with the phenomenological studies of Edward Relph and Yi-Fu Tuan.[3] There is likewise an informative body of architectural theory that examines place, primarily in the context of the modern and contemporary built environment. The formulations developed by Christian Norberg-Schulz, Alfonso Acocella and Kenneth Frampton have provided useful models in the development of this project.[4]

Although there has been no significant study of place in regards to the making of early modern architecture specifically, the concepts of space and place are foundational to the discipline. The history of early modern art is saturated with studies on the site-specific aspects of artistic production. Beginning with Vasari, historians of the period almost instinctively define their subjects according to place. A more explicit engagement with the concepts of space and place has likewise produced some of the definitive intellectual frameworks for considering early modern art. Erwin Panofsky's *Perspective as Symbolic Form* paved the way for an extensive body of scholarship on the theoretical conception of space and the Renaissance 'invention' of pictorial space.[5] His conceptualization of the Renaissance itself as a place offered an intellectual framework for historians of the discipline to draw ties between social, cognitive and technical practices.

Although not limited to the early modern period, the growing concern with world art history and the globalization of the discipline has underscored the concepts of place and space.[6] In the studies of Thomas DaCosta Kaufmann, space is traced in terms geographical coordinates and locales of cultural interchange. David Summers' call for the study of places as real social spaces, examined in terms of universal principles, provides a new framework for understanding works of art across cultural and temporal epochs. The model of *Real Spaces* has been informative to the conception of this volume and our collective aim to examine conditions of architectural planning and production across distinct contexts. The globalization of art history has also brought early modern scholars to recognize the hoary concepts of centre and periphery. Benefitting from the canonical models of Ferdinand Braudel and William McNeill, among others, historians of architecture and art have given increased attention to what were previously considered 'marginal' locales. Recent

3 Bachelard, *The Poetics of Space*; Lefebvre, *The Production of Space*; Relph, *Place and Placelessness*; Tuan, *Space and Place*. Casey, *The Fate of Place*, provides the philosophical history of the idea of place from antiquity to the modern period.

4 Acocella, *Architecture of Place*; Frampton, *Technology, Place & Architecture*; Norberg-Schulz, *Genius Loci*.

5 See, among others, Damisch, *The Origin of Perspective*; Field, *The Invention of Infinity*; and Edgerton, *Renaissance Rediscovery of Linear Perspective*.

6 DaCosta Kaufmann, *Toward a Geography of Art*, also addresses architecture, but the focus is primarily art in its geographical dimensions. See DaCosta Kaufmann, Dossin and Joyeux-Prunel, 'Reintroducing Circulations'.

years have brought incisive new studies on Renaissance architecture in Eastern Europe, Central America and South America.[7]

Related to the themes of globalization and circulation is historians' increasing interest in mobility and the urban nodes of cultural exchange. Scholars like Luca Molà, David Kim, Frits Scholten and Joanna Woodall have called attention to the physical migration of artists and craftsmen as a deeply embedded cultural practice. Travel was a determinate factor in the advancement of artistic and technological innovations, and implicitly reinforced the importance of place.[8] In the study of cities and urban planning, the predominant focus remains on social structures and sensory experience. In the past decade, the important studies of Marvin Trachtenberg and Manfredo Tafuri have been joined by those of Niall Atkinson, Donatella Calabi and Elena Svalduz, and Fabrizio Nevola, which look at the articulation of spaces of social and symbolic significance, and examine their physical forms as a reflection of local practices.[9]

The essays of this volume might be considered as extensions to this broad body of literature. Within these pages, we consider the creation of specific places, as well as the transfer of ideas and models between places, and the theoretical tools employed to envision place. The contributions are exceptional in their express interest on the systems, tools and conditions that directed early modern architecture and building practices. Paging through the index, the reader will find few references to the period's signature architect-protagonists. Indeed, in the study of Ludovica Galeazzo, a group of nuns dictate the major building developments. In Paul Brakmann and Sebastian Fitzner's contribution, the little-known Johannes Faulhaber takes centre stage. In Edward Triplett's, it is the surveyor Duarte de Armas. While the research assembled here does consider some of the era's most notable structures and sites, it is not in terms of their characteristic forms. The essay of Stefan M. Holzer and Nicoletta Marconi concerns the estimable St. Peter's Basilica, but looking past the contributions of Bramante and Michelangelo calls attention to the systems of scaffolding and building machinery that enabled the structure's continual maintenance. Merlijn Hurx looks at Amsterdam Town Hall from literally the ground up, with a focus on its subterranean foundations and piles.

7 On the importance of the work of Braudel and McNeill in the development of global history see, DaCosta Kaufmann, Dossin and Joyeux-Prunel, 'Reintroducing Circulations', 8-9. Lee, 'Introduction', underscores multidirectional cultural transfer in Europe in the fourteenth and fifteenth centuries. Among the recent studies of Renaissance architecture outside of Western Europe are those of Arciszewska, 'Architectural Crossroads', and 'Early Modern Conceptualizations of Medieval History'; and Schreffler, *Cuzco*.

8 Kim, *The Traveling Artist in the Italian Renaissance*; Molà, 'States and Crafts'; Scholten, Woodall and Meijers, *Art and Migration*.

9 Atkinson, *The Noisy Renaissance*; Calabi and Svalduz, *Il Rinascimento italiano e l'Europa*; Nevola, *Street Life in Renaissance Italy*; Tafuri, *Ricerca del Rinascimento*; Trachtenberg, *Dominion of the Eye*.

My own contribution highlights Siena's Santa Maria della Scala, with an emphasis not on the celebrated spaces of its *casa grande*, but rather on the myriad grange complexes it constructed in the Sienese *contado*. Federico Bellini's study begins in the spaces of the Baroque churches of Bernini and Borromini, examining their well-known sculptural forms in relation to the invisible mechanisms that shaped their design: music, musical composition and performance.

The book thus expands the history of early modern architecture and provides new models for understanding its creation. The European-wide focus is unique. Aware of our inherent biases, we have sought to look beyond the 'place'-specific confines of our studies, and to delineate parallels and points of intersection across geographic and temporal confines. While architectural history is still very much shaped according to distinct national 'schools', this study highlights the ubiquity of certain ideas and practices. Looking forward, historians of early modern architecture – like the remarkably transient and cosmopolitan subjects of their study – are invited to look beyond borders, geographic and disciplinary, and to consider architecture in terms of the practices by which it was made rather than the art of a single 'genius'.

'Place' in the Early Modern Period

The concept of place as a specific entity, something that *holds* and *contains*, and that in turn, generates, had a strong presence in early modern thought. The intensely self-reflexive and identity-driven nature of the period made it particularly inclined to think in terms of places.[10] In Italy, the contemporary practice among artists of assuming a moniker according to their place of origin – here, it is perhaps sufficient to name Leonardo da Vinci, Giuliano da Sangallo, and Pietro da Cortona – speaks to the close association between the individual and the identity of a given location. The artistic development of linear perspective – the 'symbolic form' of Renaissance culture – might likewise be considered to reflect a distinct concept of place. In creating perspectival landscapes, trompe l'oeil stages, and volumetric cityscapes, artists were not merely representing space – empty and infinite – rather, they were constructing specific places, delineated with concrete contours and occupied by objects and figures.[11]

10 This idea has been repeated in numerous studies, from Burkhardt, *The Civilization of the Renaissance in Italy*, to Greenblatt, *Renaissance Self-Fashioning*. Recently, Enenkel and Ottenheym, 'Introduction', linked the creation of identity in the early modern period to contemporary political, intellectual and religious developments.

11 As a system for visualizing and ordering the real world, the use of linear perspective also reflexively defined place by fixing the distance and location of visual appearances. Cropper, 'The Place of Beauty in the High Renaissance and Its Displacement in Art History', 59-60; Kanerva, *Between Science and Drawings*, 153.

Within the case studies presented here, there is little evidence that the individuals involved in the creation of architectural places explicitly recognized them as such. However, the essential concept of place, as something that bore a distinct social identity and that responded to topography, was latent in their thinking, embedded in a cultural tradition that extended back to antiquity. In writings of classical philosophy, from ancient Greece through the medieval period, 'place' is commonly understood according to the Aristotelian definition, as the immobile surface of the containing body in direct contact with the contained body. The Greek term for place, *ho topos*, was translated in Latin as *locus*, and distinguished from *spatium* (space) and *ubi* (literally 'where'). As used by classical authors, *spatium* refers to the distance between two points, and more generally, as a measure of quantity, area and time. In Latin it is often used as a geometric term, designating the area enclosed within a geometric figure, tangible and measurable, or in the heavens and infinite.[12]

Within Western history there is a strong correlation between a given locale and the cultural production it fosters. In the study of natural history, conditions related to geography, climate, location and topography are recognized as key factors that affect the quality of a place and its air (*aira*), and by extension, the people of that place and their production. The categorization of works of art and architecture according to their place of origin appears in the writings of Herodotus, Lucian and Pliny.[13] Vitruvius, in his *De architectura*, speaks of place within the context of *firmitas* (strength), *utilitas* (utility) and *venustas* (beauty).[14] Place relates to the suitability of a given site, its weather, environment and resources.[15] He likewise addresses 'places' (*locis*) in the context of a given city, distinguishing public places, including the plan of the walls and the layout of the public buildings, from private ones.[16] Places, and specific individuals and monuments located therein, are also associated with the creation of the columnar orders and their appropriate use. Although Vitruvius was certainly not concerned with theorising the concept of place as such, he clearly recognized places as specific environments, distinguished by conditions that were either natural or man-made. Space (*spatium*), in turn, was more neutral, and he used this term more generally denote an area, as in a plot of land to be surveyed.[17]

12 On the Aristotelian concept of place, see Casey, *The Fate of Place*, 50-71; see also Grant, 'The Concept of *Ubi* in Medieval and Renaissance Discussions of Place'; Rowland, 'Renaissance Ideas of Space', 1.

13 DaCosta Kaufmann, 'Introduction', 1-3; see also Kim, *The Traveling Artist in the Italian Renaissance*, 44-46; DaCosta Kaufmann, *Toward a Geography of Art*, 1-17.

14 For a basic overview of these concepts, Kruft, *A History of Architectural Theory*, 24-27, is instructive.

15 Vitruvius, *Ten Books on Architecture*, book I.4, and throughout book 2, on materials.

16 Ibid., book I.3

17 Ibid., books I.5 and I.6. Rowland underscores Vitruvius' use of *spatium* in reference to a certain location beneath the heavens, the *spatium caeli*.

Expanding upon the Vitruvian tradition, writers on early modern architecture captured the importance of place, although rarely in strict theoretical terms. Within the literature, the idea of place is evoked with multiple terms. In Italian, place is associated with '*luogo*', '*paese*' and '*terra*'; in French with '*lieu*'; in German with '*Platz*', '*Ort*', '*situs*', and '*Grund*'; and in Dutch with '*plaats*' or the nearly synonymous '*plek*'. The plurality of terms employed for 'place' speaks to the complexity of the concept, which bears both tangible and intangible qualities.

Beginning with Leon Battista Alberti, the first published theorist of early modern architecture, we see a nuanced understanding of place, which carries both metaphysical and practical connotations. The conditions of a place – in terms of its natural environment, accessibility and resources – affected the health and character of its inhabitants, and were even considered determinative of their prosperity, government and laws.[18] In his *De re aedificatoria* (c. 1450), Alberti underscores air quality as a crucial factor when selecting a building site: 'Who can have failed to notice the extensive influence that climate [*aria*] has on generation, growth, nourishment and preservation?'[19] In the second book of the treatise, he again addresses place within the context of architectural siting and foundations.

> Having constructed these models, it will be possible to examine clearly and consider thoroughly the relationship between site and the surrounding district [*situm & areae ambitum*], the shape of the area, the number and order of the parts of a building, the appearance of the walls [...] and in short the design and construction of all the [building] elements.[20]

The idea that the building plan essentially unfolds from the condition of the site is again emphasized by the German theorist Walther Ryff, in his 1548 commentary of Vitruvius, in which the terms '*Platz*' and '*Ort*' are used to describe a structure's site and foundations.[21] In the seventeenth century the English architect Henry Wotton went so far as to personify place in regards to the 'seat' and 'situation' of a construction. 'I must say that in the *Seating* of our selves (which is a kinde of *Marriage* to a *Place*) *Builders* should bee as circumspect as *Wooers*.'[22]

Francesco di Giorgio pursues a similar path of inquiry in the second rendition of his *Trattato di architettura* (c. 1490) – reflecting on the determinative qualities of

18 Alberti, *I libri della famiglia*, 228-230; Alberti, *The Family in Renaissance Florence*, 182-183. On Alberti's discussion of place, see also the contribution of Nele De Raedt in this volume.

19 Alberti, *On the Art of Building in Ten Books*, book I.3.

20 Ibid., 34. For the original Latin, Alberti, *De re aedificatoria* (Florence, N. di Lorenzo, 1485), book II.

21 See Ryff, *Vitruvius Teutsch*, book IV.

22 Wotton, *The Elements of Architecture*, 6. Italicized text is in accordance with the original.

topography, climate and materials – as does his Sienese follower, Pietro Cataneo.[23] Expounding upon city planning in his *I quattro primi libri di architettura* (1554), Cataneo explains that the conditions of place (*luogo*) determine the character of its inhabitants, and in turn, their architecture. 'And wanting to enlarge or fortify the site [...] to make it an honourable city, there are clear indications of good air, good water, and good soil, if the men who live in such places are attractive, well proportioned, with good colour, and happy appearance, and if they have many children.'[24]

Cataneo's reference to the strength of a site and its inhabitants introduces the centrality of the place concept in the field of early modern defence design, which was revolutionized with the ascendency of firearms. Francesco di Giorgio opens with the topic in his *Trattato di architettura*, as transmitted in the codex Saluzzianus 148 (c. 1485), asserting that 'First of all is to be considered the site [*sito*] and the quality of the place [*loco*]', as weak topographical features must be buttressed against attack. He then follows with a reference to Vitruvius, noting that 'we see the ancients placed [*avere posto*] all of their forts in the most strong and eminent places [*luoghi*] they could find, and most in the defended cities and for their conservation'.[25] Albrecht Dürer's *Etliche underricht, zu befestigung der Stett, Schloss und flecken* (1527) gives equal emphasis to place, methodically specifying the city's ideal site, topography, plan and organization.[26] Tellingly, Daniel Specklin of Strassburg, active as a military architect, cartographer and engineer, opened his *Architectura von Vestungen* (1589) with a discourse on the site survey, linking '*Ort*' with the practice of '*Chorographia*'.[27] The substantial *Architettura militare* (1599) of Francesco de Marchi again reiterates the importance of place, asserting that it is the architect's responsibility to design according to the dictates of a specific place. De Marchi, active in the Low Countries and Italy, advised: 'skilful and ingenious soldiers and architects will be able to build both impregnable and beautiful works,

23 In book one of the *Trattato*, conserved in the codex Magliabechianus II.I.141, Martini, *Trattati di architettura*, vol. 2, 303-310.

24 Cataneo, *I quattro primi libri di architettura*, book I.3 (3v): 'e si disiderasse con aggrandirlo e recingerlo di mura farne honorata città; seranno indicii manifesti di buon'aria, buon'acque, e buon'erbe, se gli huomini di tal luoco seranno belli, ben proportionati, di vivo colore, & lieto aspetto, con la multiplication grande di lor figli'.

25 Martini, *Trattati di architettura*, vol. 1, 3: 'In prima è da considerare el sito in qualità del loco, imperò che altro richiede un loco montuoso, altro un piano, e così secondo i luoghi più o manco debili, da quella parte dunde più offesi sieno a quella principalmente è da riparare. [...] [N]oi vediamo gli antichi avere posto tutte le fortezze ne' più forti e eminenti luoghi che hanno trovato, e massime nella città a defensione e conservazione d'essa.' This passage, which also addresses the well-composed and proportioned human body, is discussed by Noam Andrews in this volume.

26 See the commentary and transcription of Fara, *Albrecht Dürer*.

27 I am grateful to Sebastian Fitzner for this reference. See Specklin, *Architectura von Vestungen*, IV.

in accordance in with the dictates of the site [*sito*], that will comply with the rules of art, put into execution [*posta in essecutione*] by a man of skill and ingenuity'.[28]

The idea that the 'skilful and ingenious' architect should bring place- and site-specific knowledge to his work is echoed in the discussions of Philibert de l'Orme. Reflecting on the character of the architect in his *Le premier tome de l'architecture* (1567), de l'Orme reiterates that plan and theory are not enough. It's essential that the architect 'choose and find good master masons who know how to properly execute and implement'. Likewise, he must be able to draw, know well the project, and be able to 'take measures, set the schedule, and give place to the workers [*lieu aux ouvriers*]'.[29] Philibert's use of place in this context underscores the patent association between practice and place. This is similarly captured in the 1577 treatise of the Dutch architect Hans Vredeman de Vries, who emphasizes the need to align form and practice with place. Instead of following 'the antique Italian manner', he advocates for a more flexible interpretation, which takes into account local conditions and building practice. In strengthening his argument, he cites the famous Netherlandish masters Cornelis II Floris and Jacques Du Broeucq, who had accommodated ancient models to the 'necessities and customs of this country'.[30]

The discussion of Vredeman de Vries reflects early modern theories of architectural decorum, the principle, adopted from classical rhetoric, that a building's form should not only accord to its function, environment and position, but should uphold established social norms. In this context, place is understood not only as a physical locale, but also as something that can be crafted and defined according to prescribed social norms. The idea that architectural decorum was linked to place is epitomized in Sebastiano Serlio's Book VI, *Of Habitations Suitable for All Grades of Men*, which puts forth an order for domestic building types, organized

28 De Marchi, *Architettura militare*, 6v: 'Però li valenti, & ingeniosi Soldati, & Architetti, potranno in simil sito far cose inespugnabili, & belle, per la commodità del sito, che ubidirà all'arte, posta in essecutione da valent' huomo ingenioso.'

29 De l'Orme, *Le premier tome*, book IX.9: 'Je dirai encore davantage sur ce propos pour avertir les architectes et ceux qui font profession de conduire bâtiments, que ce n'est pas assez d'entendre bien tous les traits pour savoir montrer et enseigner ce qu'il faut faire, mais bien plutôt de choisir et trouver de bons maîtres maçons qui le sachent proprement exécuter et mettre en œuvre [...] et signamment si l'architecte n'a lui même tracé les pierres, jaçoit que ce ne soit son état, ni chose à propos, et à laquelle il sut fournir, pour avoir le soin à tant d'autres choses auxquelles il lui faut pourvoir, pour donner les mesures et commander en temps et lieu aux ouvriers, pour les affaires qui se présentent.' Notable also is the discussion of place by de l'Orme, *Le premier tome*, in book III.8: 'The firmness of a place to be grounded can be seen and known in various ways, and signally by the nature of the land' ('La fermeté d'un lieu pour faire fondement se peut voir et connaître en diverses sortes, et signamment par la nature des terres'). He again addressed place when speaking of antiquities and the appropriate use of specific practices and models. See de l'Orme, *Le premier tome*, book V.1.

30 Thanks to Merlijn Hurx for this reference.

according to location and social hierarchies.[31] As given by Serlio, residences placed in the country inherently differ from those placed in the city; and within a given social order, the residence of the prince finds its 'place' higher than those of the merchant, craftsman and peasant.[32]

In Serlio's widely circulated printed treatises, a building, and the place it occupies, follow certain formulae as distinct commonplaces or *topoi*.[33] Upon initial reflection, this formulation seems to invert the notion of place as something one-of-a-kind and entirely unique. But if we consider place itself as a commonplace – place as providing a framework by which architecture is structured – then the concept opens itself for further specification. The *topoi* delineated by Serlio were places for the insertion of inventions. Like so many of his contemporaries, Serlio sought to codify rules, but ultimately put forth a formulae that allowed for free interpretation and embellishment. Put in different terms, the *topoi* of early modern architectural theory constitute a pattern by which a discourse, taking the form of a building process, might be realized.

Architecture as Discursive Practice

Rhetorical metaphors are often coupled with discussions of place. Understood in literal terms, places – physical entities that may be identified by geographical coordinates – are often associated with specific languages and dialects. In the art of memory, places take form in images; they are the *loci* of the memory systems that sustained rhetoric and writing prior to the ascendancy of printing.[34] As a theoretical concept, the definition of place is also dialectical. The discourses implicit in describing place are subjective and at time even contradictory, as place is delineated both by what it is and what it is not.[35] Histories and theories of European architecture have likewise drawn analogies between language and architecture. Architecture, understood as a language or discourse, extends beyond the design of buildings; it is a means of communication, built upon specific vocabulary and grammar, and adheres to distinct social customs and practices. For Renaissance theorists, the architecture-language analogy undergirded the search for a canon

31 Serlio, *On Architecture*, book VI: 'Of Habitations'. Serlio, *On Architecture*, book VII: 'On Situations', also discusses residential building types and their placement, as well as building ornament and gates. The place-specificity of these designs is implicit, but Serlio says little about the study of place or site.

32 Here, I benefit from Summers' discussion of 'place, relation and hierarchy' (*Real Spaces*, 123).

33 For discussion on Serlio's book VI, see Carpo, 'The Architectural Principles of Temperate Classicism'. Carpo introduces the idea of Serlio's printed palace plans as a type of *topos* (p. 148).

34 Yates, *The Art of Memory*.

35 Vos, 'Introduction', xi.

of architectural forms and rules, and sanctioned practices of imitation as akin to those of the great classical authors.[36]

While the analogies between language, architecture and place are not the focus on this book, in our concern with the latter two subjects, the concept of discursive practice provides a useful heuristic. As given by Foucault, a discourse creates its subjects. Language *uses* individuals, and various forms of speaking, or discursive practices, offer places for various kinds of subjects.[37] If we define architecture as a discourse, it follows that architecture creates the architect, not vice versa. This is to say, the place of architecture – itself a *topos* – is more important than the individual there engaged. In this formulation, architecture (as language) is a continuum, into which a given architect (as a speaker) is only temporarily engaged. The actualization of the discourse, moreover, requires a certain kind of speaker, as statements and *topoi* within a given language cannot be made by anyone. The value and efficacy of such statements reside in their delivery by someone who is qualified to make them.[38] The idea of architecture as discursive practice thus draws attention to the mechanisms involved in the making of places and buildings.

The analogy helps to clarify our thinking about the notoriously vague figure of the architect in early modern Europe.[39] In this period, the architect was not defined solely by his work, as this might easily include actions that had nothing to do with art, building, or spatial design. As is well known, moreover, the architect pursued no explicitly delineated course of training or apprenticeship. His duties were defined less by a distinct professional profile than they were by the project at hand.[40] The difficulty of understanding the early modern architect is further compounded when we expand the geography of our focus or seek to draw comparisons across between distinct polities. The training and practice of 'architect' in Rome was different than that in Paris, Amsterdam and Nuremberg. Further, professional titles were often misleading, as an individual considered an 'architect' in one city might well be considered an engineer, surveyor, painter or master carpenter in another. But considering architecture in terms of discursive practices allows us to sidestep the innumerable theoretical stalemates that arise when examining the

36 For an overview on the analogy between language and the visual arts in the Renaissance, see Clarke and Crossley, 'Introduction', 1-7.

37 Schapiro, *Language and Political Understanding*, 63.

38 Ibid., 146; see Foucault, *Archaeology of Knowledge*.

39 On the character of the Renaissance architect, see Biral and Morachiello, *Immagini dell'ingegnere*, 11-15; Ettlinger, 'The Emergence of the Italian Architect during the Fifteenth Century'; Keller, *A Theatre of Machines*, 1-4; Kemp, 'From "Mimesis" to "Fantasia"'; Merrill, 'The "*professione di architetto*" in Renaissance Italy'.

40 It has been said that in the early modern period the title 'architect' was contingent on active practice. Trachtenberg, *Building-in-Time*, 106, comments that 'there was no such thing as an unemployed architect', and that in the practice of architecture, the architect defined himself.

title, background and character of the early modern architect. The essays of this volume consider the architect in relation to the work he executed. The discipline of architecture, in this context, involved not solely the artistic practices and products related to the planning, designing, and constructing of buildings; architecture also encompassed the broader spectrum of processes by which place was constructed, delineated and embodied, factors that were inseparable from context.

The protagonists of these studies vary considerably and many were not 'architects' according to a modern understanding. But regardless of how they were defined, these individuals were conversant in a common architectural language; they partook in and fostered a shared body of knowledge. In this sense, the architecture-language analogy facilitates our investigation beyond place. While each contribution examines a distinct place, the systems, practices and themes disclosed within are more universal. By defining the practices inherent in local dialogues and site-specific conditions, and then mapping their intersection across regions, cultures and epochs, we are able to better understand the creation of architecture in early modern Europe, and to further delineate the practices and knowledge that defined the 'architect'.

The Narrative

In examining early modern architecture, the historian first looks to the buildings themselves, if they remain. Secondary sources are also essential to understand a given construction, its forms, function, and making. Drawings and models help to tell this part of the story, as do printed representations, archival records, commentary and theories on architecture. But there is much in early modern architecture that cannot be captured in an image, explained in a document or even perceived in a site visit, hundreds of years after construction commenced.

In emphasizing the place of architecture – something it is embedded in and inseparable from – the chapters of this volume seek to offer a more holistic understanding of early modern architecture. In this light, our purview extends from the elemental and often intangible elements of building design – including its administrative and cultural functions, and mediated social norms that conceptually mark its place – to the more concrete processes and tools that enabled a structure's realization. The structure of this volume reflects this range, the essays divided into three parts, which address architecture's engagement with place in increasingly tangible forms.

Wolfgang Lefèvre's essay on 'Architecture on Paper' provides an instructive starting point, examining the localization of architectural production in the form of drawings. As argued by Lefèvre, the development and use of perspectival drawing across early modern Europe served as the lingua franca among practicing architects.

The wide range of drawings considered here span from those physically tied to place, including those traced on a cathedral wall, to those that, having been printed are made transient, translating what was a singular physical place into something that is ephemeral, common and mundane.

The specificity of a site is explored in terms of social, theoretical and cultural determinants in book's first part, 'Marking Place'. In these studies, the 'place-ness' of architecture is extends beyond its visual and three-dimensional character. In Federico Bellini's study of sonorous spaces in sacred buildings, the function and even the form of music is translated into the architecture of Baroque churches like Sant'Ivo alla Sapienza in Rome. In the case of the Santacroce in fifteenth-century Rome, discussed by De Raedt, the family's place along the Via in Publicolis is delineated by civic law. Following the Santacroce's conflict with the Della Valle, the Roman *civitas* sought to erase its presence, both by physically exiling certain members of the family and destroying their residential properties. For Andrews, early modern architecture may be mapped using contemporary cosmological discourses and theories on the celestial realm. Unlike the Baroque churches and Santacroce family palaces in Rome, the places addressed by Andrews are out of grasp, taking form in visualizations, outer space and theory. But the architectural practices to which they relate are real. The three essays align in showing how non-architectural discourses of the early modern period had real impact on design and building practices.

The book's second part, 'Teaching Place', casts light on places of architectural education, and the knowledge codified therein, taking examples from fifteenth-century Siena, seventeenth-century Ulm, and Rome and central Europe in the period from roughly 1650 to 1850. In my own contribution, the landholdings of the Spedale di Santa Maria della Scala in Siena may be collectively understood as a place. By managing and developing its properties over centuries, the hospital institution came to serve as both a building contractor and an architectural school, in which knowledge was developed, uniting a group of Sienese-based practitioners, and perpetuated through copy drawings and two-dimensional models. The transmission of architectural knowledge, and specifically, the knowledge amassed at a certain place, is likewise central to the articles of Paul Brakmann and Sebastian Fitzner, and Stefan M. Holzer and Nicoletta Marconi, which address, respectively, the *Kunstkammer* of Johannes Faulhaber in Ulm and the *Fabbrica* of St. Peter's in Rome. Faulhaber's *Kunstkammer*, a place of architectural production, collection and education, was mediated through a series of publications, by which knowledge of the Ulm collection came to be distributed throughout much of Europe. The technical tradition of St. Peter's *Fabbrica* was similarly codified and propagated in print, through teaching and the publication of sequential editions of *Castelli e ponti*. As discussed by Holzer and Marconi, the workshop of St. Peter's in Rome, as a distinct place, served not only as the physical backdrop for the construction of the great church, but also provided the epistemological foundation for this work. It was within the workshop that new structural systems and scaffolding were developed, which were employed in the Vatican and elsewhere in Rome. Nicola Zabaglia was one protagonist of this space, but as the authors show, the tradition of the *Fabbrica* extended far beyond this one figure.

The volume's final part, 'Excavating Place', addresses place in its most concrete form, examining practitioners' direct contact with the natural world in the physical delineation of spatial contours. The essay of Merlijn Hurx finds its place in the 'hollow land' of the Low Countries, with an analysis of seventeenth-century deep pile foundations. Citing archival reports and drawings, Hurx demonstrates that Dutch deep pile foundations constituted its own place-derived field of expertise. Yet, far from a generic, tradition bound body of knowledge, the design and construction of Dutch pile foundations were explicitly site-specific. The practices of plotting, planning and surveying outlined by Hurx bridge his essay with the final two contributions, which explore the creation of place in fifteenth-century Venice and sixteenth-century Portugal. The essays of Ludovica Galeazzo and Edward Triplett explore what might be termed 'liminal place': the articulation of place through the creation of boundaries. Both studies grow out of a close analysis of property records, which actually record or describe landscapes, in the real and legal sense. The places mapped, however, also have a 'place' dimension beyond their real spatial contours. Galeazzo's discussion of the urban construction of the *insula dei Gesuiti* in Venice provides an insightful account of property creation in the early modern period, by which the boundaries of the lagoon were physically altered. But as the product of contemporary social, political and ideological conditions, this new land also assumed an identity and form that was distinctly Venetian. Whereas in Galeazzo's study a place was physically made from where there had previously been water, in Triplett's examination of the Portuguese fortification and border maps of the *Livro das fortalezas*, the physical sites existed, but were virtually fashioned into distinct places through Duarte de Armas' chorographic representations. Triplett's own images, created using GIS and 3D modelling technology, mediate the depicted place of the *Livro das fortalezas* with the topographical place, as it exists today.

The essays of this book are intended to provide fresh insights into the history of early modern architecture in Europe and to offer new models for future study. Taken together, the contributions reveal an emphasis on the modes of architecture, including the training of the architect (or whoever designed and realized buildings in the early modern period), the means by which designs and places were virtually transmitted, networks and processes of communication, worksite structures, social conditions that drove certain ideological and formal developments, and the physical tools, foundations and machines that enabled architecture's ascent. The information and ideas presented are by no means absolute or unequivocal. A volume like this invariably has limitations, in terms of its geographic and temporal scope, the types of subjects examined, and the methods employed. Given the breadth of our guiding concept, much more can still be written on how place related to the creation of early modern architecture. In the years to come, we look forward to reading these studies. And we look forward to learning more about all the conditions and characters – extraordinary and run-of-the-mill – that shaped early modern architecture.

Bibliography

Acocella, Alfonso, *An Architecture of Place* (Rome: Laterconsult, 1992).
Alberti, Leon Battista, *De re aedificatoria* (Florence: N. di Lorenzo, 1485).
Alberti, Leon Battista, *The Family in Renaissance Florence*, trans. by Renée Neu Watkins (Columbia: University of South Carolina Press, 1969).
Alberti, Leon Battista, *On the Art of Building in Ten Books*, trans. by Joseph Rykwert, Neil Leach and Robert Tavernor (Cambridge, MA: The MIT Press, 1988).
Arciszewska, Barbara, 'Architectural Crossroads: Migration of Architects and Building Trade Professionals in Early Modern Poland 1500-1700', in Konrad Ottenheym (ed.), *Architects without Borders: Migration of Architects and Architectural Ideas in Europe 1400-1700* (Mantua: Il Rio Arte, 2014), 61-75.
Arciszewska, Barbara, 'Early Modern Conceptualizations of Medieval History and Their Impact on Residential Architecture in the Polish-Lithuanian Commonwealth', in Karl Enenkel and Konrad Ottenheym (eds), *The Quest for an Appropriate Past in Literature, Art and Architecture* (Leiden: Brill, 2019), 649-681.
Atkinson, Niall, *The Noisy Renaissance: Sound, Architecture, and Florentine Urban Life* (University Park: Pennsylvania State University Press, 2016).
Bachelard, Gaston, *The Poetics of Space* (Boston: Beacon Press, 1994).
Biral, Alessandro and Paolo Morachiello, *Immagini dell'ingegnere tra quattro e settecento* (Milan: Franco Angeli, 1985).
Burkhardt, Jacob, *The Civilization of the Renaissance in Italy* (New York: Random House, 1954).
Calabi, Donatella and Elena Svalduz (eds), *Il Rinascimento italiano e l'Europa. VI. Luoghi, spazi, architetture* (Vicenza: Angelo Colla, 2010).
Carpo, Mario, 'The Architectural Principles of Temperate Classicism: Merchant Dwellings in Sebastiano Serlio's Sixth Book', *RES: Anthropology and Aesthetics* 22 (1992): 135-151.
Casey, Edward, *The Fate of Place: A Philosophical History* (Oakland: University of California Press, 2013).
Casey, Edward, 'How to Get from Space to Place in a Fairly Short Stretch of Time: Phenomenological Prologeomena', in Steven Feld and Keith H. Basso (eds), *Sense of Place* (Santa Fe: School of American Research, 1996), 13-52.

Cataneo, Pietro, *I quattro primi libri di architettura* (Venice, 1554).

Clarke, Georgia and Paul Crossley, 'Introduction', in Georgia Clarke and Paul Crossley (eds), *Architecture and Language: Constructing Identity in European Architecture, c. 1000-c. 1650* (Cambridge: Cambridge University Press, 2000), 1-20.

Cosgrove, Denis and Veronica della Dora, 'Introduction: High Places', in Denis Cosgrove and Veronica della Dora (eds), *High Places: Cultural Geographies of Mountains, Ice, and Science* (London: I.B. Tauris, 2008), 1-17.

Cropper, Elizabeth, 'The Place of Beauty in the High Renaissance and Its Displacement in Art History', in Alvin Vos (ed.), *Place and Displacement in the Renaissance* (Binghamton, NY: Medieval & Renaissance Texts & Studies), 159-205.

DaCosta Kaufmann, Thomas, 'Introduction', in Thomas DaCosta Kaufmann and Elizabeth Pilliod (eds), *Time and Place: The Geohistory of Art* (Aldershot: Ashgate, 2005), 1-19.

DaCosta Kaufmann, Thomas, *Toward a Geography of Art* (Chicago: University of Chicago Press, 2004).

DaCosta Kaufmann, Thomas, Catherine Dossin and Béatrice Joyeux-Prunel, 'Reintroducing Circulations: Historiography and the Project of Global Art History', in Thomas DaCosta Kaufmann, Catherine Dossin and Béatrice Joyeux-Prunel (eds), *Circulations in the Global History of Art* (Surrey and Burlington: Ashgate, 2015), 1-22.

Damisch, Hubert, *The Origin of Perspective*, trans. John Goodman (Cambridge, MA: The MIT Press, 1992).

de l'Orme, Philibert, *Le premier tome de l'architecture* (Paris, 1567).

de Marchi, Francesco, *Architettura militare* (Brescia: Comino Presegni per Gaspare dall'Oglio, 1599).

de Sola-Morales, Ignasi, 'Place: Permanence or Production', in *Differences: Topographies of Contemporary Architecture* (Cambridge, MA: The MIT Press, 1996).

Edgerton, Samuel, *Renaissance Rediscovery of Linear Perspective* (New York: Harper & Row, 1976).

Enenkel, Karl and Konrad Ottenheym, 'Introduction: The Quest for an Appropriate Past: The Creation of National Identities in Early Modern Literature, Scholarship, Architecture, and Art', in Karl Enenkel and Konrad Ottenheym (eds), *The Quest for an Appropriate Past in Literature, Art and Architecture* (Leiden: Brill, 2019), 1-11.

Ettlinger, Leopold, 'The Emergence of the Italian Architect during the Fifteenth Century', in Spiro Kostof (ed.), *The Architect: Chapters in the History of the Profession* (New York: Oxford University Press, 1977), 96-123.

Fairclough, Norman, *Discourse and Social Change* (London: Polity Press, 1992).

Fara, Giovanni Maria, *Albrecht Dürer: teorico dell'architettura. una storia italiana* (Florence: Leo S. Olschki Editore, 1999).

Field, Judith Veronica, *The Invention of Infinity: Mathematics and Art in the Renaissance* (Oxford: Oxford University Press, 1997).

Foucault, Michel, *Archaeology of Knowledge*, trans. by A.M. Sheridan Smith (New York: Pantheon, 1972).

Frampton, Kenneth (ed.), *Technology, Place & Architecture: Jerusalem Seminar in Architecture* (New York: Rizzoli, 1998).

Grant, Edward, 'The Concept of Ubi in Medieval and Renaissance Discussions of Place', *Manuscripta* (1976): 71-80.

Greenblatt, Stephen, *Renaissance Self-Fashioning from More to Shakespeare* (Chicago: University of Chicago Press, 1980).

Horodowich, Elizabeth and Lia Markey (eds), *The New World in Early Modern Italy, 1492-1750* (Cambridge: Cambridge University Press, 2017).

Kanerva, Liisa, *Between Science and Drawings: Renaissance Architects on Vitruvius's Educational Ideas* (Helsinki: Finnish Academy of Science and Letters, 2006).

Keller, Alex G., *A Theatre of Machines* (London: Chapman & Hall, 1964).

Kemp, Martin, 'From "Mimesis" to "Fantasia": The Quattrocento Vocabulary of Creation, Inspiration and Genius in the Visual Arts', *Viator* 8 (1977): 359-360.

Kim, David, *The Traveling Artist in the Italian Renaissance* (New Haven: Yale University Press, 2014).

Kruft, Hanno-Walter, *A History of Architectural Theory from Vitruvius to the Present* (New York: Princeton Architectural Press, 1994).

Lee, Alexander, 'Introduction: A Wider Renaissance?', in Alexander Lee, Harry Schnitker and Pierre Péporté (eds), *Renaissance? Perceptions of Continuity and Discontinuity in Europe, c. 1300-1550* (Leiden: Brill, 2010), 245-267.

Lefebvre, Henri, *The Production of Space*, trans. by Donald Nicholson Smith (Cambridge, MA: Blackwell, 1991).

Martini, Francesco di Giorgio, *Trattati di architettura ingegneria e arte militare*, ed. by C. Maltese, 2 vols (Milan: Edizioni il Polifilo, 1967).

Merrill, Elizabeth, 'The "*professione di architetto*" in Renaissance Italy', *Journal of the Society of Architectural Historians* 76.1 (2017), 13-35, DOI: 10.1525/jsah.2017.76.1.13.

Molà, Luca, 'States and Crafts: Relocating Technical Skills in Renaissance Italy', in Michelle O'Malley and Evelyn Welch (eds), *The Material Renaissance* (Manchester: Manchester University Press, 2007), 133-153.

Nevola, Fabrizio, *Street Life in Renaissance Italy* (New Haven and London: Yale University Press, 2020).

Norberg-Schulz, Christian, *Genius Loci: Towards a Phenomenology of Architecture* (New York: Rizzoli, 1979).

Relph, Edward, *Place and Placelessness* (London: Pion, 1976).

Rowland, Ingrid D., 'Renaissance Ideas of Space: Introduction', *Memoirs of the American Academy in Rome* 58 (2013), 1-2.

Ryff, Walther, *Vitruvius Teutsch* (Nuremberg, 1548).

Serlio, Sebastiano, *On Architecture, Volume Two, Books VI-VII of "Tutte l'opere d'architettura et prospetiva" with "Castrametation of the Romans" and "The Extraordinary Book of Doors"*, trans. by Vaughan Hart and Peter Hicks (New Haven: Yale University Press, 2001).

Schapiro, Michael, *Language and Political Understanding: The Politics of Discursive Practices* (New Haven: Yale University Press, 1981).

Scholten, Frits, Joanna Woodall and Dulcia Meijers (eds), *Art and Migration: Netherlandish Artists on the Move, 1400-1750* (Leiden: Brill, 2014).

Schreffler, Michael J., *Cuzco: Incas, Spaniards, and the Making of a Colonial City* (New Haven and London: Yale University Press, 2020).

Specklin, Daniel, *Architectura von Vestungen* (Dresden: Miethe, 1712).

Summers, David, *Real Spaces: World Art History and the Rise of Western Modernism* (New York: Phaidon Press, 2003).

Tafuri, Manfredo, *Ricerca del Rinascimento: principi, città, architetti* (Turin: Einaudi, 1992).

Trachtenberg, Marvin, *Building-in-Time: From Giotto to Alberti and Modern Oblivion* (New Haven: Yale University Press, 2010).

Trachtenberg, Marvin, *Dominion of the Eye: Urbanism, Art, and Power in Early Modern Florence* (Cambridge: Cambridge University Press 1997).

Tuan, Yi-Fu, *Space and Place: The Perspective of Experience* (Minneapolis: University of Minnesota Press, 1977).

Vitruvius, *Ten Books on Architecture*, trans. by Ingrid D. Rowland (Cambridge: Cambridge University Press, 1999).

Vos, Alvin, 'Introduction', in Alvin Vos (ed.), *Place and Displacement in the Renaissance* (Binghamton, NY: Medieval & Renaissance Texts & Studies, 1995), ix-xxii.

Wotton, Sir Henry, *The Elements of Architecture* (Charlottesville: University of Virginia Press, 1968).

Yates, Frances A., *The Art of Memory* (London: Random House, 1992).

About the Author

Elizabeth Merrill is Assistant Professor in Theory, History and Criticism of Early Modern Architecture at Ghent University in Belgium. Her research focuses on architectural practices and the development of the architectural profession. She has published articles in *Architectural Histories*, the *Journal of the Society of Architectural Historians*, *Architecture Research Quarterly*, and *The Journal of the Warburg and Courtauld Institutes*, and is currently completing a monograph on the Sienese architect Francesco di Giorgio.

1. Architecture on Paper: The Development and Function of Architectural Drawings in the Renaissance

Wolfgang Lefèvre

Abstract

Drawings and the practice of drawing take centre stage in an investigation of what 'designed' Renaissance architecture, and what led the medieval master builder to gradually develop the characteristic features of the modern architect. This article focuses on the languages of drawings that were employed and developed by Renaissance architects. Examining the variety of functions that different graphical languages had within design and building processes, the article draws upon a storied argument between two Florentine architects to illustrate the conceptual and social tensions epitomized by drawing. The final section examines architectural drawings as means of communication beyond the building site, calling particular attention to the printed drawings that became increasingly important in the sixteenth century.

Keywords: linear perspective, geometry, copying, treatises, Giorgio Vasari

Introduction

> *[I]n Architecture* [...] *designs are composed only of lines, which so far as the architect is concerned, are nothing else than the beginning and the end of his art.*
>
> – Giorgio Vasari (1568)[1]

Drawings, and the practice of drawing, take centre stage if one tries to understand how Renaissance architecture was 'designed', and what prompted the development of the medieval master builder (*maître macon, Werkmeister*) in this period, as he gradually assumed the characteristic features of the modern architect.

1 Brown, *Vasari on Technique*, 206; Vasari, *Le opere di Giorgio Vasari*, vol. 1, 170.

Merrill, E. (ed.), *Creating Place in Early Modern European Architecture*.
Taylor & Francis Group 2022
DOI: 10.5117/9789463728027_CH01

The history of Renaissance architecture excels in exemplary studies on drawings, particularly on those of Italian architects.[2] Still, there is a general feeling that much remains to be done in the study of the role and practice of drawing in Renaissance architecture. There are, for instance, obvious lacunae as regards architectural drawings in the countries north of the Alps.[3] And many desiderata remain with respect to questions concerning the context and function of various architectural drawings in this period – from questions regarding their use within and beyond the construction site, in civil and military architecture, to their relationship to painterly representations of architecture and graphical representations of '*Kleinarchitektur*' by sculptors. There even remain some questions of a basic character that need further clarification, such as to the meaning of the designation 'architectural drawing' or to how these drawings shaped the communication between the various personae involved or interested in building projects.

This contribution naturally cannot address all of these questions. Rather, focus is given to one tension that challenges our understanding of drawing in this period, that which exists between the ideal character of architectural drawing and the actual planning and making of physical places. While Vasari presented the idea that the architect's work lay in the intellectual formation of a design, there is an ample record of drawings – from throughout early modern Europe – that attests to the architect's use of more tactile representations: from pictorial perspectives that captured a place and structure in two dimensions, to orthogonal plans, geometrical schemes, concept models and scaled templates that were actually passed around the worksite. If place in architecture is typically associated with a physical space or structure, drawing was also a crucial component of architecture's greater infrastructure. Although the two-dimensional drawing was itself not a place, it could, and often did, represent a greater set of processes, ideas and constructions integral to place making.

What Is an 'Architectural Drawing'?

Architectural design practices fundamentally changed in the Renaissance. In the Middle Ages, the expense of parchment and lack of readily available paper meant

2 It may suffice to mention some of the definitive studies: Ackerman, *Distance Points*, and Lotz, *Studies in Italian Renaissance Architecture*, as well as the scholarship of Frommel, Heydenreich, Saalman, Thoenes and Wittkower. For more recent studies, see, for instance, Fitzner, *Architekturzeichnungen der deutschen Renaissance*; Evans, *The Projective Cast*; Lefèvre, 'The Emergence of Combined Orthographic Projections'; Luce, *Revolutions in Parallel*.

3 This was the impetus behind a conference convened by Krista De Jonge and Konrad Ottenheym:, 'Designing Architecture in Sixteenth-Century Europe: Drawing as Motor and Medium of Architectural Innovation', which took place at the Royal Netherlands Academy of Art and Science, Amsterdam, in May 2013.

Fig. 1.1 Full-scale architectural tracing on a wall (*Ritzzeichnung*), c. 1260. Cathedral of Notre-Dame at Clermont-Ferrand. © Robert Berger, Clermont-Ferrand

that master builders planned and directed the building process largely without the help of drawings. When drawings were employed, as in the full-scale tracings on floors or walls (*Ritzzeichnungen*), their focus was unique architectural elements such as vault ribs and the tracery of windows. Similarly, the magnificent Gothic elevations on parchment (*Planrisse*) represented decorative elements or eye-catching parts of a building's design, such as rose windows, the splendid west façades, or the towers and spires of cathedrals. These plans almost never presented the building as a whole (Figures 1.1 and 1.2).[4] Even the laying-out of building foundations was, to all appearances, accomplished without scaled ground plans.[5]

But beginning in the fifteenth century, in part due to increasing availability and affordability of paper, it became customary that graphic representations of an envisaged building and its parts accompanied and aided all stages of its realization.

4 For *Ritzzeichnungen*, see Schoeller, 'Ritzzeichnungen', and Davis, 'On the Drawing Board'; for Gothic *Planrisse*, see, for instance, Köpf, *Die gotischen Planrisse der Wiener Sammlungen* and *Die gotischen Planrisse der Ulmer Sammlungen*; Recht, *Les Bâtisseurs des cathérales gothiques*; Böker, *Architektur der Gotik*.

5 See, for instance, Booz, *Der Baumeister der Gotik*, 68.

Fig. 1.2 Architectural elevation of Freiburg Münster Cathedral. Pen and ink on vellum, c. 1250. Akademie der bildenden Künste Wien, Object Nr. 16.869. From Böker, *Architektur der Gotik*, 166

Fig. 1.3 Francesco di Giorgio Martini (attributed), architectural *veduta* of an ideal city. Oil on panel, c. 1490. Staatliche Museen zu Berlin, Object Nr. 1615. © Photo: Gemäldegalerie der Staatlichen Museen zu Berlin – Preußischer Kulturbesitz; photograph by Jörg P. Anders

Drawing was employed from the incipient conception of a building to the design-consultation processes that took place between clients and architects, up to the final rendering of the working drawings that were needed in the construction process. As a consequence, the practice of drawing became a central element of the architectural profession, and with it the employment of a host of geometrical and arithmetical techniques.[6] Drawings and the practice of drawing fundamentally shaped the activity and the profession of Renaissance architects, and proved to be a driving force in the development of Renaissance architecture. As an indispensable means of the design process, construction and communication, the importance of drawings, and of the practice of drawing, can hardly be overemphasized.

Despite this uncontested truth, scholars of architecture continue to be plagued by the essential question: Of the abundance of graphical representations produced during the Renaissance, which ones can be regarded as architectural drawings? It might be suggested to first single out those images as 'architectural drawings' that render architectural subjects. However, on second thought this choice is problematic. If architectural subjects were taken as a general criterion for recognizing architectural drawings, then unavoidably drawings by painters would be included in this group, images that in reality have nothing to do with the processes of designing and erecting buildings, even if they are akin to drawings by which

6 See Gerbino and Johnston, *Compass and Rule*.

Fig. 1.4 Hartmann Schedel, chorographic urban view. *Liber chronicarum*, Nuremberg, 1493, fol. LXI. Cambridge University Library, Classmark Inc.0.A.7.2[888]

architects themselves recorded existing buildings or antique ruins. In regard to architecture rendered on *vedute* or chorographies, it goes without saying that these too can hardly be regarded architectural drawings (Figures 1.3 and 1.4).

Thus, it may be more advisable to single out those drawings as architectural ones that are drawn by architects. But this approach also proves to be problematic in an epoch in which the figurative or visual arts – painting, sculpting, and building – were not clearly separated from each other and in which one and the same artist could excel in several of them. Leonardo da Vinci is a good case in point. Should we exclude his famous drawings of architectural subjects from the category of architectural drawing given the uncertain nature of his actual involvement in any construction project?[7] Obviously, it would be too narrow a selection if we confined the genus of architectural drawings to those traced by practicing architects. Among the drawings

7 See, for instance, Heydenreich, *Die Sakralbau-Studien Leonardo da Vincis*; Pedretti, *Leonardo architteto*.

Fig. 1.5 Antoine Caron, depiction of ancient monuments. *Histoire de la Reine Arthémise*. Pen and brown ink, wash heightened with white on black chalk, c. 1562. Bibliothèque nationale de France, ark:/12148/btv1b6901591q, fol. 43r

of the long sixteenth century, there are quite a few that are undistinguishable from those of architects, but which were in fact drawn by professional painters as well as 'amateurs', such as mathematicians, scholars or interested patrons. Drawings such as Antoine Caron's (1521-1599) 'amateur drawings' for the *Histoire de la Reine Arthémise* (c. 1562) come to mind, particularly in the context of the new military architecture of the age, as the design of fortresses became an occupation that was thought befitting even a prince's rank (Figure 1.5). The architectural drawings of Landgrave Moritz of Hessen are good examples from sixteenth-century Germany (Figure 1.6).[8]

There is, therefore, no straightforward way of categorizing a fifteenth- or sixteenth-century drawing according to the genus of architectural drawing. One general reason for our uncertainty in making such classifications lies in the fact that in this period, architecture was not yet a well-demarcated field of practice. Architects were not professionals in the same sense that painters or

8 For Moritz of Hessen, see Fitzner, *Architekturzeichnungen der deutschen Renaissance*, 301-319.

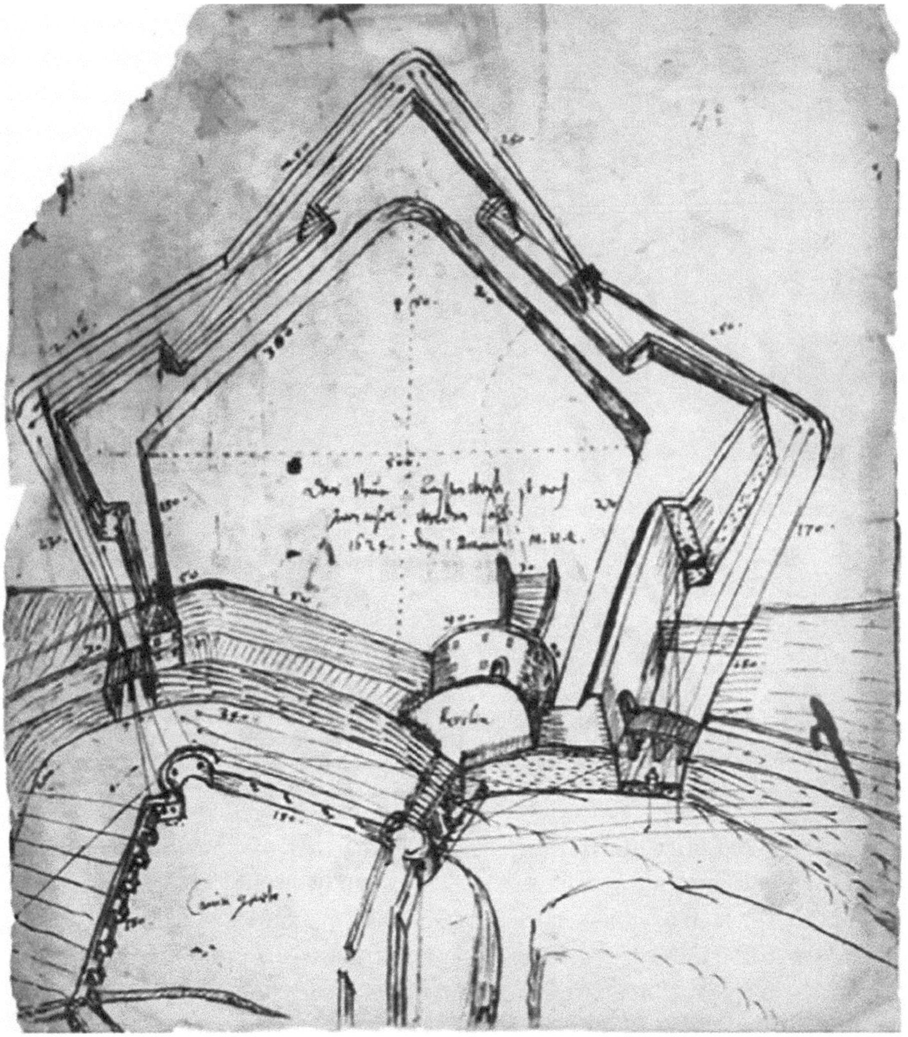

Fig. 1.6 Landgrave Moritz of Hessen, design for a castle bastion. Pen and ink, 1624. MLUB, 2° Ms. Hass., fol. 107 [278]r. Courtesy of the Universitätsbibliothek Kassel, Landesbibliothek und Murhardsche Bibliothek

sculptors were. In contrast to these artists, architects had not followed a standard course of apprenticeship, nor had they been incorporated into a guild, because for architecture, these institutions did not yet exist. Among the famous architects of the age we find craftsmen like Antonio da Sangallo the Younger (1484-1546) and Philibert de l'Orme (1510-1570), who had been apprenticed to a carpenter and to a stonemason, respectively. But the Renaissance also saw great architects who had no training in masonry or carpentry. Artists like the painters Donato Bramante

(1444-1514) and Raphael Santi (1483-1520), or the sculptor and painter Michelangelo Buonarroti (1475-1564), are prime examples. Of course, the situations south and north of the Alps differed a bit in this respect. This is to say that north of the Alps, major building projects were more regularly entrusted to practitioners with a professional background in stone masonry or carpentry. But even in this context, there still exist a number of 'architectural' drawings completed by non-architects, and likewise drawings by building practitioners that have little to do with actual architecture.

Languages of Architectural Drawings

Just as the profession of architecture was not yet clearly demarcated and institutionalized in the Renaissance, the architects' practice of drawing was also not yet standardized, but rather remained in a stage of development and experimentation.[9] In this, there appears a fundamental paradox. While drawing itself was integral to the making of architecture, the actual modes and processes of drawing were widely varied. Although it was a central component within architecture's greater infrastructure, the practice and form of drawing itself lacked definitive structure.

The theoretical foundation for Renaissance architectural drawings begins with *De re aedificatoria* of Leon Battista Alberti (1404-1472), written around 1450. In this influential text, the author assigned the then emerging practice of drawing in perspective to the art of painting, and stressed that architects should represent architectural subjects not in perspective, but by means of orthogonal plans: ground plans, elevations, and sections.[10] This demarcation of drawings made in perspective, which, by definition, do not render true angles and distances, from orthogonal plans, which give correct measurements, was restated at the beginning of the sixteenth century in Raphael's famous letter to Pope Leo X.[11] And it appears that this distinction between the two prevalent modes of drawing had to be restated given the then ubiquitous drawing practice

9 The transition from drawing practices characteristic of the Gothic period to that of the Renaissance was gradual and, in addition, not simultaneous in the countries north and south of the Alps. Moreover, as will be exemplified below, some of the new drawing techniques of the Renaissance, particularly projection techniques, must be recognized as further developments of correspondent techniques of the Gothic period.

10 Alberti, *The Ten Books of Architecture*, book II.1. See also Thoenes, 'Vitruv, Alberti, Sangallo'.

11 Di Teodoro, *La lettre à Léon X*; for a translation into English, see the appendix of Palladio, *Palladio's Rome*. See also Thoenes, 'La "Lettera" a Leone X'.

Fig. 1.7 Bernardo della Volpaia (attributed), section in perspective of San Pietro in Montorio. Pen and ink, c. 1520. Sir John Soane's Museum, Codex Coner, fol. 34r. © Sir John Soane's Museum, London

of perspectival drawing of architects. As Italian drawings from the second half of the fifteenth and the first decades of the sixteenth century unmistakably show, architects had clearly not followed Alberti's dictum, and had instead become as accomplished in perspective draughtsmanship as they were in plan construction.[12] The appropriation and employment of the pictorial language of perspective by architects was not an exclusively Italian affair. A similar development, though to a lesser degree, can be observed in the countries north of the Alps a few decades later, for instance, in sixteenth-century Netherlands.[13] In this period, the rendering of building interiors in perspective seems to have been standard practice among architects, and such renderings often replaced wooden models, which had been, at least in Italy, an indispensable medium of visualization needed in the consultation processes between client and architect (Figure 1.7).[14]

This development is not at all surprising. As is well known, the manner of rendering in perspective owed its origin and development in the West no less to architects like Filippo Brunelleschi (1377-1446) or Alberti than to painters like Masaccio (1401-1428), Piero della Francesca (1420-1492) or Albrecht Dürer (1471-1528).[15] In other words, in the Renaissance, linear perspective seems to have been the lingua franca of graphical rendering of all of the visual arts. Architects made use of and contributed to the development of this lingua franca, which was, however, by implication, not specific to architecture. Architects employed this graphical language mainly when producing drawings for the eyes of patrons or for a broader public, as well as when recording existing buildings or ancient ruins for their private 'archives' (sketchbooks, portfolios, and the like).

However, Alberti's and Raphael's advice and admonition to represent architectural subjects by means of orthogonal projections was not at all lost on the architects of the age. Besides drawings rendered in the new lingua franca of visual arts, architects executed other kinds of drawings that can be called architectural drawings proper, namely ground plans, elevations, and sections, as well as further kinds of geometrical diagrams such as stereometric layouts, templates, and the like. Moreover, Renaissance architects did not merely construct such plans and diagrams. Rather, experiencing the limits of traditional plan constructions, they refined the methods and techniques of these geometrical constructions. For example, they transformed the Gothic ground plan-elevation technique

12 See, for instance, Giuliano da Sangallo's *Taccuino Senese* (Biblioteca Communale, Siena, S.IV.8), the *Codex Mellon* (The Morgan Library & Museum, New York, 1978.44.88) or the *Codex Coner* (Sir John Soane's Museum, London).

13 See De Jonge, 'Vitruvius, Alberti, and Serlio'; De Jonge and Ottenheym, *The Low Countries at the Crossroads*.

14 See Lepik, *Das Architekturmodell in Italien 1353-1500*; see also Alberti, *The Ten Books of Architecture*, book II.1.

15 For perspective rendering in the Renaissance, see, for instance, Kemp, *The Science of Art*, part I; Panofsky, *Perspective as Symbolic Form*; Andersen, *The Geometry of an Art*.

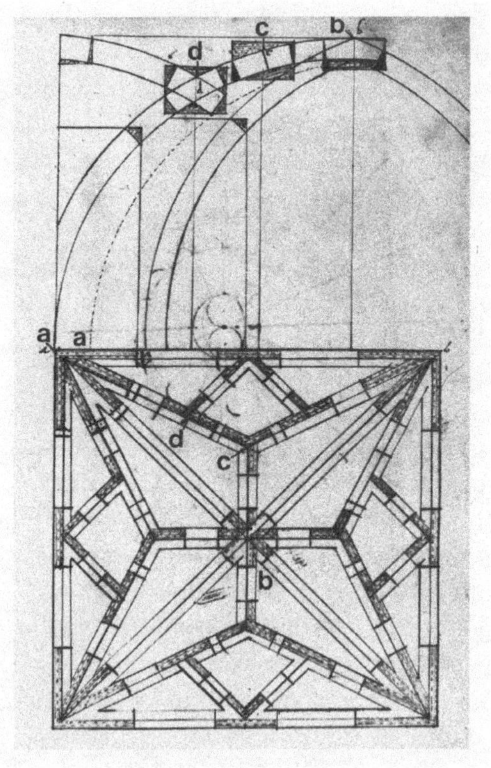

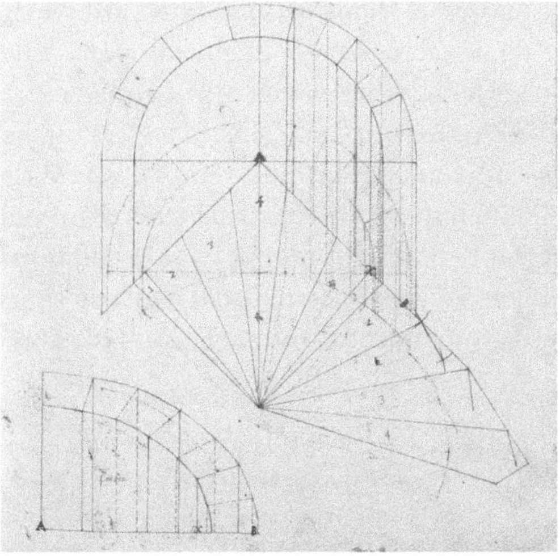

Fig. 1.8 Technical diagrams for vaulting
a) Jacob Fracht von Andernach, combined ground plan and elevation projection. Pen and ink on paper, late sixteenth century. Archiv der Stadt Köln, Ms. W° 276, fol. 29v. From Müller, *Grundlagen gotischer Bautechnik*, 178
b) Alonso de Vandelvira, combined ground plan and elevation. *Libro de cortes de cantería*. Pen and ink on paper, c. 1580. Bibl. Nacional de Madrid, Ms. 12.719

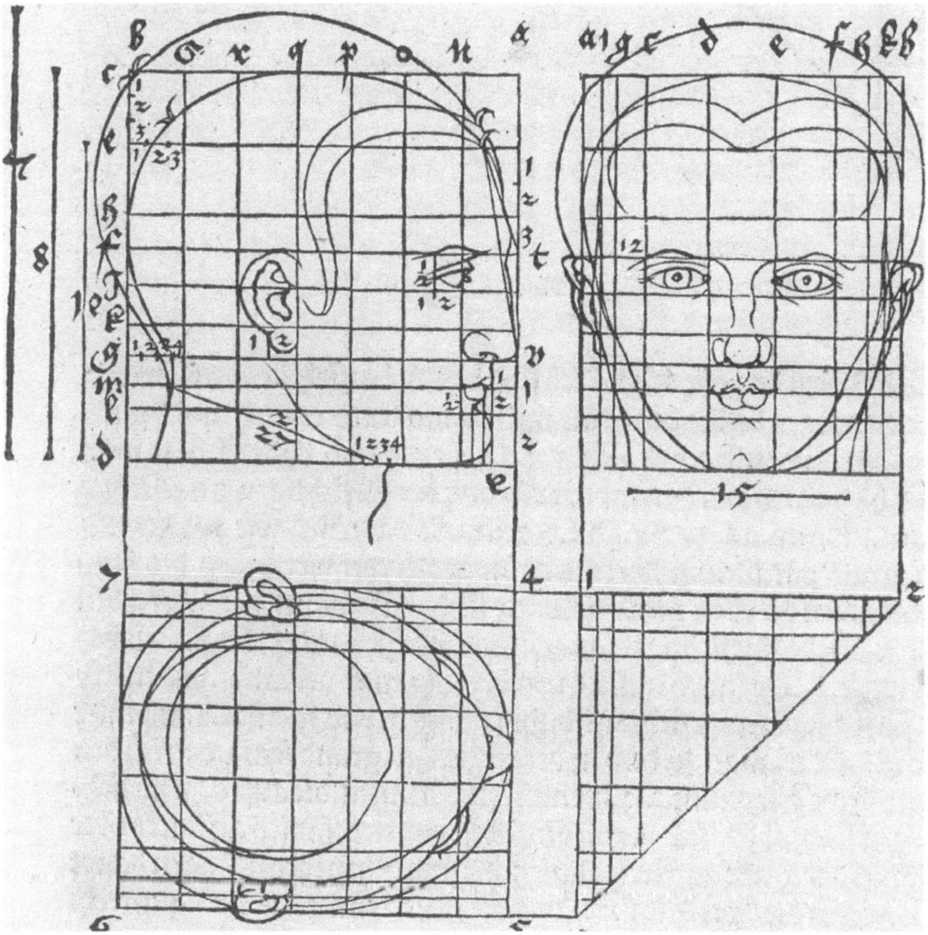

Fig. 1.9 Albrecht Dürer, combined orthogonal projections. *Hierin sind begriffen vier Bücher von menschlicher Proportion*, 1528, fol. E2v. Beinecke Library, Object Nr. 10613881

(*Bogenaustragung* or the 'Dresden method' of vault projection) into the highly sophisticated diagrams of French Renaissance stereotomy (Figure 1.8(a-b)), and developed new ones such as the combined views technique, which became the standard method of architectural plan construction, employed up to the present day (Figures 1.9 and 1.10).[16]

16 For Renaissance stereotomy, see Sakarovitch, *Épures d'architecture*; Camerota, 'Renaissance Descriptive Geometry'; Lefèvre, 'Architectural Knowledge', 61-67. For combined orthographic projections, see Lefèvre, 'The Emergence of Combined Orthographic Projections'. It has been argued that the combined views technique was not invented around 1500 (by Albrecht Dürer and Antonio da Sangallo the Younger) but had been previously employed in certain Gothic *Planrisse*, see Böker, *Architektur der Gotik*, 25. The examples adduced by Böker show coordinated plans (ground plans and elevations) drawn to approximately the

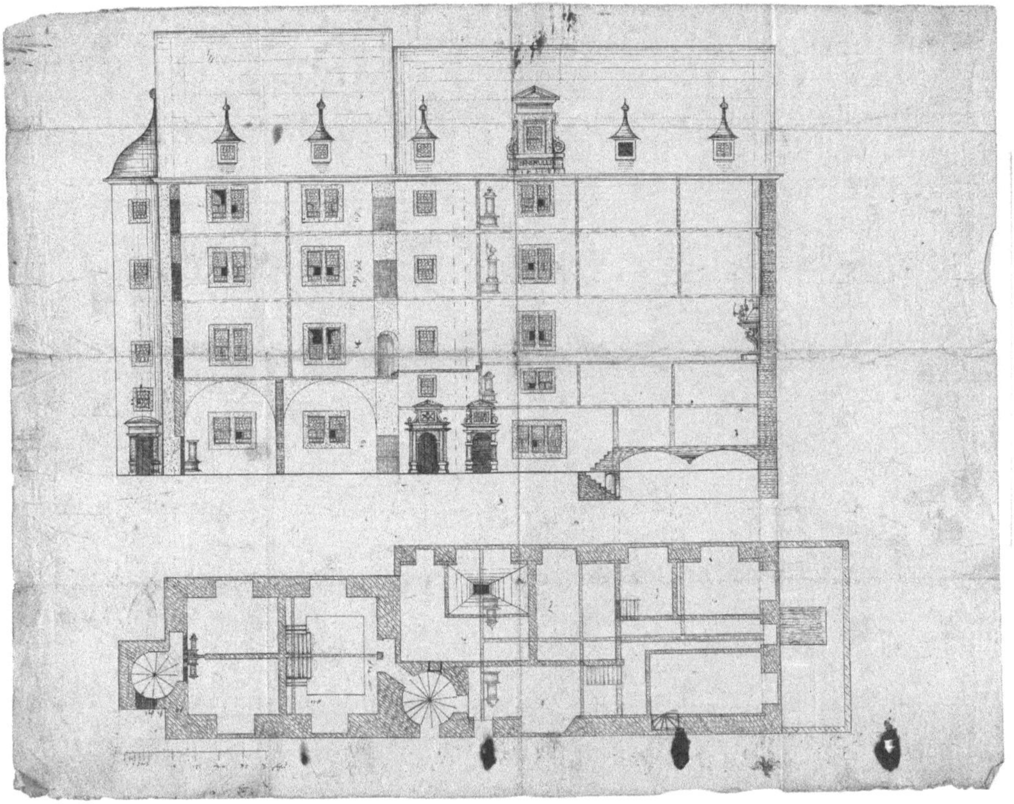

Fig. 1.10 Hans Müller, bathhouse at Ems, presented in combined orthogonal projections: elevation, section and floor plan, 1580. MLUB, 2° Ms. Hass. 107 [96]. Courtesy of the Universitätsbibliothek Kassel, Landesbibliothek und Murhardsche Bibliothek

The simultaneous and continuous use of technical drawings – diagrams, templates, orthogonal projections, combined views – alongside perspectival renderings can be simply explained by the very fact that they were, in contrast to the latter type, indispensable in the building process. They were specific architectural drawings in the sense that they served as tools in the real act of constructing a structure or place. They also had an important function in the design process.

same scale. But upon closer inspection, these do not really allow for the derivation of one plan from the other nor from a third one. Nevertheless, it has to be recognized that the invention of the combined views technique did draw on Gothic design techniques, albeit not initially from those for tracing *Planrisse*, but rather from those used by stonemasons. See Lefèvre, 'The Emergence of Combined Orthographic Projections', 237.

Disegno and Geometric Construction

Before addressing the functions of architectural drawings, their role within the greater infrastructure of early modern architectural production, an intriguing sixteenth-century debate on architectural drawing is worth mention. The argument in question was between Giorgio Vasari (1511-1574) and the Florentine military architect Bernardo Puccini (1521-1575).

In his *Introduzione alle tre arti del disegno* (1568), Giorgio Vasari distinguished between the design and execution of an architectural project by recognizing only the former as a true architectural activity of artistic merit, whereas the latter was a mere craftsman's task.[17] This distinction applied a value rating to the drawing languages used in architecture. Artistic value was granted to *disegno* only, and not to the geometrical design techniques used by master masons and military or hydraulic engineers.[18] In reaction to Vasari's proclamation, Puccini contested that drawing, in the sense of *disegno*, had practical worth in the actual practice of architecture. 'Architecture does not need their [painters' and sculptors'] *disegni*, since with simple lines it disposes the building's utility, comfort, and beauty'.[19]

Vasari's concept of *disegno*, a distinctive concept of Italian Renaissance theories of art, must be seen as belonging to the tradition of, and also standing in certain contrast to the Platonist ideals cultivated in fifteenth-century Florence.[20] According to this tradition, the idea of an artefact emerges in the intellect of the artist and is then expressed in a drawing.

> Since drawing [*disegno*], [...] having its origin in the intellect, draws out from many single things a general judgement, it is like a form or idea of all the objects in nature. [...] [F]rom this knowledge there arises a certain conception and

17 Vasari, *Le opere di Giorgio Vasari*, vol. 1, 107-213. For discussion, see Burioni, 'Die Architektur', 400; Bredekamp, *Galilei der Künstler*, 78; and Brown, *Vasari on Technique*, 206. As quoted at the start of the article: '[I]n Architecture [...] designs are composed only of lines, which so far as the architect is concerned, are nothing else than the beginning and the end of his art, for all the rest, which is carried out with the aid of models of wood formed from the said lines, is merely the work of carvers and masons' (Vasari, *Le opere di Giorgio Vasari*, vol. 1, 170).

18 Vasari and Vincenzo Borghini (1515-1580), the masterminds of the Florentine *Academia del Disegno*, understood *disegno* as an artistic outline or figurative drawing, as in the design of decor and ornament, as well as drawing in perspective, and design based on acquaintance with anatomy. See Lamberini, *Il prinicpe difeso*, 127; Barzman, *The Florentine Academy and the Early Modern State*, 161; and Burioni, 'Gattungen, Medien, Techniken', 10.

19 See Puccini, 'Trattato delle fortificazioni', quoted in Lamberini, *Il prinicpe difeso*, 335: 'Non ha bisogna l'Architettura di loro [pittori e scultori] disegni, perché con semplici linee ella divisa l'utile, commodo et il bello dell'edificio.'

20 See, for instance, Panofsky, *'Idea'*, 29; Kemp, 'Disegno'; and Barzman, *The Florentine Academy and the Early Modern State*, 145.

> judgement, so that there is formed in the mind something which afterwards, when expressed by the hand, is called design. We may conclude that design is no other than a sizable expression and declaration of our inner conception.[21]

Thus, the drawing is (first) a materialization or incorporation of an idea and the medium of drawing itself appears to be a pure neutral medium, with no impact on the idea. (The parallel of this conception to what French philosophers like Jacques Derrida criticized, with regard to ordinary language, as 'logo centrism' is obvious).[22]

In some cases, probably very simple ones, this conception of *disegno* may reflect the design process of a very experienced artist. But in more demanding cases, the artist's idea takes on its concrete shape step by step in a reflective process by which possibilities are tested and evaluated by means of graphical representations. Within this reflective process, the drawing techniques used must enable the artist to represent those aspects or dimensions of reality that are decisive for the realization of the envisioned artefact. There is no one-way road from an idea to its graphical materialization but a back-and-forth movement between the two sides in which they shape one another. While it is true that drawings are mute in regards to the practical suitability and physical behaviour of building materials, they represent the spatial conditions of the envisioned architecture. That is why plans as well as drawings in perspective were indispensable means of design in the Renaissance.

As the argument between Vasari and Puccini shows, champions of *disegno* such as Vasari regarded it not only as the chief manifestation of artistic creativity in the visual arts, but also as the very activity that distinguished the realm of fine arts from that of masons and carpenters or, for that matter, military architects. Without question, this controversy speaks to a social process, by which artists sought to distinguish themselves from mere craftsmen.[23] Antonio de Sangallo the Younger, for instance, one of the most esteemed architects of his time and no less than chief architect of New St. Peter's in Rome from 1539 until his death in 1546, was not recognized as a true architect by the famous sculptor Benvenuto Cellini (1500-1571) because he had been apprenticed – not to a master of *disegno*, that is, a

21 Brown, *Vasari on Technique*, 205; Vasari, *Le opere di Giorgio Vasari*, vol. 1, 168: 'Perché il disegno, padre delle tre arti nostre, Architettura, Scultura e Pittura, procedendo dall'intelletto, cava di molte cose un giudizio universal, simile a una forma ovvero idea di tutte le cose della natura, la quale è singolarissima nelle sue misure; di qui è che non solo nei corpi umani e degl'animali, ma nelle piante ancora e nelle fabriche e sculture e pitture, cognosce la proporzione che ha il tutto con le parti, e che hanno le parti fra loro e col tutto insieme. E perché da questa cognizione nasce un certo concetto e giudizio, che si forma nella mente quella tal cosa che poi espressa con le mani si chiama disegno; si può conchiudere che esso disegno altro non sia che una apparente espressione e dichiarazione del concetto che si ha nell'animo.'

22 See Derrida, *De la grammatologie*, ch. 2; see also Déotte, 'Alberti, Vasari, Leonardo'.

23 For the controversy's institutional context in mid-sixteenth-century Florence, see Burioni, 'Die Architektur'.

painter or sculptor – but to a master carpenter.[24] In our context, it is important above all to see that in this controversy, two essential dimensions of architecture were brought into conflict: the artistic or aesthetic dimension, epitomized by pictorial drawings, and the technical or engineering dimension, epitomized by orthogonal plans. (One is tempted to add that, in a way, the split of these two dimensions seems to be echoed in the divergent approaches to architecture by art historians and historians of science and technology.)

Languages and Functions of Architectural Drawings

Examining the actual practices of Renaissance architects, it makes little sense to play off pictorial rendering in perspective against constructing geometrical plans. Although there undoubtedly existed tensions in the design process between the technical side and the aesthetic side – the divisions between which were further accentuated with the increasing tendency towards specialization in the long sixteenth century – perspectival or pictorial drawings and orthogonal, geometrical drawings were employed in both sides of the design process.[25] The style chosen for a given drawing depended on its concrete function in the long and complex process of designing and erecting a structure.

In the beginning of a building project, plans of the building plot had to be made and sometimes – particularly for fortresses – even maps of the surrounding areas. In the design stage, sketches of the envisaged building, as a whole and in its parts, were drawn (more or less accurately) in perspective (Figure 1.11). Possible dispositions and arrangements of the various parts of a building were explored by means of ground plans. Representational drawings that were used in negotiations with the client, in addition to wooden models, were predominantly drawn in perspective or isometric projection (Figure 1.12). However, in rendering façade details, for instance, designers relied upon exact orthogonal elevations as frequently as they did views in perspective (Figure 1.13). An almost exclusive domain of plans and geometrical diagrams can be found with respect to working drawings, that is, all kinds of drawings that were used by the architect and the several craftsmen in the concrete construction process. (Unfortunately, only a few of these working drawings have survived, as they were usually disposed of after the structure's completion.)

The drawing practice of Renaissance architects was not confined to drawings related to actual building projects. The habit among architects of recording existing architecture, which can be traced back to Villard de Honnecourt's famous logbook of the thirteenth century, experienced a dramatic expansion in the course of the

24 Cellini, 'Discorso dell'archittetura', 367.
25 Lefèvre, 'Architectural Knowledge', 250-254.

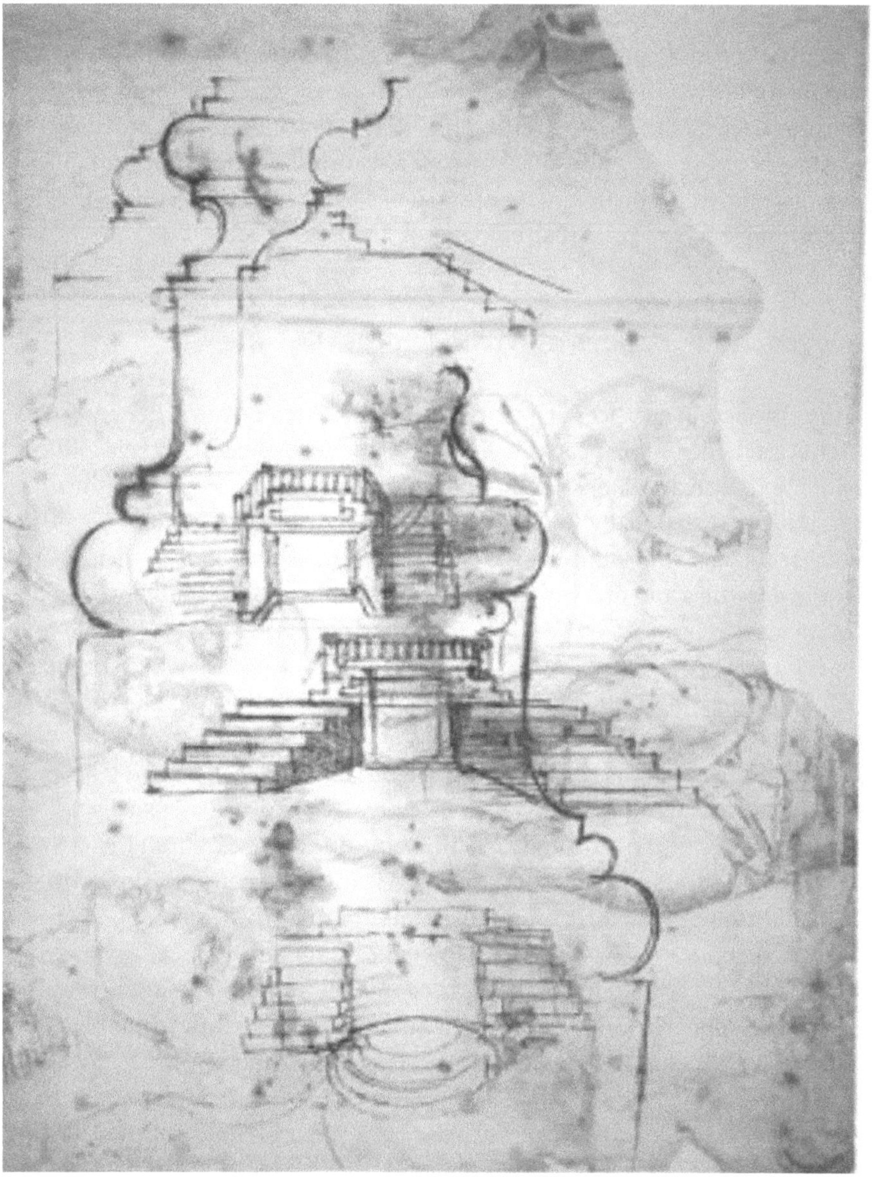

Fig. 1.11 Michelangelo, study for the vestibule of the Laurentian Library. Black chalk, pen and red chalk on paper, c. 1525. Casa Buonarroti, Florence, inv. 92 Ar. © bpk / Scala (70206536)

obsession with antiquity characteristic of the Renaissance. In this age, it became de rigueur for architects working or travelling in Italy, southern France or elsewhere within the confines of the ancient Roman Empire to record antiquarian remains. In this context, too, these ruins were recorded in perspective and by means of

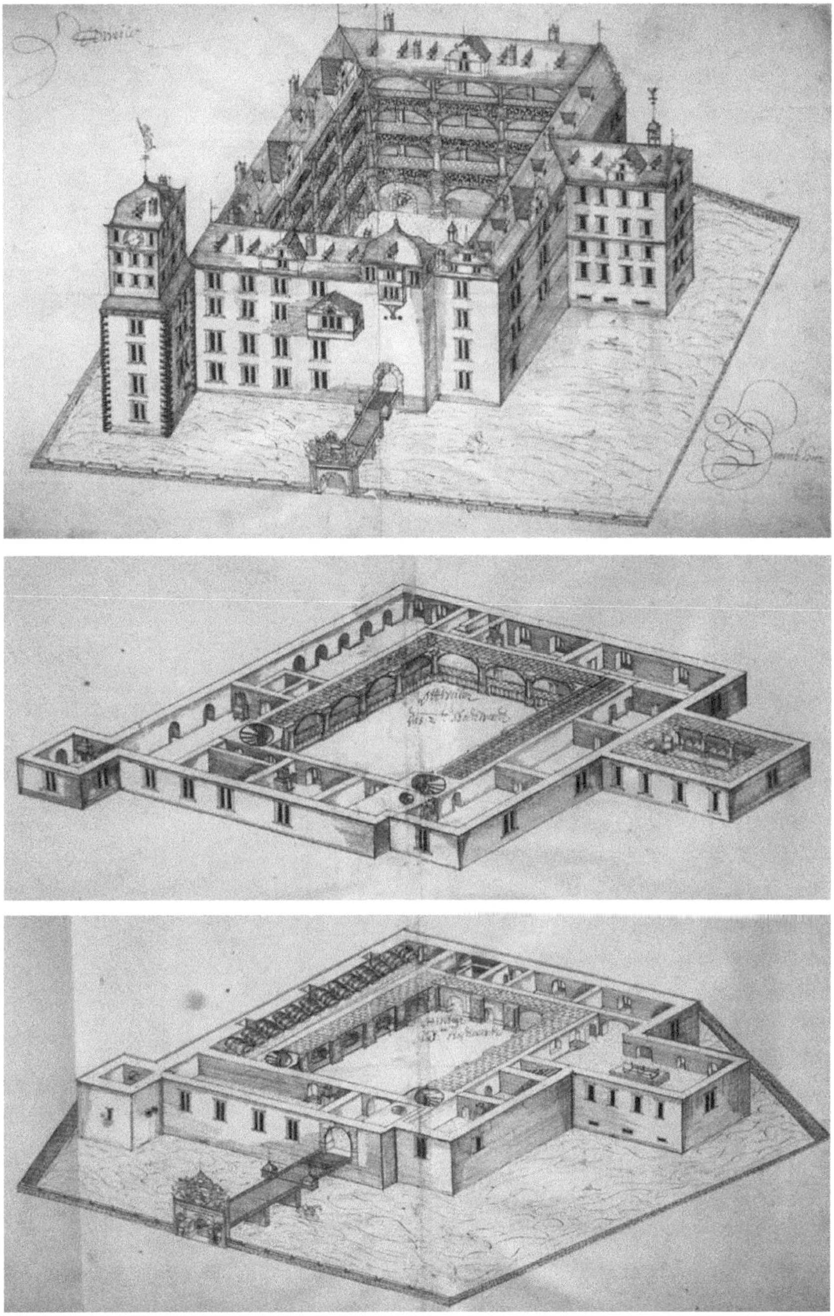

Fig. 1.12 Heinrich Höer, isometric projections of the Schloss Ottweiler. Pen and ink on paper, c. 1614/1617. Abt. 3011/1/3715 H, Hessisches Hauptstaatsarchiv Wiesbaden. From Fitzner, *Architekturzeichnungen der deutschen Renaissance*, 188

Fig. 1.13 Albrecht Altdorfer, design for a portal. (c) Wikiart

orthogonal plans (Figure 1.14). Although often recorded for the architect's private 'archive', many of these drawings were copied and circulated among architects, as well as among interested non-professionals.[26]

26 See Merrill, 'Pocket-size Architectural Notebooks'.

Fig. 1.14 Giuliano da Sangallo, the Basilica Emilia in Rome. Pen and ink on parchment, c. 1480. Biblioteca Apostolica Vaticana, Codex Vat. Barb. Lat. 4424. By concession of the Biblioteca Apostolica Vaticana, all rights reserved

Beyond the Building Site and beyond the Place

The copying and circulating of architectural drawings in the Renaissance may be directly related to the processes by which drawings helped to both define and to transcend place. Drawing allowed place-specific design ideas to be communicated beyond the parties involved in the specific site-based project. In the Middle Ages, the exchange of ideas and experiences among architects and interested clients was accomplished by travelling to exemplary buildings and, more importantly, to advanced and exemplary construction sites. In the Renaissance, travelling continued to be a major vehicle for the exchange of ideas and experiences. But now this vehicle was supplemented, and often even replaced, by circulating images of exemplary buildings or architectural elements such as columns, capitals, and window sills. Architects, clients, and interested laymen who were not fortunate enough to travel to Rome could thus achieve a basic understanding of essential features of Roman architecture thanks to the circulation of architectural drawings.

Moreover, a further new means of communication came into being in the Renaissance: the treatise on architecture. The spate of architectural treatises published in this period ranged from Alberti's famous book of the mid-fifteenth century to Andrea Palladio's *Quattro libri dell'archittetura* (1570) and Hans Vredeman de Vries' *Architectura oder Bauuung der Antiquen* (1598) in the second half of the sixteenth century, and to Joseph Furttenbach's *Architectura universalis* (1635) in the first half of the seventeenth century.[27] The image was integral to the legibility of such treatises. The reception and treatment of Vitruvius' *De architectura libri decem*, which had been passed down to the West without any images, exemplifies this fact. Renaissance editions of the canonical book, such as the famous 1521 edition by Cesare Cesariano, tried to clarify obscure passages through the addition of supplemental images, images that were not original to the text, but which were Renaissance interpretations (albeit, often interpretations grounded in sound archaeological investigations) (Figure 1.15).[28] The use of images is as important in discourses on architecture as it is in discourses on botany or other branches of natural history. Therefore, beginning with the *Trattato di archittetura* by Filarete (Antonio Averlino, c. 1400-c. 1469), written in the 1460s, it became the rule rather than an exception that treatises on architecture applied images, plans as well as drawings in perspective, to make their case.

The architectural drawings that accompanied the illustrated treatises revealed their impact most impressively in the fact that the characteristic features of what we today recognize as Renaissance-style architecture, along with its ideas and ideals, as well as its intellectual and archaeological underpinnings, spread throughout Europe within five or six decades. Within the context of place, it might thus be said that drawings, and more specifically, printed architectural drawings, allowed that which was once place-specific to become general, and even generic. The amazing

27 See Kruft, *Geschichte der Architekturtheorie*, 44-138; Hart and Hicks, *Paper Palaces*; Payne, *The Architectural Treatise in the Italian Renaissance*.

28 Cesariano, *Di Lucio Vitruvio Pollione de architectura libri dece*.

Fig. 1.15 Cesare Cesariano, proportions of Roman architectural members. *Vitruuio Pollione De architectura libri decem*, 1521, fol. 60r. © Werner Oechslin Library Foundation

pace of this propagation may be directly traced in a score of canonical, readily recognizable images.

It was not just a matter of quantity that changed the situation, or the simple fact that drawings became mass products. Along with the possibility to reproduce

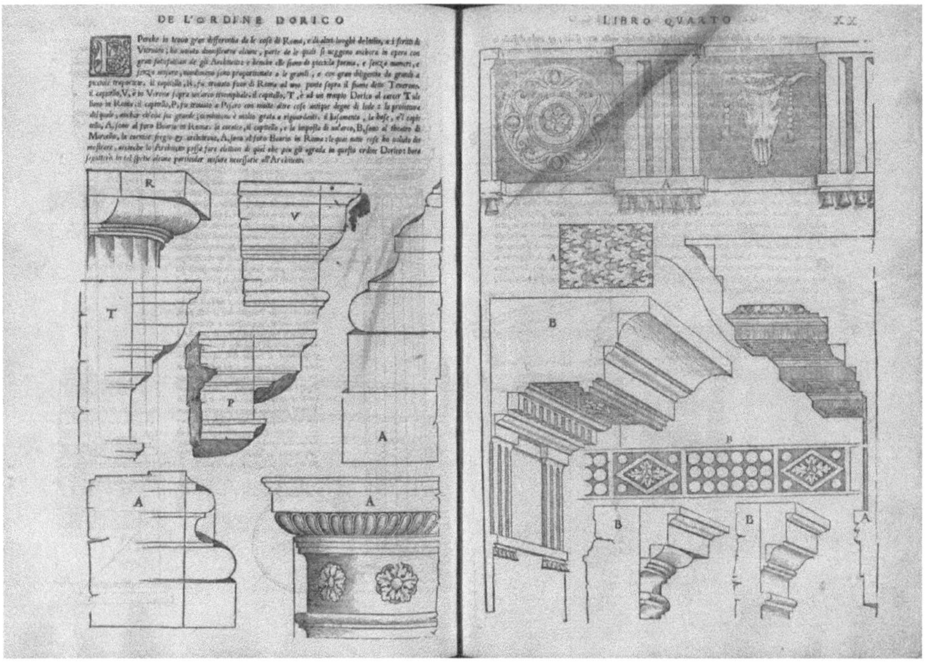

Fig. 1.16 Sebastiano Serlio, architectural patterns. *Primo libro d' architettura*, 1559, c. 20. Courtesy of the Max Planck Institute for the History of Science, Berlin

drawings mechanically came the possibility of enforcing design standardization. There is no question but that among Renaissance practitioners, the impact of Sebastiano Serlio's printed *I sette libri d'architettura*, published between 1537 and 1575, was incomparably greater than the manuscript versions of Alberti's *De re aedificatoria* or Filarete's *Trattato di architettura* in the fifteenth century. Serlio's success was due to the fact that he provided architects and clients with handy patterns with which they could design and decorate buildings according to the then fashionable style (Figure 1.16). Serlio's *Libri*, and the pattern and model books that came in its wake, did more for the spread of the Renaissance style than all the textual theory on architecture combined. These highly visual publications contributed to a standardization of architectural design that led unavoidably to a uniformity.

The invention of the printing press and of techniques of reproducing drawings mechanically by print was thus of foremost importance. Mario Carpo, in his *Architecture in the Age of Printing*, went so far as to pointedly contend that no other technical invention was as instrumental for the development of Renaissance architecture

Fig. 1.17 Andrea Palladio's Villa Rotonda. Engraving by Bernard Picart in Giacomo Leoni, *The Architecture of A. Palladio; in Four Books*, vol. II., London 1775, Table XV. The Metropolitan Museum of Art, Accession Number: 41.100.169(1.2.15). Bequest of W. Gedney Beatty, 1941

as was the invention of printing.[29] The public nature of prints contributed in a crucial way to the international spread of new ideas. But this did not mean that the practice of copying drawings by hand, and circulating such copies, ceased to be of importance for conveying and transforming ideas about architecture. Nor did it mean that architects stopped looking to the site, or that all design became place-generic.

In closing this discussion of architectural drawings, their functions and languages, as well as their social and ideological context in the long sixteenth century, one final observation may be added: the emergence of the mechanically reproduced drawing was, for dialectical reasons, necessarily connected with the emergence of the 'original' drawing. It was the mechanically produced drawing that caused the drawing by hand to take on the aura of an original.[30] Put in different terms, the generic, mechanically produced drawing re-enforced the esteem of that which was singular: that which represented a unique moment, thought, or place. This may be one reason why, just at this time, the architectural drawing became a collectible in its own right. It seems telling that, beginning in the sixteenth century, publishers began to apply a grey or a colour wash to architectural prints in order to make them look like drawings drawn by hand – like immediate records of a place, like originals (Figure 1.17).

Bibliography

Ackerman, James S., *Distance Points: Essays in the Theory and Renaissance Art and Architecture* (Cambridge, MA: The MIT Press, 1991).

Alberti, Leon Battista, *The Ten Books of Architecture* (London, 1755, rpt New York: Dover, 1986).

Andersen, Kristi, *The Geometry of an Art: The History of the Mathematical Theory of Perspective from Alberti to Monge* (New York: Springer, 2007).

Barzman, Karen-Edis, *The Florentine Academy and the Early Modern State: The Discipline of Disegno* (Cambridge: Cambridge University Press, 2000).

Benjamin, Walter, 'Das Kunstwerk im Zeitalter seiner technischen Reproduzierbarkeit', in Theodor W. Adorno (ed.), *Walter Benjamin: Schriften* (Frankfurt am Main: Suhrkamp, 1939), vol. 1, 366-405.

Böker, Johann Joseph, *Architektur der Gotik: Bestandskatalog der weltgrößten Sammlung an gotischen Baurissen der Akademie der bildenden Künste Wien* (Salzburg: Pustet, 2005).

Booz, Paul, *Der Baumeister der Gotik* (Munich: Deutscher Kunstverlag, 1956).

Bredekamp, Horst, *Galilei der Künstler* (Berlin: Akademie Verlag, 2007).

29 Carpo, *Architecture in the Age of Printing*.

30 For this dialectic and the notion of 'aura', see Benjamin, 'Das Kunstwerk im Zeitalter seiner technischen Reproduzierbarkeit'.

Brown, Baldwin G. (ed.), *Vasari on Technique: Being the Introduction to the Three Arts of Design [...] by Giorgio Vasari*, trans. by Louisa S. Maclehose (London: J.M. Dent, 1907).
Burioni, Matteo, 'Die Architektur: Kunst, Handwerk oder Technik? Giorgio Vasari, Vincenzo Borghini und die Ordnung der Künste an der *Accademia del Disegno* im frühabsolutistischen Herzogtum Florenz', *Zeitsprünge: Forschungen zur frühen Neuzeit* 8 (2004), 389-408.
Burioni, Matteo, 'Gattungen, Medien, Techniken: Vasaris Einführung in di drei Künste des *Disegno*', in Alessandro Nova (ed.), *Giorgio Vasari: Einführung in die Künste der Architektur, Bildhauerei und Malerei* (Berlin: Wagenbach, 2006), 7-24.
Camerota, Filippo, 'Renaissance Descriptive Geometry', in Wolfgang Lefèvre (ed.), *Picturing Machines, 1400-1700* (Cambridge, MA: The MIT Press, 2004), 175-208.
Carpo, Mario, *Architecture in the Age of Printing: Orality, Writing, Typography, and Printed Images in the History of Architectural Theory* (Cambridge, MA: The MIT Press, 2001).
Cellini, Benvenuto, 'Discorso dell'archittetura', in Francesco Tassi (ed.), *Ricordi prose e poesi de Benvenuto Cellini*, vol. 3 (Florence: Piatti, 1829).
Cesariano, Cesare, *Di Lucio Vitruvio Pollione de architectura libri dece: traducti de Latino in vulgare affigurati: commentati* [...] (Como: Gotardus de Ponte, 1521).
Davis, Michael T., 'On the Drawing Board: Plans of the Clermont Cathedral Terrace', in Nancy Y. Wu (ed.), *Ad quadratum: The Practical Application of Geometry in Medieval Architecture* (Aldershot: Ashgate, 2002), 183-203.
De Jonge, Krista, 'Vitruvius, Alberti, and Serlio: Architectural Treatises in the Low Countries', in Vaughan Hart and Peter Hicks (ed.), *Paper Palaces: The Rise of Renaissance Architectural Treatises* (New Haven and London: Yale University Press, 1998), 281-296.
De Jonge, Krista and Konrad Ottenheym (eds), *The Low Countries at the Crossroads: Netherlandish Architecture as an Export Product in Early Modern Europe (1480-1680)* (Turnhout: Brepols, 2013).
Déotte, Jean-Louis, 'Alberti, Vasari, Leonardo, from *Disegno* as Drawing to *Disegno* as Projective Milieu', *Appareil* (2009), DOI: 10.4000/appareil.604.
Derrida, Jacques, *De la grammatologie* (Paris: Les Éditions de Minuit, 1967).
Di Teodoro, Francesco, *La lettre à Léon X* (Besançon: Les Éd. de l'Imprimeur, 2005).
Dürer, Albrecht, *Hierin sind begriffen vier Bücher von menschlicher Proportion durch Albrechten Dürer von Nürenberg erfunden und beschriben zu nuss allen denen, so zu diser Kunst lieb tragen* (Unterschneidheim: Uhl, 1969).
Evans, Robin, *The Projective Cast: Architecture and Its Three Geometries* (Cambridge, MA: The MIT Press, 1995).
Fitzner, Sebastian, *Architekturzeichnungen der deutschen Renaissance. Funktion und Bildlichkeit zeichnerischer Produktion 1500-1650* (Cologne: MAP, 2015), DOI: https://doi.org/10.16994/bac.
Frommel, Christoph Luitpold and Nicholas Adams (eds), *The Architectural Drawings of Antonio da Sangallo the Younger and His Circle, Vol. 2: Churches, Villas, the Pantheon, Tombs, and Ancient Inscriptions* (Cambridge, MA: The MIT Press, 2000).

Gerbino, Anthony and Stephen Johnston, *Compass and Rule: Architecture as Mathematical Practice in England* (New Haven: Yale University Press, 2009).

Gerritsen, Elske, *Zeventiende-eeuwse architectuurtekeningen. De tekening in de ontwerp- en bouwpraktijk in de Nederlandse Republiek* (Zwolle: Waanders, 2006).

Hart, Vaughan and Peter Hicks (eds), *Paper Palaces: The Rise of the Renaissance Architectural Treatise* (New Haven: Yale University Press, 1998).

Heydenreich, Ludwig Heinrich, *Die Sakralbau-Studien Leonardo da Vincis: Leonardo da Vinci als Architekt* (Munich: Fink, 1971).

Kemp, Martin, *The Science of Art: Optical Themes in Western Art from Brunelleschi to Seurat* (New Haven: Yale University Press, 1992).

Kemp, Wolfgang, '*Disegno.* Beiträge zur Geschichte des Begriffs zwischen 1547 und 1607', *Marburger Jahrbuch für Kunstwissenschaft* 19 (1974), 219-240.

Köpf, Hans, *Die gotischen Planrisse der Ulmer Sammlungen* (Stuttgart: Kohlhammer, 1977).

Köpf, Hans, *Die gotischen Planrisse der Wiener Sammlungen* (Wien: Böhlau, 1969).

Kruft, Hanno-Walter, *Geschichte der Architekturtheorie* (Munich: C.H. Beck, 1985).

Lamberini, Daniela, *Il prinicpe difeso. Vita e opere di Bernardo Puccini* (Florence: Editrice La Giuntina, 1990).

Lefèvre, Wolfgang, 'Architectural Knowledge', in Matteo Valleriani (ed.), *The Structures of Practical Knowledge* (Cham: Springer, 2017), 247-269.

Lefèvre, Wolfgang, 'The Emergence of Combined Orthographic Projections', in Wolfgang Lefèvre (ed.), *Picturing Machines, 1400-1700* (Cambridge, MA: The MIT Press, 2004), 209-245.

Leonardo da Vinci, *Les manuscrits de Léonardo da Vinci de l'Institut de France – manuscrit B* (Florence: Giunti Barbèra, 1990).

Lepik, Andres, *Das Architekturmodell in Italien 1353-1500* (Worms: Wernersche Verlagsgesellschaft, 1994).

Lotz, Wolfgang, *Studies in Italian Renaissance Architecture* (Cambridge. MA: The MIT Press, 1977).

Luce, Krista M., 'Revolutions in Parallel: The Rise and Fall of Drawing in Architectural Design', PhD diss., University of Michigan, 2009.

Merrill, Elizabeth, 'Pocket-size Architectural Notebooks and the Codification of Practical Knowledge', in Matteo Valleriani (ed.), *The Structures of Practical Knowledge* (Cham: Springer, 2017), 21-54.

Müller, Werner. *Grundlagen gotischer Bautechnik* (Munich: Deutscher Kunstverlag, 1990).

Palladio, Andrea, *Palladio's Rome*, ed. and trans. by Vaughan Hart and Peter Hicks (New Haven: Yale University Press, 2009).

Panofsky, Erwin, *'Idea' – Ein Beitrag zur Begriffsgeschichte der älteren Kunsttheorie* (Leipzig: Teubner, 1924).

Panofsky, Erwin, *Perspective as Symbolic Form* (New York: Zone Books, 1997).

Payne, Alina, *The Architectural Treatise in the Italian Renaissance: Architectural Invention, Ornament, and Literary Culture* (Cambridge: Cambridge University Press, 1999).
Pedretti, Carlo, *Leonardo architteto* (Milan: Electa, 1978).
Recht, Roland, *Les Bâtisseurs des cathérales gothiques*, catalogue d'exposition (Strasbourg: Musées de la ville de Strasbourg, 1989).
Sakarovitch, Joel, *Épures d'architecture. De la Coupe des pierres à la géométrie descriptive – XVIe-XIXe siècles* (Basel: Birkhäuser, 1998).
Schedel, Hartmann, *Weltchronik. Nachdruck [der] kolorierten Gesamtausgabe von 1493*, ed. by Stephan Füssel (Cologne: Taschen, 2004).
Schoeller, Wolfgang, 'Ritzzeichnungen – Ein Beitrag zur Geschichte der Architekturzeichnung im Mittelalter', *Architectura* 19 (1989), 36-61.
Serlio, Sebastiano, *Il primo [-quinto] libro d'architettura* (Venice: Sessa, 1551).
Thoenes, Christof, 'La "Lettera" a Leone X', in Christoph L. Frommel (ed.), *Raffaello a Roma, il convegno del 1983* (Rome: Ed. dell'Elefante, 1986), 373-381.
Thoenes, Christof, 'Vitruv, Alberti, Sangallo. Zur Theorie der Architekturzeichnung in der Renaissance', in Andreas Beyer et al. (eds), *Hülle und Fülle, Festschrift für Tilmann Buddensieg* (Weimar: VDG, 1993), 379-391.
Vasari, Giorgio, *Le opere di Giorgio Vasari*, ed. by Gaetano Milanesi (Florence: Sansoni, 1981).

About the Author

Wolfgang Lefèvre was Professor of Philosophy and Science at the Freie Universität Berlin until 2006. Since 1994, he has been engaged at the Max Planck Institute for the History of Science, Berlin. He has published extensively on topics in the history of science. He is the editor of *Picturing Machines 1400-1700* (2004), and the co-creator of the Database for Machine Drawings.

Part I

Marking Place

2. The Santacroce Houses along the Via in Publicolis in Rome: Law, Place and Residential Architecture in the Early Modern Period

Nele De Raedt

Abstract
This contribution explores the place-making mechanisms at work in the law system of early modern Italy, and their relation to the design of urban residential architecture. Particular attention is directed at punishments of exclusion, whereby an individual or family was physically displaced from the *civitas* and their property was sequestered, confiscated or destroyed. As argued here, the effectiveness of these punishments depended on and further strengthened the close relation between a given family and its place of residence. The place-making mechanisms of law are explored through the specific case of the Santacroce family, whose urban property was confiscated and destroyed following their conflict with the Della Valle in fifteenth-century Rome. By reconstructing the design of the Santacroce residences, before and after their sentenced destruction, this study demonstrates how the choice of site, typology and ornamentation in urban residential architecture acquire new meaning when viewed against legal practices of exclusion.

Keywords: legal practices, urban residences, Palazzo a Punta di Diamante, Santacroce, Della Valle

Along the Via di Santa Maria del Pianto in Rome, following the course of the former Via Mercatoria, stands a proud urban residence with an imposing corner tower. Known as the Palazzo a Punta di Diamante, this residence was built by the Santacroce

Merrill, E. (ed.), *Creating Place in Early Modern European Architecture*.
Taylor & Francis Group 2022
DOI: 10.5117/9789463728027_CH02

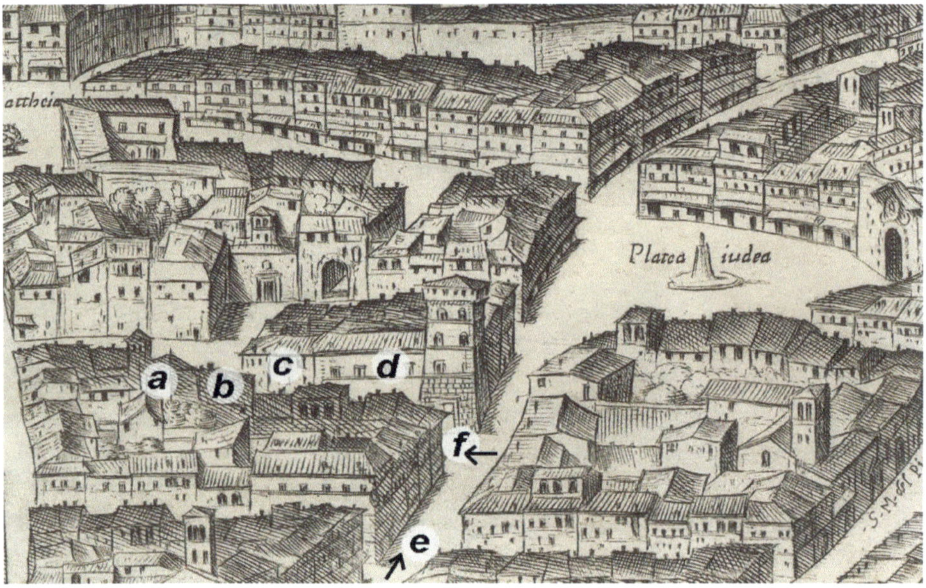

Fig. 2.1 Antonio Tempesta, plan of the city of Rome showing the Palazzo a Punta di Diamante along the Via Mercatoria. Rome: Giovanni Domenico de Rossi, 1645. The Metropolitan Museum of Art, Accession Number: 1983.1027(1-12). Edward Pearce Casey Fund, 1983

a. Santa Maria in Publicolis
b. Residence bought by the Santacroce brothers in 1439
c. Home of Prospero Santacroce
d. Palazzo a Punta di Diamante
e. Via Mercatoria
f. Via in Publicolis

family shortly after 1498.[1] In its formal typology, the home builds upon traditional Roman residential architecture, combining a corner tower with adjacent wings that surrounded a central courtyard.[2] As originally conceived, shops, to be rented out, were integrated into the plan of the ground floor along the Via Mercatoria. The home's main entrance was located on the Via in Publicolis, along with those of the family's other residences and their titular church, Santa Maria in Publicolis (Figures 2.1 and 2.2).

The Santacroce were a wealthy Roman family, which over the course of the fifteenth century acquired the unofficial title of nobles.[3] The family had risen

1 Tucci, *Laurentius Manlius*, 109-110 n. 370; Benocci, 'Palazzo Santacroce'; Tomei, *L'architettura a Roma nel Quattrocento*, 239-242.

2 Clarke, *Roman House*; Westfall, 'Alberti and the Vatican Palace Type'; Frommel, *Der römische Palastbau der Hochrenaissance*; Magnuson, *Studies in Roman Quattrocento Architecture*; Tomei, *L'architettura a Roma nel Quattrocento*.

3 On the Santracroce, Lepri, 'Alcuni documenti inediti dall'Archivio Santacroce a Roma'; Esposito, 'Per una storia della famiglia Santacroce nel Quattrocento'; Esposito, 'Famiglia, mercanzia e libri'; Visceglia,

within the social ranks of Rome from the 1430s onwards, due to the joint effort of Andrea Santacroce (1402-c. 1473) and his five brothers.[4] By the second half of the fifteenth century, under the direction of Prospero (died c. 1511) and Giorgio Santacroce (1452-c. 1499), belonging to the second generation, the family was comfortably situated among the social and political elite of the city, and was still on the rise.[5] The Palazzo a Punta di Diamante was built by Prospero's son Antonio and his newly wedded wife, Leonora Anguillara.

The construction of the *palazzo* marked the end of a tumultuous period for the family. During the 1480s, the reputation of the Santacroce had been severely damaged due to their continual conflict with the Della Valle, a Roman family of similar social and political rank.[6] This conflict had started in 1471 and had developed into a true urban warfare by the 1480s, resulting in an attack on the Della Valle houses by the Santacroce in 1482. Pope Sixtus IV, in an attempt to end the bloody private conflict, ordered the destruction of Giorgio and Prospero Santacroce's houses as the legal punishment for their attack on the Della Valle.[7] As part of the punishment, members of the Santacroce family were also excluded from the city. The absence of the Santacroce from Rome, however, was relatively short. In 1484, after the death of Pope Sixtus IV, Prospero and Giorgio were able to return to the city and to rebuild their houses. The Palazzo a Punta di Diamante was constructed a decade later on the site that had long been associated with the family, but which had also revealed, through the destruction of the previous residences, its shame and dishonour.

This essay calls attention to the conflict between the Santacroce and Della Valle families, the decreed destruction of the Santacroce residences, and the reconstruction of these properties, including the Palazzo a Punta di Diamante, as a means to explore the relation between architecture, place making, and law systems in early modern Italy. Focusing on the legal structures of the Italian communes, this contribution illustrates the place-making mechanisms at work in these systems, which were enacted both through written laws and penal sanctions. By removing contentious individuals from the *civitas*, along with their property, the penal system

La nobiltà romana in età moderna.

4 The five brothers are Paolo, Onofrio, Valeriano, Allesandro and Pietro. Esposito, 'Familiga, mercanzia e libri nel testament di Andrea Santacroce (1471)', 204-205.

5 Prospero was Valeriano's son; Giorgio was Paolo's son. On Prospero, see Esposito, 'Prospero Santacroce'; Ait and Esch, 'Aspettando l'anno Santo'. On Giorgio, see Vicarelli, 'La fabbrica "dei Famigli" del palazzo Santacroce ai Catinari'.

6 On the Della Valle, see Paoluzzi, 'La famiglia della Valle e l'origine della collezione di antichità'; Gatta, 'Lelio Della Valle'; Cherubini, 'Francesco Della Valle'; Riebesell, 'Andrea Della Valle'.

7 For a thorough analysis of the conflict in relation to larger political events, see Visceglia, 'Factions in Rome'. For contemporary accounts of the conflict, see Pontani, *Il diario romano di Gaspare Pontani*, 5; Vascho, *Il diario della città di Roma*, 44-45, 93-94; Infessura, *Diario della città di Roma*, 87-88; Conti, *Le storie de suoi tempi dal 1475 al 1510*, 134-137.

Fig. 2.2 The Palazzo a Punta di Diamante along the Via Mercatoria. © Photo: Nele De Raedt, 2018

forged a close relation between the *civitas* as a social and political community and as a physical artefact, and contributed to the construction of the *civitas* as a place. The effectiveness of this system depended on, and in turn strengthened, the close relation between a family and its place of residence. This close relation was architecturally expressed in the building's location in the city, its typology and its ornamentation. By approaching architectural design from the perspective of law and place making, this study also furthers the idea of the early modern residence as itself a distinct place, defined socially, politically and architecturally.

The Legal Construction of Place in Early Modern Italy

Over the course of the eleventh and twelfth centuries, multiple cities in northern and central Italy, such as Pisa, Milan, Arezzo and Genoa, appropriated the right for political and juridical self-government.[8] Urban magistracies were created, composed of several councils, whose representatives were chosen from the citizen body on a regular basis. In order to establish the institutional, political and legal organization of the civic community, statutes were enacted, granting legal authority to political and juridical representatives. Over the course of their existence, the governing bodies updated the statutes regularly, revising and editing the laws that would impose strict communal order.

Although Italy's individual communes developed their own statutes, the documents show similarities, as they all built upon the same legal corpus of texts, the so-called *ius commune*, and the same legal traditions.[9] As a form of punishment, the communes of early modern Italy enforced expulsion from the *civitas* (also known as banishment) for those who broke the law.[10] Two spheres of infringement were defined: reparable and irreparable acts.[11] In the case of reparable acts, the exclusion from the *civitas* was only temporary. The convicted individual could be readmitted to the commune after a given period of time or when certain conditions were met,

8 Wickham, *Sleepwalking into a New World*; Milani, *I comuni italiani*; Menant, *L'Italie des communes 1100-1350*; Coleman, 'The Italian Communes'.

9 Ascheri, *I diritti del medioevo italiano*; Pertile, *Storia del diritto italiano dalla caduta dell'impero romano alla codificazione*; Calisse, *Storia del diritto penale italiano dal secolo VI al XIX*.

10 Technically speaking, banishment was not a punishment but a suspension of the protection by the law until an obligation was fulfilled. However, when a perpetual ban was expressed, the exclusion was definitive and the ban assumed the value of a punishment. Milani, 'The Ban and the Bag', 127. The word 'banishment' is here used to refer to this legal suspension of the protection by the law. The term 'exile', on the other hand, is here used to refer to the more general condition of (forced) living outside of one's home town. I understand the two words not to be synonymous, as not everyone living in exile was by definition 'banished' in the legal sense. Within legal historical studies, however, the distinction between banishment and exile is often debated. See Milani, 'Giuristi, giudici e fuoriusciti'; Milani, *L'esclusione dal comune*; Shaw, *The Politics of Exile in Renaissance Italy*; Baxendale, 'Exile in Practice'; Stern, *Contrary Commonwealth*; Cavalca, *Il bando nella prassi e nella dottrina giuridica medievale*.

11 Milani, 'Giuristi, giudici e fuoriusciti', para. 5.

for example, after the payment of a fine, or following a settlement made between the aggressor and the offended party. Irreparable acts implied permanent exclusion. Such acts were considered unforgivable infringements against the established peace of the commune.

The *civitas* was first and foremost a social and political community, bound together through bonds of justice and peace. To be banished from that community implied the loss of protection from the law, and the obligation to reside outside of its territory. Medieval glossators described the physical displacement of the convict from the *civitas* as the defining feature of being banished. For example, comparing the punishments of deportation and relegation, which were found in Roman law, with that of banishment, Iacopo d'Arena wrote 'the deported or relegated [individual] is forbidden throughout the whole world, except on that island to which he is deported or relegated; the contrary holds for the banished [individual], because he can stay or live wherever he can, except in the city [*civitate*] from which he is banished'.[12] Alberico da Rosciate confirmed these observations, commenting that 'the deported [individual] needs to stay on the island that is assigned to him', while 'the banished can go where he wants, except for the place [*extra locum*] from which he is prohibited'.[13]

Depending on the severity of the crime, the convict's goods could also be sequestered, confiscated, and at times even destroyed.[14] Sequestration was generally applied to assure that the convict would uphold the conditions of his exclusion and stay within a certain distance from the city.[15] When these conditions were broken, the convict would be declared a rebel and his goods would be confiscated. As will be seen in the case of the Santacroce residences, the convict's goods could also be destroyed.

The place-making mechanisms at work within the legal system of early modern Italy are therefore twofold. The laws, imposed by the statutes, connected the *civitas*, as a social and political community, to a certain city and its territory.[16] What made

12 'quia deportato vel relegato totus mundus interdicitur, excepta insula in quam deportatur vel relegatur; sed in bannito est contra, quia ubique potest stare et habitare, excepta civitate ex qua exbannitur', cited in Cavalca, *Il bando nella prassi e nella dottrina giuridica medievale*, 87.

13 Cavalca, *Il bando nella prassi e nella dottrina giuridica medievale*, 87: 'deportatus manere debet in insula sibi assignata' while 'bannitus potest ire quo vult extra locum sibi prohibitum'. Apart from physical exclusion *from* the city and its hinterland, the punishment system also enforced physical displacements to a certain place (for example, confinement *in* a certain city or its prison, or *to* another city). According to Cavalca, confinement should be distinguished from banishment, although he admits that the wording is sometimes confused in the sources. See also n. 10. Cavalca, *Il bando nella prassi e nella dottrina giuridica medievale*, 55-58. See also, Brown, 'Insiders and Outsiders'.

14 Cavalca, *Il bando nella prassi e nella dottrina giuridica medievale*, 197-205.

15 Baxendale, 'Exile in Practice', 721.

16 In this volume, Elizabeth Merrill also highlights the conceptualization of the city and its larger territory as one specific place, focusing on the Spedale di Santa Maria della Scala's building activities in

the *civitas* a place was a set of rules, defined, imposed and controlled by an urban magistracy responsible for establishing peace and justice within the boundaries of the *civitas*. It was a tangible place, strengthened and defined by an intangible set of rules. Secondly, its system of punishments further strengthened the place-making mechanisms at work within this legal system. By excluding convicts from this place, and by sequestering, confiscating or even destroying their goods, the penal system continually forged a close relation between the *civitas* as a social, political and legal community, and as a physical construct. Early modern communal law strove to create a *civitas* that was legally, politically, socially and physically united. This is to say, the definition of the *civitas* was not only built upon what it contained, but also upon what and who it did not. The construction of the *civitas* as an integral whole, and as a singular place, was continually reshaped through the exclusion of dissident members.

The Importance of Site in Urban Residential Architecture

In regards to prominent social figures or families, the greater impact of their banishment from the *civitas* depended on the importance of their place of residence, whereby 'place' is understood both in terms of a city, and in terms of the buildings the family inhabited within that city. Urban residences, inhabited by prominent families, were often acquired and constructed over generations of time, marking the family's ancestry and lineage.[17] Such buildings formed the focus of familial life; they were the places where infants were born, where weddings were celebrated, and where family members passed away. In their location, size, cost and ornamentation, such residences also expressed the prominent position of the family within the city. The sequestration, confiscation or even destruction of such buildings was therefore a severe punishment, uprooting families from the place that defined their personal, social and political identity.

Within the history of architecture, the banishment of the Alberti family from Florence is exemplary, as it was addressed by Leon Battista Alberti (1404-1472) in several of his treatises.[18] In his *Libri della famiglia*, Alberti laments several times, through the voices of his characters, of the difficulties of living in exile, away from the place that defines familial honour and prestige. The location of the family residence is addressed in detail through the voice of Giannozzo, the elder character in the dialogue, who represents knowledge through experience as opposed to knowledge

Siena and its *contado* during the fifteenth century.

17 Musacchio, *Art, Marriage, and Family in the Florentine Renaissance Palace*; Lingohr, 'The Palace and Villa as Spaces of Patrician Self-Definition'; Ajmar-Wollheim and Dennis, *At Home in Renaissance Italy*; Clarke, *Roman House*.

18 On the banishment of the family, see Baxendale, 'Exile in Practice'.

gained from reading. When asked about what is necessary to maintain a family, Giannozzo states that a suitable house is among the essential requirements; the choice of a good city, and location of the home within this, also deserves special attention. Giannozzo explains he himself would seek 'a suitable city [*terra*], from which I would not have to move, and where I would be able to live healthy, without discomfort and with honour'.[19] In this city, he would buy a house in a good neighbourhood along a reputed street, where honourable citizens live.[20] In Alberti's *De re aedificatoria*, the choice of location (*regio*) for the family residence is integrated in a larger theory on architecture, where the location is put forth as one of the six elements of architecture. Regarding the selection of a site for the family residence, Alberti again emphasizes the importance of a healthy site, which offers 'every facility and every convenience to contribute to a peaceful, tranquil, and refined life'.[21]

The severity of the punishments pertaining to a family's urban residence depended on, and in turn further strengthened, the close connection between that family and the site of their residence. The following discussion of the Santacroce family, with particular attention to their social rise and subsequent banishment from Rome, the destruction of their familial residences and the eventual reconstruction of these structures, casts light on the close relationship between the legal system of exclusion and the design of urban residential architecture. By examining the Santacroce residences in terms of building site, typology and ornamentation, and by relating them to systems of law and place making, the following analysis underscores the importance of place in the creation of early modern urban residential architecture, and the means by which this association was expressed.

The 'Place' of the Santacroce in Santa Maria in Publicolis, Rome

The Palazzo a Punta di Diamante, on the corner of the Via Mercatoria and Via in Publicolis, was constructed on a site that had long been associated with the Santacroce family in Rome. The family's rise to success can be traced back to the generation of Andrea Santacroce and his five brothers, who collectively purchased a large house next to the church of Santa Maria in Publicolis in 1439.[22] It is most

19 'Cercherei quale terra a questo mi fosse atta, donde io non avessi a tramutarmi, e dove io potessi molto vivere sano senza disagio e con onore.' Alberti, *I libri della famiglia*, 200.

20 'Eleggere mi casa posta in buona vicinanza e in via famosa ove abitassono onestissimi.' Alberti, *I libri della famiglia*, 202.

21 'ut sit saluberrima, habeat opportunitates, praestet commoditates, quae ad vitam faciant pacate tranquille atque laute agendam'. Alberti, *De re aedificatoria*, 399; English citation from Alberti, *On the Art of Building in Ten Books*, 140.

22 Esposito, 'Famiglia, mercanzia e libri'.

likely that the families lived together here for at least a generation (Figure 2.1). As time went by, the members of the extended family bought, rented, and exchanged properties along the Via in Publicolis and elsewhere in the city.[23]

Within the family's investment portfolio, the Via in Publicolis received special attention as the gravitational centre of Santacroce presence in Rome. Apart from the house which Andrea and his brothers had collectively bought in 1439, the family also restored the church of Santa Maria in Publicolis in 1465.[24] From at least 1475 onwards, Prospero resided in a property on the corner of Via in Publicolis and Piazza Costaguti. That same year, he also received from the rector of Santa Maria in Publicolis the houses that lay between the Via Mercatoria, the Via in Publicolis and his own house in *enfiteusi perpetua*.[25] On these plots of land, Prospero's son Antonio would later build the Palazzo a Punta di Diamante.

From the outset, the Santacroce drew attention to the family's Roman and noble ancestry, and sought to convey this through their collection of antiquities, which were displayed in their residences.[26] *Spolia* was integrated in the buildings' façades and within the interiors, with particular emphasis to those objects that drew connections with the family's 'adopted' ancient ancestor, the Roman republican consul Publius Valerius Publicola.[27] In 1457, Andrea Santacroce, for example, attached a fragment of the *fasti consulares capitolini* to the exterior of his house, in which Publius Valerius Poplicola (wrongly confused with Publius Valerius Publicola) was named among the officials.[28] Probably around the middle of the fifteenth century, a member of the family also inscribed the words 'VALER.PUBL.CC.' ('Valerius Publicola

23 The patrimony can be reconstructed from (copies of) acts of purchase as well as testaments, preserved in the family archives. Archivio di Stato di Roma (ASR), Archivio Santacroce, b. 262 and 274; ASR, Archivio Santacroce, Pergamene IV, 4; IV, 28; VI, 7; VI, 17; XI, 284; ASR, Collegio dei Notai Capitolini, vol. 1672 and De Villa Felix, vol. 1868. Andrea's testament is published in Esposito, 'Famiglia, mercanzia e libri'. On the family's patrimony, see also Vicarelli, 'La collezione di antichità'; Tucci, *Laurentius Manlius*, 115, 212, 244-245; Benocci, 'Palazzo Santacroce'; Tomei, *L'architettura a Roma nel Quattrocento*, 239-242; Hülsen, 'Note di topografia antica e medievale', 94-100. On acquisition strategies in relation to place making, see Ludovica Galeazzo's contribution to this volume.

24 Esposito, 'Famiglia, mercanzia e libri'.

25 ASR, Archivio Santacroce, Pergamene, VI, 7. Also cited in Ait and Esch, 'Aspettando l'anno Santo', 411. The notarial document mentions that Prospero received the houses in between the *Via Recta*, *via publica* and *retro domus dicti Prosperis* in *enfiteusi perpetua*. From this document can also be concluded that Prospero was living on the corner of Piazza Costaguti and Via in Publicolis from 1475 onwards.

26 For the relation between collecting and the construction of place, see also Paul Brakmann and Sebastian Fitzner's contribution to this volume.

27 Christian, *Empire without End*, 73-74, 80-87, 372-374; Vicarelli, 'La collezione di antichità'; Modigliani, 'L'aristocrazia municipale romana nel XV secolo'; Christian, 'From Ancestral Cults to Art'; Bombardi, 'Valerio Publicola e la famiglia Santacroce'.

28 Christian, *Empire without End*, 73; Vicarelli, 'La collezione di antichità', 67; Christian, 'From Ancestral Cults to Art', 257-258.

Fig. 2.3 The *fasces et secures consulares*, as illustrated by Jacopo Mazocchi. *Epigrammata antiquae Urbis*, Rome, 1521, fol. CXXI. Courtesy of the Österreichisches Nationalbibliothek

several times consul') on the statue of an ancient *togatus*, thus transforming what had been an anonymous man into the Santacroce's immortalized ancestor.[29] In 1510, Francesco Albertini claimed to have observed a depiction of the *fasces et secures consulares*, the axes and rods carried by a Roman consul's bodyguards, on the exterior of one of the Santacroce houses (Figure 2.3). In his life of Publicola, Plutarch mentioned that the consul voluntarily removed the axes from the rods, thereby earning the love of the people and the title 'Publicola'. Most probably the *fasces et secures* on the house recalled this reference in Plutarch's text.[30]

In adopting the ancient Roman Publicola as their ancestor, the Santacroce both strengthened their family's Roman lineage and tightened their bond to their chosen neighbourhood. It was not by coincidence that the name of their ancestor was closely related to that of their patronage church, which at the time was still referred to as Santa Maria in Publico.[31] The first reference to the church as Santa Maria in Publicolis appears in the testament of Andrea Santacroce of 1471.[32] Furthermore, when Ulisse Aldrovandi visited the antiquities collection of Onofrio Santacroce in the 1550s, he recalled how the ancient *togatus* had been 'discovered in the foundations of this house'.[33] The house to which Aldrovandi referred was located adjacent to Santa Maria in Publicolis, and most probably coincided with that which was purchased by the Santacroce in 1439. It is possible that the Santacroce nourished the myth from the outset, suggesting Publius Valerius Publicola had roots in the neighbourhood. In so doing, they strengthened the history of the family's lineage to the very soil on which their residences stood.

Displacements of Bodies and Goods in the Santacroce-Della Valle conflict

In 1482, Pope Sixtus IV ordered the destruction of the houses of Prospero and Giorgio Santacroce, hitting the family in the very place where for over a half-century they had forged and displayed their Roman ancestry. At the time, Prospero was living on the corner of Via in Publicolis and Piazza Costaguti. Giorgio's whereabouts are

29 Christian, 'From Ancestral Cults to Art', 259.

30 Francesco Albertini referred to Pietro Santacroce's house in specific. Ibid.

31 See also Christian, 'From Ancestral Cults to Art'; Vicarelli, 'La collezione di antichità'.

32 Vicarelli, 'La collezione di antichità', 65 n. 22. For the testament, see Esposito, 'Famiglia, mercanzia e libri'. By the end of the fifteenth century, the church was still occasionally called 'in Publico'. In his epigraphic sylloge, written around 1489-1492, Fra Giocondo, however, is already using the term 'in Publicolis'. Christian, 'From Ancestral Cults to Art', 266 n. 25.

33 'ritrovato né fondamenti di questa casa'. Ulisse Aldrovani, *Delle statue antiche che per tutta Roma in diversi luoghi e case si veggono*, 39, cited in Vicarelli, 'La collezione di antichità', 77 n. 22.

difficult to determine; he might have been living along the Via in Publicolis, but may well have lived elsewhere in the city.

The destruction of the houses of Prospero and Giorgio Santacroce was the legal punishment for a war that they had forged against the Della Valle since 1471.[34] The conflict began during the Vacant See, when Francesco Della Valle accidentally wounded Francesco Santacroce with his sword.[35] Highly offended by the incident, Francesco Santacroce attacked Francesco Della Valle shortly thereafter on Campo de' Fiori, severely injuring him and leaving him with a permanent limp.[36] In 1478, Francesco Della Valle seized the opportunity to take revenge for his injury when his sister Livia and her husband, Prospero Santacroce, hosted their relative Francesco Santacroce for dinner. Francesco Della Valle entered his sister's home in disguise and murdered Francesco Santacroce at the table. Moved to avenge the murder of his guest and family member, Prospero then declared war upon the Della Valle.

The conflict between the two families continued to unfold over the course of the following years. In tracing key events of the conflict, it becomes evident that the legal system worked as a place-making mechanism. In repeated exclusions of bodies and goods, the legal system continuously underscored the close relation between the *civitas* as a social and political community, and as a physical artefact. The system also furthered delineated the strong connection that the Santacroce family had forged with their site of residence along the Via in Publicolis.

Following Prospero Santacroce's declaration of war, the Della Valle immediately erected extensive defensive structures around their properties along the Via Papalis.[37] As these structures inhibited Prospero's ability to take vengeance on behalf of his murdered guest, he redirected his ire upon Pietro Margani, father-in-law of Filippo Della Valle. On 15 September 1480, Prospero murdered Pietro Margani at the latter's house in Piazza Margana. The murder had direct legal consequences. On 24 October 1480, the Casale di Selva della Rocca, one of Prospero's extramural estates, was confiscated on order of the Pope.[38] It is likely that in combination with the seizure of property Prospero was forced to leave the city as well.

34 The reconstruction of events is based on a number of chronicles and diaries, as well as archival sources. Vascho, *Il diario della città di Roma*, 44-45, 93-94; Pontani, *Il diario romano di Gaspare Pontani*, 5; Conti, *Le storie de suoi tempi*, 134-137; Infessura, *Diario della città di Roma*, 87-88.

35 Francesco Santacroce was the brother of Giorgio and the cousin of Prospero.

36 This detail is specifically recalled by Sigismundo dei Conti. See Conti, *Le storie de suoi tempi*, 134. Inflicting wounds with permanent damage was considered a serious offence within the culture of *vendetta* and demanded revenge.

37 On the Della Valle houses, see Brunori, De Rubertis and Grassia, 'Palazzo della Valle-del Bufalo e l'"Isola" della Valle in Roma'; Frommel, *Der römische Palastbau der Hochrenaissance*, vol. 1, 100, 145, and vol. 3, 48-53.

38 ASR, Archivio Santacroce, b. 262, fols. 54-55, 24 October 1480.

Still, at this point, it appears that Prospero's banishment and the seizure of his property were only of a temporary nature. Just one month after he was banished, Prospero secured lawful permission to return to Rome; a peace agreement was settled between Prospero and Stefano Margani, Pietro's son, on 18 November 1480.[39] The confiscation of Prospero Santacroce's property at Selva della Rocca and his temporary exclusion from Rome probably caused some economic damage and brought a certain amount of shame upon the family. But because the punishments were soon lifted, the Santacroce were able to quickly recover. As the conflict resumed and the fight escalated over the course of the ensuing years, the consequences of the punishments would be more detrimental.

The year 1481 saw multiple peace agreements in an attempt to prevent further escalations of violence among Rome's leading citizens. By this time, the conflict between the Santacroce and Della Valle had merged with other ongoing tensions among the city's elite, including the conflict between the papal nephews, Cardinal Giuliano della Rovere and Girolamo Riario, and that between the baronial Orsini and Colonna families, and other Roman families, such as the Margani and Crescenzi.[40] On 14 January 1481, a solemn ceremony took place between Stefano Margani and Stefano di Francesco Crescenzi (principle enemies of the Margani and allies of the Santacroce) on the insistence of Pope Sixtus IV. These men, alongside a retinue of cardinals and curial members who served as witnesses, assembled in the *camera paramentorum* of the house of Cardinal Guillaume d'Estouteville. The purpose was to 'stop and contain the fights and enmities of the city and its esteemed citizens'.[41] Another peace ceremony was enacted before the pope three months later, on 12 April 1481, in the presence of representatives of Rome's baronial families, the urban magistracy and other prominent citizens.[42] Yet despite these peace agreements, Prospero wilfully pursued an attack on the Della Valle upon his return to Rome, his vitriol gaining momentum from contemporary social and political unrest in the city.

The conflict reached an apex in April 1482. By the third hour of the night of 3 April 1482, Giorgio Santacroce, Prospero's cousin and *condottiere* of the family, marched towards the Della Valle houses with 200 men and five troops. Several men also occupied Porta San Sebastiano, presumably so as to allow additional troops to enter the city, or to provide a safe escape route if necessary. During the attack on the

39 Biblioteca Apostolica Vaticana (BAV), Ottob. Lat., 2551/1: D. Iacovacci, Repertorio di famiglie, cc. 419-437, cited in Modigliani, 'Pietro Margani'.

40 Visceglia, 'Factions in Rome'.

41 'ad sedendas et componendas brigas et inimicitias Urbis et civium specialiter deputati'. Translation by author. Along with Guillaume d'Estouteville, present were Rodrigo Borgia, Stefano Nardini, Giovanni Arcimboldi, Giovanni Battista Cibo, Francesco Todeschini Piccolomini, Giovanni Colonna and Bartolomeo Marasca. ASR, Coll. Not. Cap., Notaio Camillo Benimbene, 175, cited in Modigliani, 'Pietro Margani'.

42 Vascho, Antonio de, *Il diario della città di Roma*, 44-45.

Della Valle house, Geronimo Colonna, member of the prominent baronial family, was killed. Shortly thereafter, Giorgio Santacroce fled the city, presumably driven more by fear than by legal jurisdiction. In his diary, the apostolic secretary Jacopo Gherardi da Volterra noted that 'Giorgio Santacroce, cousin of Prospero, who was until now present in the city – with Geronimo Colonna killed – left Rome more out of fear from the opposed faction than from the pope'.[43] The following day, on 4 April 1482, Pope Sixtus IV ordered the destruction of the homes of Giorgio and Prospero Santacroce.[44]

By the time Sixtus IV had ordered the destruction of the Santacroce properties, it is likely that both Giorgio and Prospero had already left Rome. Their residences destroyed, and their bodies absent, the presence of the two cousins had been physically removed from the eternal city. In the absence of these dissident members of the *civitas*, the social, political, legal and physical structure of the city could heal and realign, at least temporarily.

Construction after Destruction: The Santacroce Reclaim Social, Political and Physical Place in Rome

The absence of the Santacroce cousins from Rome was again relatively short-lived. On 12 August 1484, Pope Sixtus IV passed away. During the Vacant See that followed, the two cousins returned to Rome, and took part in a fight that broke out on Piazza Guidea.[45] It is likely that Prospero's and Giorgio's presence in Rome at this time was unlawful. Prospero's return was only legally secured a few weeks later when his son Valeriano signed a peace agreement in his father's name, promising not to offend or let others offend a number of male members of the Margani and Della Valle families

43 'Georgius Prosperi germanus, qui adhuc in Urbe se continebat, ob timorem factionis adverse, magis quam pontificis, Hyeronimo interempto, Urbe abiit'. Translation by author. Volterra, *Il diario romano*, 94. According to the Charlton T. Lewis dictionary, *germanus* translates as 'full brother or sister'. Giorgio and Prospero, however, were cousins. It appears that the use of *germanus* during the fifteenth century extended to blood relations more generally, beyond our present definition of 'brother or sister'. This might explain why, in several chronicles, Prospero and Giorgio are referred to as 'brothers' instead of 'cousins'.

44 Infessura wrote that Sixtus IV ordered the destruction of Giorgio Santacroce's house, as well as that of his brother (*fratello*). Volterra only mentioned that Prospero's house was destroyed and that Giorgio left the city. Pontani recalled how Prospero and Giorgio were declared rebels, as well as Francesco Della Valle. He did not mention any destruction. Volterra, *Il diario romano*, 94; Pontani, *Il diario romano di Gaspare Pontani*, 5; Infessura, *Diario della città di Roma*, 87. Other well-known chroniclers, such as Antonio de Vascho and Sigismundo dei Conti, make no mention of any destruction or other punishment. See Vascho, *Il diario della città di Roma*, 497; Conti, *Le storie de suoi tempi*, 134-137. Infessura referred to Prospero and Girogio as brothers, while they were cousins. See n. 43.

45 Infessura, *Diario della città di Roma*, 165-166.

Fig. 2.4 Prospero Santacroce's house on the Piazza Costaguti. © Photo: Nele De Raedt, 2018

Fig. 2.5 The loggia of Prospero Santacroce's house on the Piazza Costaguti. © Photo: Nele De Raedt, 2018

upon penalty of 20,000 golden ducats.[46] A peace agreement for Giorgio has not been found, but it is likely that he agreed to a similar contract around the same time.

Upon his return to Rome, Prospero probably moved back to the Via in Publicolis, and shortly thereafter started to restore his destroyed residence on the corner of Via in Publicolis and Piazza Costaguti. Fragments from a *loggia* date to around this time and proudly display the ownership of the Santacroce family (Figures 2.4 and 2.5).[47] The family's coat of arms is depicted on both sides of the loggia's opening, painted, along with floral motives, against a red and yellow background, the Santacroce colours. By the seventeenth century, this part of the building (number 130 on the Catasto Urbano di Roma of 1818-1824) was sold to the owners of the Palazzo a Punta di Diamante (Figure 2.6).[48] A plan of the *piano nobile* of the Santacroce properties in between the Via Mercatoria, Via in Publicolis and Piazza Costaguti,

46 ASR, Archivio Santacroce, b. 262, fol. 12. The document was signed on 3 September 1484. Pontani also recalled that a truce was made between the families of the Della Valle, the Santacroce and Stefano de Francesco for the whole month of November. Pontani, *Il diario romano di Gaspare Pontani*, 43. The astronomical amount of 20,000 ducats was undoubtedly in an attempt to prevent escalations of violence after Prospero's return to the city, and signals the threat of damage Prospero himself imposed. Other peace agreements signed by members of the Santacroce family in this period amounted to maximum 6000 ducats. ASR, Archivio Santacroce, b. 262, fols. 18, 28, 55-56.

47 The decorations became visible during a restoration of the building in 1986. Garella dates them, for formal and stylistic reasons, to the beginning of the sixteenth century. Garella, '"Pitture sopra le facciate delle case di Rome"'.

48 The construction of the Catasto urbano di Roma was attributed in 1818 to a number of architects, who used Nolli's map of Rome (1748) as a starting point. The cadastre was put in use in 1824. The maps have

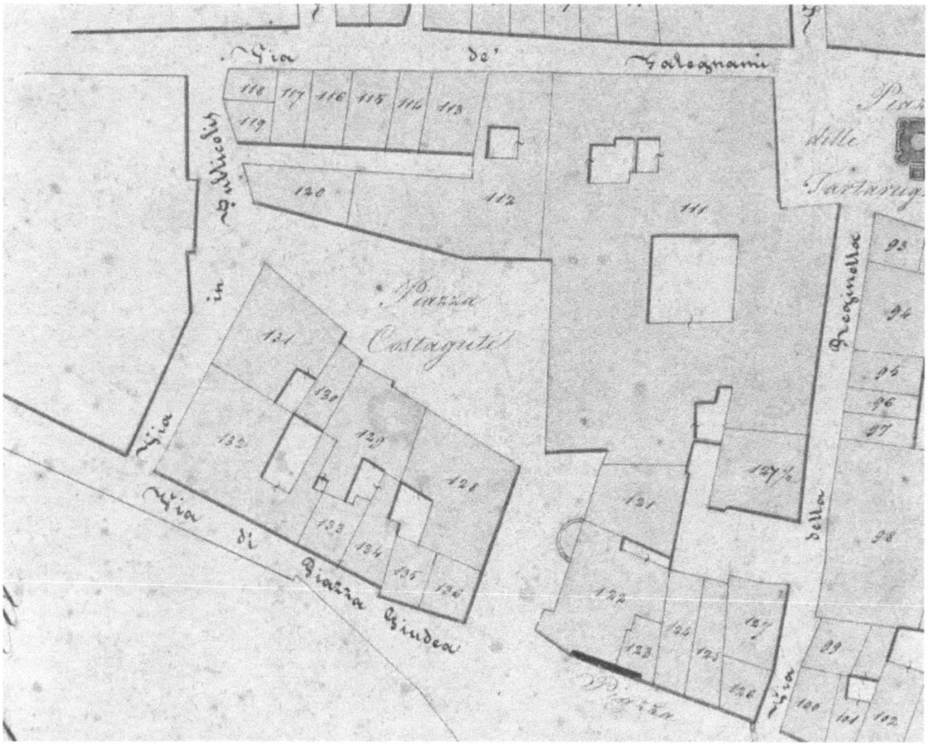

Fig. 2.6 Fragment of the Catasto Urbano showing Santacroce properties along the Via in Publicolis and Piazza Costaguti. Archivio di Stato di Roma, presidenza generale del censo, Catasto Urbano di Roma, Piante, Rione XI, I. Courtesy of il Ministero per i Beni e le Attività Culturali e per il Turismo, "ASRM/2021/1"

dated 1630-1639, shows how this part of the structure was, by this time, internally connected to the *palazzo*.[49] The larger part of Prospero's residence (number 131 on the Catasto Urbano) can no longer be discerned. At some undefined time, it was replaced by the salmon-coloured apartment building that now stands on the corner of Via in Publicolis and Piazza Costaguti (Figure 2.4).

The plan of the *piano nobile*, dated 1630-1639, gives some indication of the possible interior organization of Prospero's residence, assuming that the essential distribution of space within the building remained more or less the same.[50] An interior courtyard with open staircase led to the first floor. The *sala grande* was oriented towards Piazza Costaguti and gave access to five rooms. The entire

been digitized by the IMAGO project of the Archivio di Stato di Roma, http://www.cflr.beniculturali.it/Urbano/urbano_intro.php, accessed 5 November 2020.

49 The plan is published in Benocci, 'Palazzo Santacroce', 226-227.

50 It is not unlikely that the plan indicates a similar layout of rooms as in Prospero's time. The irregular position of the walls suggests the palace of 1630-1639 continued upon much older structures.

Fig. 2.7 Reconstruction of original Palazzo a Punta di Diamante. From Tomei, *L'architettura a Roma nel Quattrocento*, pl. 168

façade was most likely decorated with *sgraffitto* and fresco in the Santacroce colours, with decorations similar to those of the *loggia*. It is also probable that the building had its main entrance towards the Via in Publicolis, the street along which other Santacroce residences had their entrance. In his house, Prospero continued to signal the family's Roman ancestry through the display of antiquities. By the end of the fifteenth century, Fra Giocondo mentioned that he saw the *fasti consolari* displayed here.[51] Along with the ancient fragments that showed a clear connection with the Santacroce's adopted ancestor, Prospero also proudly displayed figural, life-size sculptures in the courtyard, following latest custom among Rome's elite.[52]

Apart from re-establishing his place in Rome, and displaying the Santacroce family's elevated position and Roman ancestry in the decorations of his house, Prospero also extended the family's visual presence along the Via in Publicolis, towards the more trafficked Via Mercatoria. In 1498, Prospero gained full possession of the property located on the corner of the Via in Publicolis and the Via Mercatoria (labelled as number 132 on the Catasto Urbano di Roma).[53] His son Antonio built here the Palazzo a

51 Vicarelli, 'La collezione di antichità', 67.

52 Christian, *Empire without End*, 151-213.

53 ASR, Coll. Not. Cap. Vol. 1672, cc. 180r-182r, 7.11.1498, cited in Tucci, *Laurentius Manlius*, 109-110 n. 370.

Fig. 2.8 Reconstruction of façade along the Via in Publicolis. From Tomei, *L'architettura a Roma nel Quattrocento*, pl. 170

Fig. 2.9 Reconstruction of façade along Via Mercatoria. From Tomei, *L'architettura a Roma nel Quattrocento*, pl. 169

Punta di Diamante, exploiting the highly visible site.[54] At the corner rose an imposing tower with the Santacroce coat of arms, which was fully visible to passers-by. The addition of an extra floor to the adjacent wings has reduced the visual prominence of the tower as it appears today. The main entrance of the *palazzo* was directed towards the Via in Publicolis. Towards the Via Mercatoria, shops were integrated on the ground floor, taking advantage of the location's commercial potential (Figures 2.7-2.9).

The name Palazzo a Punta di Diamante derives from the diamond-formed ornaments that are integrated on the lower register of the tower and around the doors and windows. This type of ornamentation appeared in the early modern period on multiple residences in Rome and elsewhere, and was most probably of Mediterranean origin with Catalan influences.[55] It might be that Antonio consciously chose the diamond forms as a means to visually express his marriage with Leonora Anguillara; the *casa* Anguillara was decorated with the motive in *sgraffitto* or fresco.[56] Alternatively, the diamonds might have been a tribute to Alexander VI, the Spanish pope under whom Antonio was granted permission to rebuild his residence. It might also be that the family chose this type of ornamentation for its connotations with

54 Benocci, 'Palazzo Santacroce', 228.

55 Ibid., 225.

56 Tomei, *L'architettura à Roma nel Quattrocento*, 91.

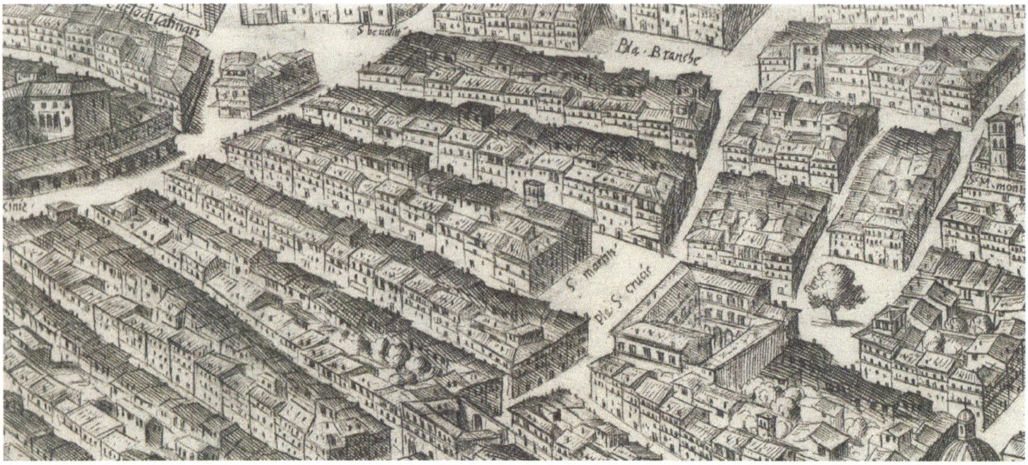

Fig. 2.10 Antonio Tempesta, plan of the city of Rome showing the Piazza Branca and Platea S. Crucis. Rome: Giovanni Domenico de Rossi, 1645. The Metropolitan Museum of Art, Accession Number: 1983.1027(1-12). Edward Pearce Casey Fund, 1983

local, *all'antica* architecture.[57] In adopting the traditional Roman typology of a tower residence, centred around a courtyard, located at the corner of the Via in Publicolis and the much more frequented Via Mercatoria, and displaying the coat of arms and diamond-shaped ornamentation, the Palazzo a Punta di Diamante emphatically proclaims the Santacroce's presence in Rome. The architectural choices might likewise be read as an attempt to further strengthen the connection between the family and the Via in Publicolis as the specific place of the Santacroce in the city.

As Giorgio Santacroce's residence in 1482 remains uncertain, it is difficult to know how he gave architectural expression to his reintegration into Rome. First mention of Giorgio's property dates to 1489, when he hired the architect Tommasso Mazzarazzi to build a house on Piazza Branca.[58] It is possible that this property was built upon the ruins of his former residence. Yet, it is equally possible that Giorgio bought these properties following the destruction of his residence, which had been located elsewhere in the city. The map of Antonio Tempesta, first printed in Rome in 1593, shows no building of particular architectural value on Piazza Branca.[59] From this we might assume that Giorgio's house was of rather modest appearance, at least in comparison to the house that his sons built on Piazza Martinelli beginning in 1502 (Figure 2.10). On Tempesta's map, the Santacroce residence on Piazza Martinelli is clearly visible, consisting of

57 Clarke, *Roman House*, 187-194.

58 ASR Coll. Not. Cap., vol. 1669, cc.346v-347r 4.11.1489. Mentioned in Tucci, *Laurentius Manlius*, 130.

59 The figure included here is a new edition of that map, dated 1645. The fragment showing Piazza Branca is similar to the original. On Tempesta's map, see Maier, 'Mapping Rome's Rebirth'; Maier, *Rome Measured and Imagined*, 167-189.

three wings organized around a central courtyard, and largely dominating the square. The fact that the Piazza Martinelli is even indicated on the map as 'Platea S. Crucis' testifies to the extent to which the square had become associated with the family.

The practice of associating squares and streets with the names of prominent families (or vice versa) allows us to make a final note on the relation between urban residential architecture and place in the early modern period. As we have seen, the Santacroce adopted an ancient ancestor whose name referred to that of the street and church next to their residence. Pietro Margani was murdered at his house in the Piazza Margana, a square that derived its name from the family living there. When Antonio Tempesta inscribed the 'Platea S. Crucis' on Piazza Martinelli in his map of Rome, he associated the square with the prominent family. Such practice of conscious association was widespread, and contributed to the extension of place, from an association with a specific family residence, into the greater public realm.[60] Apart from architectural choices, including the selection of site, building typology and ornament, and the practice of collecting and displaying antiquities in urban residential architecture, this practice of naming contributed to, and became expression of, the association between a family and their place of residence. When excluded from the *civitas*, this association was hard to undo. In case of the Santacroce, even destruction could not withhold them from reclaiming and strengthening their place in the Eternal City.

Bibliography

Manuscript Sources

Rome, Archivio di Stato di Roma
Archivio Santacroce
  b. 262 and 274
  Pergamene IV, 4; IV, 28; VI, 7; VI, 17; XI, 284
Coll. Not. Cap.
  Notaio Camillo Benimbene, 175
  vol. 1672
  vol. 1669
  vol. 1868, De Villa Felix
Rome, Biblioteca Apostolica Vaticana
  Ms. Ottob. Lat. 2551/1: D. Iacovacci, Repertorio di famiglie, c. 1620-1650

60 The practice was widespread. Piazza Farnese in front of Palazzo Farnese is one prominent example.

Printed Sources

Ait, Ivan and Arnold Esch, 'Aspettando l'anno Santo: Fornitura di vino e gestione di taverne nella Roma del 1475', *Quellen und Forschungen aus italienischen Archiven und Bibliotheken* (1993), 387-417.

Ajmar-Wollheim, Marta and Flora Dennis (eds), *At Home in Renaissance Italy* (London: V & A Publications, 2006).

Alberti, Leon Battista, *L'architettura* [*De re aedificatoria*], ed. and trans. by G. Orlando and Paolo Portoghesi, 2 vols (Milan: Il Polifilo, 1966).

Alberti, Leon Battista, *I libri della famiglia*, ed. by Ruggiero Romano, Alberto Tenenti and Furlan Francesco (Turin: Einaudi, 1994).

Alberti, Leon Battista, *On the Art of Building in Ten Books*, trans. by Joseph Rykwert, Neil Leach and Robert Tavernor (Cambridge, MA and London: The MIT Press, 1988).

Ascheri, Mario, *I diritti del medioevo italiano: secoli XI-XV* (Rome: Carocci editore, 2000).

Baxendale, Susannah Foster. 'Exile in Practice: The Alberti Family in and out of Florence 1401-1428', *Renaissance Quarterly* 44.4 (1991), 720-756.

Benocci, Carla, 'Palazzo Santacroce tra via in Publicolis e via del Pianto: Contributi e ricerche', *L'urbe* 47 (1984), 225-233.

Bombardi, Simonetta, 'Valerio Publicola e la famiglia Santacroce', *Archeologia Classica* 46 (1994), 169-198.

Brown, Alison, 'Insiders and Outsiders: The Changing Boundaries of Exile', in William J. Connell (ed.), *Society and Individual in Renaissance Florence* (Berkeley and Los Angeles: University of California Press, 2002), 337-383.

Brunori, Paola, Federica de Rubertis and Alessandro Grassia, 'Palazzo Della Valle-Del Bufalo e l'"Isola" della Valle in Roma', *Rassegna di architettura e urbanistica* 23.69/70 (1990), 138-145.

Calisse, Carlo, *Storia del diritto penale italiano dal secolo VI al XIX* (Firenze: Barbèra, 1895).

Cavalca, Desiderio, *Il bando nella prassi e nella dottrina giuridica medievale* (Milan: Giuffrè editore, 1978).

Cherubini, Paolo, 'Francesco Della Valle', in *Dizionario Biografico degli Italiani*, vol. 37 (1989), https://www.treccani.it/enciclopedia/francesco-della-valle_res-38f7af40-87ec-11dc-8e9d-0016357eee51_%28Dizionario-Biografico%29/.

Christian, Kathleen Wren, *Empire without End: Antiquities Collections in Renaissance Rome, c. 1350-1527* (New Haven and London: Yale University Press, 2010).

Christian, Kathleen Wren, 'From Ancestral Cults to Art: The Santacroce Collection of Antiquities', in Salvatore Settis (ed.), *Senso delle rovine e riusi dell'antico*, Annali della Scuola Normale Superiore di Pisa, Serie IV, Quaderni 14, Classe di Lettere e Filosofia (2002), 255-272.

Clarke, Georgia, *Roman House – Renaissance Palaces: Inventing Antiquity in Fifteenth-Century Italy* (Cambridge: Cambridge University Press, 2003).

Coleman, Edward, 'The Italian Communes: Recent Work and Current Trend', *Journal of Medieval History* 25.4 (1999), 373-397, https://doi.org/10.1016/S0304-4181(99)00010-X.

Conti, Sigismundo dei, *Le storie de suoi tempi dal 1475 al 1510*, 2 vols (Rome, 1883).

Esposito, Anna, 'Famiglia, mercanzia e libri nel testamento di Andrea Santacroce (1471)', in Arnold Esch (ed.), *Aspetti della vita economica e culturale a Roma nel Quattrocento* (Rome: Centro di ricerca, 1981), 195-220.

Esposito, Anna, 'Per una storia della famiglia Santacroce nel Quattrocento: Il problema delle fonti', *Archivio della R. Società Romana di Storia Patria* 105 (1982), 203-216.

Esposito, Anna, 'Prospero Santacroce', in *Dizionario biografico degli Italiani*, vol. 90 (2017), https://www.treccani.it/enciclopedia/prospero-santacroce_res-efe077a9-2b85-11e8-9479-00271042e8d9_(Dizionario-Biografico)/.

Frommel, Christoph Luitpold, *Der römische Palastbau der Hochrenaissance*, 3 vols (Tübingen: Wasmuth, 1973).

Garella, Luciano. '"Pitture sopra le facciate delle case di Rome". Ritrovamenti a Palazzo Santacroce ed al Palazetto Curti', *Alma Roma. Bollettino d'informazioni* 33.3-4 (1992), 124-137.

Gatta, Bruno, 'Lelio Della Valle', in *Dizionario Biografico degli Italiani*, vol. 37 (1989), https://www.treccani.it/enciclopedia/lelio-della-valle_%28Dizionario-Biografico%29/.

Gherardi, Jacopo, *Il diario romano di Jacopo Gherardi da Volterra dal 7 Settembre 1479 al 12 agosto 1484*, ed. by Enrico Carusi, (Città di Castello: S. Lapi, 1904-1911).

Hülsen, Christian, 'Note di topografia antica e medievale: Santa Maria de Publicolis', *Bullettino della Commissione archeologica comunale di Roma* 95 (1927), 94-100.

Infessura, Stefano, *Diario della città di Roma di Stefano Infessura scribasenato*, ed. by Oreste Tommasini (Rome: Forzani, 1890).

Lepri, Giada, 'Alcuni documenti inediti dall'Archivio Santacroce a Roma', in *Il tesoro della città. Strenna dell'Associazione Storia della Città* (Roma: Edizioni Kappa, 2004), 336-371.

Lingohr, Michael, 'The Palace and Villa as Spaces of Patrician Self-Definition', in Roger J. Crum and John T. Paoletti (eds), *Renaissance Florence: A Social History* (Cambridge: Cambridge University Press, 2008), 240-272.

Magnuson, Torgil, *Studies in Roman Quattrocento Architecture* (Stockholm: Almquist & Wiksell, 1958).

Maier, Jessica, 'Mapping Rome's Rebirth', in Pamela M. Jones, Barbara Wisch and Simon Ditchfield (eds), *A Companion to Early Modern Rome, 1492-1692* (Leiden and Boston: Brill, 2019), 285-304.

Maier, Jessica, *Rome Measured and Imagined: Early Modern Maps of the Eternal City* (Chicago: University of Chicago Press, 2015).

Menant, François, *L'italie des communes 1100-1350* (Paris: Belin, 2005).

Milani, Giuliano, 'The Ban and the Bag: How Defamatory Paintings Worked in Medieval Italy', in Caroline Behrmann (ed.), *Images of Shame: Infamy, Defamation and the Ethics of Oeconomia* (Berlin: De Gruyter, 2016), 119-140.

Milani, Giuliano, 'Giuristi, giudici e fuoriusciti nelle città Italiane del Duecento: Note sul reato politico communale', in Jacques Chiffoleau, Claude Gauvard and Andrea Zorzi (eds), *Pratiques sociales et politiques judiciaires dans les villes de l'occident à la fin du Moyen Âge* (Rome: Publications de l'École française de Rome, 2007), 595-642.

Milani, Giuliano, *I comuni italiani: secoli XII-XIV* (Roma: Gius. Laterza & Figli, 2005).

Milani, Giuliano, *L'esclusione dal comune: Conflitti e bandi politici a Bologna e in altre città italiane tra 12. e 14. secolo* (Rome: nella sede dell'Istituto, 2003).

Modigliani, Anna, 'L'aristocrazia municipale romana nel XV secolo: Identità politica e autorappresentazione', in Daniela Gallavotti Cavallero (ed.), *Vecchia e nuova aristocrazia a Roma e nel Lazio in età moderna* (Roma: Nuova Argos, 2006), 10-31.

Modigliani, Anna, 'Pietro Margani', in *Dizionario biografico degli Italiani*, vol. 70 (2008), https://www.treccani.it/enciclopedia/pietro-margani_%28Dizionario-Biografico%29/.

Musacchio, Jacqueline Marie, *Art, Marriage, and Family in the Florentine Renaissance Palace* (New Haven and London, Yale University Press, 2008).

Paoluzzi, Maria Cristina, 'La famiglia della Valle e l'origine della collezione di antichità', in Anna Cavallaro (ed.), *Collezioni di antichità a Roma tra '400 e '500* (Rome: De luca editore d'arte, 2007), 147-185.

Pertile, Antonio. *Storia del diritto italiano dalla caduta dell'impero romano alla codificazione*, 7 vols (Bologna: Forni, 1965).

Pontani, Gaspare, *Il diario romano di Gaspare Pontani già riferito al notaio del Nantiporto (30 gennaio 1481-25 luglio 1492)*, ed. by Diomede Toni (Città di Castello: S. Lapi, 1907).

Riebesell, Christina, 'Andrea Della Valle', in *Dizionario biografico degli Italiani*, vol. 37 (1989), https://www.treccani.it/enciclopedia/andrea-della-valle_%28Dizionario-Biografico%29.

Shaw, Christine, *The Politics of Exile in Renaissance Italy* (Cambridge: Cambridge University Press, 2000).

Stern, Randolph, *Contrary Commonwealth: The Theme of Exile in Medieval and Renaissance Italy* (Berkeley: University of California Press, 1982).

Tomei, Piero, *L'architettura a Roma nel Quattrocento* (Rome: Fratelli Palombi, 1942).

Tucci, Pier Luigi, *Laurentius Manlius: La riscoperta dell'antica Roma, La nuova Roma di Sisto IV* (Rome: Quasar, 2001).

Vascho, Antonio de, *Il diario della città di Roma dall'anno 1480 all'anno 1492 di Antonio de Vascho*, in Jacopo Gherardi, *Il diario romano di Jacopo Gherardi da Volterra dal 7 Settembre 1479 al 12 agosto 1484*, ed. by Enrico Carusi (Città di Castello: S. Lapi, 1904-1911).

Vicarelli, Francesca, 'La collezione di antichità della famiglia Santacroce', in Anna Cavallaro (ed.), *Collezioni di antichità a Roma tra '400 e '500* (Rome: De luca editore d'arte, 2007), 63-82.

Vicarelli, Francesca, 'La fabbrica "dei famigli" del Palazzo Santacroce ai Catinari', in Elisa Debenedetti (ed.), *Rome, le case, la città* (Rome: Bonsignori Editore, 1998), 81-94.

Visceglia, Maria Antonietta, 'Factions in Rome between Papal Wars and International Conflicts (1480-1530)', in Mathieu Caesar (ed.), *Factional Struggles: Divided Elites in European Cities and Courts (1400-1750)* (Leiden: Brill, 2017), 82-103.

Visceglia, Maria Antonietta (ed.), *La nobiltà romana in età moderna. Profili istituzionali e pratiche sociali* (Rome: Carocci editore, 2001).
Westfall, Carroll William, 'Alberti and the Vatican Palace Type', *Journal of the Society of Architectural Historians* 33.2 (1974), 101-121, https://doi.org/10.2307/988904.
Wickham, Chris, *Sleepwalking into a New World: The Emergence of Italian City Communes in the Twelfth Century* (Princeton and Oxford: Princeton University Press, 2015).

About the Author

Nele De Raedt is Assistant Professor of the Theory, History and Criticism of Architecture at the Faculty of Architecture, Engineering Architecture and Urban Planning (LOCI) at UCLouvain. Her research focuses on late medieval and early modern architectural history and theory, and in particular its interactions with political theory, legal history and the history of emotions. She finished her doctoral thesis, 'Injured Residences: Fame, Reputation and Self-Preservation in Renaissance Italy', in March 2019.

3. Towards a New Architecture of Cosmic Experience

Noam Andrews

Abstract

The article unfolds an account of several overlapping fields of inquiry contributing to the early modern experience of the cosmos. Traversing scale, scope, and media, from the first recorded meteorite fall to scholastic debates over the materiality of heaven and the practice of architecture as cosmic analogue, I argue in favour of bringing together a broad range of interdisciplinary source material in order to explore the spatiality of the cosmos and how it was encountered and reproduced as a place or cosmic space or non-place on earth. The accompanying examples gesture towards an open-ended model defined not solely by the built environment as much as by the ephemeral and rhetorical structures framing the cosmos for human consumption.

Keywords: cosmos, materiality, meteorite, outer space, scholasticism

On 7 November 1492, on what would otherwise have been another blustery fall day in Alsace, a young farmhand turning the soil outside the town of Ensisheim hears a sudden hiss from above. Startled, he looks up, his eyes widening, as a ball of fire hurtles out of the sky and crashes into the nearby fields with such a tremendous explosion that the impact reverberates along the valleys of the Danube and 70 miles away in Lucerne (Figure 3.1).[1] Albrecht Dürer (1471-1528), who is spending the latter part of the year working in nearby Basel as a woodcut designer, may well have witnessed the spectacle, which the humanist Conrad Lycosthenes (1518-1561) would go on to include as a 'prodigy' in his 1557 catalogue, *Prodigiorum ac ostentorum chronicon*. Today, we know it as the first recorded meteorite fall in the West.

1 Marvin, 'The Meteorite of Ensisheim', 29.

Merrill, E. (ed.), *Creating Place in Early Modern European Architecture*.
Taylor & Francis Group 2022
DOI: 10.5117/9789463728027_CH03

Fig. 3.1 Hartmann Schedel, depiction of the Ensisheim meteorite fall. *Liber Chronicarum*, Nuremberg, 1493, fol. 257r. Courtesy of the Klassik Stiftung Weimar

The farmhand creeps up to the site of impact to discover that the earth has been flattened into a crater a metre deep. At the bottom lies an alien artefact that will be described evocatively by the poet Sebastian Brant (1457-1521) in a broadsheet published later that year to commemorate the event.

> Shaped like a Grecian Delta; triangular with three sharp corners
> Singed and earthy and metalliferous.
> It fell obliquely through the air
> As though hurled from a star like Saturn.[2]

The townspeople arrive and, as crowds are wont to do, disperse, though not before hauling the meteorite, since estimated to weigh around 300 pounds, to the Ensisheim parish church, where it is hung from the choir loft as a testament to God's majesty.

2 'Von dem Donnerstein gefalle im xcii.iar: vor Ensishein', Sebastian Brant, Basel, 1492. See Marvin, 'The Meteorite of Ensisheim', 34.

Fig. 3.2 Albrecht Dürer, verso of *Saint Jerome*. Oil on panel, c. 1494. The National Gallery, Object Nr. NG6563. D1. © The National Gallery, London

Two years later, having arrived in the Venetian workshops of Alvise Vivarini and Giovanni Bellini, Dürer paints a celestial explosion on the verso of his *Penitent St. Jerome* (c. 1494). The painting depicts a meteorite streaking across the sky, its rightward, motile force alluded to by Dürer's smudged brushstrokes, as if in its velocity it had disrupted the composition of the scene and left its trace upon the careful layering of the painted surface (Figure 3.2). Rending a portentous sky asunder, the heavenly body tears the fabric of the horizon, its collision accented by spontaneous tendrils of flame that reveal a fiery domain beyond the dome of the clouds. On the painting's recto, Saint Jerome, grasping the rock that scripture tells he used to beat upon his chest as a form of atonement, is portrayed on bent knee, gazing expectantly upwards, as if, somehow, the meteorite could crack the pear wood panel that separated the two bodies, one heavenly and one heaven bound, and careen down upon him in a perversely scaled up echo of his penitence, inflicting the ultimate martyrdom by force majeure.

The universe, boundless or bounded, extra-cosmic or interstellar, for most of history hopelessly beyond reach yet ever present, preserves a repository of fears and desires, a place defined in relation to culture yet only ever encountered via terrestrial proxies. This essay presents a synoptic account of how in the early modern period the cosmos was produced as a place or cosmic space on earth, in other words, how the universe was negotiated in the first person. Bridging lay and philosophical perspectives, the currencies of this study are not limited only to buildings, but embrace other 'architectures' – both ephemeral and rhetorical – structuring modes of encounter that could never be fully embodied in the built environment nor taken to account for a self-conscious Theory of Space.[3] By sketching several contours of the cosmic experience, my intention is to gesture towards future avenues for broaching the various registers and scales of the early modern cosmos as it might have been understood, that is, *as* a place and *in* place.[4]

3 I have neither tried to de- or re-philosophize historical concepts of space, nor have I attempted to address the variegated ways that space and place were negotiated in early modern philosophical frameworks (the Aristotelian *topoi*, the Neoplatonic reimaginings of place. On the diverse semantic field of *spatium*, see Regier and Vermeir, 'Boundaries, Extents and Circulations', 2-4. On the development of arguably the first early modern science of space, see De Rizi, 'Francesco Patrizi and the New Geometry of Space'. See also Bellini's contribution in this volume on space as defined by sonic architectures.

4 Through a case study of the Santacroce family and its relation to the urban spaces of Florence and Rome, De Raedt discusses how Florentine law defined the construction of civility through the tensional dialogue between the boundedness of place and boundlessness of the space of the city – both of which apply to the law's reach. To that end, the law and the transgressions it calls for, and at times invites and accommodates, becomes another performative site for indicating what or who makes or is allowed to remain inside or outside of places and spaces (what Foucault would later locate within the penitentiary system and its subjects in *Surveiller et punir: Naissance de la prison* (1975) (*Discipline and Punish: The Birth of the Prison* [1977]), as well as in his lecture series at the Collège de France, published as *Sécurité, territoire, population* (2004) (*Security, Territory, Population* [2007]).

Siting the Aerolite

The concept of an outer-as-other space is bound into the foundation of human experience, not solely as an abstraction rendered in the diagrams of scientific treatises, but also as a domain of celestial spectacle, if only occasionally perceivable. The first half of the sixteenth century was particularly fertile for the extra-terrestrial, as wonders emerged in increasing number from the margins of the Western geographical imagination and the 'dark web' of scribal culture, now transplanted onto mainland European soil.[5] A permeable threshold stretched across the visible interface between the cosmos and human affairs, the early modern sky was anything but a blank canvas. Populated with all kinds of spectacular phenomena and fearsome portents, myriad substances were periodically ejected upon an unsuspecting population and subsequently interpreted in a wide range of responsive spatial practices and performances.[6] The 1719 Festival of the Planets in Dresden envisioned the solar system as a lavish, seven-day affair to celebrate the wedding of Fredrick Augustus II to Archduchess Maria Josepha of Habsburg. Blood rain falling on early-seventeenth-century Aix-en-Provence was theorized as having been caused by a migration of butterflies. A supernatural 'battle' fought over the skies of Nuremberg in 1561 was immortalized in the *Nuremberg Chronicle* and extra-terrestrial inhabitation was theorized (and satirized) by early modern writers and natural philosophers. Johannes Kepler (1571-1630), to name but one prominent figure, described a moon occupied by alien beings in his *Somnium* (1608).

Despite what might be presumed today to be the Ensisheim meteorite's groundbreaking strangeness – the first recording in Western history of a genuine (and still existing) material fragment undeniably from beyond the earthly sphere – and despite the fact that it had been witnessed plainly falling from the sky, what remains truly curious about the meteorite's debut was how gently it crash-landed into the European consciousness and was seamlessly absorbed into the contemporary world view. Visiting Alsace in 1528, the year of Dürer's death, Paracelsus (1493-1541) proposed that the meteor had been formed from rays of stone originating in the supralunar territory of the firmament, the very encasement of the heavens, contrary to the more general belief that the meteor had originated in the imperfect mixtures of the sublunar sphere. Suspended in molten form, according to Paracelsus, the 'conjunction of a hundred rays' had caused a singular body to coagulate, its new

5 Daston and Park, *Wonders and the Order of Nature*, 175.

6 See Pliny, 2.23, 2.25, 2.27, 2.32-2.33. Prodigy literature conspicuously did not fail to stress the presence of witnesses alongside information on the place, date and time of the event, no doubt to make the prodigy useful to those looking to read significances into its occurrence. Daston and Park, *Wonders and the Order of Nature*, 182.

solidity in turn initiating the rapid cooling of what had become the 'great stone' he was presently inspecting and its ultimate fall to earth, outlined in emanations of silver vapour.[7]

It was not until 1771, when the young Goethe visited the same church while travelling through Alsace, that anyone voiced doubt about the celestial origins of 'the monstrous aerolite hanging up in the church'. To Goethe the student, the meteorite signified blind acceptance of age-old mysteries and superstitions, as a monument to the unprovable that had aged badly in the harsh light of *Die Aufklärung*. But reflecting on the event 40 years later in *Dichtung und Wahrheit*, Goethe the statesman equivocated, pivoting towards a more nuanced stance on the nature and suspension of belief. '[We had] never suspect[ed] that such airborne beings, if they were not to fall into our corn fields, were at any rate to be preserved in our cabinets'.[8] The excretions of a material cosmos spitting iron, crosses, animals and body parts down upon the earth, a cosmos filled with things that could be collected, studied and worshiped were, after all, as close as anyone could practically get to handling the stars.

Goethe's scepticism alluded to a fundamental schism in the structure of the event as it had originally occurred, namely a disjunction between what had happened – the appearance of the aerolite and the aerolite itself as record of the event of its happening – and what the happening had come to mean to others. Its very public descent arrested, indeed ecclesiastically suspended, the intermingling of religion, natural history and humanism that had initially struck Goethe as an occasion for scepticism served to ensure the meteorite's afterlife in the burgeoning sixteenth-century literature on environmental and meteorological wonders. Within this literature, it was compared to the descriptions of falling horrors from Pliny's *Natural History* and was occasionally spliced together with shades of an impending Armageddon presaged by unnatural, meteorological phenomena.[9] Almost simultaneously, the aerolite was cast in the supporting role of cosmic pawn in the turbulent political atmosphere at the turn of the century, read first as an omen of

7 'Der groß stein zu Ensheim im Suntgau auf I centner schwer, der ist aus der materia der steinstralen, also das so zusamen komen seind ob den hundert coniunctiones der stral, und so sich coagulirt so schnel, als der ein zerlassen silber ausschüt und gestet.' See Paracelsus, *Theophrast von Hohenheim gen. Paracelsus*, 223.

8 Quotations from Goethe, *Truth and Poetry*, book III.11, 431. 'In Ensisheim sahen wir den ungeheuren Aerolithen in der Kirche aufgehängt und spotteten, der Zweifelsucht jener Zeit gemäß, über die Leichtgläubigkeit der Menschen, nicht vorahnend, dass dergleichen luftgeborene Wesen, wo nicht auf unsern eignen Acker herabfallen, doch wenigstens in unsern Kabinetten sollten verwahrt werden.' Goethe, *Gesammelte Werke*, 9: 497.

9 In addition to Lycosthenes, see Petermann Etterlin, *Kronica von der loblichen Eydtgnoschaft* (Basel, 1507); Conrad Gessner, *De rerum fossilium* (Zurich, 1565); Christian Wurstisen, *Der Basler Chronik* (Basel, 1580); and Johann Wolf, *Lectionum memorabilium* (Lauingen, 1600).

Fig. 3.3(a-b) Hartmann Schedel, the first and third days of creation. *Liber Chronicarum*, Nuremberg, 1493, fol. 2v and fol. 3v. Courtesy of the Klassik Stiftung Weimar

ensuing enmity between Archduke Maximilian of Austria and King Charles VIII of France over the independent Duchess of Brittany, and soon after, construed as having foreshadowed the death of Emperor Frederick III and Maximilian's own ascension to head the House of Habsburg.[10]

Yet at the level of immediate, lived experience, the event of the Ensisheim meteorite produced and was produced by an array of human-scale spatial logics – the horse-drawn vehicle carrying it into the nearest town, the pulley system for rigging it up in the parish church, the bespoke scaffolding and municipal permissions. Its origin story, from sky to field to city, was memorialized in circulating broadsheets and echoed in the sounds made by the hammers and chisels tasked with chipping off fragments of rock that would be ferried to Pope Pius III in Rome.[11] This choreography of ephemeral architectures, transient places, and phantom tools, only hinted at and not nearly grand enough to call for the lavish memorializations of other higher profile relocations of material, formed the humble counterpoint to the other scalar extreme to which the meteorite was related, the cosmic context of a primitive asteroid created from the accretion of dust particles over 4.55 billion years ago.[12]

10 Schedel, *Liber chronicarum*, fol. 257, 12 July 1493; and Sebastian Brant, *Varia carmina* (Basel, 1498).

11 Rowland, 'A Contemporary Account of the Ensisheim Meteor, 1492', 19.

12 See, for instance, the scaffolding required to move the Egyptian obelisk to St. Peter's Square as documented in Camillo Agrippa's *Trattato di transportare la guglia in su la piazza di San Pietro* (Rome, 1583).

A Material Space

Far from being devoid of celestial detritus, Aristotle had argued in *Physics* against the existence of an extra-terrestrial void. Wondrous yet explicable, meteorites and other 'corrupted' bodies were hence almost exclusively theorized as having been formed through combinations of the four elements (*imperfecta mixta*) in the sublunar band (the lowest celestial stratum), analysed to reveal the relations between heaven and earth and the cosmos' general influence on the health of the *anthropos*.[13] The universe was a plenum, in other words, steeped with matter even in the absence of any visibly perceivable bodies, and the categorical impossibility of true and complete emptiness carried over into later natural philosophical doctrines.[14] *Horror vacqui* was self-evident, as Gaster from *Gargantua and Pantagruel* pointedly explained, since 'the entire structure of the Universe, the heavens, the earth, the sea and the land would sooner be returned to ancient Chaos than any vacuum be admitted anywhere in the world'.[15]

For medieval Christian scholars, as well as natural philosophers working in the scholastic tradition through the seventeenth century, the constitution and scale of the universe evolved into issues of pressingly spatial and material concern. Though there were textured disagreements among different ideological camps, it was unequivocally accepted, as written in Genesis, that God had created a universe centred upon the earth through a series of concentric subdivisions. This began on the first day, with the separation of heaven from earth (*In principio creavit Deus caelum et terram*) and continued on the second day with the bisection of the waters above and below by the firmament (*firmamentum*), which God also called heaven (*Caelum*) (Figures 3.3(a-b)).[16] Scholastic disputes stemmed from the fundamental ambiguities baked into divine creation, for instance, how it was that the firmament or heaven (*Caelum*) created on the second day could be distinguished from the heaven (*Caelum*) created on the previous day. Moreover, what exactly was meant by the waters above and below the firmament.[17]

13 Martin, *Renaissance Meteorology*, 9, and Aristole, *Meteorology*, as a primary source. See also Paracelsus, *Paragranum*, 133. For a contemporary condemnation of astrological determinism, see Pico della Mirandola, *Disputationes adversus astrologiam divinatricem* (1498). See also Rutkin, 'Astrology'; Grafton, *Cardano's Cosmos*; Martin, *Renaissance Meteorology*.

14 Aristotle, *Physics*, book IV, 6-9. See also Genz, *Nothingness*, 77.

15 Rabelais, 'The Fourth Book of Pantagruel (1552)', 851. The sentence, in its immediate context, explains why air must fill a gun's chamber in the split second after firing a round of artillery.

16 'Et fecit Deus firmamentum divisitque aquas, quae erant sub firmamento, ab his, quae erant super firmamentum,' Genesis 1.7.

17 Grant, *Planets, Stars, & Orbs*, 92. Grant addresses in abundant detail these questions and many others debated by medieval commentators.

Notwithstanding agreement on the Bible's irrefutability, these few lines opened up centuries of exegesis in the *questiones* genre. Codified by Thomas Aquinas in *Summa Theologica*, Thomas, for his part, laid out a series of objections to the notion that the waters above the firmament could be of the same nature as terrestrial waters. Not only was water 'heavy by nature, and heavy things tend naturally downwards, [...] water is fluid by nature, and fluids cannot rest on a sphere, as experience shows. Therefore, since the firmament is a sphere, there cannot be water above it.'[18] He would continue to speculate at length upon the properties of these celestial waters, whether they retained the transparency of terrestrial water, whether they consisted of vapours, or another kind of formless matter lying above the fiery empyrean, while also providing ingenious counterarguments to his own philosophical deductions. In answer to his assertions that (1) fluids cannot rest upon a sphere, and thus cannot possibly be balanced upon the spherical firmament, and (2) that the waters as described in Genesis display fluid-like behaviour in the first place, Thomas referenced the *Hexameron* of the Greek theologian Basil of Caesarea.

> Basil gives two replies. He answers, first, that a body seen as concave beneath need not necessarily be rounded, or convex, above. Second, that the waters above the firmament are not fluid, but exist outside it in a solid state, as a mass of ice, and that this is the crystalline heaven of some writers.

A transparent heaven made of crystal. A spherical world contained in a rectangular-shaped cosmos with an uppermost surface that collected pooling celestial water. There were equally plausible discursions on the materiality and dimensions of the firmament itself – fire as per Plato's *Timaeus*; a composition of all four elements, as per Empedocles; or the Aristotelian fifth element, the most influential opinion held in the late Middle Ages. Questions concerning the divine territoriality of the supralunary zone, such as whether the firmament spanned continuously from the Moon to the fixed stars, and if so, whether its thickness contained distinct cavities or channels carved for the planets to move.[19] Or, as Thomas, Sacrobosco and Campanus of Novara would ultimately claim, was the firmament in actuality the eighth sphere of the fixed stars and distinct from the seven, inferior planetary orbs? Moreover, how *had* the cosmos been produced? Had it been shaped into a primordial globe via the hands of God as expressed in Pierre le Mangeur's *Historia scolastica*? Or had God inflated the centre of the finite universe like a beach ball, breathing life into the terrestrial realm through divine exhalation (Figure 3.4)?

18 Aquinas, *Summa Theologica*, I, Q. 68, Art. 2.

19 Aegidius Romanus, *Opus Hexaemeron*, quoted in Grant, *Planets, Stars, & Orbs*, 100-101.

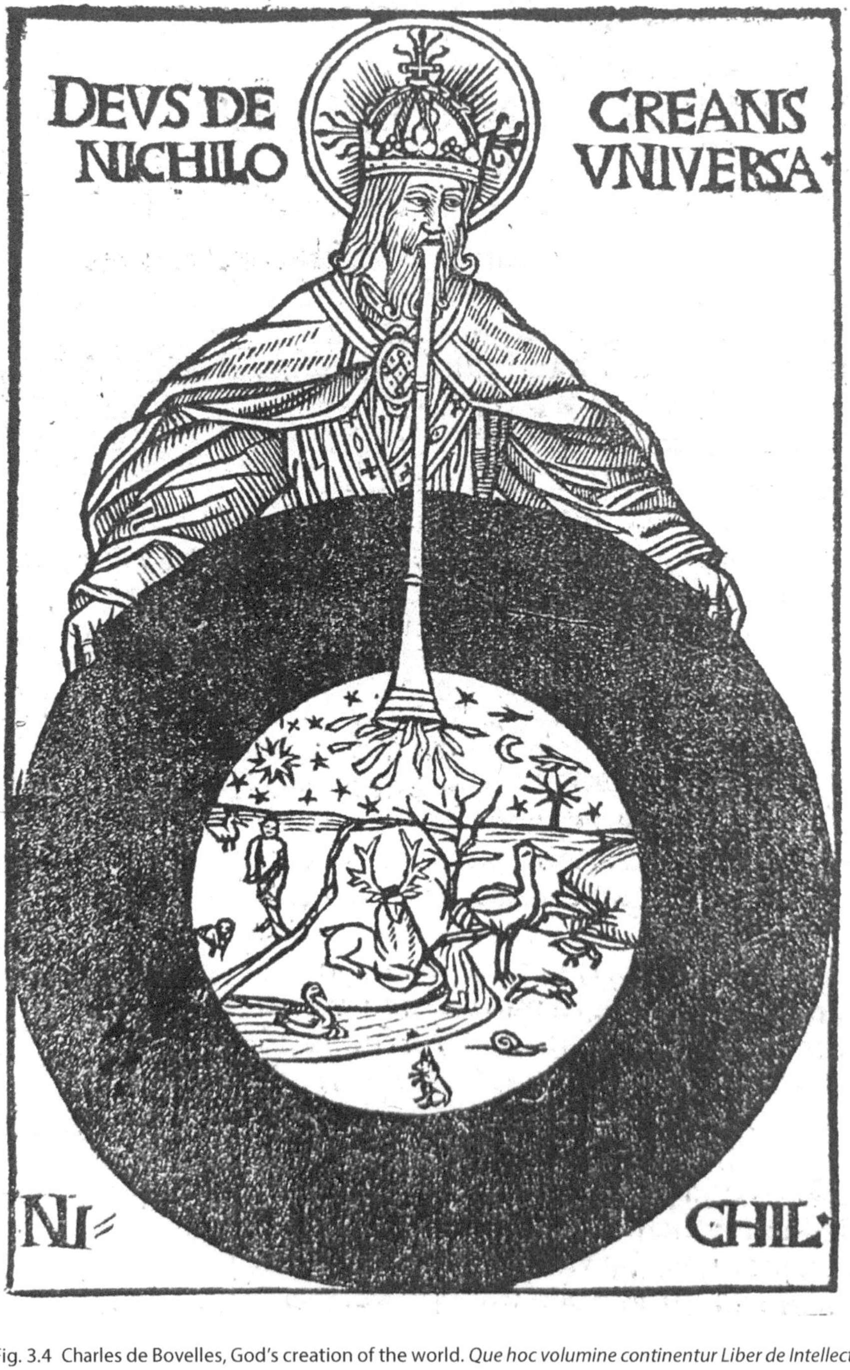

Fig. 3.4 Charles de Bovelles, God's creation of the world. *Que hoc volumine continentur Liber de Intellectu, Liber de [...] sensu. Liber de nichilo*, Paris, 1510, fol. 63r. Tolosana, Bibliothèque universitaire de l'Arsenal, Resp. 4842-2

These and other physical explanations were the dynamic spatial qualities of an unabashedly geocentric universe, not yet on the cusp of a Copernican revolution nor locatable on a Cartesian coordinate system and mired in syntheses of Christian doctrine and Aristotelian cosmology. By the thirteenth century, these cosmologies had built an uppermost stratum to heaven, the empyrean sphere (*caelum empyreum*), sometimes held to be the heaven created on the first day from Genesis and the dwelling place of God (the 'Prime Mover').[20] Creating world and world view beyond immediate perceptual phenomena through the extension of a terrestrial phenomenology was a prime modus operandi of the Aristotelian cosmos. To broach ideas or beliefs that could not be apprehended because they lay beyond the dominion of human perception, one could work through material and spatial correlations, appropriating tactics from familiar environments and places in order to develop new directions for thought and make sense of experience. 'When looked at from above,' reads Plato's *Phaedo*, 'the earth is in appearance streaked like one of those balls which have leather coverings in twelve pieces.'[21]

Architecture in the Cosmic Continuum

The practice of early modern architecture largely ignored the prodigies raining down upon the earth or the ambiguous materialities theorized by the vibrant cosmological legacy of scholastic natural philosophy. Reciprocally mapped from and onto an ideal body and extended to an ideal architecture and beyond, the cosmos was addressed via a sliding scale of proportional, rather than material, equivalences. 'The building is a form of body,' mused Leon Battista Alberti (1404-1472), who in *De statua* (1464) reimagined the body as a geographical territory and designed a site-specific measuring device called *a finitorium* consisting of a flat, gradated disc affixed to the head of a statue (or body) and a cantilevering, mobile armature suspending a plumb line.[22] Luca Pacioli (1447-1517) seconded Alberti's sentiments, adding that 'from the human body derive all measures and their denominations and it is to be found all and every ratio and proportion by which God reveals the

20 While Aristotle did not discuss the dimensions of cosmic territories, such as that of God's dwelling, the concept is addressed in al-Farghani's *Differentie scientie astrorum*, itself the source for the cosmic dimensions in Roger Bacon's *Opus majus* (prepared 1267), as well as Campanus of Novara's *Theorica planetarum* (1261-1264).

21 Plato, *Phaedo*, 258.

22 Alberti, *De re aedificatoria*, 5-6. See also Tavernor, *On Alberti and the Art of Building*, 7. Intended as an aid to corporeal measurement, the finitorium generated a three-dimensional matrix covering every point on the body relative to a central access. On the body metaphor in Alberti, see Tavernor, *On Alberti and the Art of Building*, 39-43. See also Trachtenberg, *Building-in-Time*, 80-83.

Fig. 3.5 John Shute, Corynthia. *The First and Chief Groundes of Architecture*, London, 1563. Royal Institute of British Architects, Object Nr. EW E.f526. © Royal Institute of British Architects

innermost secrets of nature'.[23] Francesco di Giorgio (1439-1501) contended that the body should serve as a model, not just for architecture but for urban planning and compared the eye to the castle, both of which should be prominently situated to survey their surroundings.[24] This theoretical tradition also extended beyond Italy. In *The First and Chief Groundes of Architecture* (London, 1563), John Shute (d. 1563) composed images comparing the proportions of the classical orders with those of different human body types, named accordingly (Figure 3.5).

Contemporary efforts to integrate architecture into the gamut of micro-macrocosms described in Plato's *Timaeus* and Aristotle's *Physics* had their most direct roots in Vitruvius' famous statements on the principles of proportion from book III.1 of *De architectura*, in which a harmonic, multiscalar relationship between ideal bodies and buildings was analogized.[25] For Vitruvius, the body could be plotted as a network of relational distances (chin to top of forehead, length of the foot equal to one-sixth the height of the body) that when translated to the architectural scale resulted in the proper arrangements for building.[26] Described in concrete/corporeal detail in *De architectura*, Vitruvius' proportionality was interpreted in kinship with the Pythagorean-Platonic *arithmos*, itself bound to a deeper articulation of the spiritual or divine structures ordering and giving form and meaning to the cosmos.[27] '*Mundus minor exemplum est, maiores mundi ordine*', as the medieval Jewish philosopher Solomon ibn Gabirol (1021-1058/1070) concisely put it in *Fons vitae*, expounding upon what would develop into a robust ontology of transcendental proportion connecting cosmic movements to human affairs, health, and bodies.[28]

23 Pacioli in *De divina proportione* (Venice, 1509), as translated in Wittkower, *Architectural Principles in the Age of Humanism*, 25.

24 'As Vitruvius has it, all art and its methods are derived from a well-composed and proportioned human body. [...] It seems to me that the city, fortress, and castle should be formed according to the human body, and that the head should have a proportional correspondence to the appropriate parts; so that the head might be the fortress, the arms its adjoining and enclosing walls, which encircling it on all sides will bind the rest of it into one body, a huge city.' Francesco di Giorgio, *Trattato di architettura* (c. 1482), quoted in Rykwert, *The Dancing Column*, 63.

25 Vitruvius devotes the majority of book IX of *De architectura* to the topic of astronomy and astrology, in which he covers the zodiac, the phases of the moon (what he calls the northern and southern constellations), as well as weather prognostications.

26 'Therefore, since nature has designed the human body so that its members are duly proportioned to the frame as a whole, it appears that the ancients had good reason for their rule, that in perfect buildings the different members must be in exact symmetrical relations to the general scheme.' Vitruvius, *Ten Books on Architecture*, book III.1.4, 73.

27 Vesely, 'The Architectonics of Embodiment', 37-38.

28 Ibn Gabirol, 'Fons vitae', 77. There are many texts addressing the micro-macrocosm correspondence. For references to the medieval period, see Wittkower, *Architectural Principles in the Age of Humanism*, 25-26 n. 68. On what he calls the 'primary' philosophical tradition of *analogia*, the structure operating upon human-architectural-cosmic proportionality, see Vesely, 'The Architectonics of Embodiment'.

Vitruvius himself had assigned credit for the constitution of a universe with 'the heaven revolving steadily round earth and sea on the pivots at the ends of its axis', to 'the architect [who] at these points was the power of Nature, and she put the pivots there, to be, as it were, centres, one of them above the earth and sea at the very top of the firmament [and] [...] the other on the opposite side under the earth in the regions of the south'.[29] Moreover, the intervening centuries had fused the concept with Christological thought to create the personage of the Divine or Supreme Architect of the Universe. Medieval manuscripts commonly depicted God holding the world in one hand and the compass, universal tool of geometry, measurement, and architecture, in the other (Figure 3.6). John Calvin (1509-1564), in his Commentary on Psalm 19:2 – The heavens are telling the glory of God, and the firmament proclaims his handiwork – explicated that 'As soon as we acknowledge God to be the supreme Architect, who has erected the beauteous fabric of the universe, our minds must necessarily be ravished with wonder at his infinite goodness, wisdom, and power.'[30] Platonic philosophy similarly accounted for an artisan-like creator of the universe, or demiurge, while Thomas Aquinas and other Christian theologians pursued the creator-as-architect metaphor, claiming that 'God, Who is the first principle of all things, may be compared to things created as the architect is to things designed.'[31]

In Vitruvius, Renaissance architects found a powerful precedent for valorising the profession of the architect in God's image and thus for occupying a critical position in a proportional continuum bridging body and cosmos.[32] Here the architectural image played a crucial role in communicating a multiscalar, geometric teleology centring upon the architect-as-creator. Landmark sixteenth-century editions of *De architectura* by Caesare Caesariano (Como, 1521) and Daniele Barbaro (Venice, 1556), as well as Sebastiano Serlio's *I sette libri dell'architettura* (Venice, 1537/1575) and Vincenzo Scamozzi's *L'idea dell'architettura universale* (Venice, 1615), all sought to visualize elements relating to the concept of a geometrically grounded, spatial order traversing the firmament to the terrestrial core of the Aristotelian cosmos.[33] Caesariano's translation even

29 Vitruvius, *Ten Books on Architecture*, book IX.4. On mechanical metaphors for the universe in Vitruvius, see Di Pasquale, 'Vitruvius's Image of the Universe'.

30 Calvin's reading does not reflect the original Hebrew, which allows for a degree of ambiguity and poetic irony as regards the act of creation.

31 Aquinas, *Summa Theologica*, Question XXVII, Reply to Objection 3.

32 Proportionality as a field of enquiry was a vast philosophical territory for ancient cultures and humanists alike, and beyond the scope of this essay. For a technical discussion of ancient mathematics and their interpretation and debate in the early modern period, see March, *Architectonics of Humanism*.

33 The most common sources remained the *Physics* and *De Caelo*, and Ptolemy's *Almagest*. This is not to say that architecture and other spatial practices (cosmology, cosmography) understood to be related through geometry and measurement, were *not* buffeted by the conflicting impulse to reconcile the classical legacy of absolute ratios and measurements with new empirical data, gleaned from surveying, navigation, developments in construction and engineering technology, and astronomical observation. See

Fig. 3.6 God as Architect. Frontispiece of *Bible moralisée*. Ink, tempera, and gold leaf on vellum, c. 1220-1230. Österreichisches Nationalbibliothek, Codex Vindobonensis 2554, fol.1v

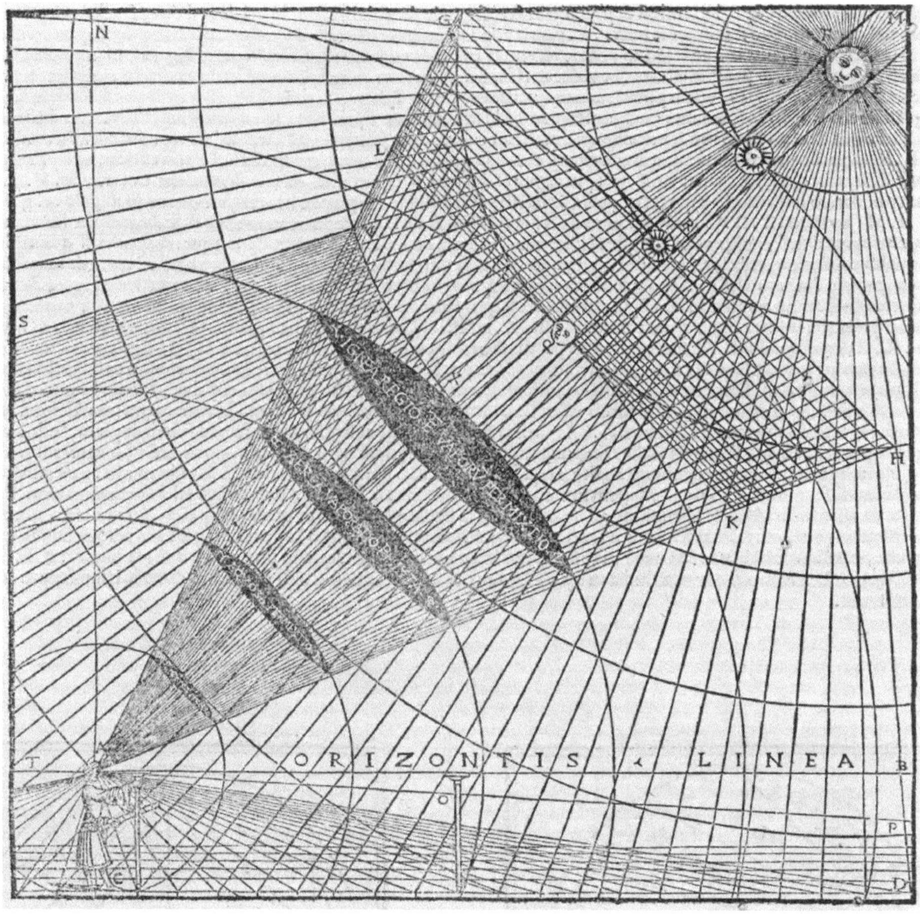

Fig. 3.7 Cesare Cesariano, declination of celestial bodies/perspectival construction. *Vitruuio Pollione De architectura libri decem*, 1521, fol. 11v. Max Planck Institute, Object Nr.: Gf 200-120 gr. raro. Courtesy of the Bibliotheca Hertziana – Max Planck Institute for Art History, Rome

included images of an armillary sphere and a heliocentric world system, and depicted the applicability of surveying tools such as the cross staff for determining both the declination of celestial bodies and the construction of linear perspective (Figure 3.7).[34]

Buildings and their surface treatments were parsed as variations on a cosmic analogue. In the exuberant dome of San Lorenzo in Turin (1668-1680), Guarino Guarini (1624-1683) aped the rotating armatures of the armillary sphere. Corrado

Cosgrove, 'Ptolemy and Vitruvius'. For more on Renaissance architecture and proportion, see Wittkower, *Architectural Principles in the Age of Humanism*, 104-137; Onians, *Bearers of Meaning*.

34 Cosgrove, 'Ptolemy and Vitruvius', 44. On the development of the discipline of cosmography and its indebtedness to new modes of visualization, see Vanden Broecke, 'The Use of Visual Media in Renaissance Cosmography'.

Giaquinto's (1703-1766) heliocentric tromp l'oeil, *Celestial Glory: The Coronation of the Virgin* (1755) at the Royal Palace in Madrid, turned the concentric circles of the Copernican universe into a play of seraphim, clouds, and saints extending backwards into a circular, heavenly space.[35] Bologna's Basilica of San Petronio, Santa Maria degli Angeli in Rome, Saint-Sulpice in Paris, and others installed brass-outlined *meridiane* running along their marble floors to track the movement of the sun (and the precise date of the equinox and solstices) in order to fix inconsistencies in the ancient Julian calendar.[36]

As theorized in its most ideal expressions, architecture had the potential to place the experience of a Classical-cum-cosmic order, even as the cosmic designs of a supreme architect, rendered as harmonic schemes of proportions, remained legible in concentric orientation of the planetary spheres. Ideal bodies were conceived as coexistent with ideal buildings and cities, and *mutatis mutandis*, architecture of sufficient ambition strove to speak to a macrocosmic condition – the immutable and paradisiacal space of the universe and heaven. Through a transcendent proportionality extending into an oscillating spatial continuum, the spatial logics of architecture could be made to bridge the human and cosmic in a 'phenomenal transparency' of overlapping spaces at incommensurate if interrelated scales.[37] Architecture, in the right hands and acting in its own self-interest, could claim to offer up charged sites teleporting one to the celestial realm, collapsing the cosmic and the cosmopolitan on pavement and page.

Outer Spatiality

The drawing possesses the intrinsic capacity to hide spatial inconsistencies only revealed with the addition of further dimensions. Leon Battista Alberti asserted as much in *De re aedificatoria* (1452) when he claimed to 'always commend the time-honoured custom, practiced by the best builders, of preparing not only drawings and sketches but also models of wood or any other material'.[38] By analogy, a fuller model of the architecture of the cosmos – much as with a fuller model of experience generally – would need to combine together and desegregate a broader set of texts, transitory demarcations, and sensoria to reveal these hidden dimensions and consistencies. Broaching what 'outerspatiality' would have mean to the early modern actor, in all of its place-making capacities, lends itself, methodologically, to

35 Hersey, *Architecture and Geometry in the Age of the Baroque*, 29.

36 See Heilbron, *The Sun in the Church*.

37 On phenomenal transparency, see Rowe, 'Transparency'.

38 Alberti, *On the Art of Building in Ten Books*, 33-34; Payne, 'The Sculptor-Architect's Drawing and Exchanges between the Arts', 60.

Fig. 3.8 Albrecht Dürer, *Martyrdom of St. Catherine* (1492). The Metropolitan Museum of Art, Accession Number: 1975.653.99. The George Khuner Collection, Gift of Mrs. George Khuner, 1975

the embrace of *all* the paradigmatic, yet paradoxical, modalities stitched together by the meteorite's landing in Alsace – the human and the celestial, the Prime Mover and the Divine Architect, their locking together in a mise en abyme of oblique interdependence forming the distorted echoes of an antique afterlife that refused to die. This was the kind of life where Pliny's description, borrowing from Aristotle, of a stone, 'wagonload in size and of a burnt appearance' that had fallen into 'a part of Thrace, at the River Ægos', returns again and again, an event experienced in its withdrawal, dramatized and multiplied in the sky above Dürer's *Martyrdom of St. Catherine* (1492) (Figure 3.8).[39] 'From the lower part of the atmosphere it rained milk and blood.'[40] This macabre episode, body parts raining down from the sky as foretold by Pliny in *Natural History*, is dated to 1513 by the *Luzerner Chronik*, the same volume to document the descent of the Ensisheim meteor.

If one were able to place themselves in that Alsatian field on that precise November day in 1492, how might the large flaming object plummeting out of the sky have been comprehended? Might the vortex created by its downward movement have spurred the imagination to linger on an otherwise invisible cosmic architecture, layers of nested, celestial spheres radiating out from the earth, their surfaces dotted with stars, their interstellar convolution now unexpectedly metonymized in a giant falling rock? In that moment, would a cross-section of the universe have revealed itself violently juxtaposed to the space of human experience? Or perhaps the thing most likely to be revealed by the meteorite as it first ploughed into the collective consciousness was the breadth and depth of the ocean of invisibility that inevitably surrounded it, a space often imagined but never visited, only encountered as it crumbled to the ground.

Bibliography

Alberti, Leon Battista, *On the Art of Building in Ten Books*, trans. by Joseph Rykwert, Robert Tavernor and Neil Leach (Cambridge, MA: The MIT Press, 1988).

Aquinas, Thomas, *Summa Theologica* (Benziger Brothers, 1947), https://dhspriory.org/thomas/summa/.

Aristotle, *Physics*, trans. R.P. Hardie and R.K. Gaye, http://classics.mit.edu/Aristotle/physics.html.

Cosgrove, Denis, 'Ptolemy and Vitruvius: Spatial Representation in the Sixteenth-Century Texts and Commentaries', in Antoine Picon and Alessandra Ponte (eds), *Architecture and the Sciences: Exchanging Metaphors* (Princeton: Princeton Architectural Press, 2003), 20-51.

39 Pliny, *The Natural History*, 2.59. See Heidegger, *Zum Ereignis-Denken*.

40 Pliny, *The Natural History*, 2.57.

Daston, Lorraine and Katharine Park, *Wonders and the Order of Nature, 1150-1750* (Cambridge, MA: Zone Books, 2001).

De Rizi, Vincenzo, 'Francesco Patrizi and the New Geometry of Space', in Koen Vermeir and Jonathan Regier (eds), *Boundaries, Extents and Circulations* (Cham: Springer, 2016), 55-106.

Di Pasquale, Giovanni, 'Vitruvius's Image of the Universe: Architecture and Mechanics', in Paolo Sanvito (ed.), *Vitruvianism: Origins and Transformations* (Berlin: De Gruyter, 2016), 49-64.

Genz, Henning, *Nothingness: The Science of Empty Space*, trans. by Karin Heusch (Cambridge, MA: Perseus Publishing, 2009).

Goethe, Johann Wolfgang von, *Sämtliche Werke*, vol. 9 (Frankfurt am Main: Deutscher Klassiker Verlag, 1989).

Goethe, Johann Wolfgang von, *Truth and Poetry*, trans. by John Oxenford (Cambridge: Cambridge University Press, 2013).

Grafton, Anthony, *Cardano's Cosmos* (Cambridge, MA: Harvard University Press, 2001).

Grant, Edward, *Planets, Stars, & Orbs: The Medieval Cosmos 1200-1687* (Cambridge: Cambridge University Press, 1996).

Heidegger, Martin, *Zum Ereignis-Denken* (Frankfurt am Main: V. Klostermann, 2013).

Heilbron, John L., *The Sun in the Church: Cathedrals as Solar Observatories* (Cambridge, MA: Harvard University Press, 1999).

Hersey, George L., *Architecture and Geometry in the Age of the Baroque* (Chicago: University of Chicago Press, 2000).

Ibn Gabirol, Solomon, 'Fons vitae', in Clemens Baeumker (ed.), *Beiträge zur Geschichte der Philosophie des Mittelalters* 3.2. (Münster: Aschendorff Buchhandlung, 1892).

Lycosthenes, Conrad, *Prodigiorum ac ostentorum chronicon* (Basel: Heinrich Petri, 1557).

March, Lionel, *Architectonics of Humanism* (West Sussex: John Wiley & Sons, 1998).

Martin, Craig, *Renaissance Meteorology: Pomponazzi to Descartes* (Baltimore: Johns Hopkins University Press, 2011).

Marvin, Ursula B., 'The Meteorite of Ensisheim, 1492 to 1992', *Meteoritics* 27.1 (1992), 28-72.

Onians, John, *Bearers of Meaning: The Classical Orders in Antiquity, the Middle Ages, and the Renaissance* (Princeton: Princeton University Press, 1988).

Paracelsus, *Paragranum*, in *Essential Theoretical Writings*, ed. by Andrew Weeks (Leiden and Boston: Brill, 2008).

Paracelsus, *Theophrast von Hohenheim gen. Paracelsus: Sämtliche Werke*, vol. 13, ed. by Karl Sudhoff (Munich and Berlin: R. Oldenbourg, 1931).

Payne, Alina, 'The Sculptor-Architect's Drawing and Exchanges between the Arts', in Michael W. Cole (ed.), *Donatello, Michelangelo, Cellini: Sculptors' Drawings from Renaissance Italy* (Boston: Isabella Stewart Gardner Museum, 2014), 57-73.

Plato, *Phaedo*, in *The Dialogues of Plato*, trans. by B. Jowett, 2 vols (London: Oxford University Press, 1892).

Pliny, *The Natural History*, trans. by John Bostock and H.T. Riley (London: H.G. Bohn, 1855), http://www.perseus.tufts.edu/hopper/text?doc=Perseus:text:1999.02.0137.
Rabelais, François, *Gargantua and Pantagruel*, trans. and ed. by M.A. Screech (London and New York: Penguin Books, 2006).
Regier, Jonathan and Koen Vermeir, 'Boundaries, Extents and Circulations: An Introduction to Spatiality and the Early Modern Concept of Space', in John Regier and Koen Vermeir (eds), *Boundaries, Extents and Circulations: Space and Spatiality in Early Modern Natural Philosophy* (Cham: Springer, 2016), 1-32.
Rowe, Colin, 'Transparency: Literal and Phenomenal', *The Mathematics of the Ideal Villa and Other Essays* (Cambridge, MA: The MIT Press, 1976), 159-184.
Rowland, Ingrid D., 'A Contemporary Account of the Ensisheim Meteor, 1492', *Meteoritics* 25.1 (1990), 19-22.
Rutkin, H. Darrel, 'Astrology', in Lorraine Daston and Katharine Park (eds), *Early Modern Science* (Cambridge: Cambridge University Press, 2006), 541-561.
Rykwert, Joseph, *The Dancing Column: On Order in Architecture* (Cambridge, MA: The MIT Press, 1996).
Schedel, Hartmann, *Liber chronicarum* (Nuremberg, 1493).
Shute, John, *The First and Chief Groundes of Architecture* (London, 1563).
Tavernor, Robert, *On Alberti and the Art of Building* (New Haven: Yale University Press, 1998).
Trachtenberg, Marvin, *Building-in-Time: From Giotto to Alberti and Modern Oblivion* (New Haven: Yale University Press, 2010).
Vanden Broecke, Steven, 'The Use of Visual Media in Renaissance Cosmography: The Cosmography of Peter Apian and Gemma Frisius', *Paedagogica Historica: International Journal of the History of Education* 36.1 (2000), 130-150.
Vesely, Dalibor, 'The Architectonics of Embodiment', in George Dodds and Robert Tavernor (eds), *Body and Building: Essays on the Changing Relation of Body and Architecture* (Cambridge, MA: The MIT Press, 2002), 29-43.
Vitruvius, *Ten Books on Architecture*, trans. by Ingrid D. Rowland (Cambridge: Cambridge University Press, 1999).
Wittkower, Rudolf, *Architectural Principles in the Age of Humanism* (West Sussex: Academy Editions, 1998 [1949]).

About the Author

Noam Andrews is a historian and curator whose interests lie in early modern history of science and its intersection with visual and material culture. He received his PhD in the history of science from Harvard University and is a postdoctoral fellow in the Faculty of Arts and Philosophy at Ghent University, Belgium.

4. Architecture for Music: Sonorous Spaces in Sacred Buildings in Renaissance and Baroque Rome

Federico Bellini

Abstract

Architectural spaces are usually considered only in their visual and three-dimensional character. However, the proper experience of space is multisensory. Sonority is undoubtedly the non-visual characteristic that most affects architecture, influencing its three-dimensional shape, and the size and distribution of its individual parts. Early modern sacred architecture is a case in point. Focusing on Rome and the development of architecture in relation to musical practices, this article demonstrates how architectural forms evolved through a process that ranged from provisional installations to the design of entirely new churches and oratories. In the Baroque period, these religious structures were conceived as synaesthetic spaces of sonority and architecture, in which vision, hearing and liturgical acts merged in an expressive unity.

Keywords: Catholic Church, Borromini, oratorio, Bernini, acoustics

Sound and Architectural Space

Remains of the nineteenth-century aesthetic theory of 'pure visibility' (*Reine Sichtbarkeit*) survive in the contemporary study of architectural history, even if not explicitly evoked. Still today, scholars commonly assume that throughout history, buildings and cities were largely formed for visual aims. In turn, much of their study is based on purely visual analysis, to which ideological interpretations, based on anachronistic values, are often superimposed. As we know, an architectural or urban place is determined by extra-formal characteristics, such as the cosmic *speculum*

Merrill, E. (ed.), *Creating Place in Early Modern European Architecture*.
Taylor & Francis Group 2022
DOI: 10.5117/9789463728027_CH04

highlighted by Andrews in his article, or the sanctions inflicted on violators of the rules of *civitas* described in De Raedt's text.

Yet, early modern architecture – as most architecture today – was built not only to be *seen*, but to be *used*, in accordance with contemporary needs. The buildings' users had a much deeper experience of architectural space than the aestheticism of our historiography would allow. To borrow from the Latin, they were not just *spectatores* (viewers) but *utentes* (users), involved in their physical, built environment on an emotional, intellectual, and often also moral level. After all, even if only from the perceptual point of view, the use of a space is a multisensory experience that goes well beyond vision. It follows that architectural space cannot be solely measured in terms of the geometry of its constituent volumes. Rather, it is characterized by expressive values that go beyond the isotropy of pure geometry, and which in some cases deform space and even contradict it. In short, in the context of architecture, it is more appropriate to speak not of neutral spaces, but of individual and unique places.

This article uses the ecclesiastical architecture of Renaissance and Baroque Rome to examine such a multidimensional understanding of space, giving particular attention to the acoustic focus integral in the buildings' design. In this period, buildings, and even cities, were ordered according to a hierarchy of their representative and symbolic values. The areas dedicated to the most prestigious functions were those that culminated in a system of paths, structures that underlined the symbolic and formal pre-eminence of individual places. The most important places and constructions were those demarcated with a series of overlapping expedients, delineated by size, illumination, ornamental richness, colour and materials. But in many cases, spatial delineation also included sound, an intangible feature that is not easily measured, and which still today is largely overlooked in architectural history.

In certain building types – theatres, auditoria and assembly halls – the primary importance of acoustics is self-evident and requires no explanation. But in the early modern period, acoustics played an equally important role in the spatial construction of a number of other architectural forms, albeit in a manner that is less immediately recognizable. Such is the case with religious buildings, in which the sound assumed different forms that ranged from the spoken word to singing and instrumental music.[1] In the period between 1450 and 1800, sound played a subtle role in conditioning the three-dimensionality and the formal hierarchy of religious spaces, as well as their conceptual representation. This is immediately recognizable in the first Protestant buildings, in both the Evangelical and Reformed traditions. The sanctity of a Protestant church was determined not by the materiality of the building or its ritual forms, but by the pronouncement of the Word, that

1 Among the few contributions on the topic, see Howard, 'Architecture and Music in Fifteenth-Century Italy'; Howard and Moretti, *Sound and Space in Renaissance Venice*.

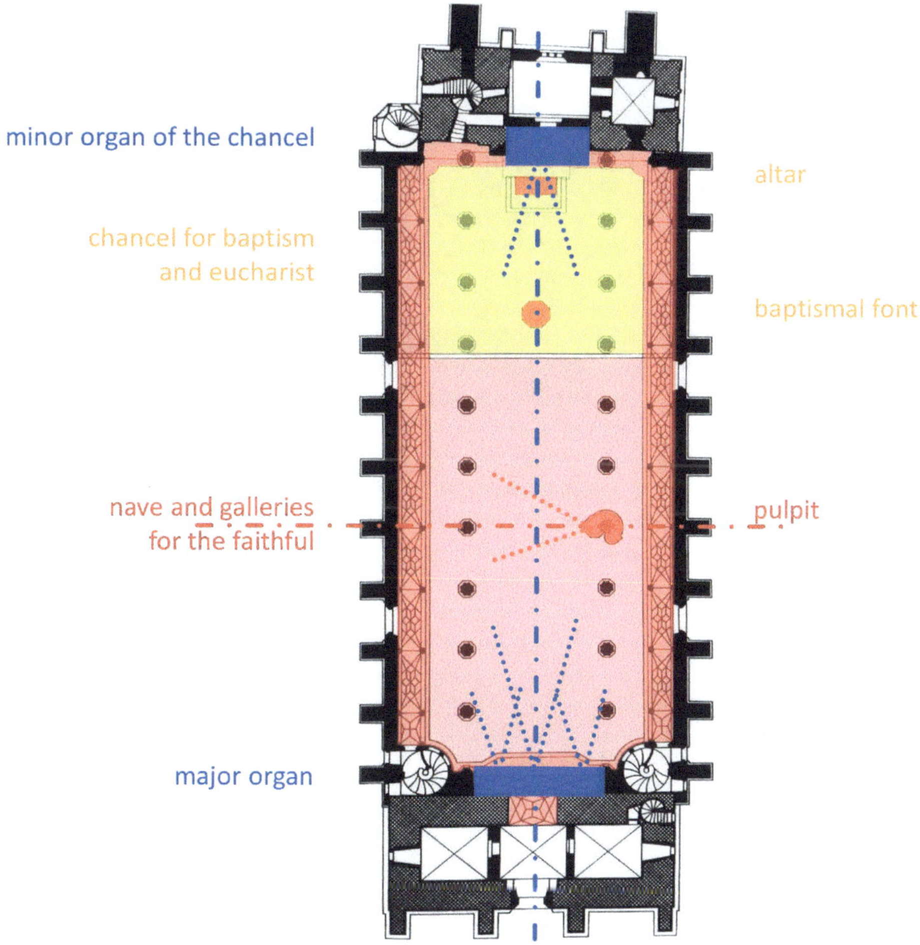

Fig. 4.1 Marktkirche, Halle, following the Lutheran renovations of 1542
a) Plan: (in red) the transverse Querkirche focused on the pulpit of the prayer; (in blue) the longitudinal axis aligned with the chancel area; (in yellow) the longitudinal axis dedicated to Eucharist and Baptism.
© Federico Bellini

is, an acoustic act.[2] The need for all the faithful to understand the readings and sermons lead to important interventions, whereby the churches were adopted from Catholicism. In the first decades of the Reform, the choirs in the naves were removed, the altars were placed in view of everyone; fixed seats were installed

2 Wex, *Ordnung und Unfriede*; Spicer, *Lutheran Churches in Early Modern Europe*; Harasimowicz, *Protestantischer Kirchenbau der Frühen Neuzeit in Europa*; see also Bellini, 'Riforma protestante e riforma dell'architettura religiosa', with wide reference to the bibliography, which cannot be summarized here.

Fig. 4.1 Marktkirche, Halle, following the Lutheran renovations of 1542
b) Nave: looking toward the altar. © Photo: Wikipedia

in the naves and balconies were built around the walls to increase the seating capacity; finally, the axes were rotated 90 degrees to concentrate the visual and auditory focus on the pulpits; pre-Reformation basilicas, which were explicitly longitudinal, were thereby transformed into transverse *Querkirchen*. St. Pierre Cathedral in Geneva (1535) for the Reformed Church, and Marktkirche in Halle (1542), for the Evangelical Church, are perhaps the most emblematic examples of these initial works (Figure 4.1(a-b)).[3]

But while the acoustic quality of Protestant churches is often contrasted with the visual aspect of Catholic churches, such differentiation is a drastic simplification, as acoustics and vision are present in both Protestant and Catholic religious

3 Bellini, 'Riforma protestante e riforma dell'architettura religiosa', 84-89.

buildings, albeit in different ways.[4] In the early modern period, the synaesthetic role of sound in Catholic architecture assumed its own forms due to the different concept of sanctity attributed to the rites and objects of worship (starting with the building itself). The Catholic ceremony is fundamentally multisensory, and involves participants, both clerical and the faithful, with a range of perceptual stimuli that help to explain the architecture of sacred buildings. In the period in question, the church was used for processional rituals, that is, as a framework for choreographed movement. The clergy and faithful moved through it in pervasive, sumptuous processions that struck the sight, sound and even smell, to then return to their assigned place in the hierarchies of religious and social order.[5] Even touch was involved, by virtue of the intrinsic sanctity recognized by Catholics in the materiality of places and sacred objects. Clerics and the faithful 'used' the religious space, touching fabrics, images, statues, relics, old walls, and columns, which they believed to contain miraculous and curative humours. With these multisensory qualities, musical sound played an important and sometimes dominant role, often modifying the three-dimensional perception of the religious space itself. Beginning in the second half of the sixteenth century, recognition of the importance of music, and sound, in the spatial experience of the church increasingly played a driving force in architectural design. Architects became not only cognizant of spatial acoustics, but began to design places that augmented and enriched this sensory component.[6]

Sacred Music and Religious Spaces

Schematically, music influenced the architectural forms of early modern church architecture on three levels. The first is at the level of the senses. Sound influences the three-dimensional perception of space. It is a well-known fact that the reflection time of a sound helps us measure the depth of a space. Music also influenced architecture at the ornamental level. In the early modern period, musical sound was used as a

4 On the role of vision in the first Lutheran churches, see Körner, *The Reformation of the Image*.

5 The celebrated printings of the *Verae imagines Ecclesiae* compare Protestant religious spaces (ordered, static, and acoustic) and Catholic spaces (chaotic, dynamic, visual): Körner, *The Reformation of the Image*, 44, fig. 10. On the procession ceremony of St. Peter's, see Rostirolla, 'Musiche e apparati nella basilica vaticana per le feste dei Santi Pietro e Paolo'. On olfactory solicitation, see Morelli, 'La vista dell'apparato superbo', 299.

6 A group of Italian scholars was formed around this topic. In March 2018, the group presented the PRIN project 'Architecture for Music: Sonorous Space and Furnishings in Sacred Buildings of the Renaissance and Baroque', Universities of Camerino, L'Aquila, Venice-Ca' Foscari, Florence, of which I was the principal investigator. The research was expanded with the international seminar 'Architecture for Music: Sonorous Space and Furnishings in Sacred Buildings of the Renaissance and Baroque', organized by Federico Bellini and Martina Frank, Venice, Ca' Foscari, 27 November 2018.

complement of architectural space, qualifying it with a type of decorative acoustic apparatus that allowed the architecture to express significance in a multisensory experience. Musical sound adds value to the space in which it is performed, and because of its temporality, it is comparable to an ephemeral apparatus, in which sound replaces colour and shape. Finally, music directed architectural design at a symbolic level. In some cases, architecture and music were integrated to shape a space – a place-specific construction – that was completely synaesthetic. In such instances, architecture was conceived in order to furnish a permanent ambience for the immaterial musical component. Architecture and music were thus in communication with one another, despite belonging to different media, and shared symbolic content.

The development of sacred music practices in the early modern period was likewise influenced by the regulations placed on the liturgy and spaces of worship during the Reformation – in northern Europe – and the Counter-Reformation – in Italy. In the context of the Catholic Church, Tridentine principles were decisive in prompting the shift of music towards the congregation. For example, medieval *tramezzi*, or rood screens that divided the clergy from the congregation, were largely demolished, especially in Florence, thereby relegating priests to retro-choirs, but also leaving organ cases half within the nave.[7] At the same time, from the middle of the seventeenth century ecclesiastical authorities were bound to constrain the unregulated expansion of musical spaces in churches.

In examining the evolution of music and religious architecture in the early modern period, it is imperative to understand that the church – in both the Roman Catholic and Protestant traditions – was not only a place of worship. It was also a social space, representing, by its forms, the dominant power of an institution (religious as well as lay), and reflecting the social ranks and the cultural identity of a community. Due to the diffusion of the sung mass accompanied by instruments, churches and oratories were the most frequented spaces in which people could listen to great music (and without cost).[8] This is not say, however, that the impact of sacred music transformed religious buildings into auditoria. In both the Catholic and Protestant churches, the impact of religious buildings remained conditioned primarily by the ritual, that is, the social modes in which worship was practiced. Music was one of the most appreciated and striking elements that contributed to defining the social practices of worship, but it was not the only defining element. The spaces dedicated to performing and listening to music remained subordinate to the general concept of religious buildings.[9] So, in the early modern period, sacred

7 Morelli, 'Sull'organo et in choro', 215-218; on *tramezzi*, see also Hall, 'The *Tramezzo* in the Italian Renaissance, Revisited'.

8 Smither, *A History of the Oratorio*, 160-161.

9 After all, even the architecture of lyrical theatres is not a direct translation of dramatic and acoustic need. The first underlying need was the topographical distribution of social classes, from which the

music and sacred architecture were not themselves independent of one another. They were both subject to the rules of liturgy, or, more accurately, to the rules of the ceremonial practices of liturgy, which could vary from church to church. The performance of religious music, and the architectural space in which this occurred, was thus a production of specific places. This question can be clarified in examining examples related to both Protestant and Catholic architecture.

The first churches conceived explicitly for the new Reformed religion were built in the Netherlands in the early 1600s.[10] In contrast to Huguenot and Swiss temples, the new Dutch *kerken* were monumental buildings realized to express the moral and economic strength of an entire community. In their design, they freely adopted systems and motifs that derived from Italian Catholic architecture, despite the overt religious differences. But the Dutch churches were by no means merely derivative. In their plan and forms, they created spatial structures in which sound played a decisive role.

The Dutch *kerken*, like all Calvinist churches, were not limited to solely religious functions. The church was deemed a sacred place only during worship services.[11] At other times, it was a lay space, an ample setting that could host public ceremonies, even sumptuous ones, accompanied by rich orchestral music. The spatial order of the church interior was adjusted according to use, as was the musical programme. During religious functions, the Dutch churches were used as transverse *Querkirchen* or cross-churches, in which the transept is considerably longer than the nave. Within this arrangement, the faithful would face the pulpit, from which the Word, recited by the presbyter, flowed. The only music allowed was homophones, sung by the faithful without any instrumental accompaniment. By contrast, during public ceremonies, the axis of the interior space was rotated to be situated longitudinally, making use of the magnificent organs whose sound spread throughout the nave. The Reformed Westerkerk in Amsterdam, designed by Hendrick de Keyser (1620-1631), and the Nieuwe Kerk by Peter Noorwits in The Hague (1649-1656), are prime examples of architectural spaces whose axial layout varied as a function of the users' experience, both visual and acoustic (Figure 4.2(a-b)).[12] The axial orientation and adjustment of space, in keeping with a musical programme, was even more pronounced in Lutheran churches, due to the centrality of music in the Evangelical rite.[13]

system of boxes (whether Italian or French is of little importance) is the clearest result. Pinelli, *I teatri*.

10 Snaet, 'For the Greater Glory of God'; Ottenheym, 'The Attractive Flavour of the Past', 105-114; Bellini, 'Riforma protestante e riforma dell'architettura religiosa', 92-93.

11 Spicer, *Calvinist Churches in Early Modern Europe*; on religious premises, see Reymond, *L'architecture religieuse des protestants*, and Isaiasz, 'Early Modern Lutheran Churches'.

12 Bellini, 'Riforma protestante e riforma dell'architettura religiosa', 92-93.

13 For a more extended discussion of this, see Range, 'The Material Presence of Music in Church'.

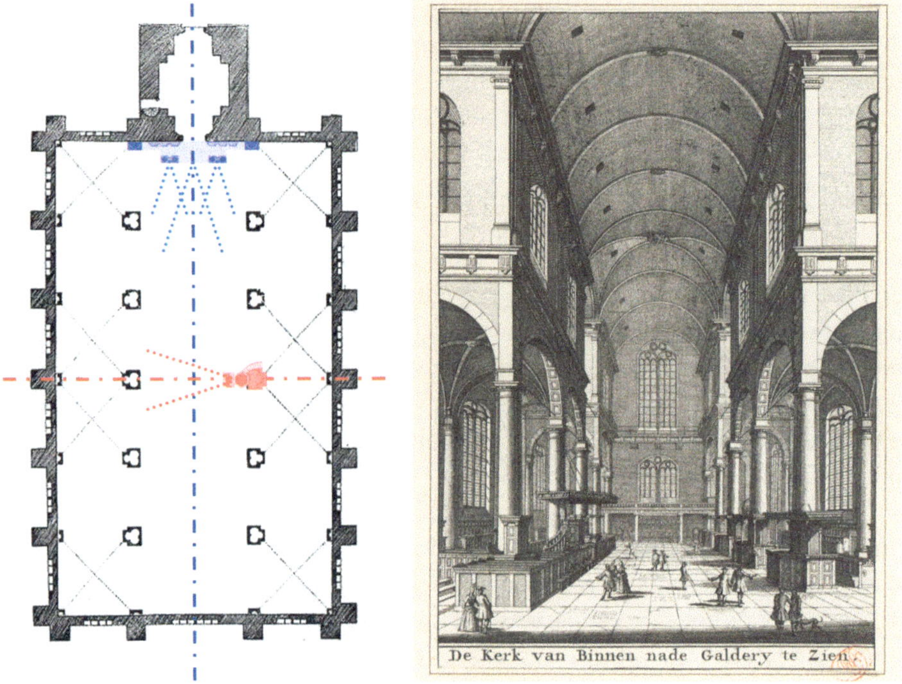

Fig. 4.2 Westerkerk, Amsterdam, designed by Hendrick Cornelisz de Keyser the Elder, 1620-1631
a) Sound plan: (in red) the axis of spoken Word; (in blue) the axis of the music and sung. © Federico Bellini
b) Daniel Stoopendaal, interior of the Westerkerk, looking towards the gallery. Engraving, c. 1700. Rijksmuseum, Object Nr. RP-P-AO-23-47B

An analogous development of acoustic-driven architecture can be seen in Catholic churches, realized in the same period. The adjustments made to St. John Lateran – the cathedral of the Bishop of Rome, the pope – in the late 1600s provide one example. The church's right transept, pointing towards the city, constituted the favoured access to the basilica for the great pontifical processions, and for this reason its façade was rebuilt in monumental form by Popes Pius IV and Sixtus V in the second half of the sixteenth century.[14] The realignment of the church was furthered by Clement VIII, who between 1597 and 1600 radically renovated the interior, entrusting the work to Giacomo Della Porta, who transformed the transept into an independent space, freeing it from the formal submission to the powerful longitudinal layout of Constantine's basilica. Pietro Paolo Olivieri erected a monumental altar on the southern end of the transept to house the Holy Sacrament.[15] To counter this, on the northern wall of the church's entrance,

14 Coffin, *Pirro Ligorio*, 50-52; Freiberg, *The Lateran in 1600*, 10-36.

15 Freiberg, *The Lateran in 1600*, 21-22.

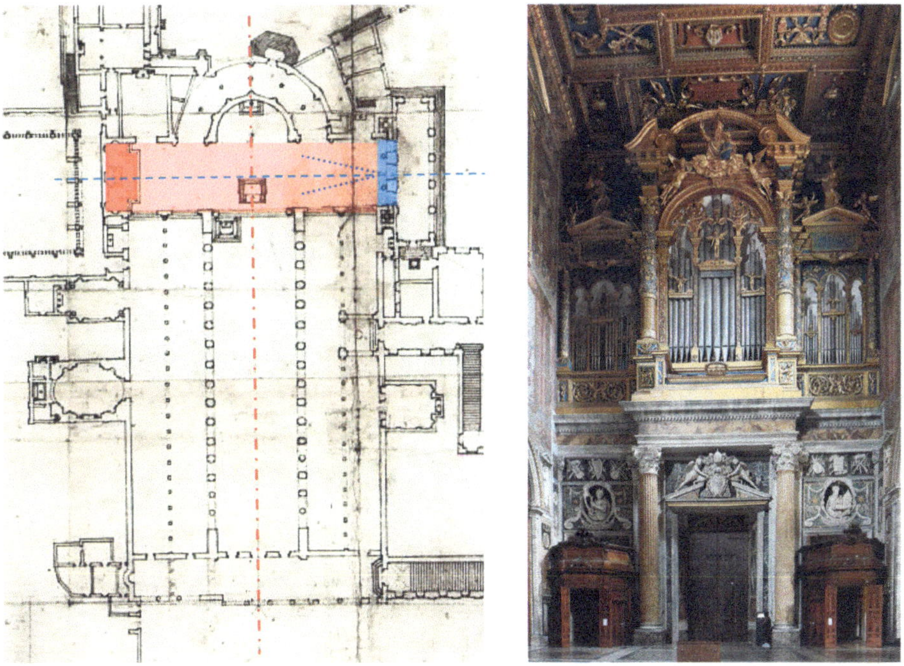

Fig. 4.3 St. John Lateran, Rome
a) Plan by Francesco Borromini, c. 1646: (in red), altar; (in blue), sound axis of the organ gallery. From Albertina Graphische Sammlung, Az. Rom 373a. © Federico Bellini
b) Organ gallery. © Photo: Federico Bellini

Giovanni Battista Montano erected a giant organ loft, the largest and first of its kind in Rome.[16] The redesign of St. John Lateran was completed in 1599-1600, when a team of masters directed by Cavalier d'Arpino painted the series of holy frescoes, following a programme designed by Cardinal Cesare Baronio.[17]

The changes made to St. John Lateran were by no means purely visual in their impact. During the celebration at the altar of the Blessed Sacrament, choral music performed at the organ radiated to the transept and defined the space by means of acoustics. The music also related to the new decorative scheme and the narrative depicted in the frescoes, creating in essence a single synaesthetic system. The parallelepiped of the transept thereby became perceptually (and functionally) independent, which was unknown in other greater basilicas, meriting the denomination 'Clementine Nave' (Figure 4.3(a-b)).

16 Battistelli et al., *Organi e cantorie nelle chiese di Roma*, 46-49.
17 Freiberg, *The Lateran in 1600*, 37-158, 288-310.

A second, even more impressive case of acoustic-driven architecture is found in the Oratorio dei Filippini by Francesco Borromini (1637-1640), to which this chapter will later return (Figures 4.13-4.15).[18] Six days per week, the Oratorio was used to pray and listen to sermons read by an Oratorian father seated on a sort of raised cathedra (*sedia*).[19] Borromini designed a rectangular plan and placed the *sedia* in the middle of the long axis, so that during the days of prayer (the so-called *oratorio piccolo*, or the 'small oratory'), the Oratorio functioned entirely as a transverse *Querkirche*, in which the spoken word dominated. In the evenings on winter holy days (from All Saints' Day to Easter), the Oratorio hosted entirely different spiritual exercises (the so-called *oratorio festivo*, or 'holy days oratory'), which attracted hundreds of believers. The spectacular choral and orchestral works performed on such occasions were described by the English traveller Francis Mortoft in 1659:

> It beginning to be night, wee went to the Chiesa Nova, where there is most incomparable Musicke every Sunday and holy day at Night, with Organs and 4 Voyces, and wee heard such sweete Musicke, tha a man could not thinke his paines be il spent, if he should come two thousand mile, if he were sure to be recompensed with nothing else, but to heare such most melodious voyces.[20]

Some years prior, Borromini had installed for these festive rites a three-level musical loft that occupied the entire altar end, and on the other end, a loggia of honour designated for cardinals and princes. The Oratorio thus became a longitudinal space between the two loggias, conceived to support the projection and audition of the sung Word. The Oratorio dei Filippini, the emblematic work of the Counter-Reformation *Ecclesia Triumphans*, therefore had a plan that – by historical paradox – recalled many spaces in Protestant churches, starting with the Schlosskapelle in Torgau founded by Luther himself. In both cases, the final form of the church was driven by the common problem of managing the acoustics of the recited and sung Word in spaces that were routinely adjusted according to different function.[21]

Both cases are also instructive in that they demonstrate how sacred music conditioned the space of religious architecture in ways that depend on the particular local conditions. While early modern acoustic-driven architectural design followed general rules, each construct was fundamentally place-specific, adapting to a

18 Bellini, 'La forma della musica'.

19 On the chair replaced the pulpit, which was prohibited by Saint Filippo Neri, see Bellini, 'La forma della musica'.

20 Smither, *A History of the Oratorio*, 162-163.

21 Bellini, 'La forma della musica'; Bellini, 'Riforma protestante e riforma dell'architettura religiosa', 97-101.

given site and location, promoting the specific ideas the clergy, and adhering to the specific needs of the congregation.

Architecture for Sacred Music: Roman Churches

Roman religious architecture adapted to the development of musical practices in terms of the typology of plans and the definition of individual elements, such as singing galleries and monumental organ cases. In these formal developments, it might be said that the entire architectural space evolved as well. The following discussion summarizes the evolutionary relationship between music and Renaissance and Baroque ecclesiastical architecture in Rome, focusing first on the design of churches and then on the design of oratories. In relation to the development of musical practices, the transformation of early modern religious architecture will be studied through processes that ranged from provisional installation of balconies and lofts, to the construction ex novo of sonorous churches and oratories. Within these synaesthetic spaces, vision, hearing and liturgical acts merge in an expressive unity.

In recent decades, Arnaldo Morelli has tried to recognize a historic trend which could explain the evolutionary relationship between sacred music and architecture in early modern Rome. According to Morelli, the influence of music on architecture was linked to the changing role of music in liturgical ceremonials. It was a cultural phenomenon. Whereas previously music had been a practice pertinent to priests, by the middle of the sixteenth century sacred music became a practice whose principal beneficiaries were the assembled faithful, who were always more attracted to attend church and the oratories depending on the quality of the music executed. Within this course of development, sacred music practices also became more theatrical and alluring. From the Gregorian plainchant and polyphony *a cappella*, sacred music evolved to incorporate polychoral forms, and later in the seventeenth and eighteenth centuries, to include narrative duets of the oratories, as well as pieces that combined voice and instrument, and in which the expressive range of organs was fundamental.[22]

This evolution of sacred music began at the end of the fifteenth century, and may be related to the development of the visual arts, including architecture, in this period. Religious chapters, orders and confraternities were encouraged to invest more and more resources – both economic and intellectual – in order to make their buildings better adapted for music, and therefore capable of attracting the greatest possible number of people. As a general consequence, the singing galleries and the organ cases moved away from the areas reserved for the clergy to the nave,

22 Morelli, 'Musica nobile e copiosa di voci et istromenti', 302-319; Morelli, 'La vista dell'apparato superbo'.

where they were closer to the faithful.[23] Yet, there were exceptions to this shift. In certain instances, the great organs remained near the presbytery or choir, although they still had to serve the aisle of the lay congregation. This is the case in the papal basilicas of St. Peter's, Santa Maria Maggiore and Santa Croce in Gerusalemme. The fact that new organs were not constructed in the naves or counter-façades of these churches may be related to the papal censure of large furnishings, including elaborate organ cases.

In the middle of the sixteenth century, the polyphony was the most common form of sacred music performed in Roman churches.[24] More complex than Gregorian monody, the contrapuntal polyphony typically accompanied solemn masses as well as more particular ceremonies, such as Vespers. During the ordinary Liturgy of the Hours (*Ufficio delle Ore*, or in Latin, *Officium Divinum*), the clergy still used to sing the Gregorian chant, or the even simpler psalmody chant.

As a general rule, the choir of the Roman polyphony adhered to a unique arrangement. Singers stood in a *cantoria* (singer loft) that also hosted a major *organo stativo* (fixed organ). On occasion, the *cantorie* were doubled, one on each side of the choir, with the addition of a smaller *organo positivo* (moveable organ) to the second *cantoria*.[25] These musical lofts were always located in the chancel of the clergy, which in the great medieval basilicas occupied the nave before the high altar, and was separated by a rood screen from the area of the lay congregation.[26] In order to allow the faithful direct vision of the high altars, the Council of Trent's decrees required the demolition of the medieval rood screens, and the movement of the clergy chancels from the naves down to the galleries, sometime back to the high altars in the *retrocori* (retro choirs). This happened throughout Italy, Rome included, but the best-documented case is that of the great basilicas of the Mendicant Orders in Florence.[27] Their renovation, ordered by Duke Cosimo I in 1565-1566, shortly after the issuing of the Tridentine decrees, was meticulously carried out by Giorgio Vasari, who tore down the rood screens and chancels, and moved the clergy into the major galleries. Still, the fact that the great organ galleries were left on the side walls, facing the faithful in the middle of the nave, is highly significant. By this time, sacred music was no longer pertinent to priests alone, but had become a practice conceived (and performed) to attract the broader public of the lay congregation.

The introduction of polychoral music in the early seventeenth century, a style that would be particularly developed in Rome, represented the next stage in the

23 Morelli, 'Sull'organo et in choro'.

24 Morelli, 'Musica nobile e copiosa di voci et istromenti', 302-314.

25 In the seventeenth century the most common type in Rome of *organo positivo* was the so-called *organo ad ala* ('wing organ'): Morelli, 'Musica nobile e copiosa di voci et istromenti', 309.

26 Hall, 'The Tramezzo in the Italian Renaissance, Revisited'.

27 Hall, *Renovation and Counter-Reformation*; Conforti, *Vasari architetto*, 209-223.

development of music and the creation of sonorous spaces. The polychoral style is a type of polyphony in which the singing choir was split in subunits: every minor choir is formed by the four principal voices (*basso, tenore, alto, soprano*), which were supported by an instrumental *basso continuo*, that normally is a positive organ.[28] Unlike the Venetian *coro spezzato*, or 'broken choir', in the Roman *policoralità* every individual choir was autonomous as regards the counterpoint harmony, although at times the choirs sang the same lines together. But the very logic of the polychoral style was not only sonorous, it was also spatial. Indeed, the minor choirs were frequently raised above the congregation in provisional lofts (*poggioli*), which were set upon timber frames and placed among the pilasters along the nave. This arrangement facilitated the distribution of sound throughout the volume of the church, exalting the three dimensional perception of both sound and space.

On the occasion of solemn liturgical celebrations, the great Roman churches competed with one another to provide the faithful the most spectacular musical ceremony, multiplying the numbers of choirs over the lofts. Reports, accounts and surviving folios of sheet music record masses performed with eight, ten and even twelve choirs.[29] In Santa Maria sopra Minerva, for example, a ten-choir mass was usually performed on the feast day of St. Dominic (Figure 4.4), as referred to in 1639 by André Maugars, a French musician who left a key source of the musical ceremonies celebrated in Rome.[30] At about the same times that Pietro della Valle recalled '*quel gran musicone*' ('that big music performance') in St. Peter's, it was reported that, because of the vastness of its interior space, masses of ten, twelve and up to sixteen choirs were usually performed in the Vatican basilica. A source reports that sometimes a couple of *cori di ripieno* (or *d'eco*), formed only by *cornetti* or other woodwind instruments, was even set '*sopra la cupola*' ('upon the dome', that is, presumably, on the lower entablature of the drum).[31] Unfortunately, no visual record has survived of the polychoral lofts, with the exception of an engraving by Barriére representing the *entrata* into Rome in 1665 of Cardinal Gondi-Retz at San Luigi dei Francesi (Figure 4.5). The image is enough to assess the effect of the polychoral music in religious spaces: exploiting the nave's arches as a reflecting ceiling, the lofts constituted a visual and acoustic *apparato* of the church.

Still, the temporary apparatuses of lofts for the polychoral music were not 'architecture' in the proper sense. As adapted to the space of the churches, they are best understood as ephemeral furnishings – visual and acoustic. The addition

28 Morelli, 'Musica nobile e copiosa di voci et istromenti', 302-310.

29 Ibid., 311-312; Morelli, 'La vista dell'apparato superbo', 294-299.

30 The *Response faite a un curieux sur le sentiment de la musique d'Italie*, published in Lionnet, 'André Maugars'.

31 Morelli, 'La vista dell'apparato superbo', 298; Rostirolla, 'Musiche e apparati nella basilica vaticana per le feste dei Santi Pietro e Paolo', 421 n. 10.

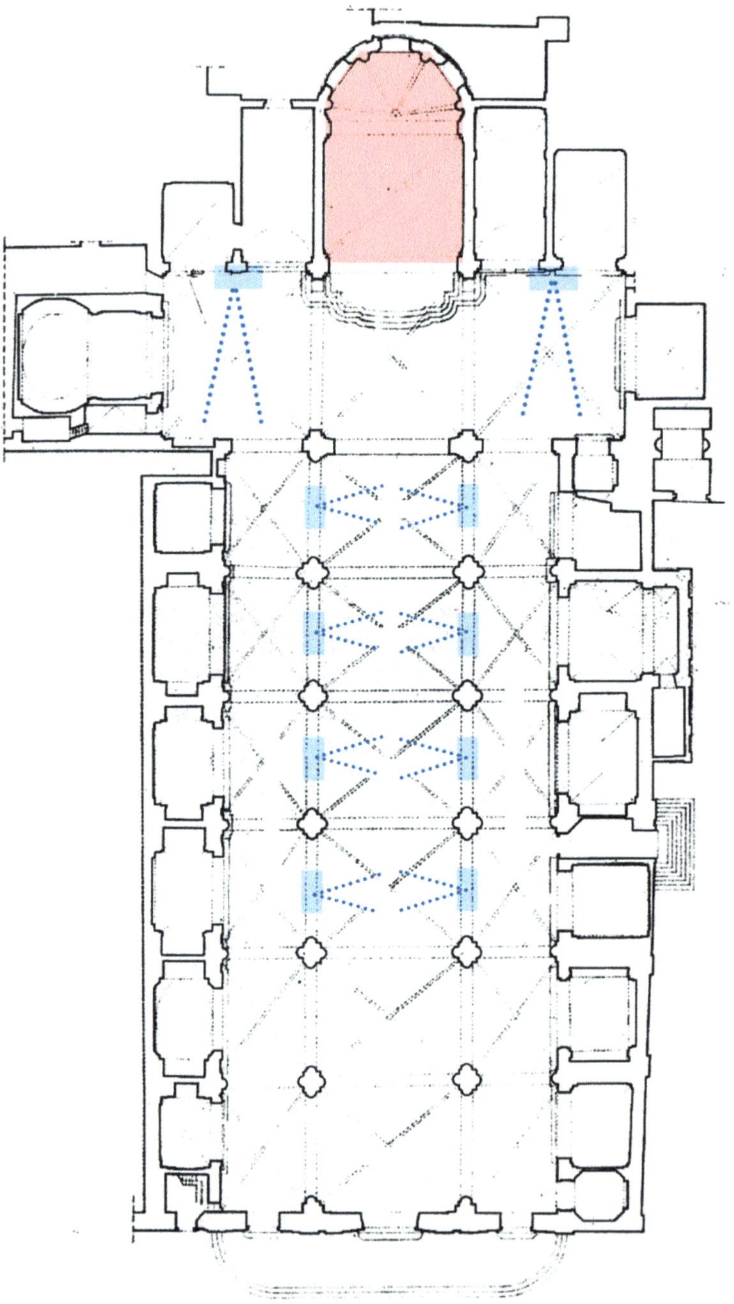

Fig. 4.4 Santa Maria sopra Minerva, Rome. Sound plan for the feast day of St. Dominic of 1639: (in red) the Dominican chancel; (in blue) the poggioli and the organ lofts. © Federico Bellini

Fig. 4.5 Dominique Barrière, San Luigi de' Francesi, Rome, with decoration for the saint's feast day, 1665. At right: the poggioli (singer lofts) prepared for the polychoral mass. The Metropolitan Museum of Art, Accession Number: 51.501.2924. The Elisha Whittelsey Collection, The Elisha Whittelsey Fund, 1951

of choir and organ lofts was most common during the golden period of polychoral music (from the end of the sixteenth century, to the third quarter of the seventeenth century), and succeeded not only in bringing the production of music closer to the congregation, but also in improving the acoustic performance by placing the choirs at greater height under the vaults. The addition of the lofts, however, is difficult to follow through plans and sections, as such architectural features are usually invisible in traditional ground plans, which represent the area just above the floor and do not detail spatial alterations at higher elevations. Moreover, singing galleries and organs – even the most monumental – are often not represented in the sections, as they are considered irrelevant to architectural space.

The interaction between music and architecture thus must be examined in the context of the buildings themselves, as is shown by the striking example of the papal 'twin chapels' of Santa Maria Maggiore. Although the two chapels share the same Greek-cross plan, the perception of their spaces was quite different. Only the Sistine Chapel, built in 1587-1588 by Domenico Fontana, is perceived as a central space, having its devotional focus (the Crypt of Nativity) in the centre. The Pauline Chapel, by contrast, was used as a longitudinal space focused on the miraculous icon of the *Virgo Salus Populi Romani* (Virgin Protectoress [i.e. Salvation] of the Roman People) framed by the lavish marble *aedicula*. As constructed, the Sistine Chapel in Santa Maria Maggiore included no device for music, as this was still considered non-essential. Just a few years later, in 1606-1616, Flaminio Ponzio endowed the Pauline Chapel with four singing galleries, supporting the specific ceremonials performed at the *Salus Populi Romani* altar.[32]

The first decades of the seventeenth century marked a turning point in the introduction of fixed musical lofts in Roman ecclesiastical architecture. The construction in 1610-1614 of the new canons' choir in St. Peter's was followed in 1624-1626 by the insertion of arches into the side walls by Carlo Maderno, which hosted organs and lofts that were instead absent in the former choir of Sixtus IV.[33] The most peculiar and remarkable case was the church of Gesù. In 1569-1582 Jacopo Barozzi da Vignola and Giacomo Della Porta built, just above the side chapels, a sort of matroneum, or gallery, connected with the Jesuit House (Figure 4.6(a-b)).[34]

32 On the Sistine Chapel, see Bellini, 'L'organismo cupolato della cappella Sistina in Santa Maria Maggiore'; on the Pauline, see Schwager, 'Die architektonische Erneuerung von S. Maria Maggiore', 248-285; see also Della Libera, 'Introduction', vii-ix.

33 The major organ was still that of Pope Alexander VI. Maderno set it beneath the arch of the right side, in common with the adjacent Clementine Chapel. A similar solution was adopted some years later at the organ of the Gregorian Chapel, see Lunelli, *L'arte organaria del Rinascimento in Roma*, 85-91; Battistelli et al., *Organi e cantorie nelle chiese di Roma*, 50-53.

34 Schwager and Schlimme, 'La chiesa del Gesù di Roma'.

Fig. 4.6 Valérien Regnart, section drawings of SS. Nome di Gesù, Praecipua Urbis Romanae Templa, Rome, 1650. From private collection
a) Interior perspective, showing the matronaea for the Jesuit fathers
b) Transformation of the matronaea into lofts for the polychoral music

This gallery was intended to be used by the fathers, who could have attended the mass from the loggias over the nave. The insertion of such a gallery was a common solution in a church of a regular order, and was also used at San Fedele in Milan, another Jesuit temple built by Pellegrino Tibaldi in the same period. Some decades later, in 1615-1616, the Roman Jesuits transformed the gallery of the Gesù into polychoral choir lofts, simply by adding marble balustrades and new gilded timber screen, the so-called *gelosie*. As given in an *avviso* (information report), the new lofts were opened on 7 August 1616 with the performance of an eight-choir mass written by Giovanni Francesco Anerio, master of the Pontifical Chapel: the eight *cantorie* were distributed among nave and transepts.[35] In 1633-1634, the organ cases and galleries of the transepts were reconstructed, so that the 'sound body' of the Gesù rose to fourteen musical lofts, all of which were permanent architectonical features.[36] With this alteration, every edge of the church could be directly reached by the sound of a choir. (It is also likely that each single choir loft could be used separately during private masses that were celebrated in the side chapel in front of it).

From the middle of the seventeenth century onward, singing galleries were always integrated into the architectural design of new churches, enhancing the stereophonic effect of the space. In SS. Luca e Martina (begun in 1635) there are four lofts (Figure 4.7). Sant'Agnese in Agone (begun in 1652), which follows a similar plan, has eight singer lofts, to which a great organ's balcony was subsequently added

35 Morelli, 'Musica nobile e copiosa di voci et istromenti', 306-307.
36 Battistelli et al., *Organi e cantorie nelle chiese di Roma*, 80-81.

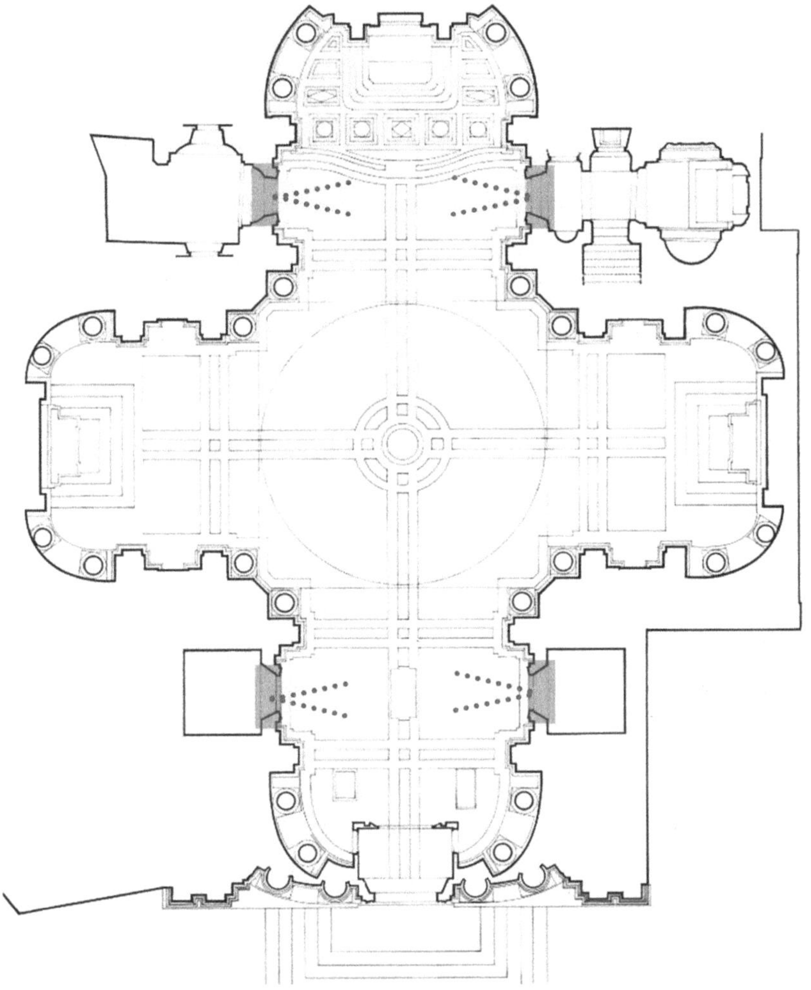

Fig. 4.7 Santi Luca e Martina, Rome, 1635-1672. Sound plan with singer lofts. © Federico Bellini.

(Figure 4.8).[37] Some years later, in 1662-1667, Carlo Rainaldi and Giovanni Antonio de' Rossi installed thirteen singer lofts into the architectural body of Santa Maria in Campitelli, which are distinguished by their size and position. The four major lofts, together with the great organ gallery in the counter-façade, acoustically dominated the space of the nave. The eight smaller lofts were evenly divided between the false transept and the domed shrine. This made it possible to celebrate separately

37 On Santi Luca e Martina, see Noehles, 'La chiesa dei Santi Luca e Martina'; on Sant'Agnese in Agone, see Bellini, *Le cupole di Borromini*, 205-215, 233-241.

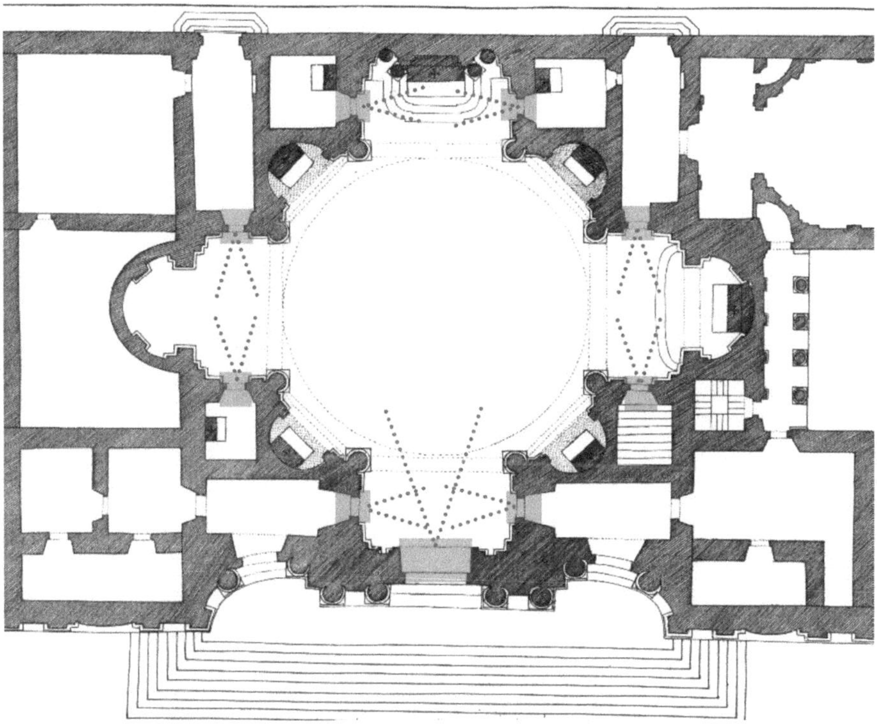

Fig. 4.8 Sant'Agnese in Agone, Rome, c. 1652. Sound plan with singer lofts. © Federico Bellini

musical rites in every part of the church (nave, chapels, transept, shrine), using only the adjacent cantories and without engaging the others (Figures 4.9 and 4.10). The same principle was followed by Francesco Fontana in the reconstruction of the SS. Apostoli (1702-1717). Here, the fifteen cantories no longer served for the production polychoral music, as this had been replaced by the practice of the *concerto*. But they made it possible to chant masses separately within each of the private side chapels. Public masses, of course, were chanted at the Franciscan's chancel, which was equipped with four lofts and two great organs.

In a few limited cases, musical sonority within the church assumed symbolic and even theological values.[38] The most striking example of the musical construct granting space such immaterial charge is, without doubt, the triple galleries of Sant'Ivo alla Sapienza. Sant'Ivo is the chapel of the *Studium Urbis*, the university of Rome, and was actually to be dedicated to the Holy Wisdom, the *Sapientia*, who

38 One notable example is the Angelic balcony above the Santa Casa di Loreto (realized 1533-1534). On this, see Frommel, *L'architettura del santuario e del palazzo apostolico di Loreto*, 63.

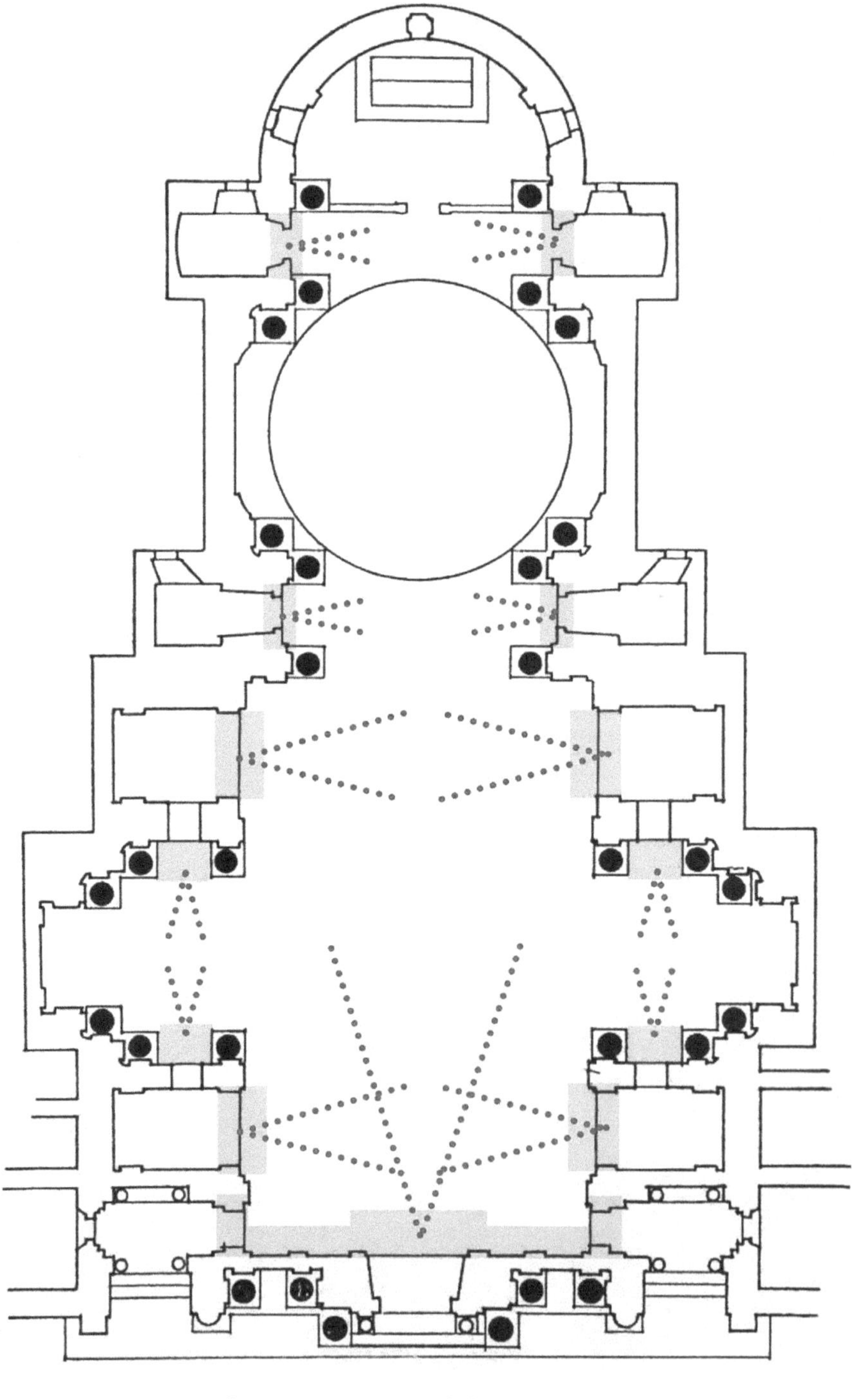

Fig. 4.9 Santa Maria in Campitelli, Rome, 1662-1667. Sound plans with singer lofts. © Federico Bellini

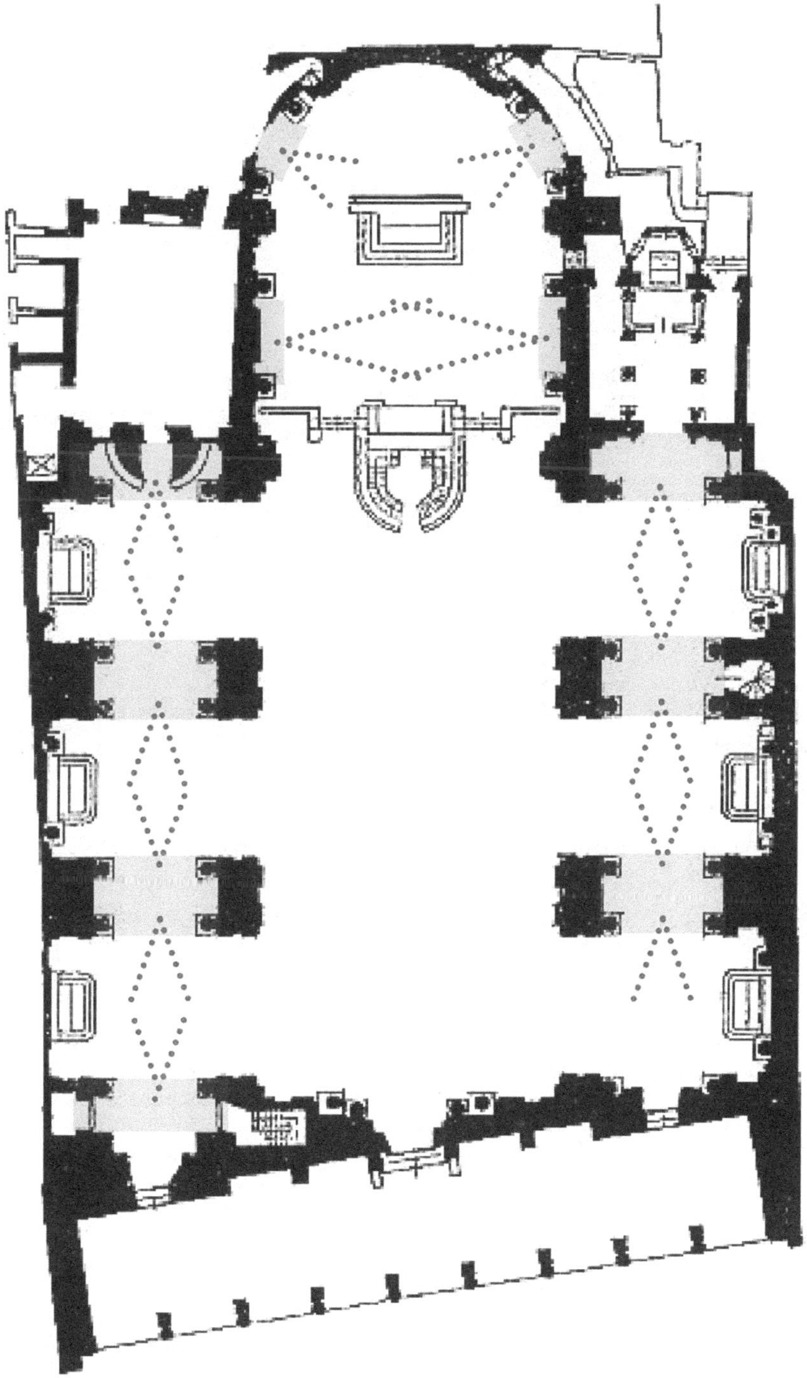

Fig. 4.10 SS. Apostoli, Rome, 1702-1717. Sound plan with singer lofts. © Federico Bellini

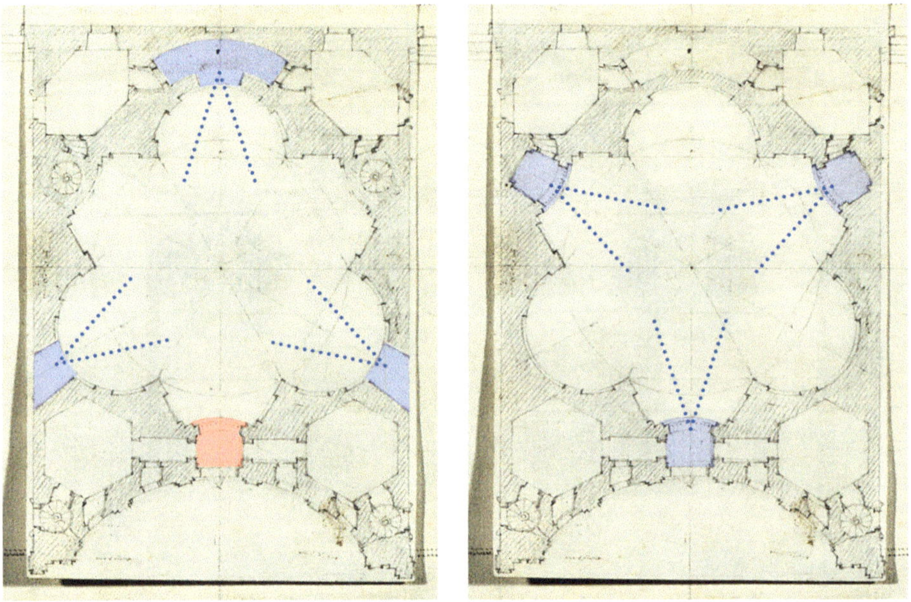

Fig. 4.11 Holy Wisdom chapel at the Studium Urbis (the so-called Sant'Ivo alla Sapienza), 1643-1659. Sound plans. From Albertina Graphische Sammlung, Az. Rom 500k. © Federico Bellini
a) Prior to the layout imposed by Borromini, 1643-1644, with the cantorie (in blue) and the cardinals' loggia (in red)
b) Final layout, 1658-1659, with the cantorie (in blue)

gave the name to the *Studium* itself.[39] In 1640-1642, the university commissioned Francesco Borromini to design the church in the location of an existing palazzo. The perimeters of site were thus limited, and Borromini conceived a place-specific plan that both accommodated the location and ingeniously referenced the dedication to Wisdom, an attribute of the Holy Trinity (according to the Scholastic theology). The plan is based on Trinitarian symbolism: an equilateral triangle generated by a circle, that is to say, the Three Persons emanated from the Unity of God. In the first phase of construction (1643-1644), Borromini arranged the space for the organ over the high altar, most likely intending that the two loggias on the side apses function as choir lofts.[40] Following this, in 1658-1660, Borromini changed the chapel's layout. He closed the former loggias and removed the two spiral staircases in the chapel's corners, recreating the triangle of choirs in a 60-degree rotated layout (Figure 4.11(a-b)).

The peculiar plan of the Sapienza forced the site-specific composition of three-choir masses, a quite unusual solution in Roman polychoral music. On 30 May 1661,

39 Bellini, *Le cupole di Borromini*, 155-203; the trinitarian simbology has been proposed in Bellini, 'Lo spazio dell'inesprimibile'.
40 On this point I agree with Smyth-Pinney and Smyth, 'Borromini and Benevoli', 22.

Sant'Ivo alla Sapienza was inaugurated with a famous three-choir mass written by Orazio Benevoli, at that time master of the Cappella Giulia.[41] Recently, some pieces of the Benevoli mass were performed in the church of Sapienza by a vocal choir (unfortunately without the *basso continuo* of the organs).[42] The most striking effect was not the impressive stereophony of the sound, but its uneven richness. Since the choirs play different musical lines, alternating with one another at different volumes, the listener feels immersed in a changing, unpredictable and fluid sound, which is emitted from three sources. The 'triangular' sonority of the Sapienza is perfectly integrated into its unique architectural form, and both sonority and architecture contribute to express the Trinitarian symbolism in an emotional synaesthetic experience.

The Sonorous Architecture of the Oratories

More so than church architecture, the design of early modern Roman oratories underwent a marked evolution in keeping with contemporary advancements in music. Unlike a church, an oratory is a religious space conceived primarily for the prayer, not for communal mass.[43] Moreover, the oratories of the lay confraternities were expected to host ceremonies, which were always accompanied by music. In terms of architecture, oratory plans were quite simple: a rectangle, with the altar set in an arched recess, and encircled by the seats for the brothers (Figure 4.12(a-c)). But the simplicity of the plans also allowed for a significant degree of modification and innovation. From the second half of the sixteenth century in Rome, the individual design of a series of oratories reflected the ceremonial practices and musical preferences on the individual confraternities.

The oratory of the SS. Crocifisso was among the first to adapt its architecture to new musical preferences. With no fixed *cantorie* in 1562-1566, the confraternity was later compelled to add a great timber choir on the counter-façade. In 1571-1572, the oratory of the Gonfalone was instead arranged with two marble *cantorie*, placed on the sides of the small gallery and topped with pediments.[44] The oratories of SS. Marcello and Gonfalone both featured a wooden ceiling, beautifully decorated but acoustically absorbing. When building the Jesuit oratory of the Caravita in 1630-1633, Giovanni Antonio de' Rossi adopted the two-loft plan of the Gonfalone (later adding an another

41 Smyth-Pinney and Smyth, 'Borromini and Benevoli'; Della Libera, La musica a Sant'Ivo alla Sapienza nel Seicento'.

42 The *Missa Ecce Sacerdos magnus* was executed by the Schola Romana. The ensemble was directed by Stefano Sabene, 17 March 2018. See online video: https://www.accademiasanluca.eu/it, accessed 26 November 2020.

43 Moroni, *Dizionario di erudizione storico-ecclesiastica da S. Pietro*, 41-43.

44 On Gonfalone, see Wisch and Newbigin, *Acting on Faith*, 398-399; on SS. Crocifisso, see Henneberg, *L'oratorio dell'arciconfraternita del Santissimo Crocifisso di San Marcello*, 18-26.

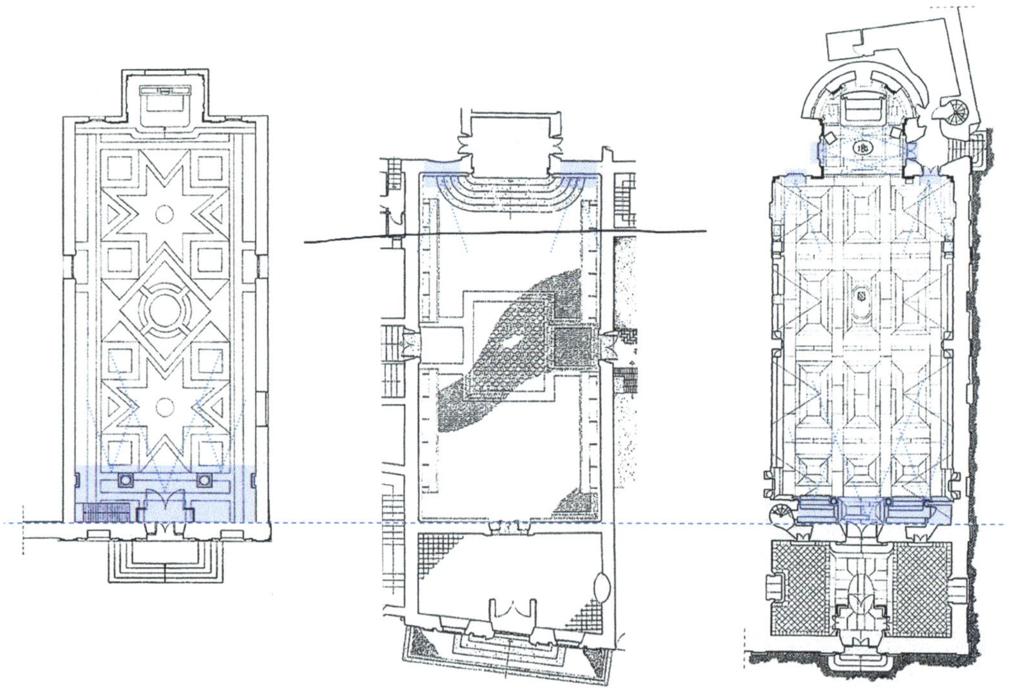

Fig. 4.12 Placement of singer lofts in Roman oratories. For the comparison, the transversal length of the churches has been made equal and the counter-façades aligned. © Federico Bellini
a) SS. Crocifisso di San Marcello, 1562-1568
b) Santa Lucia del Gonfalone, 1556-1571
c) San Francesco Saverio del Caravita, 1632-1633, and c. 1670-1677

pair of lofts in the apse), but used a masonry vault instead of a timber roof, following the no longer existing example of the oratory of the Trinità dei Pellegrini. At that time, de' Rossi and the Jesuits were fully aware that a vault is able to reflect and amplify the sound. This fact had been asserted a century prior by Francesco Zorzi in his report on San Francesco della Vigna in Venice (1537), and was also well-known in Rome.[45]

The oratory designed by Borromini in 1639-1640 for the House of Oratorians, the congregation founded by Filippo Neri, represents an even more exceptional case.[46] The so-called Oratorio dei Filippini provides clear testimony to some of the primary motives behind religious building design in this period. The motives that directed its unique design were neither formal, nor acoustic, nor even devotional; in the Oratorio, the key issue was the arrangement of space so that it could properly accommodate three ranks of the faithful, who would remain socially, and physically,

45 As demonstrated by a comment of Emilio Cavalieri in 1602, see Morelli, 'Space for Music in RomanResidences', 312; on Zorzi's report, see Howard and Moretti, *Sound and Space in Renaissance Venice*, 100-102.
46 Connors, *Borromini e l'Oratorio romano*; Connors, 'Introduzione', xi-xl; Morelli, *Il tempio armonico*.

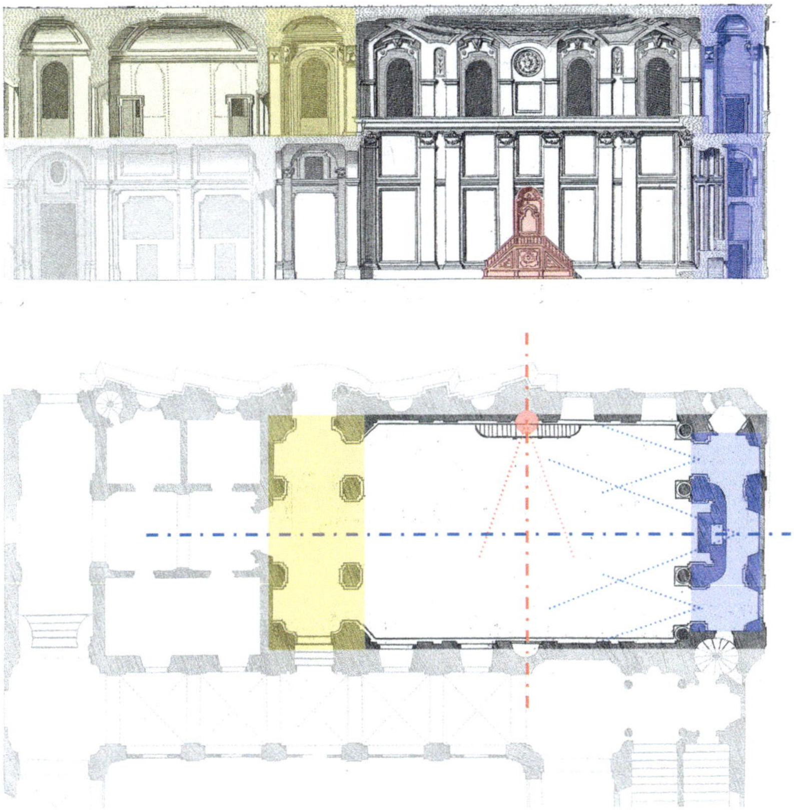

Fig. 4.13 Oratorio dei Filippini, Rome, 1637-1640. Section and sound plan: (in red) the transverse axis of the spoken Word during the oratorio piccolo (short oratorio); (in blue) the longitudinal axis between the singer lofts and cardinals loggia; (in yellow) lofts used during the oratorio festivo (holydays oratorio). From Borromini, Opus architectonicum Equitis Francisci Boromini, 1725, tav. III, XLII. © Federico Bellini

separated from one another.[47] The design was further complicated by conditions and function specific to the House of the Oratorians. The Oratorio served different functions, depending on the season and even on the day of the week. Throughout the year, the Oratorio was used daily by the company of the '*fratelli esterni*' (literally 'outside brothers'), a kind of third order of oratorian laymen. The musical element of their ceremonies was limited: the brothers would sing two antiphons *a cappella* only at the end of their devotions. The most appealing religious service was instead celebrated every Sunday in the winter, from All Saints' Day to Easter. This included prayer, sermons, and litanies, and was concluded by the exciting performance of two musical *laudi concertate*, for voices and instruments. Indeed, the *laudi*

47 Bellini, 'La forma della musica'.

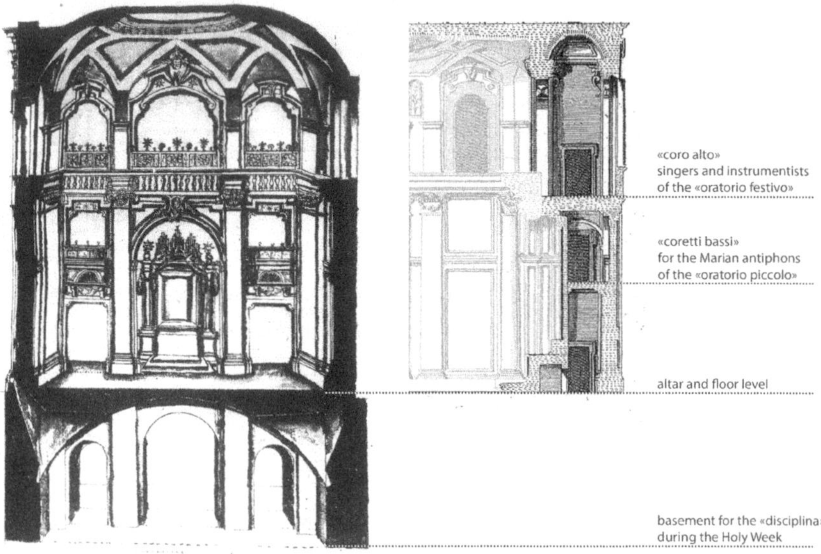

Fig. 4.14 Oratorio dei Filippini, Rome, 1637-1640. Section view of the singers' and organ lofts. From Borromini, Opus architectonicum Equitis Francisci Boromini, 1725, tav. XLII. © Federico Bellini

performed in the Oratorio were not of the medieval kind. As in other parts of Italy, the musical *lauda* had developed in a modern form influenced by the *mottetto concertato.* Two professional soloists, supported by singers and instrumentalists, sang in Italian a sacred story, introducing a dramatic feature that soon would be adopted by the modern *oratorio* (in the musical sense of the term).[48] These elements of drama, similar to the nascent Florentine *dramma in musica,* made the oratorian *laudi* extremely popular. Their success was tremendous. The Oratorio dei Filippini attracted an enthusiastic audience drawn from all the parts of the city and incited the professional development of singers, who were chosen among the stars of Rome and paid by the richest families. In fact, at times the Oratorio generated too much enthusiasm. It was not unusual for the people in the Oratorio to come to blows in defending the honour of their favourite singers. The Oratorians themselves remained somewhat detached, baffled by the fervour their ceremonies induced.[49]

In the Oratorio, Borromini needed to provide lofts for singers and instrumentalists, as well as the seats reserved to the high-ranking people during the winter Sunday celebrations (Figure 4.13).[50] In 1637-1638 he reviewed the solution of Giovanni

48 Smither, *A History of the Oratorio,* 118-142; Morelli, *Il tempio armonico,* 63-81.

49 Morelli, *Il tempio armonico,* 29-30.

50 Bellini, 'La forma della musica'.

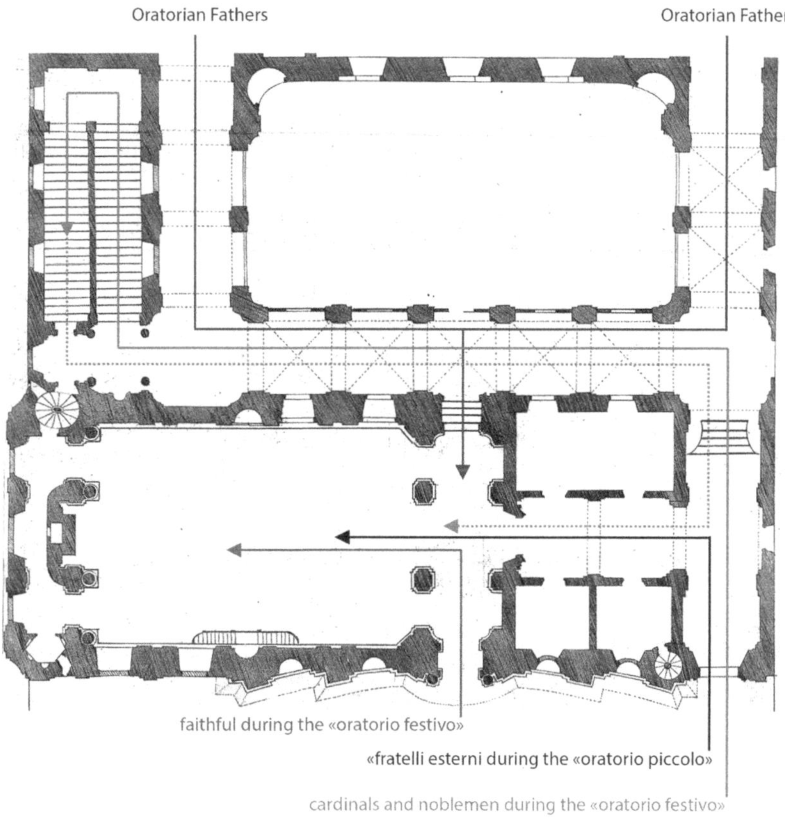

Fig. 4.15 Oratorio dei Filippini, Rome, 1637-1640. Diagram of the separate paths taken by the faithful, depending on spiritual practice and social standing. From Borromini, Opus architectonicum Equitis Francisci Boromini, 1725, tav. III. © Federico Bellini

Antonio de' Rossi for the recently completed Caravita, and arranged two lofts for singers, one above the other, on the side of the altar. The loft on the higher level provided a great gallery for an organ and instruments, and was set just below the vault in order to reflect the sound (Figure 4.14). On the front side of the Oratorio, Borromini built a second loggia, falsely symmetrical. This was actually dedicated to cardinals, nobles and their followers, who could attend the ceremonies from this sort of *piano nobile*, which functioned akin to a stage of honour in a theatre. The paths of circulation to be followed within the Oratorio were also carefully separated: cardinals, '*fratelli esterni*' and common people entered the Oratorio through different entrances (Figure 4.15).

In its originality, the Oratorio dei Filippini could not be imitated. Just a year later Gianlorenzo Bernini, Borromini's bitter rival, adopted the idea of two lofts, one above the other, in the reconstruction of the apse of San Lorenzo in Damaso.

But within this context, the device was less successful. In the subsequent design of oratories in Rome, the gallery for the organ and instruments was generally set on the counter-façade, while singers' lofts were distributed evenly along the adjacent walls. This arrangement led the way to the proper *auditoria* of the eighteenth century, such as the oratories of the Angelo Custode and the Annunziata in Borgo. Again, each was unique in its design, responding to the conditions of the site, the culture of the confraternity and the evolution of the role of music in religious ceremonies.

The Architecture of Singer Lofts and Organ Cases

Although polychoral music survived in Rome until the eighteenth century, in the last decades of the seventeenth century the *concerto* emerged as the more established practice of sacred music. Soloist voices were now accompanied by a unique choir, and supported by a small orchestra of instruments led by a major organ.[51] The *concerto* posed entirely new questions to patrons, architects and artists. No longer was the musical performance determined solely by the distribution of small choirs in the ecclesiastical space; it was now necessary to focus and harmonize the visual and symbolic quality in an individual, monumentalized galleries. The great organ lofts of the 1700s, in Rome as elsewhere, sensationalized acoustics: as plastic representations of sound, they concentrated synaesthetic expression on individual objects, which were formally defined. The design of site-specific organ cases comprise a type of architecture, and ecclesiastical architecture specifically, that has been substantially understudied in architectural history. As a way of conclusion, the following offers an overview of such extraordinary constructions, shedding light on a different aspect of music-driven design. In terms of their positioning, the organ cases not only shaped the spatial distribution of music, just as the elevated and purposely placed choir lofts also did. Moreover, as imposing physical constructions, the cases substantially conditioned the interior dimensions of church architecture. Each was inherently unique in its massive form and considerable expense, further delineating the singularity and place-specificity of individual churches.

Great organs had existed in Rome as early as the fifteenth century, and there had developed a rich tradition by which architects endeavoured to give them an architectural shape. The organ installed in St. Peter's (1496) is one notable, early example.[52] But the very first organ designed in Rome as proper '*Kleinarchitektur*'

51 Morelli, 'Musica nobile e copiosa di voci et istromenti', 317-324.

52 Antinori, 'La cantoria con organo di Alessandro VI'; Rostirolla, *Musica e musicisti nella Basilica di San Pietro*, 31, 222.

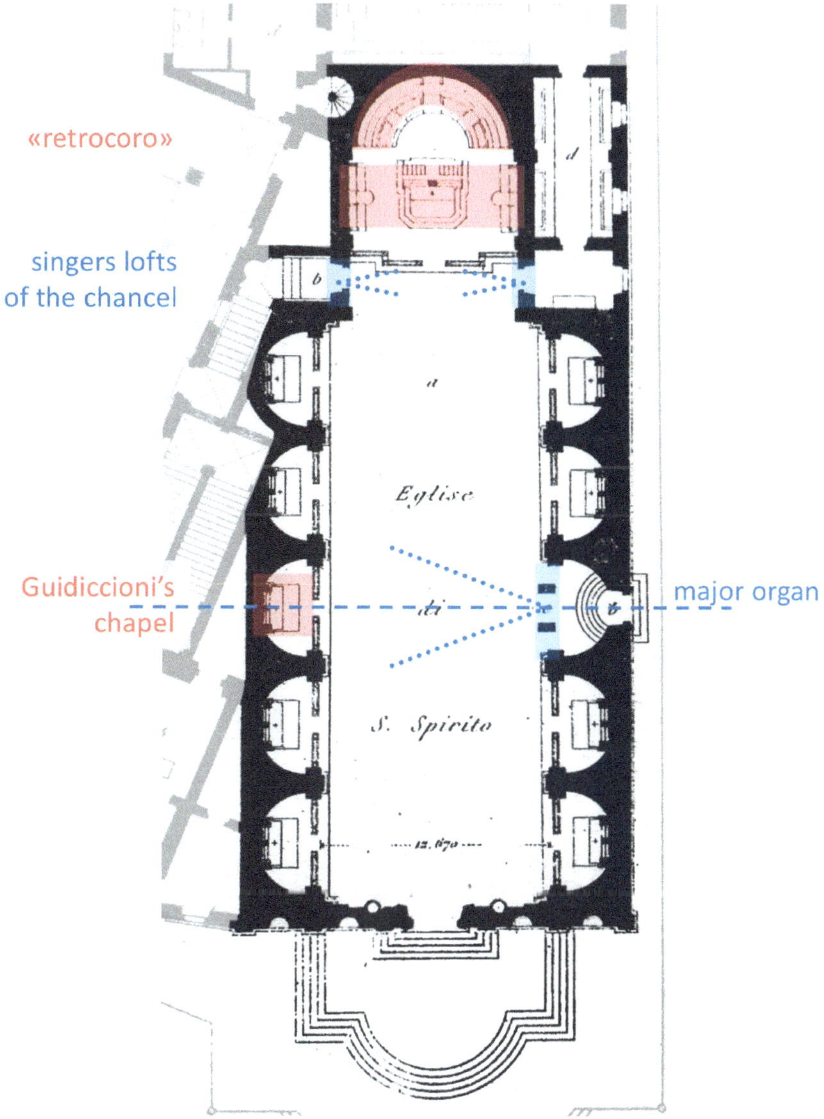

Fig. 4.16 SS. Spirito, Rome
a) Sound plan: (in red) the sacred areas of the chancel and Guidiccioni's chapel; (in blue) the singer lofts.
© Federico Bellini

(or 'small architecture') was that of SS. Spirito, attributed to the *bottega* of Antonio da Sangallo il Giovane (1546-1547). The organ pipes in SS. Spirito are set into a triumphal three-spanned Serlian arch, providing a model that would be followed for over a hundred years, as in the aforementioned great organ case of San Giovanni

Fig. 4.16 SS. Spirito, Rome
b) Nave, looking towards the altar. © Photo: Federico Bellini

in Laterano.[53] Apart from the physical body of the organ itself, the organ case of SS. Spirito stood upon two granite columns, which framed the side entrance of the church. The position of the organ also aligned with the chapel of Commendatore Alessandro Guidiccioni, patron of both the organ and the chapel. In this way,

53 The organ of Nicola da Cremona was kept in tune in May 1554, see Colonna, 'Il ciborio della corsia sistina', 83-87; Howe, 'Architecture for "Divine Hymns"'.

Fig. 4.17 Organ galleries
a) Santa Maria del Popolo, Rome, designed by Bernini, 1655. © Photo: Wikimedia
b) Santa Maria in Vallicella, Rome, designed by Camillo Rusconi, 1698. © Photo: Wikimedia

Guidiccioni was able to build into the longitudinal plan of SS. Spirito a spatial transverse axis, which was generated by the music played at the organ loft during the ceremonies celebrated within his own chapel (Fig. 4.16(a-b)).

It became common in the seventeenth century for paired organ cases to be built into transept walls of existing churches. Placed beside the chancel, these organ cases faced the nave and aisles, in order to serve both naves and chancels.[54] In the first decades, the architecture of the organ cases followed more or less the Serlian type implemented by the Sangallo workshop at SS. Spirito. The cases installed in Santa Maria sopra Minerva by Paolo Maruscelli (1628) are a prime example. But as ecclesiastical architecture and music became increasingly multifaceted, the design of organ cases likewise became more of a plastic exercise in Baroque decoration. This movement is epitomized in the marvellous organ loft of Santa Maria del Popolo by Gianlorenzo Bernini (1655), or the spectacular great organs at Santa Maria in Vallicella by Camillo Rusconi (1698) (Figure 4.17(a-b)).

54 On the following organ cases, see Battistelli et al., *Organi e cantorie nelle chiese di Roma*.

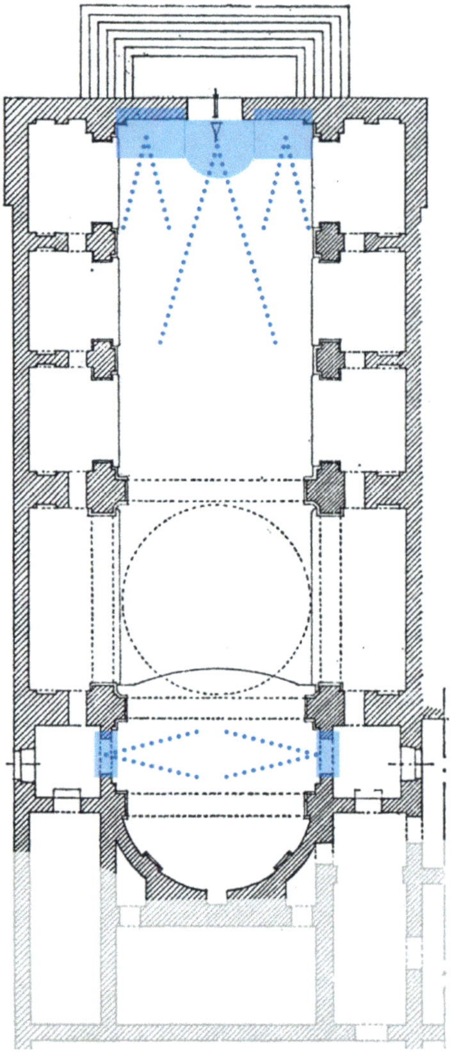

Fig. 4.18 Santa Maria della Vittoria, Rome
(a) Sound plan, with singer lofts (in blue). © Federico Bellini

At the end of the seventeenth century, loggias for musicians were progressively enlarged in order to accommodate singers and instrumentalists, who were ever more numerous with the increasing practice of the *concerto*.[55] Following the example of the Lateran Nave Clementina, organ lofts were set against the internal façade in order to accommodate an entire orchestra. With the astonishing two-level loft at Santa

55 Morelli, 'Musica nobile e copiosa di voci et istromenti', 312-319.

Fig. 4.18 Santa Maria della Vittoria, Rome
((b) Counter-façade organ gallery, attributed to Mattia de Rossi, 1682. The upper balcony is an eighteenth-century addition for the concerto grosso. © Photo: Livio Andronico, Wikipedia

Maria della Vittoria, attributed to Mattia de Rossi (1682), organ lofts on the internal façade became a design theme in themselves. There are many examples of churches with similar organ lofts in Rome, which still merit study, including Sant'Antonio dei Portoghesi, Santa Maria Maddalena, Sant'Eustacchio, and Santa Maria della Scala (Plate 4.18(a-b)). In the eighteenth century, the great organ galleries and cases functioned almost as shrines to religious music, increasingly drawing attention away from ciboria and altar baldachins. These constructions, were repeatedly censured for their decadence – by Popes Alexander VII, Innocent XII and Benedict XIV – although such decrees will be rarely implemented.[56]

The centrality of sacred music and religious architecture, and the link that had been established between the two arts, thus gradually declined in the eighteenth century. In the nineteenth and twentieth centuries, the main places dedicated to listening to music were no longer be churches and oratories, but theatres and

56 Ibid., 316-317 (on Alexander VII and Innocent XII), 322-324 (on Benedict XIV).

auditoria, to which the creative attention of the architects refocused. By this time, even composers of sacred music were aware that their music would likely be performed in theatres, and not only in religious buildings. (Prime examples include the sacred productions by Anton Bruckner and Benjamin Britten, or Wagner's *Parsifal*, a work of sacred character written to be presented in an opera house.) But even if the sonorial-spatial experience of Renaissance and Baroque religious architecture has expired, through history, it is still possible to understand how sound can contribute to defining a multisensory space, attributing to it specific qualities that make it a place.

Bibliography

Antinori, Aloisio, 'La cantoria con organo di Alessandro VI e la "cappella del S. Pietro di Bronzo"', *Quaderni dell'Istituto di Storia dell'Architettura*, 25-30 (1995-1997), 129-136.

Battistelli, Giovanni, Oscar Mischiati, Arnaldo Morelli and Claudio M. Strinati, *Organi e cantorie nelle chiese di Roma* (Rome: Istituto Poligrafico e Zecca dello Stato, 1994).

Bellini, Federico, 'La forma della musica: l'Oratorio di Francesco Borromini alla Vallicella', paper presented at the conference 'Francesco Borromini 1599-1667', Rome, 11-13 December 2017.

Bellini, Federico, *Le cupole di Borromini. La 'scientia' statica in età barocca* (Milan: Electa, 2004).

Bellini, Federico, 'L'organismo cupolato della cappella Sistina in Santa Maria Maggiore', in Giovanna Curcio, Nicola Navone and Sergio Villari (eds), *Studi su Domenico Fontana* (Mendrisio-Cinisello Balsamo: Mendrisio Academy Press-Silvana Ed., 2011), 105-125.

Bellini, Federico, 'Lo spazio dell'inesprimibile: la rappresentazione del Paracleto nella Cappella della Sapienza', paper presented at the conference 'Lo spazio della Roma barocca: il paesaggio ideale e l'illusionismo', Rome, 30 June-1 July 2015.

Bellini, Federico, 'Riforma protestante e riforma dell'architettura religiosa', in Stefano Biancu (ed.), *Riforma e modernità. Prospettive e bilanci a 500 anni dalle Tesi di Lutero* (Rome: Studium, 2018), 79-101.

Borromini, Francesco, *Opus architectonicum Equitis Francisci Boromini ex ejusdem exemplaribus petitum* [...] *Romæ Sebastianus Gianninus edidit, ac excudit* (1725).

Coffin, David R., *Pirro Ligorio: The Renaissance Artist, Architect, and Antiquarian* (University Park: Pennsylvania State University Press, 2004).

Colonna, Flavia, 'Il ciborio della corsia sistina, l'organo e il ciborio della chiesa di Santo Spirito in Sassia', in Guido Beltramini and Adriano Ghisetti Giavarina (eds), *Studi in onore di Renato Cevese* (CISA Palladio: Vicenza, 2000), 83-91, 515-525.

Conforti, Claudia, *Vasari architetto* (Milan: Electa, 1993).

Connors, Joseph, *Borromini e l'Oratorio romano. Stile e società* (Turin: Einaudi 1989).

Connors, Joseph, 'Introduzione', in Joseph Connors (ed.), Francesco Borromini, *Opus Architectonicum* (Milan: Polifilo 1998), xi-lxxxviii.

Della Libera, Luca, 'Introduction', in *Alessandro Melani: Music for the Pauline Chapel of Santa Maria Maggiore* (New Haven: Yale A-R Editions, 2017), vii-xvi.

Della Libera, Luca, 'La musica a Sant'Ivo alla Sapienza nel Seicento', in Federica Nardacci (ed.), *Musica tra storia e filologia. Studi in onore di Lino Bianchi* (Rome: Istituto Italiano per la Storia della musica, 2010), 135-152.

Freiberg, Jack, *The Lateran in 1600: Christian Concord in Counter-Reformation Rome* (Cambridge: Cambridge University Press, 1995).

Frommel, Christoph L., *L'architettura del santuario e del palazzo apostolico di Loreto da Paolo II a Paolo III* (Loreto: Tecnostampa, 2018).

Hall, Marcia B., *Renovation and Counter-Reformation: Vasari and Duke Cosimo in Sta. Maria Novella and Sta. Croce, 1565-1577* (Oxford: Clarendon Press, 1979).

Hall, Marcia B., 'The Tramezzo in the Italian Renaissance, Revisited', in Sharon E.J. Gerstel (ed.), *Thresholds of the Sacred: Architectural, Art Historical, Liturgical, and Theological Perspectives on Religious Screens, East and West* (Cambridge, MA: Harvard University Press, 2006), 214-232.

Harasimowicz, Jan (ed.), *Protestantischer Kirchenbau der Frühen Neuzeit in Europa. Grundlagen und neue Forschungskonzepte* (Regensburg: Schnell-Schneider, 2015).

Henneberg, Josephine von, *L'oratorio dell'arciconfraternita del Santissimo Crocifisso di San Marcello* (Rome: Bulzoni 1974).

Howard, Deborah, 'Architecture and Music in Fifteenth-Century Italy', in Anna Maria Busse Berger and Jesse Rodin (eds), *The Cambridge History of Fifteenth-Century Music* (Cambridge: Cambridge University Press, 2015), 333-359.

Howard, Deborah and Laura Moretti, *Sound and Space in Renaissance Venice: Architecture, Music, Acoustics* (New Haven: Yale University Press, 2009).

Howe, Eunice D., 'Architecture for "Divine Hymns": The Organ of Antonio da Sangallo the Younger for the Church of Santo Spirito in Sassia', in Katherine A. McIver (ed.), *Art and Music in the Early Modern Period* (Burlington: Aldershot, 2003), 57-90.

Isaiasz, Vera, 'Early Modern Lutheran Churches: Redefining the Boundaries of the Holy and the Profane', in Andrew Spicer (ed.), *Lutheran Churches in Early Modern Europe* (Farnham: Ashgate, 2012), 17-37.

Körner, Joseph Leo, *The Reformation of the Image* (London: Reaktion Books, 2004).

Lionnet, Jean, 'André Maugars: risposta data a un curioso sul sentimento della musica d'Italia', *Nuova rivista musicale italiana* 19 (1985), 681-707.

Lunelli, Renato, *L'arte organaria del Rinascimento in Roma e gli organi di S. Pietro in Vaticano dalle origini a tutto il periodo frescobaldiano* (Florence: Olschki, 1958).

Morelli, Arnaldo, *Il tempio armonico. musica nell'oratorio dei Filippini in Roma (1575-1705)*, Analecta Musicologica 27 (Laaber: Laaber Verlag, 1991).

Morelli, Arnaldo, 'La vista dell'apparato superbo, l'udito della musica eccellente. Spazio ecclesiastico e dimensione sonora', in Marcello Fagiolo and Paolo Portoghesi (eds), *Roma barocca. Bernini, Borromini, Pietro da Cortona* (Milan: Electa, 2006), 294-301.

Morelli, Arnaldo, '"Musica nobile e copiosa di voci et istromenti". Spazio architettonico, cantorie e palchi in relazione ai mutamenti di stile e prassi nella musica da chiesa fra Sei e Settecento', *Analecta musicologica* 33 (2004), 293-330.

Morelli, Arnaldo, 'Space for Music in Roman Residences', in Deborah Howard and Laura Moretti (eds), *The Music Room in Early Modern France and Italy: Sound, Space, and Object* (Oxford: Oxford University Press, 2012), 309-320.

Morelli, Arnaldo, '"Sull'organo et in choro": spazio architettonico e prassi musicale nelle chiese italiane durante il Rinascimento', in Jörg Stabenow (ed.), *Lo spazio e il culto: relazioni tra edificio ecclesiale e uso liturgico dal XV al XVI secolo* (Venice: Marsilio, 2006), 209-226.

Moroni, Gaetano, *Dizionario di erudizione storico-ecclesiastica da S. Pietro sino ai nostri giorni* (Venice: Tipografia Emiliana, 1848).

Noehles, Karl, 'La chiesa dei Santi Luca e Martina dal prebarocco al barocco maturo', in Marcello Fagiolo and Paolo Portoghesi (eds), *Roma barocca. Bernini, Borromini, Pietro da Cortona* (Milan: Electa, 2006), 214-255.

Ottenheym, Konrad, 'The Attractive Flavour of the Past: Combining New Concepts for Ecclesiastical Buildings with References to Tradition in Seventeenth-Century Holland', in Jan Harasimowicz (ed.), *Protestantischer Kirchenbau der Frühen Neuzeit in Europa. Grundlagen und neue Forschungskonzepte* (Regensburg: Schnell-Schneider, 2015), 99-114.

Pinelli, Antonio, *I teatri. Lo spazio dello spettacolo dal teatro umanistico al teatro dell'opera* (Florence: Sansoni, 1973).

Range, Matthias, 'The Material Presence of Music in Church: The Hanseatic City of Lübeck', in Andrew Spicer (ed.), *Lutheran Churches in Early Modern Europe* (Farnham: Ashgate, 2012), 197-220.

Reymond, Bernard, *L'architecture religieuse des protestants. Histoire, caractéristique, problèmes actuels* (Genève: Labor et Fides, 1996).

Rostirolla, Giancarlo, *Musica e musicisti nella Basilica di San Pietro. Vol I: Dalle origini al 1804* (Vatican City: Ed. Capitolo Vaticano, 2014).

Rostirolla, Giancarlo, 'Musiche e apparati nella basilica vaticana per le feste dei Santi Pietro e Paolo e della Dedicazione dalla fine del XVI al primo quarto del XVII secolo', *Analecta musicologica* 33 (2004), 417-474.

Schwager, Klaus, 'Die architektonische Erneuerung von S. Maria Maggiore unter Paul V. Bauprogramm, Baugeschichte, Baugestalt und ihre Voraussetzungen', *Römisches Jahrbuch für Kunstgeschichte* 20 (1983), 241-312.

Schwager, Klaus and Hermann Schlimme, 'La chiesa del Gesù di Roma', in Richard J. Tuttle, Bruno Adorni, Chrisoph L. Frommel and Christof Thoenes (eds), *Jacopo Barozzi da Vignola* (Milan: Electa, 2002), 277-299.

Smither, Howard E., *A History of the Oratorio, Vol. I: The Oratorio in the Baroque Era: Italy, Vienna, Paris* (Chapel Hill: University of North Carolina Press, 1979).

Smyth-Pinney, Julia and David Smyth, 'Borromini and Benevoli: Architectural and Musical Designs in a Seventeenth-Century Roman Church', *Center* 18 (2014), 19-32.

Snaet, Joris, 'For the Greater Glory of God: Religious Architecture in the Low Countries 1560-1700', in Krista De Jonge and Konrad Ottenheym (eds), *Unity and Discontinuity: Architectural Relations between the Southern and Northern Low Countries 1530-1700* (Turnhout: Brepols, 2017), 251-298.

Spicer, Andrew, *Calvinist Churches in Early Modern Europe* (Manchester: Manchester University Press, 2007).

Spicer, Andrew (ed.), *Lutheran Churches in Early Modern Europe* (Farnham: Ashgate, 2012).

Wex, Reinhold, *Ordnung und Unfriede. Raumprobleme des protestantischen Kirchenbaus im 17. und 18. Jahrhundert in Deutschland* (Marburg: Jonas, 1984).

Wisch, Barbara and Nerida Newbigin (eds), *Acting on Faith: The Confraternity of the Gonfalone in Renaissance Rome* (Philadelphia: Saint Joseph's University Press, 2013).

About the Author

Federico Bellini is Full Professor at the Scuola di Ateneo di Architettura e Design (SAAD) of the University of Camerino, Italy. His research examines the relationship between form, symbolism and construction in Renaissance and Baroque architecture. His publications include *Le cupole di Borromini. La 'scientia' costruttiva in età barocca* (2004) and *La basilica di San Pietro da Michelangelo a Della Porta* (2011).

Part II

Teaching Place

5. The Spedale di Santa Maria della Scala and the Construction of Siena

Elizabeth Merrill

Abstract
The Spedale di Santa Maria della Scala was central to the development of architecture and infrastructure in early modern Siena. A major landowner and patron, the hospital institution oversaw the construction of a wide range of buildings throughout the commune, and also played a crucial role in the perpetuation of a distinctly Sienese corpus of technical knowledge. Archival records attest to the presence of the Spedale's building workshop, which contributed workers, materials and expertise to both the institution's projects, as well as those involving Siena's infrastructure and defences. Several fifteenth-century model books trace the technical tradition spearheaded by the Scala. Assembled by individual practitioners, the books bolstered a collective memory, delineating the ideas and structures that made Siena a place.

Key Words: *contado*, granges, technical knowledge, Jacopo Mariano Taccola, Francesco di Giorgio

Introduction

As a distinct place, Siena is most overtly delineated in its built environment: its undulating terrain, narrow winding streets, imposing palaces and abundance of terracotta brick (Figure 5.1).[1] In the early modern period, Siena's infrastructure was also essential to making it a singular place. Within the city, this included the impressive fountains, the fabled *bottini*, the brick paved streets and piazzas, and the extensive network of subterranean workshops and storage areas.[2] Outside of

1 On the use of brick in Siena, see Balestracci, 'La corporazione dei muratori', 27.
2 Siena's underground spaces are discussed in Comune di Siena, *I bottini*, 14.

Merrill, E. (ed.), *Creating Place in Early Modern European Architecture.*
Taylor & Francis Group 2022
DOI: 10.5117/9789463728027_CH05

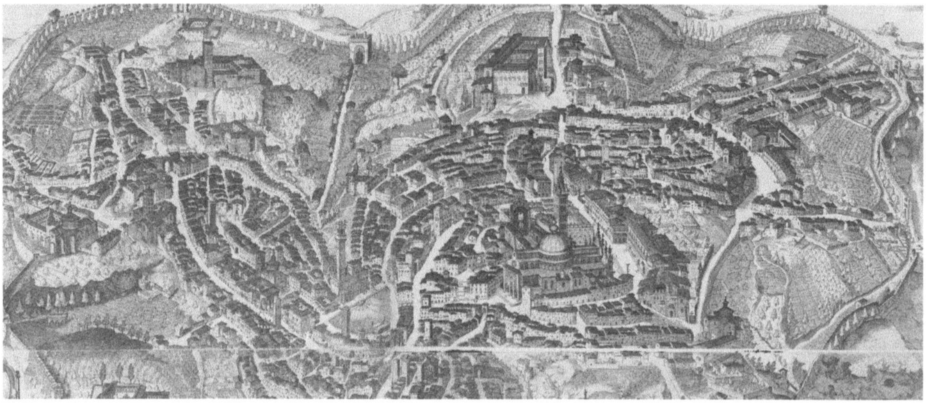

Fig. 5.1 Map of Siena. Detail from etching by Francesco Vanni, c. 1597. Rijksmuseum, Object Nr. RP-P-OB-207.709

the city, in the *contado*, the landholdings and production that took place in the granges, mills, quarries and kilns were equally fundamental to the life of Siena. The building industry was thus a leading protagonist in the history of early modern Siena, and instrumental within this was the city's great welfare institution: the Spedale di Santa Maria della Scala.[3]

This article examines the role of the Spedale di Santa Maria della Scala in the development of early modern Siena as a place: in the realization of its architecture and infrastructure, and in the perpetuation of a distinctly Sienese corpus of technical building knowledge. The Santa Maria della Scala was a, if not the, primary force in the development and maintenance of Siena's iconic tradition of early modern technical design, which as exhibited in numerous anonymous copybooks, as well as the notebooks of Jacopo Mariano Taccola and Francesco di Giorgio, encompassed machine design, hydraulic infrastructure, armament production and fortification architecture.

The importance of the Spedale – as an economic and administrative centre, a welfare institution and a patron of the arts – is the subject of a large body of scholarship. The majority of this literature focuses on the *casa grande*, the institution's administrative centre, which served as the hub of its myriad activities, and was the location of its great public and ceremonial spaces, as well as of storerooms, technical facilities and workshops. The celebrated spaces of the *casa grande* include the Sala di Pellegrinaio, the old sacristy, and the hospital church, SS. Annunziata.

But the Spedale di Santa Maria della Scala also had an enormous footprint outside the city, as one of Siena's major landowners, and as an operator of mills, granges and kilns. Far less has been said about the cultural and artistic importance of Santa Maria della Scala's activities in the *contado*, and more generally, its broader

3 On Siena's building culture, see Balestracci, 'La corporazione dei muratori', 25-26.

function as a harbinger of Siena's fabled technical culture. Records held in the hospital archive attest to the presence of an active building workshop within the *casa grande*, which directed the institution's construction projects – both in and outside the city. The workshop likewise contributed workers, materials and expertise to the projects involving Siena's infrastructure and defences. The scope of technical design initiatives spearheaded by the Santa Maria della Scala is echoed in a series of fifteenth-century model books. The drawings, recipes and notes contained within these personal repositories trace communal building traditions and practices. The individual architect or designer assembled these materials in a process of training his memory. In doing so, he also bolstered a collective memory, further delineating the ideas and structures that made Siena a place.

Siena's Spedale di Santa Maria della Scala

The Spedale di Santa Maria della Scala was established in the late eleventh century under the auspices of the church. Initially, its primary functions were the housing of pilgrims and the care of the sick. It was also a foundling hospital and bestowed alms to needy families within the city.[4] Over the course of the thirteenth and fourteenth centuries, however, the Santa Maria della Scala significantly expanded, and its administration and power did as well. In this period, it became one of Siena's principle institutions, alongside the Duomo and the Palazzo Pubblico.[5] It was regarded as an autonomous lay institution, independent from the city and the church, but closely aligned with the commune, as well as the Duomo and the Studio of Siena. By the fourteenth century, the Santa Maria della Scala was far more than a hospital and welfare institution.[6] The multifunctional institution was Siena's primary producer of foodstuffs, to such a degree that it set market values. The Scala was also a significant producer of material products, including bricks, lime, travertine and metalwork, and as one of Siena's most dominant institutions, it commonly provided financial assistance to diverse subjects, including the Commune of Siena. Beyond this, in granting administrative rights over its extensive possessions, the Santa Maria della Scala fulfilled important social, political and economic functions.[7]

4 Balestracci and Piccinni, 'L'Ospedale di la Città', 21. During times of plague, the Spedale cared for all who were ill. In times of famine, citizens relied on the hospital for the supply of essential foodstuffs.

5 Bellosi, 'Il terzo polo artistico di Siena', 35-39.

6 On the multifunctionality and economic and political importance of the Spedale di Santa Maria della Scala, see Ascheri, 'Storia dell'ospedale e/o storia della città', 65.

7 For a detailed review of the administrative development of the Spedale di Santa Maria della Scala, as reflected in the documents, see Balestracci and Piccinni, 'L'Ospedale di la Città', 22-24. See also Di

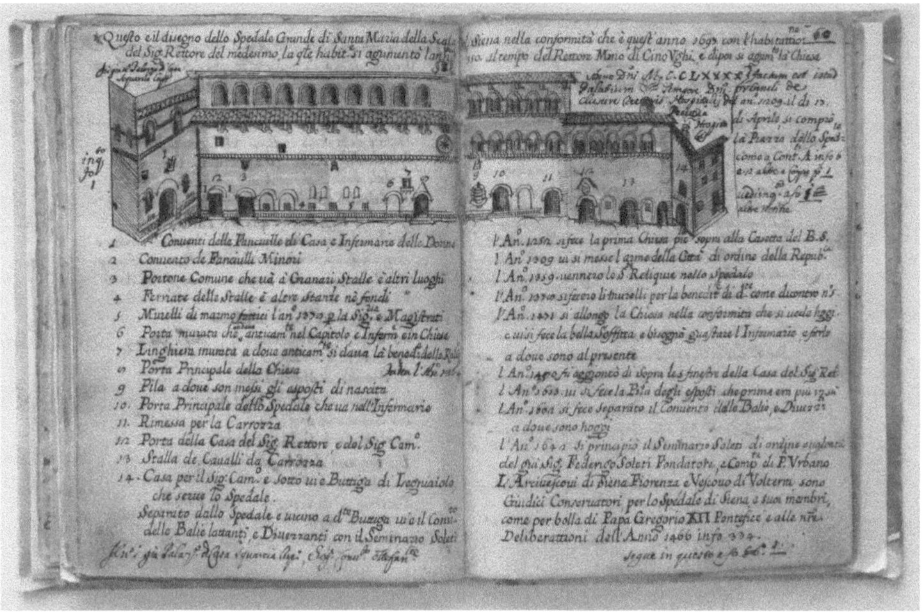

Fig. 5.2 Girolamo Macchi, façade of the Spedale di Santa Maria della Scala in Siena, c. 1700. Archivio di Stato di Siena, Origine dello Spedale di S. Maria della Scala di Siena, D-113, cc. 59v-60r

The heart of the Spedale di Santa Maria della Scala was the extensive hospital complex, the *casa grande*, located on the piazza del Duomo directly across from Siena's great cathedral (Figure 5.2). As will be discussed subsequently, this conglomerate compound provided the spaces for the Santa Maria della Scala's manifold activities, from the housing of pilgrims, to the storage and production of foodstuffs, and various artisanal activities. But the Santa Maria della Scala also extended outside of the *casa grande* – significantly so – literally occupying a substantial portion of Siena. By the fourteenth century, the Santa Maria della Scala was Siena's largest landholder, controlling a portfolio of property that equalled over a third of the entire Sienese territory. Within the city of Siena, the hospital owned 107 houses, three apartments, seven *botteghe*, one garden and four plots of land, a warehouse, a heated bath facility (*stufa*) and a small hospital.[8]

The vast majority of the Scala's real estate holdings were located outside of the city proper in the Sienese *contado*. A large portion of these properties were donated to the Santa Maria della Scala by its rectors, individuals from Siena's most wealthy families, and who, upon taking office, were obligated to grant the institution a

Toro, *Amministrazione e contabilità*, 49-52. Nevola, *Siena*, 130-131, discusses the close links between the Spedale and the commune.

8 Numbers relate to records from 1428. See Balestracci and Piccinni, *Siena nel Trecento*, 141-142.

portion of their ancestral land holdings.[9] Other properties were purchased by the Scala or granted by the commune, often to fill out and consolidate holdings that were already in the hospital's possession. The lands, which encompassed mountainous areas, marshlands, valleys and rivers, were all utilized for their productive capacities.[10] Their primary purpose was the provision of foodstuffs for the institution's numerous charges. The food and material products of the hospital's properties were also sold on the open market, serving as Siena's primary supply of food, and in turn, providing monetary support for the institution's manifold activities.[11]

Administratively, the rural holdings of the Santa Maria della Scala were structured within a network of granges (*grancie*), which oversaw the cultivation of farms, vineyards and orchards, the raising of livestock, the harvesting of wood and stone, and the production of bricks, lime and metalwork objects. It was undoubtedly due to the fact that the Santa Maria della Scala produced the majority of Sienese grain that it was also granted a virtual monopoly on the milling industry.[12] Beginning in the fourteenth century, the commune of Siena gave the Scala licence to control key waterways with the construction and operation of mills. The commune also gave the institution communal land for the development of new mills.[13] In the fourteenth, fifteenth and sixteenth centuries, a large portion of the mills within the commune of Siena were owned and operated by the Spedale.[14]

The *casa grande* was the Spedale di Santa Maria della Scala's central reference point, the administrative hub of its activities within Siena, and as distributed throughout its network of granges.[15] A city within a city, the *casa grande* reflected the diversity and breadth of the institution and might be seen as a microcosm of Siena.[16] A detailed inventory of the complex, made in the fourteenth century, allows us to reconstruct the manifold activities of this place. On the ground level, there were public and ceremonial spaces, including the well-known Sala del Pellegrinaio

9 Di Toro, *Amministrazione e contabilità*, 45.

10 On the Spedale's acquisition of its rural properties, see Epstein, *Alle origini della fattoria toscana*, 29-58.

11 Balestracci, 'La politica di gestione', 294, notes that food supply was a principle preoccupation of the commune.

12 Ibid., 294-296.

13 Acocella and Turrin, *Travertino di Siena*, 46-48; Balestracci and Piccinni, 'L'Ospedale di la Città', 25; Cecchini, 'Le grance dell'Ospedale di S. Maria della Scala di Siena'.

14 Balestracci, 'Approvvigionamento e distribuzione', 139.

15 Di Toro, *Amministrazione e contabilità*, 49.

16 Sordini, *Dentro l'antico ospedale*, 279. The renown of the Spedale's structure and administration was such that in 1456 the Duke of Milan asked for a full report of the complex. See Leverotti, 'L'ospedale senese di Santa Maria della Scala in una relazione del 1456'.

and the Cappella del Chiodo. Offices, dormitories and apartments occupied the upper levels of the complex, accessible by two stair ramps.

The Spedale complex also extended under the ground – three levels – following the slope of the hill. The inventory describes the internal street of the centre – the former Via di Vallepiatta – which served as the principal axis of distribution for the hospital's extensive utilitarian spaces.[17] Within the massive walls and the great vaults, there were granaries, cisterns, storage facilities, kitchens, slaughterhouses, animal pens, cellars of wine and oil, foundries, the seats of lay companies and artisan workshops.[18] On the lowest level of the hospital complex, near a large water well and next to a slaughterhouse, the inventory also locates 'the room of the carpenter and builder'. The description of the workshop space specifies that it was here that 'carpentry and metalwork takes place for projects not only within the hospital, but also in all the houses, workshops and properties scattered throughout the city'.[19]

The Bottega of the Santa Maria della Scala

The 'the room of the carpenter and builder', which in other documents was referred to as the '*buttigha del legname*' or simply the '*butiga*' was the Santa Maria della Scala's building workshop.[20] As such, it was also one of Siena's principle building workshops. Within the *casa grande* itself, the second half of the fifteenth century saw considerable building and decorative activity. In the Pellegrinaio, or great pilgrim's hall, a series of frescoes were completed by Domenico di Bartolo, Vecchietta and Priamo della Quercia. Between 1445 and 1467, the Spedale's church and sacristy were expanded and decorated in a programme that included the construction of a new façade elevation, a coffered ceiling, the realisation of altarpieces and panels, and the facture of a bronze ciborium.[21] In 1479, work commenced on the amplification of the palatial residence of the Scala's rector.[22]

17 Ibid., 279. Originally, this was a public street, open to the air, located close to the city wall. But as the Spedale sequentially developed outward into the valley, the street was incorporated into the structure.

18 Ibid., 281, 314-315.

19 Ibid., 316.

20 Documentary examples: 'A Maio di Jacomo nostro sta in chasa alla butiga [in the Spedale] e di 3 di Iulio soldi venti contanti a lui e son posti a sua ragione a libro della famiglia [...] a folio 101' and 'A Paolo di Giovanni di [A]ciano nostro garzone alle buttigha del[']legname [in Spedale] a di 16 di detto [ottobre] soldi 20 contanti a lui e son posti a libro della famiglia a folio 122.' Archivio di Stato di Siena (ASSi), Ospedale di Santa Maria, vol. 859 (Fasc. I), fols. 44r, 53v.

21 Cavallero, *Lo Spedale di Santa Maria della Scala in Siena*, 147-200.

22 Milani, 'L'attività costruttiva del Quattrocento dalle fonti archivistiche', 116-117. In the fourteenth century, the multifold building activities of the Spedale di Santa Maria della Scala – both in the city

The Quattrocento was also a period of marked growth and building activity within Siena and its *contado*, more generally. The city alone saw the contemporaneous development of the Palazzo Piccolomini (1469-1495), the Loggia del Papa (1462), the Oratorio di Santa Caterina in Fontebranda (1465-1472) and the church of Santo Spirito (c. 1460-1490). Within the *contado*, significant resources were poured into the rebuilding of Sienese defences, the formation of Pienza and the construction of the massive Bruna River dam.[23] The grange network of the Santa Maria della Scala, which might be likened to a divided company (each office worked independently but remained under a central control and retained part of a unified identity), also witnessed marked growth and building activity.[24] Supervised by the hospital's rector, the individual *granciere* – overseers of the granges – were responsible for all construction and maintenance work on the rural properties, from the repair of roads and bridges, to the reclamation of swampy areas, and the construction of mills, dams and aqueducts.[25] Records from the *Entrate e Uscite* of the Santa Maria della Scala account for the centralized oversight of the projects undertaken at the granges. In March and April 1471, for example, a payment was made to one *granciere*, Goro di Paolo, for the needs of a granary and mill.[26] Similarly, in December 1474, payments were made to the *grancia* of Montisi for the construction of a brick tower, and to the *grancia* of Cuna, for 'expenses of the *grancia*'.[27]

The Santa Maria della Scala's building workshop, as the central node of this activity, was thus not a meagre one-man operation, but rather, a vibrant centre of manifold activity. It was here that labourers would have met carpenters, stonecutters,

and in the *contado* – were managed by an '*operaio*'. Although the position no longer existed in the late fifteenth century, documents from the period suggest that the job was filled by other means.

23 The extensive building activities in Quattrocento Siena necessitated augmented building teams. A significant numbers of migrants joined project sites in low-population areas, such as in the areas of Talamone, Fighine and Saturnia. See Cecchini, 'Maestri Luganesi e comaschi a Siena nel secolo XV', 133. On the structure of work teams and the motivations of the immigrant workers, see Balestracci, 'L'immigrazione di manodopera nella Siena medievali', 179-180; Bianchi, 'Maestri costruttori lomabardi nei cantieri della Toscana', 158-161.

24 Di Toro, *Amministrazione e contabilità*, 53.

25 Ibid., 49, 53-54; Milani, 'L'attività costruttiva del Quattrocento dalle fonti archivistiche', 118.

26 The documents in reference, for March 1471: 'A Frate Goro di Paolo grancere a piano a di 28 di marzo L. 33 e soldi 22 contanti per bisongnio della grancia e mulino e sono posti a lo S morello [...] folio 398'; and April 1471: 'A Frate Goro di Paolo nostro grancere a piana a di 28 [di Aprile] L[ire] 44 e soldi sedici contanti a lui per la uopere del mulino e son posti a lui a L. S morello [...] folio 420'. ASSi, Ospedale di Santa Maria, vol. 858 (Fasc. I and II), fol. 69v and 73v.

27 Two payments appear on the same folio: (1) 'A la grancia di Monticiello a di 26 dicembre lire 5 e soldi 12 contanti demo [abbiamo dato] a torre da Monteciello per mantone porto a valerisse e sono posti a Libro Verde T [...] folio 56'; and (2) 'A la grancia di Chuna a di detto [26 dicembre] lire 5 e soldi 12 demo [abbiamo dato] a frate Giovanni di Bartolomeo piu tempo fa per spese della grancia a Libro Verde T [...] folio 552'. ASSi, Ospedale di Santa Maria, vol. 860 (Fasc. I), fol. 67v.

brick workers and other skilled artisans. What is more, the wealth of properties and projects overseen by the Scala meant that it regularly employed a considerable number of practitioners. The names of the vast majority of these individuals are unknown, as a given project was typically assigned to a single named *operaio* or *capomaestro*, who assumed full responsibility for overseeing the organization and the evolution of work, appointing workers, sourcing material, fixing salaries and compensation, and orchestrating the execution of various operations.[28] For reasons of economy and scale, moreover – we must remember Siena's relatively small size and population in the Quattrocento – individuals employed by the Santa Maria della Scala necessarily moved between projects that required various levels and types of expertise. The work of '*scarpellino*' Francesco di Bartolomeo in the years 1475-1476 is a good example. Within the Spedale church, he constructed a threshold and reliquary chapel, the marble for which he had quarried and transported. In this same period, Francesco di Bartolomeo completed a variety of tasks related to the completion of a '*chasa*' for the Santa Maria della Scala, including the construction of a loggia on the second level of the house, which was to serve as a dovecote.[29]

The building workshop of the Santa Maria della Scala was well positioned to assume a wide range of technically and geographically disparate projects not only due to its size and administrative infrastructure, but also given its close political and economic ties with the communal government, and its physical proximity to the Opera del Duomo.[30] Siena's Opera del Duomo was responsible for the construction of the cathedral, and often assumed building projects for the commune. At any given period, it employed dozens, if not hundreds, of workers.[31] But the Opera del Duomo was not the only entity that contracted for Sienese building projects, and ample evidence shows that the Santa Maria della Scala workshop functioned as an extension of the Opera del Duomo. It has been noted, for example, that in the

28 Pinto, 'L'organizzazione della difesa', 266-267, details such a hierarchy in regards to fortification construction in Siena in the fourteenth and fifteenth centuries.

29 All records are kept in the ASSi, Ospedale di Santa Maria, vol. 524. The account for the construction of the threshold (fol. 92v): 'Francesco di Bartolomeo Scarpellino de avere a di 27 di guigno L. 5 e soldi 22 denari o ebbe per noi da Misser. Nicolo Ricoveri. Detti denari se gli darano per cherte pietre se murarano per la soila dove e fermata su la graticola e s[ono] e messer in questo.' The chapel is noted in multiple documents. On fol. 97v: 'Francesco di Bartolomeo Scarpellatore che apreso a fare la chappela del marmo per gli nostri relique denno dare L. 168 soldi o sono per tanti fattalo creditore gli doveva dare.' In January 1475, his travel to the quarry is noted (fol. 7v): 'Francesco di Bartolomeo scarpelmatore che apresso a fare la chappella del marmo per gli nostri reliquie di dare a di 8 di genaio L. 11 e S. – per aiuto a lui disse per andare alla chava e so[no] aiuscita di Frate Giovanni di M. Martino camerlegno [...] folio 69.' Payments made between 12 June and 14 August 1476 (fol. 229r) relate the construction of the 'chasa': 'portano il grano alla cava' and '[fare] l'allogagone dei collombiai della casa'.

30 On the Opera del Duomo, see Giorgi, *Costruire una cattedrale*. Balestracci, 'La corporazione dei muratori', 26, underscores the Spedale building workshop as a place continually open to change.

31 Balestracci, 'La Corporazione dei muratori', 29.

construction and maintenance of the *bottini*, an operation that required hundreds of workers annually, the Santa Maria della Scala, along with the commune, acted as a contractor, providing workers, tools and materials.[32] As will be discussed in greater detail below, the expertise the Santa Maria della Scala developed in the construction of rural fortifications and its mills positioned it to serve as a defence contractor on behalf of the commune. Finally, in tracing the careers of a select group of practitioners active in the Spedale workshop in the second half of the fifteenth century – the subject of the final section of this chapter – it is readily apparent that the operations of this major workshop often merged with projects involving major communal building endeavours.

The Architecture of the Granges

It was outside of city centre that most of the building initiatives and production activities of the Santa Maria della Scala took place. Inventories compiled by the central administration, along with payment receipts, filed in the Spedale's *Entrate e Uscite*, provide a partial image of the granges, both as productive centres and as architectural complexes.[33] The granges were not merely stand-alone structures, but were themselves small precincts, with farms, houses, mills and lands given out to sharecropping. Additional insight into the grange complexes is gained from the few constructions that remain, as well as early modern written and visual material. The Spedale granges should not be dismissed as merely utilitarian farms, without formal or technical merit. Rather, these substantial facilities presented many exemplary features of early modern architecture, as manifest in their thick brick and masonry foundations, wide cross and umbrella vaults, covered ramps, mechanical infrastructure, sculptural ornament and defensive features.

In 1500, the network of Santa Maria della Scala granges numbered twelve: at Castelletto, San Quirico, Camigliano, Montisi, San Giusto, Grosseto, Montepescali, Prata, Spedaletto, Cuna, Serre and Masse (Figure 5.3). Within this network, there were a total of at least 164 farms, 189 houses, fifteen mills, seven taverns, six olive farms, four fulling mills, fourteen kilns, 32 dovecotes and eleven workshops.[34] The

32 Balestracci, Costantini and Vigni, *La memoria dell'acqua*, 34; Prager and Scaglia, *Mariano Taccola and His Book* De Ingeneis, 4.

33 In examining the granges as individual nodes of architectural production, the archival records are often insufficient. Not only do the inventories bear notable inconsistencies in scope and detail, and as they were not composed specifically as architectural or building accounts, they often gloss over details regarding certain constructions. See Epstein, 'Inventari di beni di grance dell'Ospedale di S. Maria della Scala di Siena'.

34 Balestracci and Piccinni, 'L'Ospedale di la Città', 25.

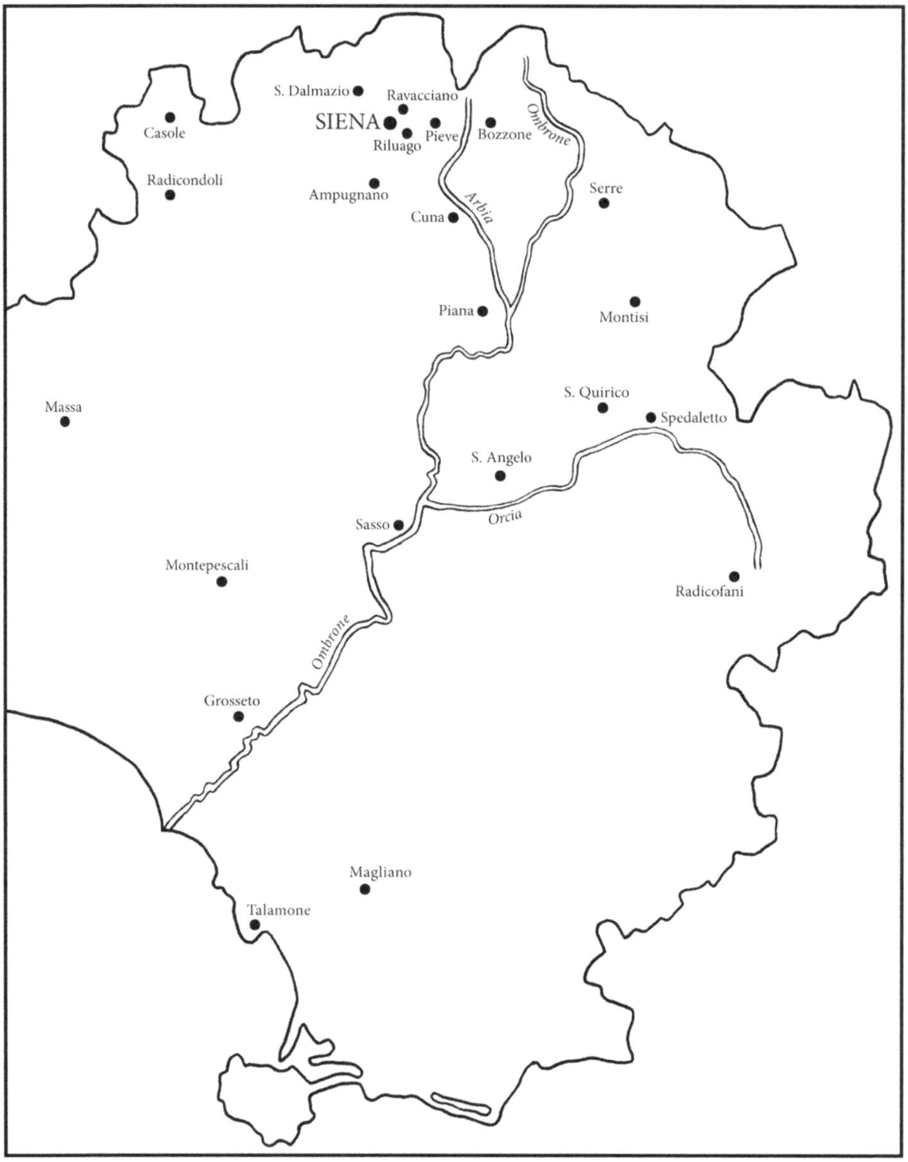

Fig. 5.3 Locations of the granges owned by the Spedale, c. 1500. © Photo: Elizabeth Merrill

granges – all of which were located south of Siena, with a concentrated number in the Val d'Orcia – were each specialized in terms of location and the given productive capabilities. But as nodes within a greater network, the granges were frequently engaged in reciprocal agreements, whereby, for example, the grain harvested at one centre would be sent to another for processing, or the animals raised at one grange (Grosseto) would be exchanged for foodstuffs from another (Cuna).[35]

The scale of the individual grange properties sheds light on the extensive corpus of buildings and the mechanical infrastructure that each supported. It also provides a sense of the Scala's economic and social influence, and the very real role it played in the generation and application of architectural and technical building knowledge.[36] The granges of Cuna and Serre – the most productive and extensive of the Scala's holdings – are instructive points of reference. Around 1450, the grange at Cuna included 670 hectares of farmland, as well as numerous houses and workshops, three mills, two inns, a kiln, a small hospital, a church and two chapels.[37] The grange at Serre, in turn, covered nearly 600 hectares, with at least 36 farms, numerous houses, four mills, and a travertine quarry (Figure 5.4).[38] The real estate and infrastructure of such grange systems could not be managed by a few, but was ever evolving, with new structures being added and existing facilities requiring continual maintenance.

The grange facilities centred on a composite complex, a compact architectural block organised around two or more courtyards that might be likened to an enclosed compound or a small village. These structures did not adhere to a single typology – as functional facilities that had to accommodate a variety of conditions and environmental factors such coherence was not even desirable – but they did bear notable formal similarities.[39] Distributed on two or more levels, the grange compounds were equipped to fulfil the same set of residential and productive functions, with spaces for the housing of workers and animals, and the storage of grain and other foodstuffs. The lower levels of the grange house were composed of wide, vaulted spaces – necessary to maximize storage and productive facilities. At Serre, these spaces were occupied by stables, barns, kitchens, tanning rooms, ovens and braziers, storage facilities and places of production and conservation – of olives, grapes, cheese and grain (oats, rye and barley).[40] The upper levels of the grange was often accessible by a stair ramp and featured open loggias.[41] Typically, the space here was at least in part occupied by the apartment of the *granciere* and

35 Coscarella and Franchi, *La grancia di Cuna*, 8. On the distribution of the Scala's network of granges, see also Franchi and Coascarella, 'Le grance dello Spedale', 68-69.

36 Epstein, *Alle origini della fattoria toscana*, 191.

37 Franchi and Coscarella, 'Le grance dello Spedale', 78-79.

38 Balestracci, 'La politica di gestione', 294, notes that four mills existed at Serre di Rapolano around 1600. An overview of the holdings of the Grancia of Serre is provided in *Grancia delle Serre*, 2. On the quarry at Serre, see Acocella and Turrin, *Travertino di Siena*, 47-49.

39 Coscarella and Franchi, *La grancia di Cuna*, 8.

40 *Grancia delle Serre*, 5.

41 Ibid., 6. Serre, Cuna, Spedaletto and likely also Montisi, all had stair ramps.

Fig. 5.4 Giuseppe Maria Zaccheri, elevation of the grange and houses of Serre, 1751. Archivio di Stato di Siena, Ospedale S. Maria della Scala n. 1441: 'Grancia di Serre', c. 79: 'Casa del Podere di Torciano'

Fig. 5.5 Grancia di Serre, rib vaults of the loggia. © Photo: Elizabeth Merrill

Fig. 5.6 Grancia di Serre, main courtyard. © Photo: Elizabeth Merrill

Fig. 5.7 Grancia di Spedaletto, crenellated wall and tower, developed c. 1446. © Photo: Elizabeth Merrill

his 'family', individuals who helped manage the grange and activities of the house, and numbered between 25 and 30. There was often also an office, rooms for the accommodation of pilgrims and more storage spaces.[42] Aside from their productive functions, the granges, as nodes within the greater Spedale network, were also welfare centres. Every grange complex included a church or a chapel, as well as places for the accommodation and care of pilgrims, the sick and the poor. As central points of reference and security for a greater population of rural inhabitants – farmers and sharecroppers of the Scala properties, as well as other private individuals who lived in the vicinity – the grange complexes had to be physically solid and visually reassuring. The imposing brick walls, expansive courtyards, remarkably formal vaulted halls and modest yet artful decorative features were in keeping with the moral solidity and security that the Scala espoused.[43]

While there are few records that name the individuals involved in the design and construction of Scala granges, the building fabric attests to the involvement of highly skilled workers: stonemasons who knew the stereotomy necessary to form the vaults, builders with the technical acumen to scale and engineer the palatial foundations and load-bearing walls, hydrologists who could design the cisterns and wells, and sculptors who could execute the decorative portals, window mouldings and crests (Figures 5.5 and 5.6). Moreover, as almost all the grange compounds were fortified – a topic to which we will subsequently return – individuals expert in defence design would have been involved in the buildings' construction (Figure 5.7). While few, if any, of these figures would have borne the title '*architetto*' – the term was not consistently used prior to the sixteenth century – collectively they contributed to the creation of a distinctly Sienese, early modern architecture.[44]

Mills and Production

The Spedale di Santa Maria della Scala's role as a primary impetus for Sienese architectural production and technical design extended beyond its patronage of the expansive grange compounds. As previously noted, the Scala's rural properties frequently contained mechanical infrastructure for the processing of foodstuffs and for the production of building supplies (brick, lime and stone). Principle among these constructions were the Scala's network of mills, which were not only vastly

42 Franchi and Coscarella, 'Le grance dello Spedale', 76-77. On the layout of spaces within the grancia of Cuna, see Coscarella and Franchi, *La grancia di Cuna*, 17-22; for a discussion on the *granciere*, his job description and his 'family', see ibid., 25.

43 Coscarella and Franchi, *La grancia di Cuna*, 9.

44 Merrill, 'The "professione di architetto" in Renaissance Italy', 14-16.

important to the operations of the hospital, but were also crucial to life of commune at large.[45]

In architectural terms, the mills represented an advanced field of technical design, a sector in which the Scala was not merely causally invested. By the end of the sixteenth century, the Santa Maria della Scala owned at least fifteen mills. Of these, five were located at Cuna, four were at Serre di Rapolano, and there was one each at Buonconvento, Montisi, Castelluccio, Spedaletto, San Quirico, Prata and Montespescali.[46] The need for adequate milling facilities, and the paucity of mills, was a recurrent theme in early modern Siena. The scarcity of water – and therefore also of water-powered production facilities – meant that the majority of Sienese industry was located outside of the city centre. The development of mills on the Merse River, and throughout the *contado*, was therefore vital to the sustenance and economy of Siena.[47] It was here that grain was ground, and paper, cloth and ironworks were produced. The desire to maximize production and efficiency also meant that there was a near continual interest to improve the mills and to devise mechanisms that could process more, operate more quickly, and function with less power.

Records – both written and graphic – from the fourteenth and fifteenth centuries attest to a keen interest in mill construction and design. Documents of 1334 and 1385 presented to the Siena's General Council record complaints filed by citizens in thirteen provinces that lacked adequate mills.[48] Tellingly, it was in this same period that the Scala acquired a great many of its mills, either through direct acquisition or inheritance.[49] The inventories and account books of the Scala attest to the enormous energy that was continually poured into the development of its mills, which were powered by water, as well as by humans and animals. In 1380s, the Scala's mills at Ravacciano and Valiano were repaired; the following decade, those at Monteroni, Scrofiano and Serre di Rapolano underwent improvements.[50] Care for the milling network often also required more large-scale interventions. In 1375, a draught in the Val d'Arbia had severely limited milling operations at Monteroni, Buonconvento and Isola, and the Scala requested permission to build barriers and to divert water to the Bozzone stream.[51] In 1439, two years after the plague, it was written that mills that were previously 'fruitful and useful', had become 'almost all non-useful and largely clogged, so that they do not mill'.[52] Even after the repairs

45 Di Toro, *Amministrazione e contabilità*, 48.
46 Balestracci, 'Approvvigionamento e distribuzione', 139.
47 Topic is addressed in Comune di Siena, *I bottini*, 10-11.
48 Balestracci, 'Approvvigionamento e distribuzione', 131.
49 Epstein, *Alle origini della fattoria toscana*, 86-90.
50 Ibid., 189 (and n. 55).
51 Ibid., 85.
52 Balestracci, 'La politica di gestione', 299 n. 33.

were made, maintenance was continuous. A series of payments made by the Santa Maria della Scala to the *granciere* at Buonconvento in 1471 and 1472 account for extensive work done on the mill there.[53]

For graphic documentation of this endless preoccupation with mill design and construction, we can turn to the treatise-turned-notebook of Jacopo Mariano Taccola, *De ingeneis*. While there is no immediate, known link between Taccola (1382-1453/1458) and the Spedale di Santa Maria della Scala, the fact that *De ingeneis* is teeming with designs of construction types that the Scala would have regularly undertaken – mills, gear drives, water wheels, piledrivers, pump mechanisms and bucket wheels – is highly suggestive.[54] Taccola, who was trained as a sculptor, assumed a role akin to that of a modern-day engineer or inventor. In addition to his artistic activities, he was an academic administrator in Siena's Studio, and served the city as communal estimator and superintendent of roads.[55] He was certainly aware of the infrastructure needs of the commune and its *contado*. Moreover, his tenure as secretary within Siena's Studio (1424-1434), which was closely linked to the Spedale, would have given him ample opportunity to engage with, and perhaps consult on, mechanical projects undertaken by the latter institution. His illustration of a fulling mill on folio 40r, which sits in front of a modest yet well-built farm house, recalls a Spedale grange (Figure 5.8). At the base of the drawing, the pair of water scoops (on the right), and the man surveying land by means of a measured cord tied to an arrow (to the left), might likewise be related to projects that occupied the builders and technicians employed by the Scala. Among his many annotations, Taccola addresses the grinding of grain without the use of water, and the construction of a wheel that could function for sixteen hours straight.[56] Whether or not the material of Taccola's book relates, in any sense, to properties of the Scala is largely irrelevant. Indisputable is its relationship to local infrastructure needs and Sienese-specific building types.

53 See, for example, ASSi, Ospedale di Santa Maria, vol. 858 (Fasc. I), fol. 69v: 'A Frate Goro di Paolo grancere a piano a di 28 di marzo L. 33 e soldi 22 contanti per bisongnio della grancia e mulino e sono posti a lo S morello [...] folio 398'; ASSi, Ospedale di Santa Maria, vol. 858 (Fasc. I), fol. 73v: 'A Frate Goro di Paolo nostro grancere a piana [Buonconvento] a di 28 [di Aprile] L[ire] 44 e soldi sedici contanti a lui per la uopere del mulino e son posti a lui a L. S morello [...] folio 420'; ASSi, Ospedale di Sta. Maria, vol. 858 (Fasc. II), fol. 65r: 'La grancia di piana a di detto L. 5 a soldi 8 contanti per lui a pasthinno di nanni per huopere dodici avito al mulino come che ne fece polizie frate goro e sono e frate goro a L. Verde T [...] a folio 47'.

54 On the history of *De Ingeneis*, and Taccola's purpose in preparing it, see Prager and Scaglia, *Mariano Taccola and His Book* De Ingeneis, 10-16.

55 On the life of Taccola, see the introduction to Taccola, *De Ingeneis*, vol. 1, 11-15; Prager and Scaglia, *Mariano Taccola and His Book* De Ingeneis, 3-21.

56 Mills, waterwheels and bucket wheels appear throughout *De Ingeneis*. On a mill that grinds without water and that can run for sixteen hours, see text fol. 57r of Bayerische Staatsbibliothek, Munich, codex Monacensis 197 II as transcribed and translated in Mariano Taccola, *De Ingeneis*, vol. 1, 79.

Fig. 5.8 Jacopo Mariano Taccola, illustration of a fulling mill. *De Ingeneis*, c. 1430. Bayerische Staatsbibliothek, Munich, codex Monacensis 197 II, fol. 40r

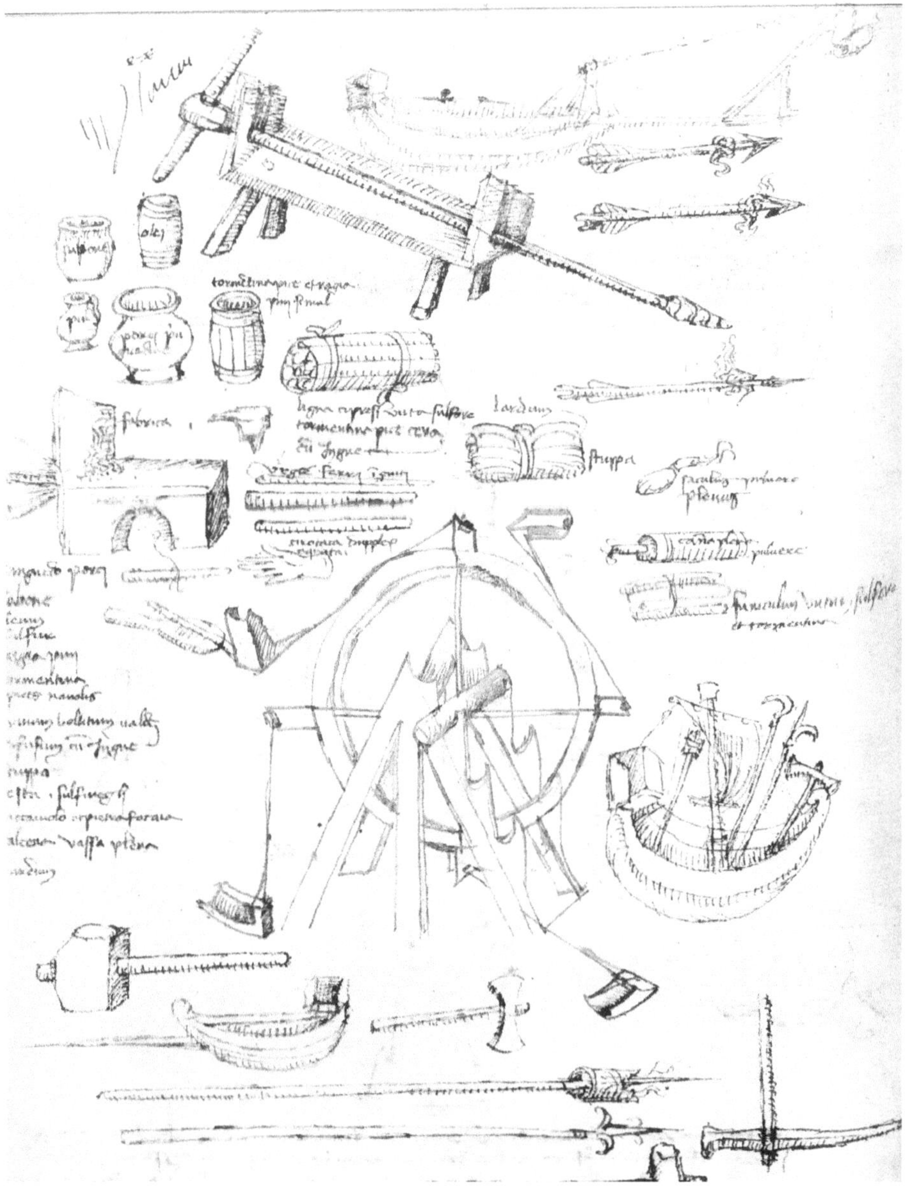

Fig. 5.9 Jacopo Mariano Taccola, illustrations of excavation equipment. *De Ingeneis*, c. 1430. Bayerische Staatsbibliothek, Munich, codex Monacensis 197 II, fol. 69v

Within the pages of *De ingeneis*, it is also possible to find illustrations of kilns and furnaces, and excavation equipment (mallets, picks, axes, drills), devices that relate to the Santa Maria della Scala's other primary fields of production (Figure 5.9). The travertine quarries located on Spedale properties – at Querciolaie and Serre di Rapolano – were Siena's most productive. The relationship between the Scala and the supply of travertine to the city was important, and as an extension of this, the ties between the hospital and Siena's leading patrons of architecture were noteworthy. The white travertine that faced the city's most grandiose Renaissance constructions – the Palazzo Piccolomini most conspicuously – was quarried on the land of the Scala hospital.[57]

The kilns owned and operated by the Scala produced the bricks, lime and ironworks that the hospital used in constructing its own properties. The hospital also sold and distributed these products to the commune.[58] Siena was a city of bricks. In the fifteenth century, the *Ufficiali sopra l'ornato* classified buildings based on their appearance and material, and ordered the destruction and reconstruction of a great many non-brick buildings. The city's streets were also paved in brick, as were a great many of its churches and institutions, the *casa grande* of the Spedale di Santa Maria della Scala included.[59] The hospital's role in realizing this brick-lined place – '*siena di mattoni*' – was thus not inconsequential. The Santa Maria della Scala both provided the city with the physical building blocks of its built environment, and supplied many of the workers who crafted this place.

The paramount role of the Santa Maria della Scala as a kiln operator is attested to in the extensive corpus of items its facilities produced. Documentation from the fifteenth century records the Scala kilns producing bricks – of many shapes and types – as well as lime, gutters, eaves and cannons of various measures.[60] The last item, firearms, is particularly interesting, in light of both the defensive element of the granges and Siena's specialized artillery industry in the fifteenth century. While the work of Siena's great artillerists is frequently associated with the commune, it is highly plausible that the Santa Maria della Scala played an important role in the Sienese development of casting technology and its production of the leading experts in defensive design.[61]

The Spedale Fortifies Siena

By the fifteenth century, the granges and mills of the Santa Maria della Scala were the leading productive facilities within the Commune of Siena. They were

57 Acocella and Turrin, *Travertino di Siena*, 47-49. This is also noted by Tozzetti, *Relazioni d'alcuni viaggi fatti in diverse parti della Toscana*, 273.

58 Alongside the commune itself, the Santa Maria della Scala was one of Siena's most notable proprietors of kilns, with facilities at Cuna, Costa al Pino and Costa Fabbri, among other locales. Balestracci, 'Produzione ed uso del mattone', 421-422. On the kilns of the Spedale, see Valacchi, 'Dislocazione delle Foraci'.

59 Balestracci, 'Produzione ed uso del mattone', 424-428.

60 Corsi, 'Forma dimensioni e caratteristiche del mattone senese', 25.

61 Ermini, 'Campane e cannoni', 389-390.

also important locales in its defensive network. Frequent incursions into the Sienese *contado*, especially devastating in the fourteenth century, proved that the destruction of livestock, foodstuffs and other vital resources were the prime target of Siena's enemies.[62] While the destruction of communal properties was an obvious and dangerous threat, damages made to the Scala properties were equally precarious, as it was within these facilities that the majority of Siena's grain was cultivated, processed and sold. The threat of famine demanded the fortification of the rural granges, production centres and mills. As summarized in a document of October 1391, regarding the fortification of Molin del Pero, on the Merse River, such a facility 'animates the whole citizenry', and once fortified, would 'be able to secure all of the citizens from the enemy', and with the other fortified mills, would provide protection in times of war.[63] While few Sienese mills from the early modern period remain extant today – exemplars of a unique type of part industrial, part military architecture – the rich archival records of the Santa Maria della Scala again, along with ample visual records, offer striking insight into these unique constructions.[64] The Santa Maria della Scala initiated the fortification of its granges and mills in the mid-Trecento, and by 1400, many of these complexes shared much in common with medieval fortification architecture: high walls, barbicans, corner towers, crenellations, and dungeons.[65]

The first grange to be fortified was that of Cuna, with work beginning in 1367 and extending until approximately 1380. Here, a large amount (more than 500 gold florins) was invested in the construction of walls, the reinforcement with iron of the main portal and the construction of a stone barbican.[66] Additional elements of fortification were added in subsequent decades. Most important was a thick and angled wall, which extended around the entire perimeter. On the west side of the compound there was a walkway, outfitted with slits and machicolations, which would have been used to the launch of offensive material on the assailants. Two long braces extending on the north end of the compound evidence the presence of a guard tower. The eastern side of the compound had additional fortification. Here, two 4-metre-tall battlements, which feature semi-inverted pyramid-shaped

62 Epstein, *Alle origini della fattoria toscana*, 253-254.

63 Balestracci, 'Approvvigionamento e distribuzione', 137, quotes the document: 'ibi fortilitium quod teneri et custodiri possit ab onmi gente inimica [...] istud videtur esse utilitissimum pro vestra civitate, quia si casus accideret quod gens inimica veniret super territorium senesem, istud novum molendium [...] fulcient de macinato totam vestram civitatem; et de aliis molendinis que sunt in vestro comitatu et massis tempore compagnie et guerre modica ratio fieri potest'.

64 Balestracci, 'Approvvigionamento e distribuzione.'

65 Coscarella and Franchi, *La grancia di Cuna*, 9; Epstein, *Alle origini della fattoria toscana*, 253-254.

66 Epstein, *Alle origini della fattoria toscana*, 253.

corbels, supported blind arches, a motif typical in fourteenth- and fifteenth-century Sienese architecture.[67]

The work done to fortify the other granges was similar. The commune mandated that the Spedale secure its properties with its own funds. However, when the need arose, the commune proved more than willing to support the Scala in its fortification endeavours.[68] For the defence of Sant'Angelo in Colle, for example, the Sienese government granted to the hospital, against the opposition of the local government, the rights to a palace, which could be developed as a fortification.[69] Similarly, in seeking a means to protect its holdings at Piana, a small village not far from Buonconvento, the Scala was granted funds to fortify the nearby village of Santa Innocenza. The rector was placed in charge of the project, which was to be of mutual benefit to the commune and the hospital.[70]

The collaborative relationship that developed between the hospital institution and the commune in the defence of mills is overtly demonstrated in the case of the mill at Monteroni. In the 1370s, the General Council filed a complaint against the Scala's rector regarding the poor and unfortified condition of the Monteroni mill, which was located in an area of great value to the Scala and to Siena. The Santa Maria della Scala, in turn, responded by requesting the commune for the funds – a thousand florins – to restore the structure.[71] These were granted, and by the end of the 1380s, the Monteroni mill was not only restored, but fully fortified. What is more, the mill, which was often referred to as the '*forteza*', appears to have assumed the role of a defensive outpost. In 1391 the Scala asked, and obtained, from the Balìa of Siena permission to quarter soldiers at the mill, who were considered the exclusive protectors of the mill and exonerated from other commitments. In establishing this defensive hold, the Santa Maria della Scala demonstrated its economic power, as well as its military and political strength. By the fifteenth century, the Scala had not only the means to restore and fortify its mills, it also had the authority to suppress private mills, to regulate and deviate watercourses, and to place military garrisons.[72]

The Santa Maria della Scala's investment and experience in defensive design had unquestionable significance. Beginning in the fourteenth century, and continuing

67 Coscarella and Franchi, *La grancia di Cuna*, 14-15; Franchi and Coscarella, 'Le grance dello Spedale', 78.

68 Still, the role of the commune in the expansion and fortification of the Scala's landholdings was not determinative. See Epstein, *Alle origini della fattoria toscana*, 269.

69 Epstein, *Alle origini della fattoria toscana*, 254. This occured in 1380.

70 Franchi and Coscarella, 'Le grance dello Spedale', 70. The fortification of Stigliano was similar, including heavy ironworks and a tower, see Epstein, *Alle origini della fattoria toscana*, 255.

71 Epstein, *Alle origini della fattoria toscana*, 85

72 Balestracci, 'La politica di gestione', 301.

in the fifteenth, the Scala often served the commune as a defensive contractor, supplying workforces and designers to complete fortification projects. On a least one occasion – at Buonconvento – the Scala was asked to direct and fund the fortification of a location that was strategically important to the commune, but was of little interest to their own activities.[73] In the mid-Quattrocento, there are records of Spedale-employed practitioners realizing defences for the commune. The '*maestro del legname*' and architect Guidoccio d'Andrea (active 1440-1479), who served as *capomaestro* and salaried architect of the Spedale, was involved in the design of the communal defences at Fighine and Arcidosso (1462), and at Sarteano (1467). The fact that another of the Spedale's favoured artists, Vecchietta, partnered with Guidoccio on the latter project suggests that the institution itself was responsible for the defence project. The hospital's involvement in communal defences is further signalled by the fact that Vecchietta also worked on the fortifications at Orbetello, Talamone and Monte Acuto, which were not Spedale properties.[74]

Protagonists of Place: The Spedale Architects

Describing the role of the Spedale's rural landholdings within the greater administrative structure of the institution, the Sienese historians F. Cecilia Franchi and Giuseppina Coscarella underscore the productive function of the granges and the representative function they filled. The granges signalled the presence of the pious institution throughout the region of Siena. 'They constituted a pole, a determined place of reference for the *contado*, and through them the Spedale exercised and reaffirmed its own dominance on the territory.'[75] The infrastructure and building executed by the hospital institution was pivotal in establishing this dominance and in delimiting the environment that was reflective both of the Spedale and of the Sienese city-state as a whole.

In the extensive literature on the Spedale di Santa Maria della Scala in the early modern period, much attention is given to the importance of the welfare institution as a major landowner and patron of the arts, yet almost nothing has been said about its role in the germination, development and perpetuation of artistic and architectural knowledge. The Spedale was instrumental in the development of Sienese architecture and its distinct tradition of technical design, not only because it was itself a major landowner, and therefore was directly responsible for

73 Epstein, *Alle origini della fattoria toscana*, 256-259.

74 Romagnoli, *Biografia cronologica de' bellartisti senesi*, vol. 5, 54-58; Milanesi, *Documenti per la storia dell'arte Senese*, vol. 2, 281-282.

75 Franchi and Coscarella, 'Le grance dello Spedale', 70.

much building production, but also because in its workshops, kilns and quarries, it produced both the materials and knowledge that came to form Siena's built environment.

The builders, designers and architects who physically designed and constructed this environment are the often-overlooked protagonists of this history. This is in part due to the documentary records – a great many practitioners are unnamed in the accounts – and is in part due to the deep-seated historical interest in the 'fine arts'. But the architect-protagonists of the Spedale are not entirely unknown. Archival records offer insight into the technical diversity of a select group of individuals who led the Scala's workshop in the mid-fifteenth century. And a unique set of anonymous model books, also from this period, provide evidence as to how knowledge was perpetuated within a community of technicians and designers. As a way of conclusion, the limited review of a handful of these figures, and of the drawings that epitomized their wide-ranging technical knowledge, helps to solidify, in more tangible terms, the real importance of the Spedale in the creation of Siena as a place.

The previously cited '*scarpellino*' Francesco di Bartolomeo, as well as Guidoccio d'Andrea and Vecchietta, each exemplify the Spedale architect-practitioner whose expansive job description precluded specialization. Dionisio da Viterbo is yet another example of an individual who served the Santa Maria della Scala in the second half of the fifteenth century, and whose simultaneous involvement in multiple commissions attests to the fertile and porous nature of the Spedale *bottega*. A metalworker and clockmaker, Dionisio first arrived in Siena with his brother Pierdomenico in 1467. Their first assignment was to fix the clock of the Torre di Mangia. Not long after, the two brothers were entrenched in projects in the Spedale di Santa Maria della Scala, and it appears that the institution served as host to the talented young metalworkers. Not only did the pair rent rooms from the hospital in the Palazzo dei Capitano, but it is noted that Dionisio was allowed to borrow the necessary tools from the Santa Maria della Scala for his work there.[76] Between 1471 and 1476 – before being called to Florence by Lorenzo de' Medici – the brothers executed metal mounts and decoration for over 22 codices held within the church of the SS. Annunziata. By 1474, they were also involved in the library of the sacristy of the Duomo, where they executed ten book mounts, as well as a lattice grate to enclose the books.[77]

The dynamism of the Santa Maria della Scala workshop not only brought practitioners with varied skill sets and diverse backgrounds into contact with one another, it also necessitated collaboration and the exchange of knowledge. Because

76 Ermini, 'Campane e cannoni', 421.

77 Ibid., 415, 420-421.

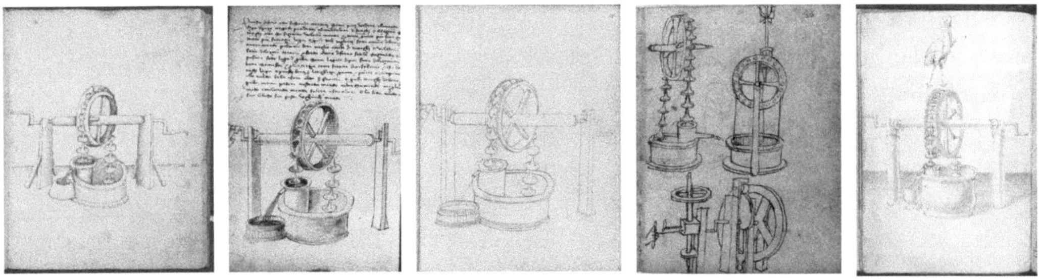

Fig. 5.10 Design for a chain pump
a) Jacopo Mariano Taccola, De Ingeneis, c. 1430. Biblioteca Nazionale Centrale Firenze, codex Palat. 766, fol. 30r. © Biblioteca Nazionale Centrale Firenze, by permission of the Ministry for Cultural Heritage and Activities and Tourism
b) Anonymous Sienese, c. 1480. The British Library, Ms. Add. 34113, fol. 23v. © The British Library Board
c) Anonymous Sienese, c. 1480. Sächsische Landesbibliothek, Staats- und Universitätsbibliothek, Dresden, codex Ob. 13 Dresden, fol. 123r.
d) Francesco di Giorgio, Codicetto, c. 1465-1480. Biblioteca Apostolica Vaticana, Vat. Urb. Lat. 1757, fol. 96r. By concession of the Biblioteca Apostolica Vaticana, all rights reserved
e) Anonymous Sienese, c. 1480. Biblioteca Nazionale Centrale Firenze, codex Palat. 767, fol. 33r. © Biblioteca Nazionale Centrale Firenze, by permission of the Ministry for Cultural Heritage and Activities and Tourism

so many projects involved vital infrastructure, it was often necessary for work to proceed quickly. The extensive demands placed on individuals like Francesco di Bartolomeo, Guidoccio d'Andrea and Dionisio da Viterbo indicate that work had to be delegated. As in so many early modern workshops, therefore, teaching was essential to the health of the Scala *bottega*.

The survival of a unique group of technical model books, all composed in Siena between 1465 and 1485, might be testimony to this activity. Only one of these volumes has a known author: the *Codicetto* of Francesco di Giorgio.[78] The remaining four books – the Ms. Additional 34113, the codex Ob. 13 Dresden, the Album-Codex S.IV.5, and the Codex Palatino 767 – are of unknown authorship.[79] But the close relationship of the books to one another is indisputable. These volumes share a standard canon of models. A portion of this material clearly derives from Taccola's *De ingeneis*. One example is the chain pump (Figure 5.10(a-e)). But a good many other drawings are not Taccola derivations. Traditionally assigned to Francesco di

78 Francesco's autograph *Codicetto* is held today in the Biblioteca Apostolica Vaticana (BAV), Vat. Urb. lat. 1757.

79 The British Library, London, Ms. Additional 34113; Sächsische Landesbibliothek, Staats- und Universitätsbibliothek, Dresden, Ob. 13 Dresden; Biblioteca Comunale Siena, Ms. S.IV.5; Biblioteca Nazionale Centrale Firenze, Codex Palatino 767. The Ms. Additional 34113 and the codex Ob. 13 Dresden are discussed at length in Merrill, 'Fifteenth-Century Sienese Copybooks'. For an overview of the S.IV.5 and the Palatino 767, see Scaglia, *Francesco di Giorgio*, 70-73, 141-142.

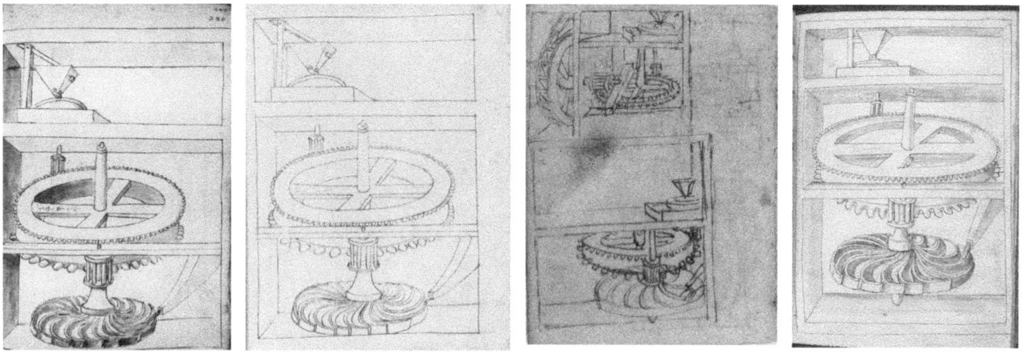

Fig. 5.11 Design for water-powered mills
a) Anonymous Sienese, c. 1480. The British Library, Ms. Add. 34113, fol. 230r. © The British Library Board
b) Anonymous Sienese, c. 1480. Sächsische Landesbibliothek, Staats- und Universitätsbibliothek, Dresden, codex Ob. 13 Dresden, fol. 146r.
c) Francesco di Giorgio, Codicetto, c. 1465-1480. Biblioteca Apostolica Vaticana, Vat. Urb. Lat. 1757, fol. 162v. By concession of the Biblioteca Apostolica Vaticana, all rights reserved
d) Anonymous Sienese, c. 1480. Biblioteca Nazionale Centrale Firenze, Codex Palat. 767, fol. 74r. © Biblioteca Nazionale Centrale Firenze, by permission of the Ministry for Cultural Heritage and Activities and Tourism

Giorgio, they are perhaps more accurately characterized as belonging to a Sienese school of technical design.

Within this corpus of material, there are numerous designs for building machinery: hoists, pulleys, wheel drives and cranes. Mills are another design type that proliferates, as are water pumps, wells and drilling machinery. To varying degrees, the model books also include designs for ships and military devices. If the authors of the five books were not copying directly from one another, they were unquestionably drawing upon a common, shared source. For example, the design for a distinct water-powered mill appears in nearly analogous form in four of the five books (Figure 5.11(a-d)). Likewise, we find the authors repeating the exact same drilling machinery (Figure 5.12 (a-d)). There is a distinct four-part piston pump, which might derive from a simpler construction recorded by Taccola, copied in near identical form in four of the volumes (Figure 5.13(a-e)).

The visual material recorded in these five books should be regarded as the inheritance of a distinct group of Sienese practitioners, and arguably, to practitioners who were either engaged in the Spedale workshop or came into contact with its activities through their involvement in communal projects. The graphic models so meticulously recorded within the volumes reflect technical problems confronted by the Commune of Siena. More specifically, they were instructive to those polyvalent individuals who commonly oscillated between projects involving building, infrastructure development, hydrology and defence, individuals typified in the likes of Guidoccio d'Andrea. The manner in which the models were copied – freely and

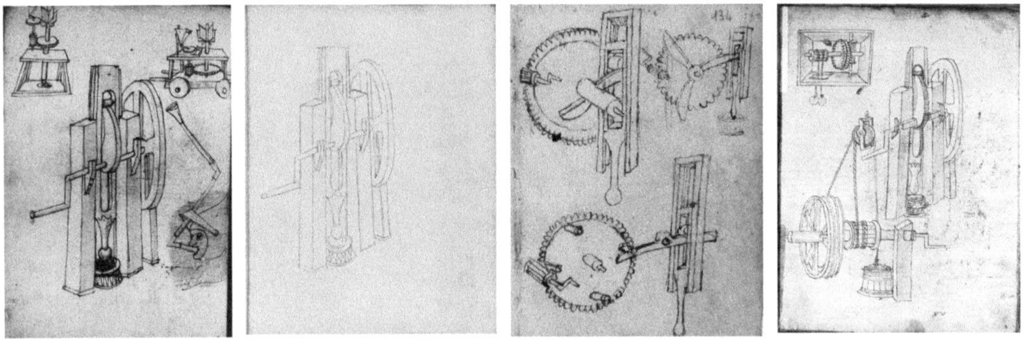

Fig. 5.12 Design for drilling machinery
a) Anonymous Sienese, c. 1480. The British Library, Ms. Add. 34113, fol. 75v. © The British Library Board
b) Anonymous Sienese, c. 1480. Sächsische Landesbibliothek, Staats- und Universitätsbibliothek, Dresden, codex Ob. 13 Dresden, fol. 127
c) Francesco di Giorgio, Codicetto, c. 1465-1480. Biblioteca Apostolica Vaticana, Vat. Urb. Lat. 1757, fol. 134r. By concession of the Biblioteca Apostolica Vaticana, all rights reserved
d) Anonymous Sienese, c. 1480. Biblioteca Comunale, Siena, Ms. S.IV.5, fol. 66r. © Biblioteca Comunale degli Intronati, Siena, by permission of the Ministry for Cultural Heritage and Activities and Tourism

without recourse to citation – indicates that these were part of a common body of knowledge and were made readily accessible for reference.

That the model books were in some way instructional aids, related to the teaching activities of the Scala workshop or the need to communicate design ideas between the nodes of institution, is supported in Spedale's established reputation in supporting young artists. Francesco di Giorgio is just one individual whose monumental career was bolstered by the patronage of the Spedale di Santa Maria della Scala. A series of documents from 1470 and 1471 trace Francesco di Giorgio's activities, partnered with Lotto di Domenico, on the production of the soffit of the Spedale church.[80] It was in this same period that Francesco held the position of *operaio dei bottini*, overseer of the city's extensive system of subterranean aqueducts. Francesco's pocket-sized *Codicetto*, in which he carefully copied models, dates to this period. The fact that his work in the Spedale and *bottini* overlapped, as did his compilation of the *Codicetto*, is unlikely coincidental. Rather, it reflects the degree to which the Scala controlled major civic projects, like the *bottini* maintenance, and developed the technical skills of young talents.[81]

The workshop of the Spedale appears to have also played an important role in the early career of Giacomo Cozzarelli, and might have served as the locus of his first contact with Francesco di Giorgio, with whom he would continue to collaborate

80 On Lotto di Domenico, see Romagnoli, *Biografia cronologica de' bellartisti senesi*, vol. 5, 119-121.
81 Francesco appointment as *operaio dei bottini* was well known, and the position might have been cause for him to receive the commission for SS. Annunziata soffit.

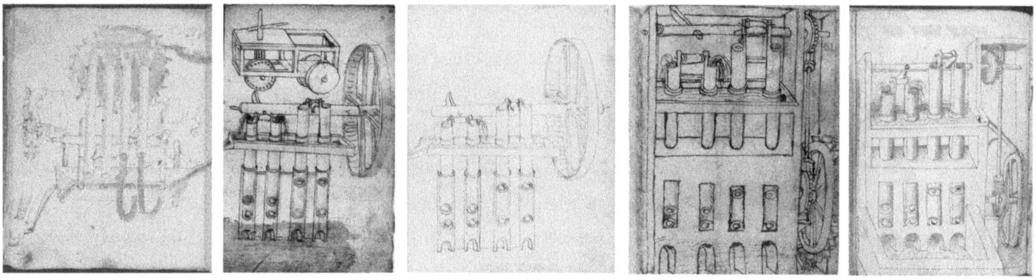

Fig. 5.13 Design for piston pump
a) Jacopo Mariano Taccola, *De Ingeneis*, c. 1430. Biblioteca Nazionale Centrale Firenze, Codex Palat. 766, fol. 18r. © Biblioteca Nazionale Centrale Firenze, by permission of the Ministry for Cultural Heritage and Activities and Tourism
b) Anonymous Sienese, c. 1480. The British Library, Ms. Add. 34113, fol. 70r. © The British Library Board
c) Anonymous Sienese, c. 1480. Sächsische Landesbibliothek, Staats- und Universitätsbibliothek, Dresden, codex Ob. 13 Dresden, fol. 118r
d) Francesco di Giorgio, *Codicetto*, c. 1465-1480. Biblioteca Apostolica Vaticana, Vat. Urb. Lat. 1757, fol. 132r. By concession of the Biblioteca Apostolica Vaticana, all rights reserved
e) Anonymous Sienese, c. 1480. Biblioteca Nazionale Centrale Firenze, Codex Palat. 767, fol. 55r. © Biblioteca Nazionale Centrale Firenze, by permission of the Ministry for Cultural Heritage and Activities and Tourism

for three decades.[82] The first record of Cozzarelli is found in a Scala record of October 1471, which accounts for his receipt of a payment on the behalf of Francesco.[83] In subsequent records of the *Entrate e Uscite* of the Scala, Cozzarelli's name appears independent of Francesco's. He is routinely referred to as '*nostro M.º in casa*' – that is, one of the principal artists employed by the Spedale, and like Dionisio da Viterbo, he possibly resided in one of the hospital's properties.[84] Notable projects he completed for the Scala between 1473 and 1475 include the design of a carriage for the festival of Santa Maria del Agosto, and the decoration of two marble coats of arms.[85]

82 A document of 1483 notes that Cozzarelli was then in Urbino with Francesco, see Weller, *Francesco di Giorgio*, 352. In the final decade of the fifteenth century, the two worked together on numerous prestigious projects for the Duomo and the city of Siena. According to Chironi, 'Politici e ingegneri', 382, Cozzarelli was the alter ego of Francesco at this time.
83 Document is reproduced by Weller, *Francesco di Giorgio*, 342.
84 Confusion arises in the different appellations given to Cozzarelli in the documents, and the different spellings of his name. In records from June to November 1473 (ASSi, Ospedale di Santa Maria, vol. 859), he is alternatively referred to as 'Jacomo d'Agnolo detto Cozzarello nostro maestro', 'Jacomo di Angolo Cozzarelli', 'Jacomo di Bartoloemeio Cozzarelli', and 'Jacomo detto Cozzarello nostro maestro in casa'.
85 See ASSi, Ospedale di Santa Maria, vol. 859 (Fasc. I), fol. 48r: 'A Jacomo di Bartolomeo Cozzarelli e Sandro suo conpagno dipintori ha dipinto el charo e son posti a Libro Verde T [...] a folio 362'. The notes of Romagnoli, *Biografia cronologica de' bellartisti senesi*, vol. 5, 214, suggest that this work was for the festival of Santa Maria del Agosto. Also: 'A Iacomo di Bartolomeo Cozzarelli dipentore a di detto [13 agosto] soldi 56 contanti a lui per dipentura di due armi [stemme] una di missera e una della Scala fatte di marmo e sono a Libro di Verde T [...] a folio 511' (ASSi, Ospedale di Santa Maria, vol. 860, fol. 52r).

Although we lack detailed accounts of the activities of the Scala *bottega*, it is still possible to reconstruct in part the intensity and diversity of this compound space. The practitioners tied to the workshop in the second half of the fifteenth century – Francesco di Bartolomeo, Guidoccio d'Andrea, Dionisio da Viterbo, Francesco di Giorgio and Giacomo Cozzarelli, among many others – attest to the agglomeration of information, skills and ideas that were fostered there. Similarly, the survival of the unique group of Sienese model books points to an impressive collective of Sienese practitioners. The work of these individuals, reflected in the conscientiously copied drawings, was closely related to a set of distinctly Sienese design problems. The building works of the Spedale di Santa Maria della Scala constituted a significant part of this and were fundamental in furthering the delineation of a specifically Sienese place.

Bibliography

Manuscript Sources

Dresden, Sächsische Landesbibliothek, Staats- und Universitätsbibliothek
Codex Ob. 13 Dresden: Anonymous Sienese, late fifteenth century
Florence, Biblioteca Nazionale Centrale Firenze
Codex Palatino 766: Jacopo Mariano Taccola, *De Ingeneis*, c. 1430
Codex Palatino 767: Anonymous Sienese, late fifteenth century
London, The British Library
Ms. Additional 34113: Anonymous Sienese, late fifteenth century
Rome, Biblioteca Apostolica Vaticana
Ms. Vat. Urb. lat. 1757: Francesco di Giorgio Martini, *Codicetto*, c. 1475
Siena, Archivio di Stato di Siena
Ospedale di Santa Maria
vol. 858 (Fasc. I and II): 1470-1472
vol. 859 (Fasc. I): 1473-1474
vol. 860 (Fasc. I): 1474-1475
vol. 524: 1475-1476
Siena, Biblioteca Comunale degli Intronati
Ms. S.IV.5: Anonymous Sienese, late fifteenth century

Printed Sources

Acocella, Alfonso and Davide Turrin (eds), *Travertino di Siena. Sienese Travertine* (Florence: Alinea Editrice, 2010).

Ascheri, Mario, 'Storia dell'ospedale e/o storia della città', in Carlo Infantino and Enrico Toti (eds), *Spedale di Santa Maria della Scala. Atti del Convegno Internazionale di Studi, 20-22 novembre 1986* (Siena: Comune di Siena, 1988), 65-71.

Balestracci, Duccio, 'Approvvigionamento e distribuzione dei Prodotti Alimentari a Siena nell'Epoca Comunale. Mulini, Mercati e Botteghe', *Archeologia medievale* 8 (1981), 127-154.

Balestracci, Duccio, 'La corporazione dei muratori dal XIII al XVI secolo', in Maurizio Boldrini (ed.), *Il Coloro della Città: Siena* (Siena: Protagon Editori Toscani, 1993).

Balestracci, Duccio, 'La politica di gestione delle acque e dei mulini nel territorio senese nel basso medieovo', in Paola Galetti (ed.), *I mulini nell'Europa medievale: atti del convegno di San Quirico d'Orcia, 21-23 settembre 2000* (Bologna: CLUEB, 2003), 287-302.

Balestracci, Duccio, 'L'immigrazione di manodopera nella Siena medievale', in *Forestieri e stranieri nelle città basso-medievali. Atti del Seminario Internazionale di Studio Bagno a Ripoli (Firenze), 4-8 giugno 1984* (Florence: Salimbeni, 1988), 163-180.

Balestracci, Duccio 'Produzione ed uso del mattone a Siena nel Medioevo', in Patrick Boucheron and Henri Broise (eds), *La brique antique et médiévale* (Rome: École Française de Rome, 2000), 417-428.

Balestracci, Duccio and Gabriella Piccinni, 'L'Ospedale di la Città', in Daniela Gallavotti Cavallero (ed.), *Lo Spedale di Santa Maria della Scala in Siena. Vicenda di una committenza artistica* (Pisa: Pacini Editore, 1985), 19-42.

Balestracci, Duccio and Gabriella Piccinni, *Siena nel Trecento: Assetto urbano e strutture edilizie* (Florence: Edizioni Clusf, 1977).

Balestracci, Duccio, Armando Costantini and Laura Vigni, *La memoria dell'acqua: i bottini di Siena* (Siena: Protagon, 2006).

Balestracci, Duccio, Daniele Lamberini and Mauro Civai, *I bottini medievali di Siena* (Siena: Edizioni Alsaba, 1993).

Bellosi, Luciano, 'Il terzo polo artistico di Siena', in Carlo Infantino and Enrico Toti (eds), *Spedale di Santa Maria della Scala. Atti del Convegno Internazionale di Studi, 20-22 novembre 1986* (Siena: Comune di Siena, 1988), 35-39.

Bianchi, Giovanna, 'Maestri costruttori lombardi nei cantieri della Toscana centro-meridonionale (secoli XII-XV). Indizi documentarie ed evidenze materiali', in Stefano Della Torre, Tiziano Mannoni and Valeria Pracchi (eds), *Magistri d'Europa: eventi, relazioni, strutture della migrazione di artisti e costruttori dai laghi lombardi* (Milan: Nodo libri, 1996), 155-166.

Cantini, Federico, *Archeologia urbana a Siena: l'area dell'Ospedale di Santa Maria della Scala prima dell'Ospedal: altomedioevo* (Florence: All'insegna del giglio, 2005).

Cavallero, Daniela Gallavotti (ed.), *Lo Spedale di Santa Maria della Scala in Siena. Vicenda di una committenza artistica* (Pisa: Pacini Editore 1985).

Cavallero, Daniela Gallavotti and Andrea Brogi (eds), *Lo Spedale Grande di Siena. Fatti urbanistici e architettonici del Santa Maria della Scala* (Florence: La Casa Usher, 1987).

Cecchini, Giovanni, 'Le grance dell'Ospedale di S. Maria della Scala di Siena', *Economia e storia* 6 (1959), 405-422.

Cecchini, Giovanni, 'Maestri Luganesi e comaschi a Siena nel secolo XV', in Edoardo Arslan (ed.), *Arte e artisti dei laghi lombardi. I: Architetti e scultori del Quattocento* (Como: Tip. Editrice Noseda, 1959), 131-150.

Chironi, Giuseppe, 'Politici e ingegneri. I provveditori della Camera del comune di Siena negli anni '90 del Quattrocento', *Ricerche storiche* 23 (1993), 375-395.

Comune di Siena (ed.), *I bottini: acquedotti medievali senesi* (Siena: Edizioni Gielle, 1984).

Corsi, Rita, 'Forma Dimensioni e Caratteristiche del Mattone Senese', in *Fornaci e mattoni a Siena: dal XIII secolo all'azienda Cialfi* (Siena: Fornaci Cialfi, 1991), 21-30.

Coscarella, Giuseppina and Franca Cecilia Franchi, *La grancia di Cuna in Val d'Arbia: un esempio di fattoria fortificata medievale* (Florence: Salimbeni, 1983).

Di Toro, Pierre, *Amministrazione e contabilità nel XV e XVI secolo: lo spedale senese del Santa Maria della Scala attraverso i libri contabili* (Padua: CEDAM, 1999).

Epstein, Stephan R., *Alle origini della fattoria toscana: l'Ospedale della Scala di Siena e le sue terre (metà '200-metà '400)* (Florence: Salimbeni, 1986).

Epstein, Stephan R., 'Inventari di beni di grance dell'Ospedale di S. Maria della Scala di Siena (1356, 1385)', *Archeologia Medievale* 15 (1988), 535-549.

Ermini, Giampaolo, 'Campane e cannoni. Agostino da Piacenza e Giovanni da Zagabria: un fonditore padano ed uno schiavone nella Siena del Quattrocento', in Matteo Ceriana and Victoria Avery (eds), *L'industria artistica del bronzo del Rinascimento a Venezia e nell'Italia settentrionale, 2007* (Verona: Scripta, 2008), 387-446.

Franchi, Cecilia R. and Giuseppina Coscarella, 'Le grance dello Spedale di Santa Maria della Scala nel Contado Senese', *Bullettino senese di storia patria* 93 (1986), 66-92.

Giorgi, Andrea, *Costruire una cattedrale: l'Opera di Santa Maria di Siena tra XII e XIV secolo* (Munich: Deutscher Kunstverlag, 2005).

Grancia delle Serre, Centro Documentazione sulle Antiche Grance del Santa Maria della Scala, Serre di Rapolano, Rapolano Terme, Siena, Musei Senesi.

Leverotti, Franca, 'L'ospedale senese di Santa Maria della Scala in una relazione del 1456', *Bullettino senese di storia patria* 91 (1984), 276-291.

Merrill, Elizabeth, 'Fifteenth-Century Sienese Copybooks and the Origins of Francesco di Giorgio's *Codicetto*', *Journal of the Warburg and Courtauld Institutes* 83 (2020), 37-80.

Merrill, Elizabeth, 'The "*professione di architetto*" in Renaissance Italy', *Journal of the Society of Architectural Historians* 76.1 (2017), 13-35, DOI: 10.1525/jsah.2017.76.1.13.

Milanesi, Gaetano, *Documenti per la storia dell'arte Senese*, 3 vols (Siena: Presso Onorato Porri, 1854-1856).

Milani, Angela, 'L'attività costruttiva del Quattrocento dalle fonti archivistiche', in Enrica Boldrini and Roberto Parenti (eds), *Santa Maria della Scala. Archeologia ed edilizia sulla piazza dello Spedale* (Florence: Ed. All'Insegna del Giglio, 1991), 115-134.

Nevola, Fabrizio, *Siena: Constructing the Renaissance City* (New Haven: Yale University Press, 2007).

Pinto, Giuliano, 'L'immigrazione di manodopera nel territorio senese alla metà del Quattrocento', *La Toscana nel tardo medioevo. Ambiente, economia rurale, società* (Florence: Sansoni Editore, 1982), 421-429.

Pinto, Giuliano, 'L'organizzazione della difesa: i cantieri delle costruzioni militari nel territorio senese (secoli XIV-XV)', *Castelli* 3 (1984), 259-268.

Prager, Frank and Gustina Scaglia, *Mariano Taccola and His Book* De Ingeneis (Cambridge, MA: The MIT Press, 1972).

Romagnoli, Ettore, *Biografia cronologica de' bellartisti senesi 1200-1800*, 13 vols (Florence: Edizioni S.P.E.S, 1976).

Scaglia, Gustina, *Francesco di Giorgio: Checklist and History of Manuscripts and Drawings in Autographs and Copies from ca. 1470 to 1687 and Renewed Copies (1764-1839)* (Bethlehem, PA: Lehigh University Press 1992).

Sordini, Beatrice, *Dentro l'antico ospedale: Santa Maria della Scala; uomini, cose e spazi di vita nella Siena medievale* (Siena: Protagon Editori, 2010).

Taccola, Jacopo Mariano, *De Ingeneis*, ed. by Frank Prager and Gustina Scaglia, 2 vols (Wiesbaden: Dr. Ludwig Reicher Verlag, 1984).

Tozzetti, Giovanni Targioni, *Relazioni d'alcuni viaggi fatti in diverse parti della Toscana per osservare le produzioni naturali, e gli antichi monumenti di essa*, vol. 4 (Florence: Stamperia Imperiale, 1754).

Valacchi, Federico, 'Dislocazione delle Foraci e Loro Continuità d'uso sul territorio dello stato senese tra Medioevo ed Età Moderna', *Fornaci e mattoni a Siena: dal XIII secolo all'azienda Cialfi* (Siena: Fornaci Cialfi, 1991), 41-52.

Weller, Allen Stuart, *Francesco di Giorgio, 1439-1501* (Chicago: University of Chicago Press, 1943).

About the Author

Elizabeth Merrill is Assistant Professor in Theory, History and Criticism of Early Modern Architecture at Ghent University in Belgium. Her research focuses on architectural practices and the development of the architectural profession. She has published articles in *Architectural Histories*, the *Journal of the Society of Architectural Historians*, *Architecture Research Quarterly*, and *The Journal of the Warburg and Courtauld Institutes*, and is currently completing a monograph on the Sienese architect Francesco di Giorgio.

6. Places of Knowledge between Ulm and the Netherlands in the Seventeenth Century: The *Kunstkammer* of Johannes Faulhaber*

Paul Brakmann and Sebastian Fitzner

Abstract

This article investigates how the *Kunstkammer* of Johannes Faulhaber, renowned mathematician and engineer of Ulm, functioned as a place dedicated to the advancement of mechanical-architectural knowledge. Examining several unstudied publications associated with his *Kunstkammer* and a previously unknown inventory, we reconstruct the collection and examine Faulhaber's advertisement of it in printed catalogues. A comparison of Faulhaber's collection with that of his contemporary Joseph Furttenbach the Elder highlights specifics of its focus and scope. The *Kunstkammer* was also a place of technology transfer, whereby aspects of Dutch military technology were introduced into the German context, and were in turn further disseminated through Faulhaber's publications. In this sense, Faulhaber's *Kunstkammer* can be understood as an entanglement of 'places' – both physical and printed.

Keywords: art chamber, technical model, fortification, secrecy, technology transfer, engineer

In 1628 Johannes Faulhaber (1580-1635), mathematician and engineer in Ulm, published his brief brochure *Geheime Kunstkammer* (secret art chamber).[1] This

* Our greatest gratitude goes to Elizabeth Merrill for her intriguing discussion on the 'places of architectural knowledge' and her helpful advice. Paul Brakmann is responsible for sections three and four of the article, which are the result of an inspiring research project. Special thanks goes to Paul Brakmann and his unswerving enthusiasm and research. Further thanks goes to Hole Rößler for his advice and to Marcus Popplow for sharing his instructive preprint (Popplow, 'Models of Machines').

1 For a general overview, see Hawlitschek, *Johann Faulhaber 1580-1635*; Hawlitschek, 'Niederländische Mathematik'; Hawlitschek, *Johann Faulhaber 1580-1635 und René Descartes 1596-1650*; Schneider,

Merrill, E. (ed.), *Creating Place in Early Modern European Architecture*.
Taylor & Francis Group 2022
DOI: 10.5117/9789463728027_CH06

essentially unstudied publication is one of the earliest printed records of a *Kunstkammer* of an engineer or technical designer.[2] Faulhaber's unique collection exhibited machines and fortification models, technical and mathematical manuscripts and drawings, as well as drawing and measuring instruments, rather than the *artificialia*, *naturalia*, and *exotica* typical of *Kunst*- and *Wunderkammern*.[3] This article focuses on Faulhaber's *Kunstkammer* as a dedicated place of mechanical and architectural knowledge.[4] The didactic function and use of the collection, and its related publications, may be likened to an entangled space of engineering knowledge production and distribution. Still, as Faulhaber's *Kunstkammer* does not survive, it is necessary to reconstruct it by reverting to his *Geheime Kunstkammer* and similar publications, as well as a previously unpublished handwritten inventory, the so-called *Specification*, which enumerates his models, drawing and measuring instruments, fortification and machine drawings, and other items.

Johannes Faulhaber's *Kunstkammer* was part of his estate and famous school of mathematics, founded in 1600, which was visited by a numerous young scholars, as well as members of the high-ranking nobility.[5] Both the collection and the school formed a dedicated place for education and the transfer of mechanical-architectural knowledge within Ulm and abroad. Consequently, Faulhaber sought to ensure his establishment's success by means of printed publications – notably his *Geheime Kunstkammer* – in effect 'spreading out' the theoretical equalization of the collection's physical place within an imaginative space of the textual *Kunstkammer*.[6] This article highlights several ways in which he advertised his services and knowledge, analysing, on the one hand, the relationship between the physical place of Faulhaber's premises and the place-less, intellectual realm of circulating books, on the other. Faulhaber's collection existed within an intellectual milieu that went beyond the immediate

Johannes Faulhaber. See also Zweckbronner, 'Rechenmeister, Ingenieur und Bürger'; Faulhaber, *Geheime Kunstkammer*.

2 There is a short mention in Popplow, 'Court Mathematicians', 299. Recent publications on Faulhaber, which do not discuss the *Geheime Kunstkammer*, include: Gnehm and Büchi, 'Johannes Faulhaber'. On 'textual art chambers', see Schock, 'Die imaginäre Kunstkammer'.

3 In particular on *Kunstkammern*, see, for instance, Grote, *Macrocosmos in microcosmo*. On civic chambers of the early modern period, see Beßler, 'Vormoderne städtische Sammlungen'.

4 To date there are several studies engaged with similar phenomena by Faulhaber's contemporary Joseph Furttenbach the Elder (1591-1667). In particular, see Lazardzig, *Theatermaschine und Festungsbau*; Siebenhüner, 'Entwerfen'; Zaugg, '"bey den Jtalienern"'; Lazardzig and Rößler, *Technologies*; also see Rößler, 'Wissensmarketing der Frühen Neuzeit'; Becker, 'Der Transfer technischen Wissens'. Also see Günther, 'Joseph Furttenbachs Architekturmuseum', which, unfortunately, has a few inaccuracies.

5 The council of the city of Ulm entrusted Faulhaber on 28 May 1600 to run a school of mathematics. See Hawlitschek, *Johann Faulhaber 1580-1635*, 20-21.

6 Schock, 'Die imaginäre Kunstkammer', 546.

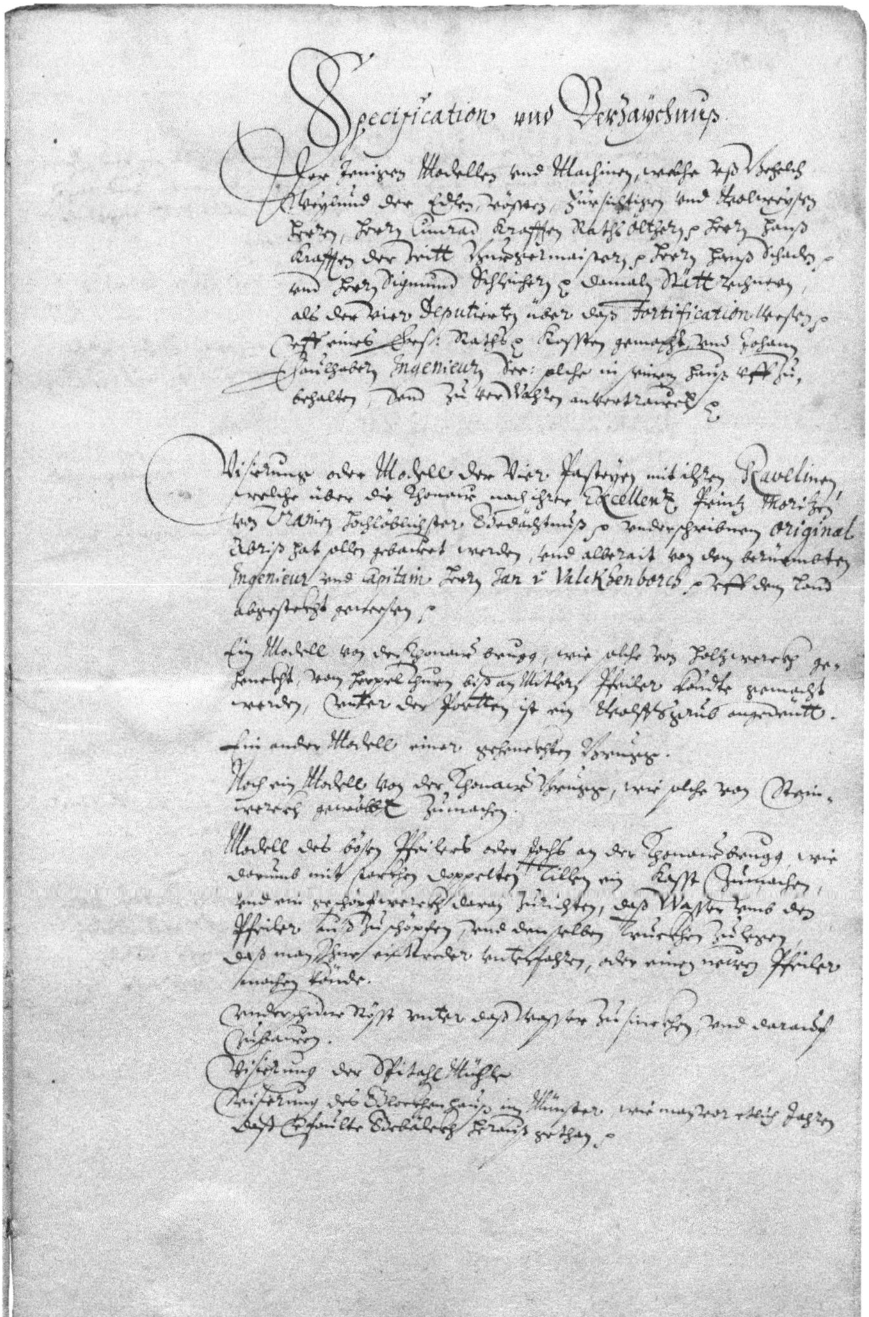
Specification und Verzaichnus

Fig. 6.1 Johann Matthäus Faulhaber, handwritten inventory of the *Kunstkammer* of Johannes Faulhaber. *Specification*, title page, 1 April 1636. © Landesarchiv Baden-Württemberg, StAL, D 55 Bü 40

context of Ulm. This study considers how, from a certain decisive point onward, Faulhaber's collection became a means of 'international' technology transfer, introducing, for example, aspects of Dutch military technology to a German audience. In order to better contextualize the characteristics of Faulhaber's practices of collecting, mediating, and teaching mechanical-architectural knowledge, the comparison of his collection with that of his contemporary, Joseph Furttenbach the Elder (1591-1667), is instructive.[7] By focusing on the *Kunstkammer* as a dedicated place of knowledge production and circulation, this article is closely linked to ideas concerning the 'circulation and diffusion of technical knowledge', which have been primarily discussed within the history of science.[8] This article, therefore, seeks to reveal the nature of the knowledge contained in Faulhaber's collection and how his *Kunstkammer* functioned as a place of knowledge production. Within this place, the study, education, and transfer of mechanical-architectural knowledge were entangled. They were also interwoven in the 'places' of the various publications of Faulhaber, and the physical 'places' of their initial conception.

Faulhaber's Collection in Detail

The *Kunstkammer* of Johannes Faulhaber was part of his private estate that was located near the Munster of Ulm at Platzgasse 4.[9] We do not know when exactly Faulhaber started collecting, but it is likely that he established his *Kunstkammer* in the late 1620s after having returned from the Netherlands in 1624.[10] Unfortunately, there are no sources that provide insight into the inner structure of his house, the *Kunstkammer* or his school of mathematics. But using the so-called *Specification* from 1636, an inventory written a year after Faulhaber's death by his son Johann Matthäus, we are able to largely reconstruct his collection (Figure 6.1).[11] This inventory lists more than 90 items (including models and inventions for fortifications, mills, water-lifting devices, bridges, military equipment), a printing press and coins, and

7 See n. 4.

8 Becker, 'Der Transfer technischen Wissens', 54. See also Martens and van de Vijver, 'Engineers and the Circulation of Knowledge'; Reith, 'Know-how, Technologietransfer'.

9 On 22 September 1604 Faulhaber paid a final fee (200 gulden) for his estate. See Hawlitschek, *Johann Faulhaber 1580-1635*, 21.

10 The earliest known sources of that collection are printed lists like the *Continuatio, deß Newen Mathematischen Kunstspiegels* (1620), the *Zwey und Viertzig Secreta* (1621), and the *Erste Teutsche Lection* (1621), in which Faulhaber promoted his knowledge. The earliest source revealing his *Kunstkammer* is the *Geheime Kunstkammer* (1628).

11 Ludwigsburg Staatsarchiv D 55 Bü 40. See appendix.

about more than 30 drawing and measuring instruments (compass or *astrolabia*).[12] Also documented are numerous drawings, most of which, unfortunately, are only generally referenced, in addition to prints, manuscripts and treatises written by 'most noble authors' addressing fortifications, arithmetic and geometry.[13]

Tellingly, the inventory distinguishes between models that Faulhaber had ordered and paid for himself, and models he had commissioned under instruction of the city council of Ulm. Faulhaber's estate thus contained not only his private models, but also 24 models of the city council of Ulm, including several models for a bridge over the River Danube, and models for fortification works.[14] Interestingly, the civic models were crafted for the city council on the recommendation of Faulhaber. According to the *Specification*, all the models that belonged to the city of Ulm were stored separately from the private collection in Faulhaber's house, and were not officially part of his *Kunstkammer*.[15] Faulhaber's custodial care of important models of the imperial city apparently coincides with his official role as civic engineer.[16] However, in 1628, the council did not renew Faulhaber's contract as 'engineer of the city of Ulm', and instead paid him a 'waiting fee'. Therefore, on 4 April 1628 he was prompted to refile his holding of all civic models at the tax office.[17] He was also urged to designate himself only as 'engineer' and no longer as 'engineer of the city'. A few weeks later, on 26 May 1628, the day when the waiting fee was finally enacted, Faulhaber was pleased to discuss with the council in detail those 'models, instruments and commitments he was allowed to keep and which ones he had to finally hand over to the council'.[18] Still, Faulhaber was ultimately allowed to keep the models at his house, where they must had been on display until his death on 10 September 1635 and were then listed in the *Specification* a year later.

The appointment as civic engineer of Ulm was thus obviously connected with a privileged access to civic models. Even more, we can deduce that these fortification and machine models were not stored in civic places, nor in the town hall or the

12 Although the *Specification* listed 'models, machines, and drawing and measuring instruments', it is worth noting that only 28 items were explicitly characterized as models, while about another 64 were denoted with other terms.

13 Appendix, folio 5v.

14 Appendix, folios 2r, 2v.

15 Appendix, folio 6v.

16 Similar instances of the private custody of municipal or princley drawings and models by court architects and engineers occurred in the sixteenth century north of the Alps. See Fitzner, *Architekturzeichnungen der deutschen Renaissance*, 79-81.

17 Hawlitschek, *Johann Faulhaber 1580-1635*, 96. This instruction did not pertain to Faulhaber's private models.

18 See Hawlitschek, *Johann Faulhaber 1580-1635*, 96-97: 'und uff die H. Deputirten gestelt, mit ime zu handlen, was er an Modellen, Instrumenten und Rechnungen, die er noch bey seinen Handen, zu eines Ers. Raths Gewalt liefern, und dagegen er bey seinen Handen behalten soll'.

armoury. This circumstance is particularly important in reconstructing the early modern practice of model collecting, and reveals more general practices of collecting and storing models.

According to little-studied examples of the late seventeenth century, model collections of fortifications or technical infrastructure were usually stored in civic town houses, armouries, arsenals or academies.[19] As Marcus Popplow points out, the first known public presentation of a machine model took place in Paris in 1683.[20] But the example of Faulhaber's collection reveals that civic models also functioned as objects of knowledge, working tools for the engineer, which were not only part of displays or memorializing collections. Another source indicates that city council of Ulm even had its own '*Kunstkammer*', but we have to assume that this *Kunstkammer* was presumably the so-called 'model floor' in the civic armoury, which was later used for housing models, treatises and drawings concerned to fortifications, architecture and mechanics.[21]

The *Kunstkammer* of Faulhaber, by contrast, was more public and educational in its nature and function, visited and studied by burghers, scholars, engineers and architects, as well as 'various princes, counts and noble men'.[22] Furthermore, it is likely that the collection of models and instruments was also used by students of Faulhaber. In 1609, for example, Johann Carl, a 22-year-old engineer from Nuremberg, trained in perspectival drawing and measuring under Faulhaber.[23] In February 1631 an engineer named Hermann Müller visited Ulm and was shown notable civic buildings like the 'armoury, fortification works, town hall, and a waterworks', before

19 See Beßler, 'Vormoderne städtische Sammlungen', 309-315, 318-319; Fitzner, *Architekturzeichnungen der deutschen Renaissance*, 89-90; Günther, 'Joseph Furttenbachs Architekturmuseum'. On technical models as objects related to 'oddities' and 'utilization', see Meyer, 'Perspektiven der Popularisierung', 167. On collecting and epistemic functions of models, see Popplow, 'Models of Machines'.

20 Popplow, 'Technisches Modell', with reference to Birembaut, 'L'exposition de modèles de machines'.

21 It is reported that the 'mechanic' and 'water engineer' Andreas Liebmann of Ulm granted three mechanical models (a 'boat bridge', a 'spindle', and a 'boat mill') to the council of Ulm at the end of the seventeenth century, which were then evaluated by 'Johann Faulhaber' (probably Johann Matthäus Faulhaber, the son of Johannes) and stored in a '*Kunstkammer*'. See Weyermann, *Neue historisch = biographisch = artistische Nachrichten*, 277. The inventory of 1793 ('Inventory of the most humble and wise Council's armoury of Ulm. Anno 1793') documents 'a huge collection of fortification models, models of bridges, mills, buildings, machines etc.' and describes 'model floors' ('n.o. 18 model floors n.o. XX-XXIV'). See Häberle, 'Das Schicksal', 7-8. On the armoury, see Neumann, *Das Zeughaus*, vol. 1, 241, and vol. 2, nos. 215-217.

22 They inspected Faulhaber's invention of a '*sphœra materialis*'. See Faulhaber, *Academia*: 'vnderschiedliche[n] Reichs Fürsten / Grafen vnnd Herren'; see also Schneider, *Johannes Faulhaber*, 37. The treatise is dedicated to Landgrave Philip of Hesse-Butzbach. See discussion below.

23 Doppelmayr, *Historische Nachricht*, 230; Zweckbronner, 'Rechenmeister, Ingenieur und Bürger', 116.

being guided by Faulhaber through the *Kunstkammer*.[24] Besides foreign scholars, engineers and noblemen, local individuals with an interest in mechanical design also knew of Faulhaber's *Kunstkammer*. In 1630, for example, the town engineer, Joseph Furttenbach the Elder, sent Faulhaber a container with all of his recently published treatises, with the hope that he would keep them in his 'magnificent and most famous *Kunstkammer*', in 'memory' of Furttenbach himself.[25] Furttenbach presumably gave these documents to Faulhaber in exchange for Faulhaber's gift to him of a copy of the *Ingenieurs-Schul*, which was dedicated to Furttenbach and nine others.[26]

Promoting a Model Collection in Print

In 1628, Faulhaber's *Geheime Kunstkammer* was published by Jonas Saur, Ulm's municipal printer (Figure 6.2). The short publication consists of a hundred catalogue entries, which, rather than listing an actual inventory of Faulhaber's collection, provide potential uses of its models, drawings and treatises. The catalogue entries represent a *pars pro toto* of a hypothetical body of technological knowledge. The concise entries, organized according to the objects' media (e.g. drawings or models), do not document the function of the objects, their provenance or materiality, but rather link them by topic. The entries are based on thematic classification criteria and not according to the objects' location in a given room, cabinet or grouping. Thus, the printed 'imaginary art cabinet' does not present substantial information on the actual nature of the objects contained within Faulhaber's collection, but paints a picture of their possible fields of application.[27]

The *Geheime Kunstkammer* was not the first catalogue of this kind that Faulhaber had published. Eight years prior, two brochures of similar content appeared in Ulm and Augsburg, advertising Faulhaber's knowledge and his willingness to teach numerous useful inventions, techniques and recipes in return for appropriate compensation.[28] Except for marginal variations, the *Continuatio, deß Newen*

24 Ulm Stadtarchiv Faulhaber H 5/1, sheet 564. Letter of Johannes Faulhaber to Sebastian Kurz, 22 February 1631. Transcribed by Hawlitschek, *Johann Faulhaber 1580-1635*, 324.

25 Presumably five treatises were published by Joseph Furttenbach prior to 1630: *Newes Itinerarium Italiae* (1627); *Halinitro-Pyrobolia* (1627); *Architectura Civilis* (1628); *Architectura Navalis* (1629); *Architectura Martialis* (1630). Ulm Stadtarchiv Faulhaber H 5/1, sheet 557-558. Letter of Joseph Furttenbach the Elder to Johannes Faulhaber, 23 November 1630. Transcribed by Hawlitschek, *Johann Faulhaber 1580-1635*, 100.

26 See Hawlitschek, *Johann Faulhaber 1580-1635*, 100, 175. Faulhaber, *Ingenieurs-Schul, Erster Theil*, 5.

27 The term is from Schock, 'Die imaginäre Kunstkammer'.

28 Faulhaber, *Continuatio*; Faulhaber, *Zwey und Viertzig Secreta*.

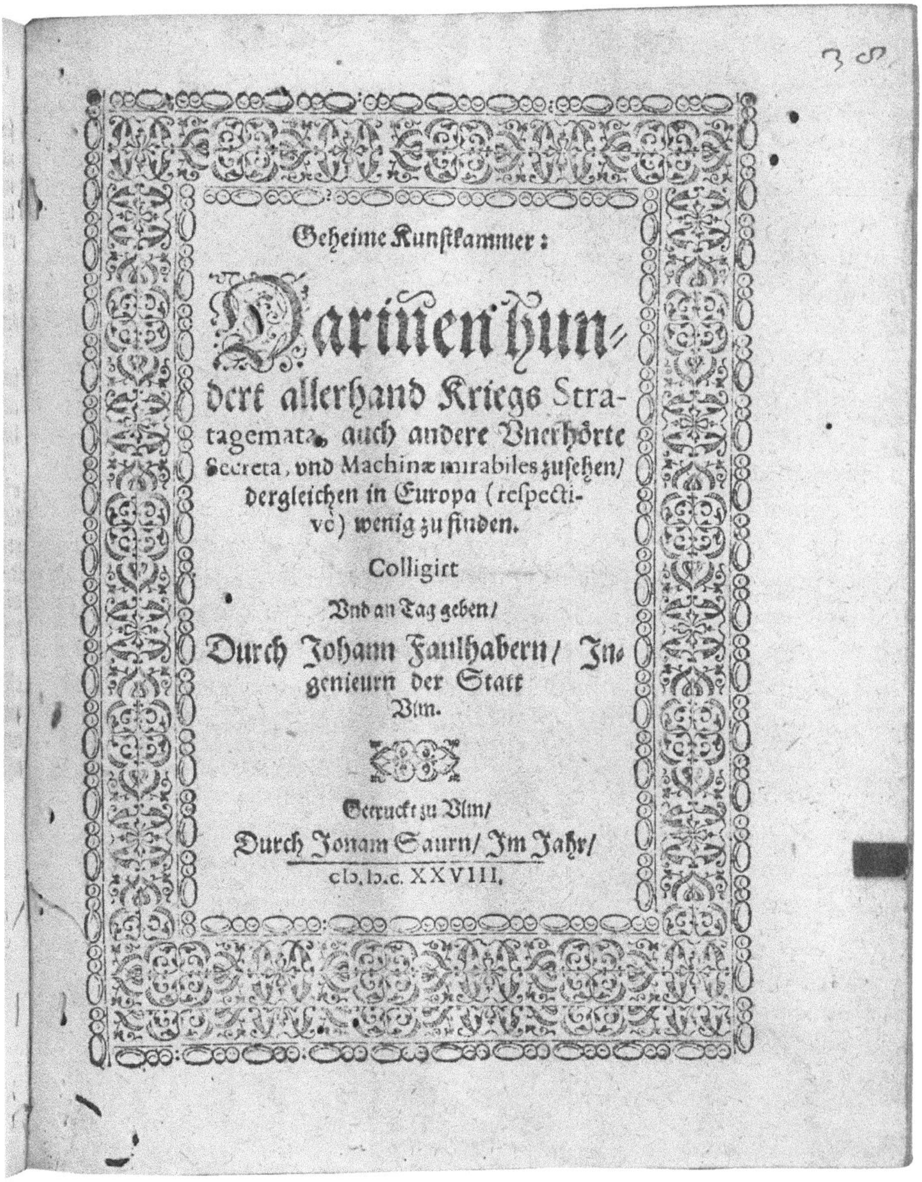
Geheime Kunstkammer:
Darinnen hundert allerhand Kriegs Stratagemata, auch andere Vnerhörte Secreta, vnd Machinæ mirabiles zusehen/ dergleichen in Europa (respective) wenig zu finden.
Colligirt
Vnd an Tag geben/
Durch Johann Faulhabern/ Ingenieurn der Statt Vlm.
Getruckt zu Vlm/
Durch Jonam Saurn/ Im Jahr/
cIↄ.Iↄc.XXVIII.

Fig. 6.2 Johannes Faulhaber, *Geheime Kunstkammer*, title page, 1628. © Zentralbibliothek Zürich, Inv. Nr. 18.15,38

Mathematischen Kunstspiegels (1620) and *Zwey und Viertzig Secreta* (1621) both feature the same instruments, machines and tricks of the trade, a good number of which were later adapted for the *Geheime Kunstkammer* (Figures 6.3 and 6.4). The main difference between the two short texts can be found in the circumstances of

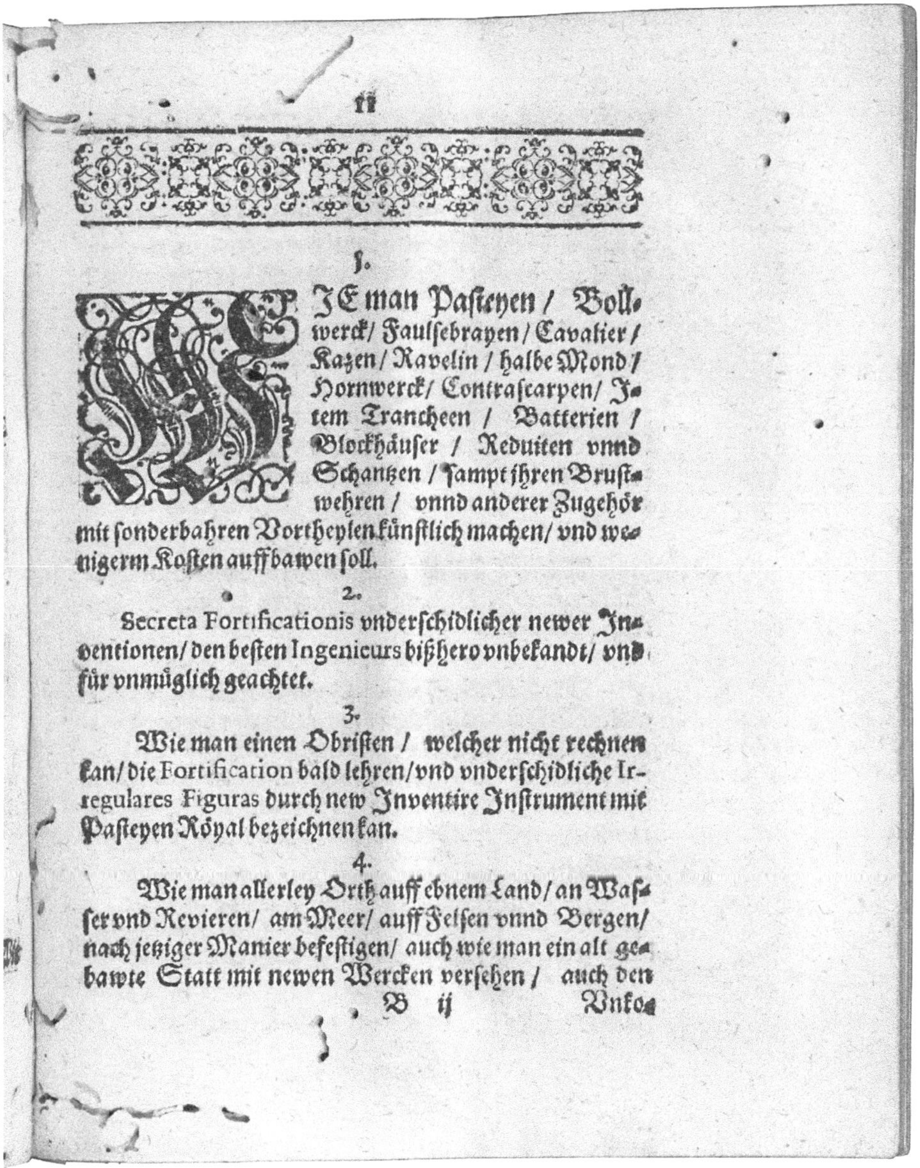

ij

1.

WJE man Pasteyen / Bollwerck / Faulsebrayen / Cavalier / Kazen / Ravelin / halbe Mond / Hornwerck / Contrascarpen / Item Trancheen / Batterien / Blockhäuser / Reduiten vnnd Schantzen / sampt jhren Brustwehren / vnnd anderer Zugehör mit sonderbahren Vortheylen künstlich machen / vnd wenigerm Kosten auffbawen soll.

2.

Secreta Fortificationis vnderschidlicher newer Inventionen / den besten Ingenieurs bißhero vnbekandt / vnd für vnmüglich geachtet.

3.

Wie man einen Obristen / welcher nicht rechnen kan / die Fortification bald lehren / vnd vnderschidliche Irregulares Figuras durch new Inventire Instrument mit Pasteyen Röyal bezeichnen kan.

4.

Wie man allerley Orth auff ebnem Land / an Wasser vnd Revieren / am Meer / auff Felsen vnnd Bergen / nach jetziger Manier befestigen / auch wie man ein alt gebawte Statt mit newen Wercken versehen / auch den

B ij Vnko-

Fig. 6.3 Johannes Faulhaber, *Geheime Kunstkammer*, entries 1-4, 1628. © Zentralbibliothek Zürich, Inv. Nr. 18.15,38

their publication – in Ulm and Augsburg – and, accordingly, in the target audience of each. Faulhaber's move to Augsburg in 1621 stemmed from his ongoing conflict with Ulm's civic authorities, sparked by his prophetic interpretation of the influential 1618 comet and continuous number speculations. From his contact with apocalyptic

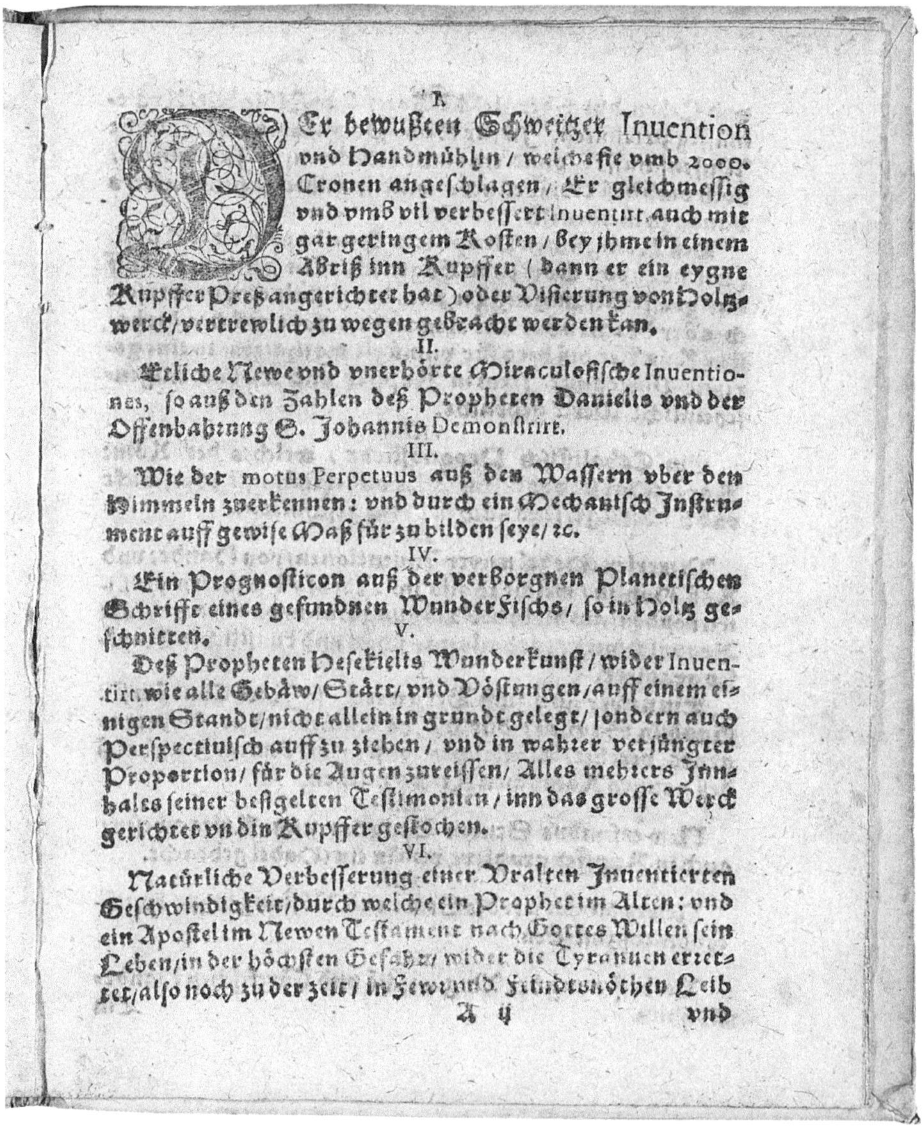

I.

Der bewußten Schweitzer Inuention vnd Handmühlin / welche sie vmb 2000. Cronen angeschlagen / Er gleichmessig vnd vmb vil verbessert Inuentirt auch mit gar geringem Kosten / bey jhme in einem Abriß inn Kupffer (dann er ein eygne Kupffer Preß angerichtet hat) oder Visierung von Holtzwerck / vertrewlich zu wegen gebracht werden kan.

II.

Etliche Newe vnd vnerhörte Miraculosische Inuentiones, so auß den Zahlen deß Propheten Danielis vnd der Offenbahrung S. Johannis Demonstrirt.

III.

Wie der motus Perpetuus auß den Wassern vber den Himmeln zuerkennen: vnd durch ein Mechanisch Instrument auff gewisse Maß für zu bilden seye / etc.

IV.

Ein Prognosticon auß der verborgnen Planetischen Schrifft eines gefundnen WunderFischs / so in Holtz geschnitten.

V.

Deß Propheten Hesekielis Wunderkunst / wider Inuentirt / wie alle Gebäw / Stätt / vnd Vöstungen / auff einem eynigen Standt / nicht allein in grundt gelegt / sondern auch Perspectiuisch auffzuziehen / vnd in wahrer verjüngter Proportion / für die Augen zureissen / Alles mehrers Innhalts seiner besigelten Testimonien / inn das grosse Werck gerichtet vnd dein Kupffer gestochen.

VI.

Natürliche Verbesserung einer Vralten Inuentierten Geschwindigkeit / durch welche ein Prophet im Alten: vnd ein Apostel im Newen Testament nach Gottes Willen sein Leben / in der höchsten Gefahr / wider die Tyrannen erretet / also noch zu der zeit / in Fewr vnd Feindtsnöthen Leib

A ij vnd

Fig. 6.4 Johannes Faulhaber, *Zwey und Viertzig Secreta*, entries no. I-VI, 1621. © Niedersächsische Staats- und Universitätsbibliothek, Göttingen, Inv. Nr. 8 MATH I, 4059

enthusiast Noah Kolb, Faulhaber even claimed to be in possession of heavenly given knowledge, especially in regards to his ability to interpret biblical numbers.[29] Settled in Augsburg only shortly after the publication of the *Continuatio* in Ulm, he

29 For a detailed account of Faulhaber's activities in this regard, see Schneider, *Johannes Faulhaber*, esp. 4-30.

resumed his practice in trading useful and technically erudite knowledge.[30] The republication of *Continuatio* as *Zwey und Viertzig Secreta* was due to this change in location.

Similarities between the *Geheime Kunstkammer* and Faulhaber's earlier publications are also discernible. While most of these works are structured as brief how-to treatises on a certain subject, their functional approach bears resemblance to the genre of the register or the list, akin to the *Geheime Kunstkammer*. As promised in their titles, they provide information on particular subjects, such as the construction of mills and mathematical instruments, solutions to arithmetical problems, and number speculation. But at the same time, Faulhaber routinely emphasizes that he holds additional information about a given subject or a series of compelling inventions, which, for various reasons he has not published.[31] If the reader wants more information, he should await the publication of a forthcoming pamphlet or, in numerous cases, contact Faulhaber directly.[32] Occasionally Faulhaber adds testimonies of noblemen and other notables as proof of his competence.

Mediating between a demonstration of professional knowledge and the promise of forthcoming information, Faulhaber's publications thus carefully maintained a balance between openness and concealment. Efforts were made to assure that the texts remained rewarding while still retaining enough secrecy to allow the author to further commodify his knowledge. Many of Faulhaber's publications can be likened to the two genres of so called '*usus et fabrica*' literature and paper instruments, which Mario Biagioli delineated in the circulation of early modern printed books of instruments.[33] Faulhaber's earlier publications, including *Ein sehr nützlicher new erfundener Gebrauch eines niderländischen Instruments* (1610), *Newe Geometrische und Perspectivische Inventiones* (1610) and *Newer Mathematischer Kunstspiegel* (1612), often describe in considerable detail the manufacture and use of particular instruments.[34] Sometimes Faulhaber also provided the reader with copper plates of the items in full scale, which could be cut out and pasted onto wood to obtain a simple makeshift version.[35] Among

30 Schneider, *Johannes Faulhaber*, 30.

31 See, for instance, Faulhaber, *Newe Geometrische vnd Perspectivische Inventiones*, 38; Faulhaber, *Warhafftige und Gründliche Solution*, 22; Faulhaber, *Erste. Teutsche Lection*, 12; Faulhaber, *Ein sehr nützlicher new erfundener Gebrauch eines niderländischen Instruments*, 6; Faulhaber, *Newer Mathematischer Kunstspiegel*; Faulhaber, *Weitere Continuation*, 22.

32 Faulhaber, *Ein sehr nützlicher new erfundener Gebrauch eines niderländischen Instruments*, 6.

33 Biagioli, 'From Print to Patents', 162-166.

34 These include a device used in building surveys, in a version with added dioptres or a six-pointed reduction compass. Faulhaber, *Ein sehr nützlicher new erfundener Gebrauch eines niderländischen Instruments*, 5-12, 13-14.

35 The presence of such an instrument in its assembled state is documented for the art chamber of the dukes of Württemberg: Stuttgart Hauptstaatsarchiv A20a Bü 23, 12. We would like to thank Irmgard

the paper instruments he published was a proportional compass attributed to Galileo Galilei and a circular instrument for field and building surveys based on a Dutch design.[36]

As noted by Biagioli, however, it is unclear if such paper instruments presented satisfactory consumer commodities, or if they were rather part of '"distance learning" packages', aimed at expanding the market for mathematical teachers and instrument makers.[37] Faulhaber, in any case, leaves no doubt in his publications that much more knowledge awaits anyone who 'may as he desires announce himself here in Ulm'.[38] In contrast to the typical '*usus et fabrica*' literature, which often recommend the reader to certain manufacturers, Faulhaber's publications did not do so.[39] The intent, it seems, was rather to attract readers to his own business of technological hands-on tutorials. The topics of his publications were not limited to mathematical instruments; Faulhaber also distributed knowledge about horse and hand mills, as well as descriptions of technical aids for perspective drawing and gunnery.[40]

Faulhaber's earliest written account of this 'advertisement strategy' dates four years after he founded his school, with the 1604 publication of the *Arithmetischer Cubiccossischer Lustgarten*, a disquisition of mathematical problems and their numerical solutions.[41] But in order to reproduce each exact solution, Gerolamo Cardano's method for cubic equations was required: a fact not disclosed in the text. Faulhaber instead suggested that the procedure could be conveniently learned from him in person.[42] The *Arithmetischer Cubiccossischer Lustgarten* capitalized on Faulhaber's ability to teach methodological knowledge he himself had acquired through German translations of classical and more recent mathematical works.[43] His market was only damaged after the competing mathematician Peter Roth

Müsch, Landesmuseum Württemberg, for this observation

36 Faulhaber, *Inventiones*, 27-30, 19-26. Faulhaber's publications were part of a lively trade in paper instruments that developed in sixteenth-century southern Germany. For a discussion of its origins and a recent research overview, see Schmidt, *Interactive and Sculptural Printmaking*, 205-240.

37 Biagioli, 'From Print to Patents', 163.

38 'Wann aber sonst einer geheime Instrument / welche mit gar geringem Kosten könden gemacht werden / zu allerlery Sonnenuhren / Büchsenmeisterey / Feldmessen / Visiren / Perspectiv / sampt den demonstrirten Fundamenten / zum aufftragen der Proportional und newerfundenen VisierZirckeln / auch andern nutzlichen Sachen / vom Buchhalten / Schrifftätzen / und wunderbarlichen Cossischen Rechnungen / darvon in meinen zwey außgangenen Aurithmetischen und Geometrischen Büchlein gar nichts vermeldet worden / von mir als freye Künsten zu lernen begert / der mag nach seiner Gelegenheit bey mir zu allhie Ulm sich anmelden / soll ihme guter gründlicher Bericht / nach Gebür ertheilet werden.' Faulhaber, *Ein sehr nützlicher new erfundener Gebrauch eines niderländischen Instruments*, 6.

39 Biagioli, 'From Print to Patents', 164-165.

40 Faulhaber, *Inventiones*; Faulhaber, *Mechanische Verbesserung*; Faulhaber, *Weitere Continuation*.

41 Faulhaber, *Arithmetischer Cubiccossischer Lustgarten*.

42 Schneider, *Johannes Faulhaber*, 54.

43 Ibid., 56.

published Cardano's rules, and with them the entire 'secret' solution paths for the *Arithmetischer Cubiccossischer Lustgarten*, effectively obliterating Faulhaber's business model of a 'sales catalogue of mathematical knowledge'.[44] In turn, from late 1609 onward, Faulhaber invested considerable energy in the acquisition of imperial and local privileges for his inventions and their teaching.[45] Thus protected, he began to publish the aforementioned pamphlets and small treatises. In addition to these texts, which mostly present a single or few inventions, publications like the *Continuatio, deß Newen Mathematischen Kunstspiegels* and *Zwey und Viertzig Secreta* presented a more general overview of Faulhaber's offerings in the form of registers and lists. The title page of the *Continuatio* prominently states that infringement upon the privilege would be penalized, and within the text, further information is given about the modalities of payment and the learning conditions in his school.[46] In promoting his knowledge in publication – knowledge that was linked with an actual collection of the machine models, instruments and inventions – it might be said that Faulhaber diffused the charge of his *Kunstkammer* and school as a physical place. Yet, in the strategy of publication he pursued, Faulhaber was also careful to conceal specific details pertaining to his mechanical knowledge and his practices as a teacher, and thereby reinforced the fundamental, non-transferable value of his model collection and school. His most extensive list of knowledge, after all, was cast with an aura of secrecy with the name *Geheime Kunstkammer*, and here and elsewhere, he made frequent use of the expression '*secretum*' to refer to the knowledge he provided. In this context, the early modern notion of secrecy appears to refer to knowledge that is in principle informative, but is also intentionally concealed from public awareness.[47] With the term '*secreta*' Faulhaber referred to skills and designs, the circulation of which he sought to control. This included technological items of literally explosive nature such as inventions for military mining, which he explained, are, 'due to [potential] abuse, not to be made public but to be kept secret and only to be communicated confidentially to Christian princes and gentlemen'.[48] In this, Faulhaber gave the impression that he was offering craft secrets in the sense of '*arcana artis*', although many of his secrets actually derive from existing literature.[49]

At the same time, Faulhaber's publications also share a certain semantic proximity to the so-called books of secrets. In the sixteenth century, this genre of vernacular

44 Ibid., 54.

45 Ibid., 94-95.

46 Faulhaber, *Weitere Continuation*, [6].

47 For an overview and further literature on the early modern sematical field of 'secrecy', see Jütte, *The Age of Secrecy*, 2-22.

48 Faulhaber, *Inventiones*, 38: 'welche Sachen doch wegen deß Mißbrauchs nit zu divulgiren / sondern in geheim zu halten / und Christlichen Fürsten und Herrn allein vertrewlich zu communiciren sind'.

49 Schneider, *Johannes Faulhaber*, 49.

how-to literature popularized practical know-how and recipes beyond the oral tradition of guild apprenticeship, thereby promoting technical literacy and drawing attention to empirical workshop knowledge that had traditionally remained outside the scope of scientific scholarship.[50] The so-called 'professor of secrets' was associated with this type of applied literature, an individual who sought to collect unknown, lost, or hidden knowledge and then offered it to an enthusiastic public.[51] While publications typically composed by a 'professor of secrets' listed actual how-to knowledge, rather than merely outlining what might be acquired from the author in person, Faulhaber can still be associated with this professional profile. As underscored by Daniel Jütte, '*secreta* literature' was only in part a commercial disquisition of knowledge; such publications also functioned as a means of self-fashioning and advertisement for their authors within a veritable 'economy of secrets'. In publishing a 'book of secrets', the charlatan, and likewise the accepted scholar, could raise his social prestige and recommend himself to the courts, which remained the most dominant patrons in the market for secrets.[52] Faulhaber used the genre to similar effect. In 1618 he received an appointment from Landgrave Philip III of Hesse-Butzbach, who was particularly interested in mathematics and to whom Faulhaber promised to disclose his secrets and inventions in exchange for appropriate compensation.[53] Faulhaber subsequently sent mechanical models to Butzbach, but was soon released from the appointment due to the ongoing investigations in Ulm, which did not permit him to freely disclose his speculations about biblical numbers. This preoccupation with mystical number speculation, also mirrored in his publications, placed Faulhaber within the esoteric tradition from which the books of secrets originate.[54]

Still, over time, Faulhaber's proclivity to publicly disclose knowledge increased. The *Continuatio* was accompanied with the announcement that the author would have 'one or two' of his secrets printed as a proof of his competence.[55] Subsequently more items from his catalogues appeared in print, such as gun-laying techniques for returning ordnance to defined elevation and azimuth angles between firings.[56] When, in the 1630s, Faulhaber released his four-volume fortification manual

50 Eamon, *Science and the Secrets of Nature*, 113.

51 Ibid., ch. 4.

52 Jütte, *The Age of Secrecy*, 14-16.

53 Hawlitschek, *Johann Faulhaber 1580-1635*, 232-234. For an overview about Phillip's erudite activites and his library, see Schenk, 'Geheimnis – Herrschaft – Wissen'.

54 Eamon, *Science and the Secrets of Nature*, chs. 1, 2.

55 Faulhaber, *Weitere Continuation*, 5.

56 Ibid., 19-21.

Ingenieurs Schul (1630-1633), he briefly disclosed several of '*secreta*' that he had previously shared only confidentially.[57]

The *Geheime Kunstkammer* came at the end of a long list of publications that served comparable purposes. More explicitly than his '*usus et fabrica*' and paper instrument books, the *Geheime Kunstkammer* was an advertisement of Faulhaber's services as a teacher of practical know-how. While following the general character of *Continuatio* and *Zwey und Viertzig*, the *Geheime Kunstkammer* lacks their legal placement within a distinct regional context. But like the other publications, its chief purpose was to induce a personal encounter between vendor and client, either by persuading prospective students into a visit to Faulhaber's premises or by encouraging them to employ him independently. The *Geheime Kunstkammer* is thus not merely a description of a collection, but rather a catalogue that served commercial purposes within an economy of knowledge, although still closely linked with the actual collection that provided most of the machine models, drawings, instruments and inventions it listed.[58]

The Knowledge of the *Geheime Kunstkammer*

Although the *Geheime Kunstkammer* shared much in common with the 'book of secrets' in terms of its genre, the actual knowledge it put forth was substantially different. The know-how disclosed by 'professors of secrets', such as the prototypical Alessio Piemontese, typically involved the realms of pharmacy, domestic chemistry and alchemy, and at times natural magic. While Faulhaber's early lists of secrets at least partially participate in this kind of knowledge, meeting the practical needs of a curious upper-class public, his main focus lay in mechanical-mathematical knowledge.[59] This is even more so the case in the *Geheime Kunstkammer*. Here, the 'magical' items have virtually all been replaced by fortification designs, siege

57 For example, he included information on an instrument for designing regular and irregular fortresses without the need for calculations, which he had previously only referenced. Faulhaber, *Ingenieurs Schul Dritter Theil*, ch. 10. Another example is a roller mill, presumably after one published by Agostino Ramelli, which previously was listed in the *Geheime Kunstkammer*. See Faulhaber, *Ingenieurs Schul Vierdter Teil*, 150-152.

58 Interestingly Daniel Mögling, physician and court mathematician of Philip III of Hesse-Butzbach, named his 1629 compilation, translation and discussion of mechanical treatises and problems *Mechanische Kunstkammer*. As suggested by Popplow, 'Court Mathematicians', 299, Mögling was aware of Faulhaber's publication and his treatise 'might perhaps be read as a response to Faulhaber's "secrets," in defiance of which Mögling, in *Kunst-Kammer*, now freely presented his readers with basic knowledge on mechanics'.

59 Eamon, *Science and the Secrets of Nature*, 144-146. In *Continuatio* and *Zwey und Viertzig Secreta* even a lengthy advertisement for a profitable recipe for the transmutation of silver into gold is presented, side by side with more or less pragmatic mechanical inventions and items regarding the interpretation of divine signs and numerical speculation.

technology and mills. Although Faulhaber, even before the publication of the *Geheime Kunstkammer*, was one of the few engineers to classify his know-how with the term '*secreta*', in term of content, the knowledge he provided was substantially different.[60]

Faulhaber's publications mirror his professional biography, the course of which can be traced within the time that elapsed between these works. The first two of his published works, *Continuatio* and *Zwey und Viertzig Secreta*, depict a mathematical practitioner who was also engaged in astrology and alchemy. In contrast, the *Geheime Kunstkammer* exhibits the canonical knowledge of a fortification engineer. In the seven year period that separates the two groups of publications, Faulhaber travelled extensively. As supervisor of fortification works he was commissioned by the city of Basel to complete projects there. Even more importantly, he was sent to the Netherlands, where he acquired new technical knowledge. His year of travel within the United Provinces was one of the most decisive periods in Faulhaber's professional life, and according to a brief description in the posthumous *Specification*, it seems that his time in the province of Holland had a major impact on his decision to extend his collection of models to an entire *Kunstkammer*.[61] The waterworks, fireworks, boats, floats, pontoon bridges, catapults, ladders, stratagems and other items listed in the *Specification* are said to have been encountered in the 'Prince of Orange's *Kunstkammer*' in The Hague, as well as in arsenals in Delft and Dordrecht (and also others within German states).[62] Besides his presumable studies within the military infrastructure of the Dutch Republic and possibly even a visit to the *Stadhouderlijk Kwartier*, the visitor from Ulm exchanged inventions with military officials.[63] Unfortunately, few records survive relating to the conditions and events of this stay in the Netherlands, which lasted from February 1623 to February 1624.[64] In April 1624, having just returned from his travels, Faulhaber wrote to his good friend Sebastian Kurz:

> I was called to the city of Basel whose senate had requested me from the city of Ulm for fortification works, and I was also sent in the Netherlands to Prince Maurice on important business; however, the prince wanted me to stay for an indefinite commission and offered me three times as much as my salary was in

60 One other example is Keßler, *Unterschiedliche bißhero mehrern Theils Secreta*.

61 His presence in these locations can be inferred from a paragraph within the *Specification* that summarizes numerous inventions Faulhaber acquired from other collections, including the '*Kunstkam[m]er*' in The Hague, the armouries in Delft and Dordrecht, as well as the '*Kunstkam[m]ern*' in Dresden, Kassel and Stuttgart. See appendix, 5r.

62 See appendix, 5r. The *Geheime Kunstkammer* also states an expandable siege ladder Faulhaber has seen in Maurits' *Kunstkammer*, as well as in others. See Faulhaber, *Geheime Kunstkammer*, no. 26.

63 For example, he received a newly conceived petard from a certain colonel Dänhoff in exchange for some of his own '*secreta*'. Faulhaber, *Geheime Kunstkammer*, 15.

64 Hawlitschek, 'Niederländische Mathematik', 33.

Fig. 6.5 Sebastian Furck, portrait of Johannes Faulhaber with gold medal, surrounded by four *'Miraculorum'*, an opened book of *'secreta'*, and holding a compass, 1630/1631. © Herzog August Bibliothek Wolfenbüttel, Inv. Nr. I 4107

> Basel; but I declined such offered employment as I resolved to first and foremost serve my fatherland. After an exam I was subsequently declared engineer and the prince bestowed to me his portrait in gold.[65]

Faulhaber is depicted wearing this portrait medal in the 1630/1631 portrait of him by Sebastian Furck, where, as a central iconographical element, it signals his expertise as a provider of mathematical and mechanical secrets (Figure 6.5).

Faulhaber used his stay in the Netherlands to heighten his social prestige – upon his return, the city council decided to appoint him engineer of the fortifications of Ulm – and to obtain technological knowledge from one of the most progressive military cultures of the age. Since the late sixteenth century, Prince Maurits van Nassau together with his cousin Willem Lodewijk had begun to transform the Dutch military into an innovative, disciplined army that could match the power of the opposing Spanish forces. Borrowing from classical Roman and Byzantine military treatises, structural and tactical innovations were established, including the introduction of volley fire and standardized manoeuvres, which required the rigorous drill of elementary movements as well as a specialized language of command.[66] While a core aspect of the army's reform consisted of the implementation of novel infantry tactics (it has been called a tactical revolution), it also encompassed technological aspects in terms of fortification design, siege technology and the standardization of guns.[67] Within the so-called 'military revolution' of the sixteenth and seventeenth centuries, Dutch expertise in the art of fortification was in great international demand.[68] Reforms undertaken by the Dutch army included efforts to standardize equipment – guns and artillery pieces, as well as the entire range

65 'Ich bin nacher der Statt Basel / zum Festungsbau / beschriben und von selbigem Senat bey der Statt Ulm ausgebetten, auch in die Niederland zu Printz Moritzen in wichtigen Geschäfften verschickht worden, unnd aber der Printz mit mir tractiren lassen wöllen, daß ich mich bey seiner Excellenz in ein ewige Bestallung einlassen solle, da mir dan 3mal souil anerbonen worden, als ich in Basel Besoldung gehapt, als hab ich solche angebotne Bestallung glimpflich abgeschlagen und meinem Vatterland zuvorderst zu dienen mich resolvirt. Darauff ich nach vorhergegangenem Examen für ein Ingenieur erklärt, und der Printz mir sein Brustbild von Gold verehrt.' Ulm Stadtarchiv Faulhaber H 5/1, sheet 475. Letter of Johannes Faulhaber to Sebastian Kurz, 30 April 1624. Transcribed by Hawlitschek, *Johann Faulhaber 1580-1635*, 316-317.

66 The far-reaching and extensively discussed question of the House of Orange's army reform and its role within a 'military revolution' can only be outlined very briefly here. The classical study on this process is that of Hahlweg, *Die Heeresreform der Oranier und die Antike*. For a more detailed overview of the changes in Dutch military practice during the late sixteenth and early seventeenth centuries, see Wijn, 'Het krijgswezen in den tijd van prins Maurits', and van Nimwegen, *The Dutch Army and the Military Revolutions*, part 1.

67 Van Nimwegen, *The Dutch Army and the Military Revolutions*, 85; van Nimwegen, 'Maurits van Nassau and Siege Warfare', 122; Parker, *The Military Revolution*, 7-16.

68 Davids, *The Rise and Decline of Dutch Technological Leadership*, vol. 1, 289-292.

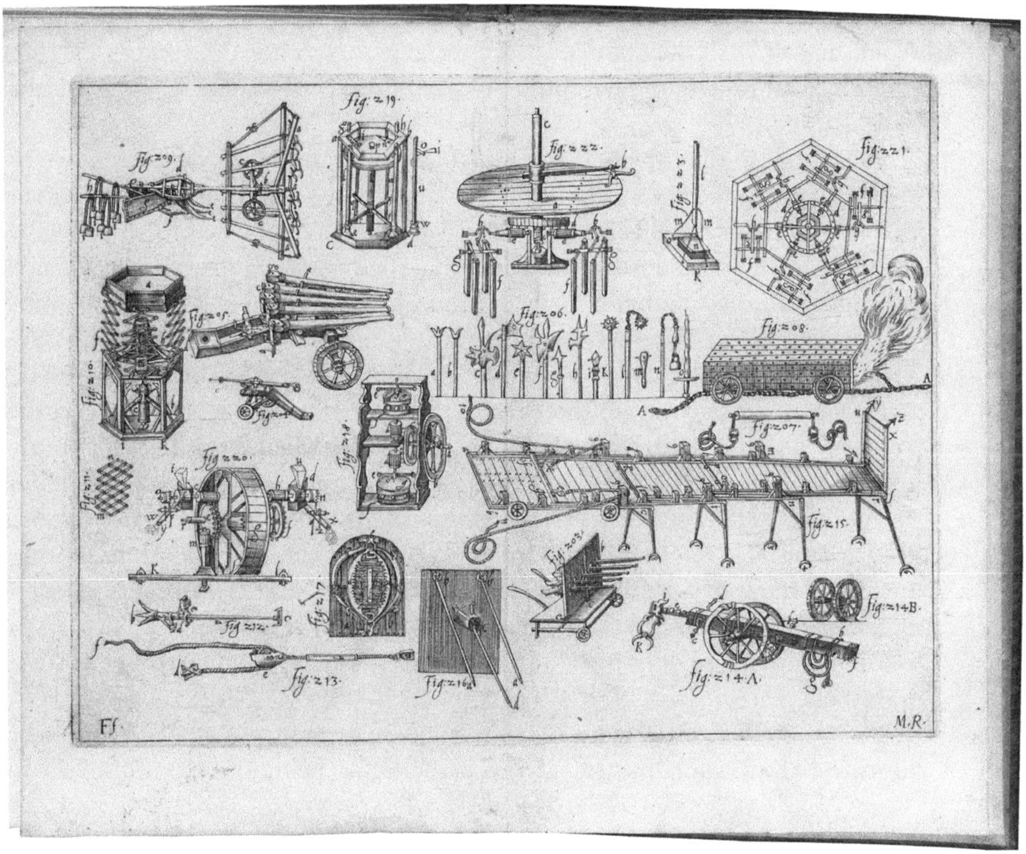

Fig. 6.6 Johannes Faulhaber (engraved by Matthäus Rembold), inventions of military objects. *Ingenieurs-Schul*, 1637, table *Ff.* © Niedersächsische Staats- und Universitätsbibliothek, Göttingen, Inv. Nr. 4 ARS MIL 506/1

of equipment for earthwork, mining and besiegement.[69] The Dutch army also promoted modern fortification techniques through the foundation of an engineering school in Leiden, which was supervised by distinguished mathematician Simon Stevin.[70]

Many of the items Faulhaber published in the *Geheime Kunstkammer* and his other publications are directly linked to Dutch military and technological developments. For instance, alongside layouts of numerous Dutch fortresses (most of them Faulhaber had personally visited), the *Geheime Kunstkammer* provides siege methods from the Dutch War of Independence, an account of a method of laying out military camps according to Prince Maurice's design, as well as

69 De Jong, 'Militaire hervormingen', 482-483.
70 See Krüger, 'Actoren en factoren', ch. 2.

battle orders employed by the prince and countless stratagems that originated from the war with the Spanish. Moreover, visitors to both Faulhaber's printed and physical *Kunstkammer* could admire a model of Simon Stevin's peculiar sailing wagon.[71]

Even more so than the *Geheime Kunstkammer*, Faulhaber's *opus magnum*, the four-volume *Ingenieurs Schul* (1630-1633), might be read as an engineering manual of the old Dutch system of fortification design, supplemented with the innovative use of logarithms.[72] The second and third tome of the publication include numerous examples of hitherto unpublished fortresses, which Faulhaber had visited himself and whose ground plans were communicated to him by Dutch engineers David van Orliens and Johan van Valckenburgh, among others.[73] The fourth and last tome contains aspects of poliorcetics, stratagems and siege machinery (Figure 6.6). Some of these related to seventeenth-century Dutch practice, while others derive from most important contemporary engineering treatises such as Diego Ufano's *Tratado dela artilleria*, Adam Freitag's *Architectura Militaris*, and Samuel Marolois' *Fortification ou architecture militaire*, as well as from 'theatre of machine' volumes, including those of Agostino Ramelli's *Diverse et artificiose machine* and Joseph Boillot's *Modelles, artifices de feu et divers instrumens de guerre*.[74] Throughout the volume, Faulhaber added anecdotes from the Dutch war and made use of Dutch terminology.[75]

But Faulhaber's knowledge of foreign advancements was not solely linked to his travel. Even before his time in the Netherlands, he maintained close ties to a

71 Faulhaber, *Geheime Kunstkammer*, nos. 8, 11, 12, 14-15, 19, 22, 29, 44; see appendix, folio 3v.

72 Schneider, *Johannes Faulhaber*, 167-170. Interestingly, Faulhaber planned to publish a synopsis of the second, third, and fourth part of his *opus magnum*, entitled *Academia Fortificatoria*. On 13 October 1630 he stated his intention to publish the work with Halbmayer in Nuremberg in a letter to his friend Sebastian Kurz. Four years later, on 24 December 1634, the council of Ulm confirmed Faulhaber's printing of the *Academia Fortificatoria*. See Hawlitschek, *Johann Faulhaber 1580-1635*, 102, 321-322. By contrast, Büchi, *Fortifikationsliteratur*, 154, 362-363 suggests that the manuscript's diagramatical plates were used by Faulhaber in courses on the *Academia Fortificatoria*. See also Büchi, '"Synopsis architectonicæ"', 195. This planned publication was likely part of Faulhaber's strategy in advertising his knowledge, attracting scholars to his school and *Kunstkammer*, and encouraging the purchase his *Ingenieurs-Schul, Erster Theil*. On the importance of this treatise, see Bürger, *Architectura Militaris*, 309-311.

73 Faulhaber, *Ingenieurs Schul Dritter Theil*, 75, figs. 93-102.

74 Such as an account of the armament of foot and cavalry soldiers according to the 'Ordre op de waapeninge van het voetvolk' issued by Maurice and William Louis in 1599. Faulhaber, *Ingenieurs Schul Vierdter Teil*, 104-105; see van Nimwegen, *The Dutch Army and the Military Revolutions*, 85-99. For example, an iron trap against enemy petardiers, Faulhaber, *Ingenieurs Schul Vierdter Teil*, 145-147, derived from Boillot, *Modelles*, 78-80; an expandable siege tower with a scissor mechanism derived from Vegetius and Ramelli: Faulhaber, *Ingenieurs Schul Vierdter Teil*, 134-137; Ramelli, *Le diverse et artificiose macchine*, fig. 146, and appear questionable in their feasibility.

75 Hawlitschek, 'Niederländische Mathematik', 39.

Fig. 6.7 Johann Carl, *Kleines Zeughaus* with various models of military equipment, c. 1625. © Sebastian Fitzner, courtesy of the Germanisches Nationalmuseum, Nuremberg

distinguished protagonist of Dutch military reform: Ludolph van Ceulen, mathematician and professor at the *Duytsche Mathematique*, the Leiden engineering school founded by Prince Maurice in 1600.[76] Their relationship was characterized by mutual sympathy and the letters from Ulm reveal Faulhaber's attempts to obtain Dutch local privileges through van Ceulen. Faulhaber had also persuaded another friend, the Dutch adventurer Philibert Vernatti, to help him extend his business territory by finding customers for his inventions in the Netherlands. But apparently it was only by presenting himself in person that Faulhaber succeeded in initiating fruitful professional relationships with the Dutch experts.[77]

Faulhaber's activities in the Netherlands can be compared to those of his former student Johann Carl, who a decade before had visited the Low Countries with similar intent. Carl, who was primarily interested in the newly standardized Dutch artillery, had meticulously copied all sorts of guns and siege equipment in scaled drawings. After returning to Nuremberg, his home town, he supervised the manufacture of elaborate models from these delineations, creating a unique collection of miniature military equipment, the so-called *Kleines Zeughaus* (small armoury) (Figure 6.7). This *Kleines Zeughaus*, which is preserved to this day, represents state-of-the-art standardized Dutch artillery pieces next to basic military camp equipment and individual armaments.[78]

76 Krüger, 'Actoren en factoren', 50.

77 For a more in-depth discussion of Faulhaber's exchange of letters with Ludolph von Ceulen, see Hawlitschek, 'Niederländische Mathematik', 24-31.

78 Königer, *Zeughaus*.

Like Carl's *Kleines Zeughaus*, Faulhaber's model collection similarly functioned as a means of technology transfer that extended from the Netherlands to the Holy Roman Empire.[79] Both Faulhaber and Carl had witnessed a highly innovative military culture, knowledge of which they conserved in drawings and models.[80] In the sense that Faulhaber's model collection represents his professional travels, it may be compared to that of his fellow engineer, Joseph Furttenbach the Elder, whose *Kunstkammer* extended from his twelve years of study in Italy.

A Competition of Engineers? The Collection of Joseph Furttenbach the Elder in Ulm

The famed collection of Joseph Furttenbach in Ulm contained far more models than that of Faulhaber. Whereas Faulhaber's collection consisted of about 90 items, which were mostly related to the fields of mechanics and military technology, Furttenbach assembled far more items, including numerous non-architectural and non-mechanical objects, like corals and a fossil of an elephant tooth.[81] Yet comparison of the two collections helps shed light on the formation and structure of Faulhaber's collection, of which comparably less is known. Joseph Furttenbach began to form his collection around January 1620 when he settled in Ulm.[82] According to a manuscript in Furttenbach's hand entitled *Architectura universale*, dated 1632, it is possible to partially reconstruct his first *Kunstkammer*.[83] As given in a short explanation and ground plan of his home, the collection was mainly on display in three rooms on the second floor (Figure 6.8).[84] The first, a 'small art chamber' ('*kunstcämerlin*') contained a 'grotto, drawings, and a model of an armoury'. The second, a small 'room dedicated to the arts' ('*kunststüblein*'), was equipped with a 'table, a chest of weapons', an additional 'table', two 'globes', 'drawings and fortifications'. The third room, the 'art chamber' ('*Kunstcamer*'), contained an enormous wooden chest of models.[85] It is on the collection contained within this model-chest, as documented in 1632, that the comparison with Faulhaber's *Kunstkammer* is based. The chest

79 Davids, *The Rise and Decline of Dutch Technological Leadership*, vol. 1, 275-279.

80 For instance, the description and drawings of military equipment in ONB, 265941-E.

81 It is not easy to distinguish real models from written inventions or drawings of models, due to the fact that Faulhaber's list mostly describes objects without specifying their materiality. The objects were stored in a drawer that was part of the room denominated '*Kunst Kammer*', Furttenbach, *Architectura Privata*, 26.

82 See Furttenbach Ulm Stadtarchiv H Furtenbach 1, 1; Berthold, 'Joseph Furttenbach', 9 n. 4.

83 Ulm Stadtarchiv Furttenbach H 5, 223-233. See Günther, 'Joseph Furttenbachs Architekturmuseum', 42-43.

84 Ulm Stadtarchiv Furttenbach H 5, 223-233.

85 Ibid., 229.

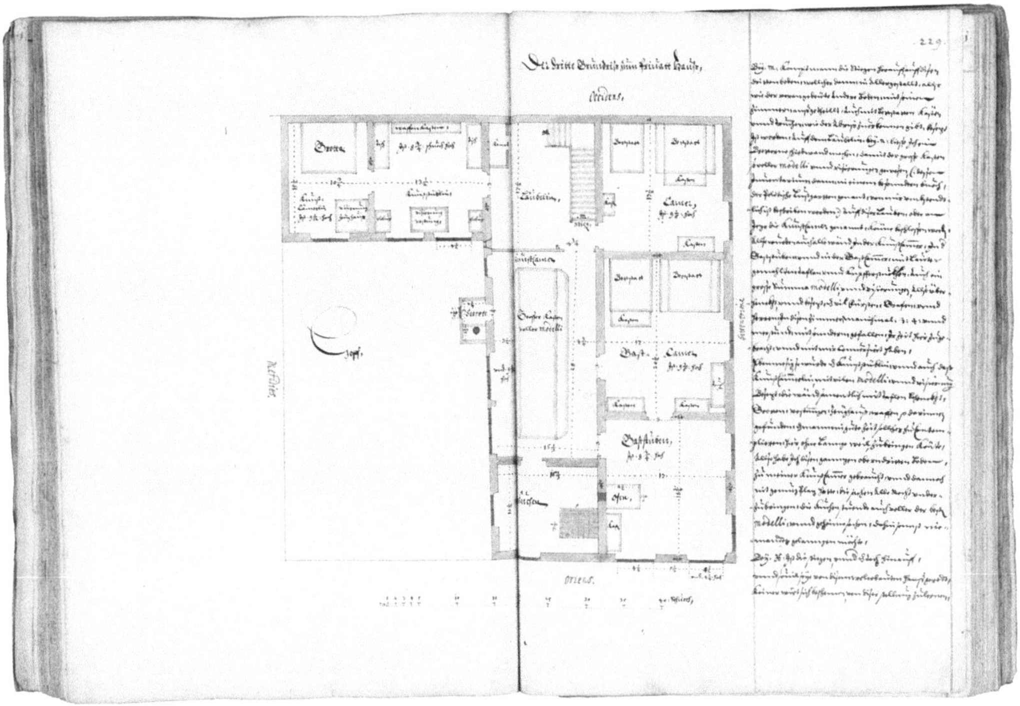

Fig. 6.8 Joseph Furttenbach, ground floor of the *Kunstkammer. Architectura universale*, 1632. © Stadtarchiv Ulm, Furttenbach H 5

was on display during Faulhaber's lifetime, and it is possible, through Furttenbach's description in his 1641 *Architectura privata*, to reconstruct its contents.[86]

Composed of wood and glass, Furttenbach's model-chest was elaborately decorated with coloured columns, arches, entablatures, pyramids, and balls. It measured approximately 6.49 metres in length, 1.47 metres in width, and 1.3 metres in height, and contained in total ten compartments, which held about 64 models and more than 28 instruments.[87] The most important compartments, according to Furttenbach, were those dedicated to the '*Principal Artes*', with models concerning *architectura civilis* (fourteen), mechanics (twelve), *architectura militaris* (eleven), and *architectura navalis* (eleven). Besides the so-called '*Principal Artes*', elsewhere in his collection he displayed a model for a theatre, a grotto, as well as

86 Apparently, the three rooms were not sufficient to store all of the models, so Furttenbach also used the kitchen, which was 'filled with the best models and secret things of matter'. Ulm Stadtarchiv Furttenbach H 5, 229.

87 See Furttenbach, *Architectura Privata*, 34-35. For the measurements, see Trautmann, 'Heillose Groschen'.

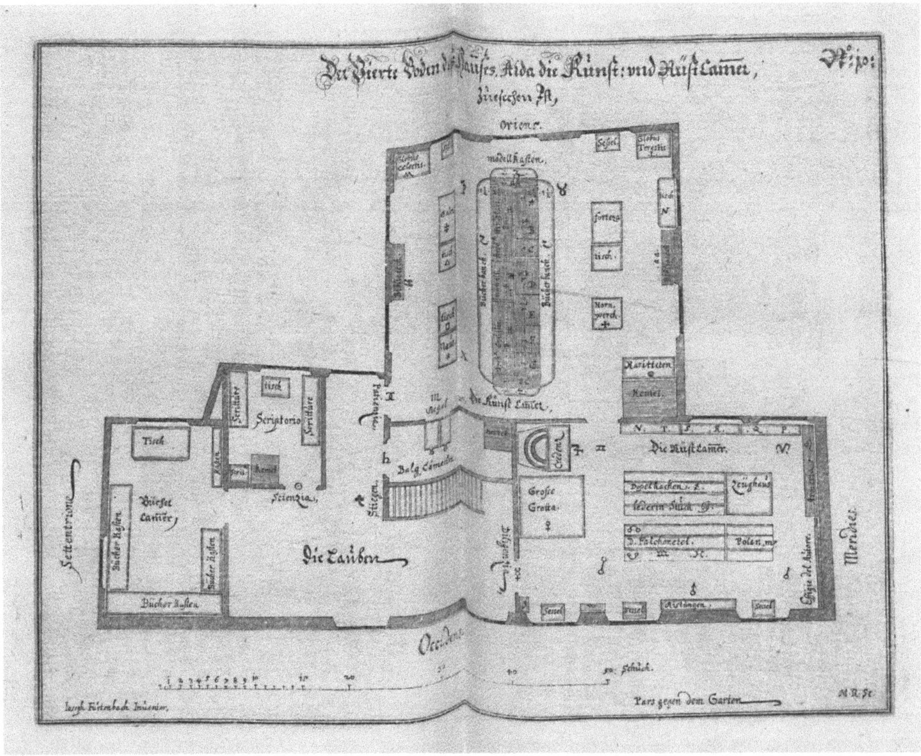

Fig. 6.9 Joseph Furttenbach (engraved by Matthäus Rembold), ground floor plan of the *Kunstkammer. Architectura privata*, table N° 10, 1641. © Sächsische Landesbibliothek, Staats- und Universitätsbibliothek, Dresden, Shelfmark Archit.146, misc. 1

three models concerning fireworks.[88] By 1632, Furttenbach's collection was already highly regarded. Numerous visitors, including princes, counts and noblemen, would come to the collection and 'could contemplate here for some time without ennui'.[89] According to Furttenbach's handwritten *Curriculum vitae*, he also advised several persons like Doctor Johann Schultes and his cousin Gabriel Furttenbach in tasks such as the layout of regular and irregular fortifications and measuring the height of a tower.[90]

Within his *Architectura universale*, Furttenbach left a telling note, indicating that all of the models and drawings in the large model-chest had been 'described'

88 See Furttenbach, *Architectura Privata*, 35, 38-46.

89 Ulm Stadtarchiv Furttenbach H 5, 229. It was said that 'ein gute Zeit sollches zu Contemplieren, hier ohne Lange weil, zubringen könte', and visitors could engage in discussion with Furttenbach for up to three or four hours ('d[as] vil Fürsten, Grafen, vnd herren, In disen zimmern manichmal .3: 4: vnnd mer stunde mit mir Conversiert haben').

90 See Greyerz, Siebenhüner and Zaugg (eds), 'Joseph Furttenbach, *Lebenslauff*', 234-235.

by himself with 'great diligence' in a 'particular book', entitled *Political Pleasure Garden*.[91] Although this book is unknown today, the reference indicates that by 1632 Furttenbach had finished documentation of his model and drawing collection. His extensive and well-known *Kunstkammer* was assembled in his newly erected house (between 1638 and 1640) and published in the *Architectura privata* from 1641 (Figure 6.9). The *Architectura privata*, a complete description of Furttenbach's estate, included elaborate etchings of elevations and floor plans.[92]

The *Kunstkammer*, located on the home's third floor, functioned similarly to that of Faulhaber, as a dedicated place for collecting, distributing and discussing mechanical-architectural knowledge with burghers, professionals, as well as visitors from the higher and lower ranked nobility.[93] While the majority of Furttenbach's collection has not survived, according to the *Architectura privata*, it united fifteen different disciplines, which were represented through architectural, mechanical, and military models, drawing and measuring instruments, *artificalia* and *naturalia*, as well as paintings, prints, and personal memorabilia, including his certificate of apprenticeship within the Italian '*Arte della Bombardieri*' granted by the German colonel Adrian of Sittinghausen.[94] This disparate material was represented under his broad understanding of the '*Mechanica*'. Together with her fourteen sons and daughters, the allegory of '*Mechanica*' was used to outline the *ars mechanica*, based upon the partition of the arts of architecture and mechanics into theory and practice (Figure 6.10).[95] The models stored in Furttenbach's model-chest also reflect this concept of the *ars mechanica*.[96]

Interestingly, Furttenbach chose to distinguish his earlier *Kunstkammer* of 1632 from the one in Sterngasse 4 by altering the title to *Kunst- und Rüstkammer* (art and armoury chamber). By renaming the collection, Furttenbach underscored its composition according to two different fields of interest, linked to the concepts

91 Ulm Stadtarchiv Furttenbach H 5, 229: 'in einem besondern buch, der Politische Lustgartten genant [...] vmbstendtlich ist beschriben worden'.

92 Further inventories of his collection were published in 1660 and 1666.

93 Furttenbach documented the visits in a visitor's book. See in detail Siebenhüner, 'Entwerfen', 60-64.

94 See Siebenhüner, 'Entwerfen', 57. An inventory of the armoury in Ulm of 1793 lists three models of Furttenbach. See Häberle, 'Das Schicksal', 7. Interestingly, two models or copies of them were presumably part of Furttenbach's own *Kunstkammer*: 'a board about 22 inches long and 17 inches wide with an new invented model, by the author, showing a bastion useful against the hereditary enemy, the Turk' and 'two different models carved from wood, depicting partition walls'. See Furttenbach and Furttenbach, *Inventarium*, 55. On the models, see Berthold, 'Joseph Furttenbach', 179.

95 For further discussion, see Fitzner and Weitemeier, 'Das Frontispiz'.

96 On the 'fictious classification' of the objects according to Furttenbach's publications, see Rott, 'Die Rüst- und Kunstkammer'.

Fig. 6.10 Joseph Furttenbach (engraved by Raphael Custos), frontispiece with '*mechanica*' and her daughters and sons. *Mechanische Reißladen*, 1644. © Universitätsbibliothek Technische Universität Darmstadt, Hs 2795

of *arte* and *marte*.[97] The private *Rüstkammer*, exceptional at this time, was a place for the storage of weapons, which were kept in the event of warfare as well as for representational purposes.[98] Furttenbach further extended his *Rüstkammer* with the addition of several other military-related objects, including treatises of gunpowder, images of fireworks, and a wooden model of an armoury with 200 canons. Within the same room, these were placed alongside more or less non-military objects, like the model of a princely grotto, sea seals and a tumbler.[99]

Faulhaber's collection, in turn, was almost entirely dedicated to mechanics and military technology (Figure 6.11). And while Furttenbach foregrounded the *ars mechanica* as a core objective of his collection, Faulhaber's in fact seemed more focused on the advancement of military, mechanical and mathematical issues of his time. The distinction between the two *Kunstkammern*, and the different methodological focus of each, is underscored in comparing their contents. In terms of physical models, Faulhaber's *Kunstkammer* contained seven models for mills, four models of waterworks, four models of military bridges, and five models of lifting devices. By contrast, the fourth compartment of Furttenbach's model-chest, entitled 'about bridges, lifting devices, pounding mills and more of

97 Although the concept of *arte et marte* expressed the ideal character of a ruler as well as the foundation of a good government from the fifteenth to the seventeenth centuries, we might consider that Furttenbach refers to this concept. Thus, he himself represented as a guarantor of the liberal arts as well as the art of warfare. See Brink, *Arte et Marte*.

98 Neumann, *Das Zeughaus*, 39.

99 Furttenbach, *Architectura Privata*, 20, 25.

Fig. 6.11 Johannes Faulhaber, *Ingenieurs-Schul*, frontispiece with *'sapentia'* educating the liberal arts and the *artes mechanicae*, 1630. © Herzog August Bibliothek Wolfenbüttel, Shelfmark 15.3 Arithm.(1)

such *mechanical* instruments', included a total of twelve mechanical models.[100] Elsewhere, it is possible to account for an additional three mills and four military bridges in Furttenbach's collection.

The thematic distinction between the two collections is made clearer if we consider that Furttenbach's assemblage of architectural models included not just fortifications (eleven in total), but also palaces, private houses and pleasure gardens (about thirteen). Faulhaber's collection featured no models that might be properly defined as *architectura civilis*. The collections of Faulhaber and Furttenbach were – besides the items of the *mechanica* – more aligned in their holdings of instruments for drawing and measurement, treatises concerning military and technical design, and drawings and prints of fortification works. But based on Furttenbach's 1641 *Architectura privata*, it seems that his collection was much more extensive than that of Faulhaber. What is more, whereas Faulhaber's holdings were largely focused on objects and the latest military knowledge that stemmed from the Netherlands, Furttenbach had drawn the core parts of his collection from Italy.[101]

Still, the underlying order of the two *Kunstkammern* followed a similar logic, as revealed in the printed *Architectura privata* and Faulhaber's *Geheime Kunstkammer.* Although the *Architectura privata* contains an entire description of Furttenbach's private house, as well as etchings, it is based upon on entries that inform the reader of different categories of knowledge. Beyond this, Furttenbach made sure to link the objects described in the entries with symbols on the printed floor plan, thus enabling the reader to complete a virtual tour of the art chamber.[102] This framework would have enticed the contemporary reader to visit the *Kunstkammer*, as well as to buy Furttenbach's various treatises, which were extensively cited in the entries. Within the entries, Furttenbach also highlighted his connections with the most famous engineers of his time.[103] This strategy seems closely linked to Faulhaber's offerings of specific secret knowledge as provided in his *Geheime Kunstkammer.*

In professionalising the genre of the *Geheime Kunstkammer* in form and style, Furttenbach succeeded in bringing heightened attention to the knowledge it contained, while also memorializing himself and his family.[104] In 1704, 37 years after

100 Furttenbach, *Architectura Privata*, 37-38.

101 In particular, regarding Furttenbach`s formative travels, see Lazardzig, *Theatermaschine und Festungsbau*, 115-123; Zaugg, '"bey den Jtalienern"'.

102 See Lazardzig, *Theatermaschine und Festungsbau*, 127.

103 For example, the entry of a lifting device, the so-called 'Argano', notes that it was invented by Dominico Fontana, improved by Galileo Galilei, and presented by Galilei to Furttenbach in 1617 in Florence. Furttenbach, *Architectura Privata*, 37-38. In detail, see Siebenhüner, 'Things That Matter'.

104 On the self-fashioning and *memoria* of Furttenbach, see Lazardzig, *Theatermaschine und Festungsbau*, 127, and Siebenhüner, 'Entwerfen', 49.

Furttenbach's death, the famous architect Leonhard Christoph Sturm published his *Geöffnete Raritäten- und Naturalien-Kammer*, in which he gave a historic description of Furttenbach's *Kunstkammer* and tellingly characterized the collection as 'oddities of models of all sorts of artificial machines and buildings'.[105] Sturm thus understood Furttenbach's *Kunstkammer* as an extended comprehension of mechanics and architecture. The writer and geographer Martin Zeiller also described Furttenbach's collection. In his *Topographia Sueviae*, published 1643, he described the *Kunstkammer* as containing 'some models, instruments, architectural drawings; full of rare and strange natural and artificial things'.[106]

While further research on Furttenbach's and Faulhaber's *Kunstkammern* is still needed, we might safely deduce that the two technical designers of Ulm were not necessarily in competition with one another, but were merely both highly engaged in developing collections of mechanical-architectural knowledge and creating places for the sharing, teaching and marketing of this information. While the collections were contemporaneous and shared similar features, they were established by the two men in very different ways.[107] In future research, it would be interesting to compare the specialized collections of Faulhaber and Furttenbach with the more classic *Kunstkammer* of Christoph Weickmann (1617–1681) in Ulm.[108]

Faulhaber's Legacy and the Afterlife of His Collection

According to Martin Zeiller's *Topographia Sueviae* (1643), the *Kunstkammer* of Johannes Faulhaber was well-known in its day in Ulm and abroad. Zeiller tells us that following Johannes Faulhaber's death (10 September 1635), the private portion of the collection – including models, drawings and 'rare mathematical and mechanical instruments' – was inherited by his son, Johann Matthäus (1604-1683), who kept

105 Sturm, *Raritäten- und Naturalien-Kammer*, 167: 'curieusen Modellen von allerhand künstlichen Machinen und Gebäuden'. Upon the death of Furttenbach the Elder, the art chamber was transferred to the ancestral seat of castle Leutkirch in 1667 by Gabriel Furtenbach of Leutkirch. See Berthold, 'Joseph Furttenbach', 179. Only a few objects of this collection are known today.

106 Zeiller, *Topographia Sueviae*, 203: 'so mit mancherley Modellen / Jnstrumenten / Architectonischen Handrissen; rar- vnnd wunderlichen / Natur- vnd künstlichen Sachen besetzt'. However, architecture was not the primary focus, as Günther has recently suggested. See Günther, 'Joseph Furttenbachs Architekturmuseum', 55. On the specifics of this collection, see Lazardzig, *Theatermaschine und Festungsbau*, 123-132, and Siebenhüner, 'Entwerfen'.

107 Concerning advertising knowledge by Furttenbach, see the forthcoming study by Rößler, 'Wissensmarketing der Frühen Neuzeit'.

108 See Bujok, 'Die Ulmer Kunstkammer'.

these objects as a 'beloved treasure'.[109] As given in the *Specification*, most of the civic models passed to the ownership of the town council. Unfortunately, we do not know how Johann Matthäus – who acted as the '*Bauschreiber*' and '*Visierer*' in Ulm, as well as superintendent of the civic brewery, mills and peat digging – used the collection or whether he made it accessible to interested members of the public.[110] But, according to handwritten and illustrated manuscripts, a portion of which he obviously inherited from his father, we can deduce that Johann Matthäus was dedicated to enriching his knowledge in the fields of mechanics and architecture.[111]

Still, by the mid-eighteenth century, Faulhaber's former *Kunstkammer* was no longer well-known outside of Ulm. Leonhard Christoph Sturm, for example, failed to mention it in his famous *Geöffnete Raritäten- und Naturalien-Kammer* (1704), although he did include other collections in Ulm, including that of Joseph Furttenbach the Elder. It is through an exacting study of two essentially unstudied sources, the *Geheime Kunstkammer* and the *Specification*, that this article has attempted to reconstruct the exceptional collection, one of the earliest known *Kunstkammern* of an engineer in the German territories. As demonstrated here, Faulhaber's collection was mostly dedicated to the fields of mechanics, and he used his collection as part of his well-known school of mathematics.

The scope and influence of Faulhaber's physical collection is further complicated by its association with several printed lists, the purpose of which was to provide an overview of Faulhaber's offerings and to encourage personal encounters between the vendor and client. While the public nature of Faulhaber's activities, and the commercial structure he built up around his collection, may seem incongruous with modern notions of knowledge acquisition and academic study, this practice was very much in keeping with contemporary norms. Faulhaber's peer and contemporary, Joseph Furttenbach, also advertised his collection and his knowledge in print. Thirteen years after Faulhaber had published his *Geheime Kunstkammer* (1628), Furttenbach published his own elaborate description, which was supplemented by wonderfully printed etchings of his estate, including his *Kunst- and Rüstkammer*. What is more, each of the printed *Kunstkammern* were dedicated to a patron of

109 Zeiller, *Topographia Sueviae*, 202-204, describes the art chamber of Furttenbach in greater detail. This is probably not coincidential, as Zeiller is named in the *Architectura privata* (1641) as the 'author's [Joseph Furttenbach] beloved and intimate friend' ('deß Authoris sehr lieber vnd wolvertrawter Freund'). See Furttenbach, *Architectura*.

110 Hawlitschek, *Johann Faulhaber 1580-1635*, 358.

111 For instance, Bayerische Staatsbibliothek, Munich (BSB)-Hss Cod.icon. 229 a, BSB-Hss Cod.icon. 229 b. Further study is needed on volumes of manuscripts and drawings preserved in the BSB, which were inherited by several members of the Faulhabian dynasty of engineers (including Johannes, Johannes Matthäus and Anton Faulhaber). See BSB-Hss Cod.icon. 225 a, 225 b, 226, 227 a, 227 b, 228, 230, BSB-Hss Cgm 4532 a, as well as the volumes of manuscripts and drawings preserved in the town archive of Ulm.

the arts of the higher nobility. Faulhaber's book was dedicated to count Wratislaw I of Fürstenberg (1584-1631), later president of the Aulic Council in Vienna, and Furttenbach's was granted to Maximilian Willibald of Waldburg-Wolfegg (1604-1667), imperial marshal and Bavarian state holder of the Upper Palatinate, as well as the founder of the well-known collection of Wolfegg.[112] But as shown, Faulhaber's idea to publish his *Kunstkammer* was inspired by *secreta* literature, which he conceptualized as advertising knowledge in the sense of a 'professor of secrets'. We should assume that Faulhaber was reliant on visitors who paid him for various mechanical and architectural 'secrets' he kept in his *Kunstkammer*.

The study of the *Kunstkammern* of early modern engineers is revealing in what it tells us about collection practices, knowledge acquisition and, more generally, knowledge transfer and education. The *Kunstkammer* of Johannes Faulhaber was a place of 'international' technology transfer, whereby some of the newest advancements in Dutch military technology were introduced into a German context, and which in turn were further disseminated through Faulhaber's printed lists and treatises. Consequently, the place of the *Kunstkammer* was not only physical and spatial; the knowledge it contained was also connected to the 'places' of Faulhaber's publications – especially his *Geheime Kunstkammer* – and the 'places' of where the ideas and models contained within were initially conceived.

Bibliography

Manuscript Sources

Ludwigsburg, Staatsarchiv

D 55 Bü 40: Johann Matthäus Faulhaber, *Specification*, handwritten inventory of the *Kunstkammer* of Johannes Faulhaber, 1 April 1636

Stuttgart, Hauptstaatsarchiv

A20a Bü 23: Johann Schuckard, Inventory of the Württembergian *Kunstkammer*, fascicle 8: Box N and O, 1705/1723

Ulm, Stadtarchiv

Furttenbach H 5: Joseph Furttenbach, *Architectura Vniuersale, Erster Tail, Darinnen Angedeüt wirt, waß Innerhalb einer Jarsfrüst, in deß Haÿ: Reichs Statt Vlm, An merlaÿ Gebäwen, zue Krieg, vnnd frid, zu wasser vnd Land, zum Leben, vnnd Kranckhen Personen, zuunderhalten, Ist Auffgebawen, Coregirt, vnnd Repariert worden. Alles auß Aigener Experienza, Im werckh selbsten, vffgericht, Erbawen, delinirt, vnnd hiezugegen*, 1632.

Vienna, Österreichische Nationalbibliothek

112 On Faulhaber and the count, see Hawlitschek, *Johann Faulhaber 1580-1635*, 96.

265941-E: Johann Carl, *Beschreibung und Abbildung der Artillerie. Wie diesselbe der Durchleuchtigste Hochgebohrne Fürst und Herr, Herr Mauritius von Nassaw Christmiltest gedächtnus ins werckh gerichtet und zu Feld geführet, auch von den verainigten Niederlanden annoch unverendert gebraucht wird*, seventeenth century.

Printed Sources

Becker, Sebastian, 'Der Transfer technischen Wissens in der Frühen Neuzeit: Vorüberlegungen', in Sabina Brevaglieri and Matthias Schnettger (eds), *Transferprozesse zwischen dem Alten Reich und Italien im 17. Jahrhundert. Wissenskonfigurationen – Akteure – Netzwerke* (Bielefeld: Transcript, 2018), 29-60.

Berthold, Margot, 'Joseph Furttenbach 1591-1667. Architekturtheoretiker und Stadtbaumeister in Ulm. Ein Beitrag zur Theater- und Kunstgeschichte', PhD diss., Ludwig-Maximilians-Universität, 1953.

Beßler, Gabriele, 'Vormoderne städtische Sammlungen: Erinnerung und Identifikation', in Joachim J. Halbekann, Ellen Widder and Sabine von Heusinger (eds), *Stadt zwischen Erinnerungsbewahrung und Gedächtnisverlust* (Ostfildern: Jan Thorbecke, 2015), 301-332.

Biagioli, Mario, 'From Print to Patents: Living on Instruments in Early Modern Europe', *History of Science* 44.2 (2006), 139-186.

Birembaut, Arthur, 'L'exposition de modèles de machines à Paris en 1683', *Revue d'histoire des sciences et de leurs applications* 20.2 (1967), 141-158.

Boillot, Joseph, *Modelles, artifices de feu et divers instrumens de guerre, avec les moyens de s'en prévaloir pour assiéger, battre, surprendre et deffendre toutes places* (Chaumont-en-Bassigny: Mareschal, 1598).

Brink, Claudia, *Arte et Marte. Kriegskunst und Kunstliebe im Herrscherbild des 15. und 16. Jahrhunderts in Italien* (Munich and Berlin: Deutscher Kunstverlag, 2000).

Büchi, Tobias, *Fortifikationsliteratur des 16. und 17. Jahrhunderts: Traktate deutscher Sprache im europäischen Kontext* (Basel: Schwabe, 2015).

Büchi, Tobias, '"Synopsis architectonicæ" von Henning Hasemann', *Scholion* 10 (2016), 195-205.

Bujok, Elke, 'Die Ulmer Kunstkammer Christoph Weickmanns (1617-1681) und der Erwerb seiner arabischen Mumie', *Ulm und Oberschwaben* 53/54 (2007), 180-191.

Bürger, Stefan, *Architectura Militaris. Festungsbautraktate des 17. Jahrhunderts von Specklin bis Sturm*, Kunstwissenschaftliche Studien 176 (Berlin: Deutscher Kunstverlag, 2013).

Davids, Karel, *The Rise and Decline of Dutch Technological Leadership: Technology, Economy and Culture in the Netherlands, 1350-1800*, 2 vols (Leiden: Brill, 2008).

de Jong, M.A.G., 'Militaire hervormingen in het Staatse leger en de opbouw van het wapenbedrijf, 1585-1621', *BMGN – Low Countries Historical Review* 118.4 (2003), 467-493.

Doppelmayr, Johann Gabriel, *Historische Nachricht von den Nürnbergischen Mathematicis und Künstlern* [...] (Nuremberg: Peter Conrad Monaths, 1730).

Dupré, Sven and Michael Korey, 'Optical Objects in the Dresden Kunstkammer: Lucas Brunn and the Courtly Display of Knowledge', in Giorgio Strano et al. (eds), *European Collections of Scientific Instruments, 1550-1750* (Leiden and Boston: Brill, 2009), 61-85.

Eamon, William, *Science and the Secrets of Nature: Books of Secrets in Medieval and Early Modern Culture* (Princeton: Princeton University Press, 1996).

Faulhaber, Johannes, *Academia Algebræ, Darinnen die miraculosische Inventiones / zu den höchsten Cossen weiters continuirt und profitiert werden* [...] (Augsburg: Johann Ulrich Schönigk, 1631).

Faulhaber, Johannes, *Anderer Theil der Ingenieurs Schul: Darinnen die Regular Fortification, sampt den Aussenwercken / durch und ohne Rechnung mit newen Inventionibus gelhrt werden* [...] (Ulm: Saur, 1633).

Faulhaber, Johannes, *Arithmetischer Cubiccossischer Lustgarten: Darinnen Hundert und Sechtzig Blümlein / das ist auserlesner schöner künstlicher Exempel mit Newen Inventionibus gepflanzet werden* [...] (Tübingen: Cellius, 1604).

Faulhaber, Johannes, *Continuatio, deß Newen Mathematischen Kunstspiegels. Das ist Privilegierte Newe Inventiones, Wissenschafften und Secreten von mancherley Wunderkünste / [et]c. Welche der gantzen Landschaff / deß Hochlöblichen Herzogthumbs Württember / neben deß Heiligen ReichsStatt Ulm angeboten werden* [...] (Tübingen: Werlin, 1620).

Faulhaber, Johannes, *Ein Mathematische Newe Invention, Einer sehr nutzlichen und geschmeidigen Hauß oder Handmühlin: Welche gleichwol kein Kampff oder Schwingrad hat / aber dannoch gut zart Mehl mahlet* [...] (Augsburg: Michelspacher, 1616).

Faulhaber, Johannes, *Ein sehr nützlicher new erfundener Gebrauch eines niderländischen Instruments zum Abmessen und Grundtlegen mit sehr geschwindem Vortheil zu Practiciren* (Frankfurt am Main: Humm, 1610).

Faulhaber, Johannes, *Erste Teutsche Lection: so er im löblichen Fürstenthumb Württemberg offentlich angeschlagen und gehalten Welche begreifft das Prognosticon vom Gog und Magog* [...] (Augspurg: Franck, 1621).

Faulhaber, Johannes, *Geheime Kunstkammer. Darinnen hundert allerhand Kriegs Stratagemata, auch andere Unerhörte Secreta, und Machinae mirabiles zusehe / dergleichen in Europa (respectivè) wenig zu finden* (Ulm: Saur, 1628).

Faulhaber, Johannes, *Ingenieurs Schul Dritter Theil. Darinnen Die Irregular Figuren zu Fortificirn, durch unnd ohne Rechnung mit underschidlichen Newen Inventionibus gelehrt werden* [...] (Ulm: Saur, 1633).

Faulhaber, Johannes, *Ingenieurs-Schul, Erster Theil: Darinnen durch den Canonem Logarithmicum alle Planische Triangel zur fortification, oder Architectura Militari, Optica, Geodaesia, Geometria, &c. gelährt wird* [...] (Frankfurt am Main: Stolzenberger, 1630).

Faulhaber, Johannes, *Ingenieurs Schul Vierdter Teil. Von Fortificatione Practica Offensiva Et Defensiva* [...] (Ulm: Saur, 1633).

Faulhaber, Johannes, *Mechanische Verbesserung einer Alten Roßmühle / welche vor diesem der Königliche Ingenieur Augustinus Ramellus, & c. an tag geben* [...] (Ulm: Saur, 1625).

Faulhaber, Johannes, *Newe Geometrische und Perspectivische Inventiones Etlicher sonderbahrer Instrument / die zum Perspectivischen Grundreissen der Pasteyen unnd Vestungen / wie auch zum Planimetrischen Grundlegen der Stätt / Feldläger und Landtschafften / deßgleichen zur Büchsenmeisterey sehr nützlich unnd gebrauchsam seynd* (Frankfurt am Main: Humm/Richter, 1610).

Faulhaber, Johannes, *Newer Mathematischer Kunstspiegel: Darinnen fürnemblich dreyerley Stück zusehen. Als erstlich / ein gründtliche Verzeichnuß / der wunderbarlichen Natur unnd Eigenschafften / etlicher Zahlen / Danielis / und der Offenbahrung Sanct Johannis. Zum andern / ein newerfundner gebrauch / Daniel Specklins Instruments / zu abmessung der höhe / tiefe / weite und breyte* [...] *Zum driten / ein Kurtzer doch klärlicher Bericht / vonn einem sechsspitzigen ProportionalZirckel* [...] (Ulm: Barth, 1612).

Faulhaber, Johannes, *Warhafftige und Gründliche Solution oder Aufflößung einer Hochwichtigen Frag. Wie mann die Fristen: welche ohne Interesse / auff gewisse Ziel und Zeit hinauß zubezahlen verfallen / wann manns auff einmahl vorher mit Abzug eines gewissen percento, einfachen Interesse deß Jars anticipirt oder Baar vor ein bezahlt / Abrechnen soll / das nit Interesse auff Interesse unvermerckt darunder einschleiche* (Ulm: Meder, 1618).

Faulhaber, Johannes, *Weitere Continuation des Privilegierten Mathematischen Kunstspiegels / darinnen alle Ingenieur Bawmeister / vnd andere Künstler Newe Inventiones, so bißhero für vnmüglich gehalten worden / Augenscheinlich sehen könden* (Tübingen: Werlin, 1626).

Faulhaber, Johannes, *Zwey und Viertzig Secreta / welche er in deß H. ReichsStatt Augspurg offentlich zu Affigieren / und männigklich zulehren von dem Löbichen Magistrat Gnädige Bewilligung erlangt hat* (Augsburg: Franck, 1621).

Fitzner, Sebastian, *Architekturzeichnungen der deutschen Renaissance. Funktion und Bildlichkeit zeichnerischer Produktion 1500-1650* (Cologne: Modern Academic Publishing, 2015), doi: http://dx.doi.org/10.16994/bac.

Fitzner, Sebastian and Lars Weitemeiner, 'Das Frontispiz', in Joseph Furttenbach, *Mechanische Reißladen*, FONTES. E-Quellen und Dokumente zur Kunstgeschichte, 2017, doi: https://doi.org/10.11588/artdok.00005383, 38-50.

Freitag, Adam, *Architectura Militaris Nova et aucta, oder Newe vermehrte Fortification Von Regular Vestungen, von Irregular Vestungen und Hussen wercken, Von praxi Offensiva und Defensiva: auff die neweste Niederländische praxin gerichtet und beschrieben* (Leiden: Elzevier, 1631).

Furttenbach, Johann Gabriel and Johann Baptista Furttenbach, *Inventarium, Vieler Nutzbarn immer Denckwürdigen so wohl von Militar: als Civil: auch Navalischen Gebäuen und dergleichen Architectonischen Modellen* [...] (Augsburg: Schultes, 1666).

Furttenbach, Joseph, *Architectura Privata Das ist: Gründtliche Beschreibung Neben conterfetischer Vorstellung inn was Form und Manier ein gar Irregular, Burgerliches Wohn-Hauß* (Augsburg: Schultes, 1641).

Gnehm, Michael and Tobias Büchi, 'Johannes Faulhaber', in Werner Oechslin, Tobias Büchi and Martin Pozsgai (eds), *Architekturtheorie im deutschsprachigen Kulturraum 1486-1648* (Basel: Colmena, 2018), 487-498.

Greyerz, Kaspar von, Kim Siebenhüner and Roberto Zaugg (eds), *Joseph Furttenbach, Lebenslauff 1652-1664* (Cologne: Böhlau, 2013).

Grote, Andreas (ed.), *Macrocosmos in microcosmo: Die Welt in der Stube. Zur Geschichte des Sammelns 1450 bis 1800* (Opladen: Leske + Budrich, 1994).

Günther, Hubertus, 'Joseph Furttenbachs Architekturmuseum: Ein Rundgang durch das Haus des Ulmer Stadtbaumeisters', in Simon Paulus and Klaus Jan Philipp (eds), *'Um 1600' – Das Neue Lusthaus in Stuttgart und sein architekturgeschichtlicher Kontext* (Berlin: LIT Verlag, 2017), 39-58.

Häberle, A., 'Das Schicksal der Ulmer Zeughäuser, des einstigen Stolzes der Reichsstadt', *Ulmer Historische Blätter* 6 (1927), 7-8.

Hahlweg, Werner, *Die Heeresreform der Oranier und die Antike: Studien zur Geschichte des Kriegswesens der Niederlande, Deutschlands, Frankreichs, Englands, Italiens, Spaniens und der Schweiz vom Jahre 1589 bis zum Dreißigjährigen Kriege* (Osnabrück: Biblio, 1987).

Hawlitschek, Kurt, *Johann Faulhaber 1580-1635. Eine Blütezeit der mathematischen Wissenschaften in Ulm* (Ulm: Stadtbibliothek, 1995).

Hawlitschek, Kurt, *Johann Faulhaber 1580-1635 und René Descartes 1596-1650* (Ulm: Stadtbibliothek, 2006).

Hawlitschek, Kurt, 'Niederländische Mathematik und Technik. Ihr Einfluß auf Ulm im 17. Jahrhundert', *Ulm und Oberschwaben* 51 (2000), 23-41.

Jütte, Daniel, *The Age of Secrecy: Jews, Christians, and the Economy of Secrets, 1400-1800* (New Haven: Yale University Press, 2015).

Keßler, Franz, *Unterschiedliche bißhero mehrern Theils Secreta Oder verborgene geheime Künste: Deren die Erste genant / Ortforschung* [...] *Die ander / Wasserharnisch* [...] *Die dritte / Luffthosen* [...] *Samt beygefügtem wolerdachten Schwimgürtel* [...] (Oppenheim: Johann Theodor de Bry, 1616).

Königer, Ernst, *Das Kleine Nürnberger Zeughaus* (Nuremberg: Germanisches Nationalmuseum, 1967).

Krüger, Jenneke H. J., 'Actoren en factoren achter het wiskundecurriculum sinds 1600: Actors and Factors behind the Mathematics Curriculum since 1600', PhD diss., Universiteit Utrecht, 2014.

Lazardzig, Jan, *Theatermaschine und Festungsbau: Paradoxien der Wissensproduktion im 17. Jahrhundert* (Berlin: Akademie Verlag, 2007).

Lazardzig, Jan and Hole Rößler (eds), *Technologies of Theatre: Joseph Furttenbach and the Transfer of Mechanical Knowledge in Early Modern Theatre Cultures* (Frankfurt am Main: Vittorio Klosterman, 2016).

Marolois, Samuel, *Fortification ou architecture militaire tant offensive que defensive* (The Hague: Hondius, 1615).

Martens, Pieter and Dirk van de Vijver, 'Engineers and the Circulation of Knowledge in the Spanish Netherlands', in Sven Dupré et al. (eds), *Embattled Territory: The Circulation of Knowledge in the Spanish Netherlands* (Ghent: Academia Press, 2015), 73-106.

Meyer, Torsten, 'Perspektiven der Popularisierung von Technik in der Frühen Neuzeit (1500-1800)', in Lars Bluma, Karl Picol and Wolfhard Weber (eds), *Technikvermittlung und Technikpopularisierung. Historische und didaktische Perspektiven* (Münster and New York: Waxmann, 2004), 145-170.

Neumann, Hartwig, *Das Zeughaus. Die Entwicklung eines Bautyps von der spätmittelalterlichen Rüstkammer zum Arsenal im deutschsprachigen Bereich vom XV. bis XIX. Jahrhundert*, 2 vols (Bonn: Bernard und Graefe, 1992).

Parker, Geoffrey, *The Military Revolution: Military Innovation and the Rise of the West, 1500-1800* (Cambridge: Cambridge University Press, 1988).

Popplow, Marcus, 'Court Mathematicians, Rosicrucians, and Engineering Experts: The German Translation of Guidobaldo del Monte's *Mechanicorum liber* by Daniel Mögling (1629)', in Antonio Becchi, Domenico Bertoloni Meli and Enrico Gamba (eds), *Guidobaldo del Monte (1545-1607): Theory and Practice of the Mathematical Disciplines from Urbino to Europe* (Berlin: Edition Open Access, Max Planck Institute for the History of Science, 2013), https://www.mprl-series.mpg.de/proceedings/4/.

Popplow, Marcus, 'Models of Machines: A "Missing Link" between Early Modern Engineering and Mechanics?', Max-Planck-Institut für Wissenschaftsgeschichte: Preprint 225 (2002).

Popplow, Marcus, 'Technisches Modell', in Friedrich Jaeger (ed.), *Enzyklopädie der Neuzeit*, 16 vols (Stuttgart: Metzler, 2005-2012), vol. 13, 298-303.

Ramelli, Agostino, *Le diverse et artificiose macchine del capitano Agostino Ramelli* (Paris, 1588).

Reith, Reinhold, 'Know-how, Technologietransfer und die Arcana Artis im Mitteleuropa der Frühen Neuzeit', *Early Science and Medicine* 10.3 (2005), 349-377.

Rößler, Hole, 'Wissensmarketing der Frühen Neuzeit. Joseph Furttenbach (1591-1667) und die Vermarktung von technischem Wissen', forthcoming.

Rott, Herbert Wilhelm, 'Die Rüst- und Kunstkammer Joseph Furttenbachs in Ulm', in Hanno-Walter Kruft (ed.), *'vom Schönen gerührt ...'. Kunstliteratur des 17. und 18. Jahrhunderts aus Beständen der Bibliothek Oettingen-Wallerstein* (Huisheim: Verein Rieser Kulturtage, 1988), 13-17.

Schenk, Gerrit J., 'Geheimnis – Herrschaft – Wissen. Theoretisches und praktisches Wissen in der frühneuzeitlichen Hofkultur am Beispiel von Beständen der Darmstädter

Universitäts- und Landesbibliothek', lecture delivered on the occasion of the opening of the exhibition *Geheimnis – Herrschaft – Wissen. Forscherdrang hessischer Landgrafen'*, Darmstadt, 17 July 2017, accessed 10 January 2018, http://tuprints.ulb.tu-darmstadt.de/6760/.

Schock, Flemming, 'Die imaginäre Kunstkammer. Frühneuzeitliche Sammlungsräume zwischen Materialität und Textualität', in Karin Friedrich (ed.), *Die Erschließung des Raumes. Konstruktion, Imagination und Darstellung von Räumen und Grenzen im Barockzeitalter*, 2 vols (Wiesbaden: Harrassowitz, 2014), vol. 2, 545-562.

Schmidt, Suzanne Karr, *Interactive and Sculptural Printmaking in the Renaissance* (Leiden: Brill, 2018).

Schneider, Ivo, *Johannes Faulhaber 1580-1635. Rechenmeister in einer Welt des Umbruchs* (Basel: Birkhäuser, 1993).

Siebenhüner, Kim, 'Entwerfen, Modelle bauen, ausstellen. Joseph Furttenbach und seine Rüst- und Modellkammer', in Kaspar von Greyerz, Kim Siebenhüner and Roberto Zaugg (eds), *Joseph Furttenbach, Lebenslauff 1652-1664* (Cologne: Böhlau, 2013), 45-65.

Siebenhüner, Kim, 'Things That Matter: Zur Geschichte der materiellen Kultur in der Frühneuzeitforschung', *Zeitschrift für Historische Forschung* 42 (2015), 373-409.

Sturm, Leonhard Christian, *Die Geöffnete Raritäten- und Naturalien-Kammer: / Worinnen Der Galanten Jugend / andern Curieusen und Reisenden gewiesen wird / wie sie Galerien, Kunst- und Raritäten-Kammern mit Nutzen besehen und davon raisoniren sollen.* [...], *Des Geöffneten Ritter-Platzes Dritter Theil* (Hamburg: Schiller, 1704).

Trautmann, Andreas, 'Heillose Groschen in wohlfeilen Zeiten: Ein wirtschaftsgeschichtlicher Kommentar', in Kaspar von Greyerz, Kim Siebenhüner and Roberto Zaugg (eds), *Joseph Furttenbach, Lebenslauff 1652-1664* (Cologne: Böhlau, 2013), 67-85.

Ufano, Diego, *Tratado dela artilleria y uso della platicado por el capitan Diego Ufano en las guerras de Flandes* (Brüssels: Momarte, 1613).

van Nimwegen, Olaf, *The Dutch Army and the Military Revolutions, 1588-1688* (Woodbridge: Boydell, 2010).

van Nimwegen, Olaf, 'Maurits van Nassau and Siege Warfare (1590-1597)', in Marco van der Hoeven (ed.), *Exercise of Arms: Warfare in the Netherlands, 1568-1648* (Leiden: Brill, 1997), 113-152.

Weyermann, Albrecht, *Neue historisch = biographisch = artistische Nachrichten von Gelehrten und Künstlern, auch alten und neuen adelichen und bürgerlichen Familien aus der vormaligen Reichsstadt Ulm* (Ulm: Stettinischen Buchhandlung, 1829).

Wijn, Jan W., 'Het krijgswezen in den tijd van prins Maurits', PhD diss., Rijks-Universiteit, 1934.

Zaugg, Roberto, '"bey den Jtalienern recht sinnreiche Gedancken [...] gespürt". Joseph Furttenbach als kultureller Vermittler', in Kaspar von Greyerz, Kim Siebenhüner and Roberto Zaugg (eds), *Joseph Furttenbach, Lebenslauff 1652-1664* (Cologne: Böhlau, 2013), 25-43.

Zeiller, Martin, *Topographia Sueviae* [...] (Frankfurt am Main: Matthäus Merian, 1643).
Zweckbronner, Gerhard, 'Rechenmeister, Ingenieur und Bürger zu Ulm. Johann Faulhaber (1580-1635) in seiner Zeit', *Technikgeschichte* 47.2 (1980), 114-132.

About the Authors

Paul Brakmann is a research associate in the Research Centre 'The Technical Image' in the Department of Art and Visual History and the Hermann von Helmholtz Centre for Cultural Techniques at Humboldt University, Berlin. His interests include the visual culture of early modern science and technology, and the social history of photography.
Sebastian Fitzner was Assistant Professor of European and American Architectural History, 1500-1800 and visiting Professor for Art History, in the Art History Department of the Freie Universität Berlin. His primary research concerns Northern Renaissance architecture and early modern material culture. His forthcoming book is dedicated to 'Hercules's house' and princely architectural model collections in Kassel, Berlin, St. Petersburg and Paris, 1700-1900.

Appendix

Here follows a transcription of the inventory of the *Kunstkammer* of Johannes Faulhaber (5 May 1580-10 September 1635), which was part of his estate and school of mathematics at Platzgasse 4 in Ulm. The inventory consists of two parts. The first section documents those 'architectural and machine models' that were entrusted to Johannes Faulhaber by the town council. The second part (beginning on folio 3r) documents the 'models, machines, and drawing and measuring instruments' that Johannes Faulhaber had commissioned at his own expense, and which were displayed in his private *Kunstkammer*. Both parts of the inventory were issued on 1 April 1636 by Johann Matthäus Faulhaber, the son of Johannes Faulhaber. The inventory is written in brown ink on paper and folded into a non-paginated brochure. The transcription is to the letter, and additions by the authors are marked in brackets. Indistinct readings are denoted with brackets and a question mark. Illegible words are denoted with brackets and ellipsis. Source of the original: State archive of Ludwigsburg / *Ludwigsburg Staatsarchiv D 55 Bü 40.*

[folio 1r]

[Cover sheet designated with number] 7

[folio 1v]

[folio 2r]

Specification vnd Verzaÿchnuß.
Der Jenigen Modellen vnd Maschinen, welche vß Befelch weÿlund der Edlen, vösten, fürsichtigen vnd Wolweÿßen Heren, Heren Cunrad Krafften Raths Ölthern etc. Heren Hanß Krafften der dritt Burgermaistern etc. Heren Hanß Schachen etc. vnd Heren Sigmund Schleichern etc. damals Stättrechnern, als der vier *Deputierten* über daß *Fortification* wesen etc. uff eines Ers: Raths etc. kosten gemacht, vnd Johann Faulhabern *Ingenieuren* See:[ligen] solche in seinen hauß uff zubehalten, vnd zu verWahren anvertrauert
Visierungen oder Modell der Vier Pasteÿen mit ihren *Ravelinen*, welche über die Dhonau nach ihrer Excellentz Printz Moritzen von Oranien hochlöblichsten Gedächtnuß etc. vnderschreibenen *Original* abriß hat alles gebawet werden, vnd alberait was den berüembten *Ingenieur vnd Capitain* heren *Jan v[on] ValcKhenborch* etc. vff den land abgesteckgt gewesen etc.
Ein Modell von der Dhonau brugg, wie solche von holtzwerkg gemakgt, von herpel dhuren biß an Mitlern Pfeiler köndte gemacht werden, vnter der Portten ist ein Wolffsgrub angedeutt.
Ein ander Modell einer gehenckhten Brugge.
Noch ein Modell von der Dhonau Brugge, wie solche von Stainwerkh gewölbt zumachen.
Modell des bösten Pfeilers oder Jochs an der Dhonau brugg, wie darumb mit starkhen doppelten Tillen ein kast zumachen, und ein geschöpfwerkg daran zurichten, das Wasser vmb des Pfeiler auß zu schöpfen, vnd den selben Truckhen zu legen, daß man Ihne nicht vnder vnterfahren, oder einen neuen Pfeiler machen könde.
Vnderschidene Röst vnter daß Wasser zu sinckhen, vnd drauf zu bawen.
Visierung der Spitahl Mühle
Visierung des Glockhen hauß im Münster, wie man voretlich Jahren deß vefaulte Gebälkh herauß gethan etc.

[folio 2v]

Modell des Geschöpfs beÿ der Walckg zwischen dem frauen vnd Ganß Thor, welches man zu außgrabung deß fundaments, vnd aus schöpffung des Wassers an grosen Wuhor daselbst hatte angericht, dardurch ein Ers:[samen] Raht etc. etlich fl. 200 ersparth etc.
Ein Zug Ehl, wie die Pföhl auß d[er] Thonau vnd Ihler herauß geEhlrt werden.

Ein Zug, mit welchem vermitelst eines eÿsenen Rechen, die grose [...] vnd Schemen vß den Stattgräben mit [...] außzuwössern.
Modell eines Salpeter Kessels.
Ein Stuckh einer *Cortin*, daran ein Portall vnd Bruggen übern Graben.
Brugg über ein *Ravelin* mit einer Schnellbrugg vnd Gatter.
daß hornwerckh vnd die zwo Ober Pasteÿen, welche haben sollen über die Thonau gelegt werden.
Modell wie daß egige der Obern Pasteÿ vor dem Herdprugg Thor im fundament wieder daß vngestüm anlauffen vnd Gewallt, der Dhonau zu bewahren.
dreÿerleÿ Manieren von däm[m]en oder schlochten ins wasser zu bauen.
Zweÿ *Mantekens* oder Khnie Schantz Körblin für die Mußquetieren wie die in Niderland in Belägerungen gebraucht werden.
Brugg über d[er] halben Mohn vor den herdprugg thor
daß hornwerkh zwischen der Ersten vnd andern Pasteÿ vor dem Glöggler Thor welches Ao 1635 vff *ortinantz* heren *General Major* Schneidenwinds etc. gemacht worden, Vff Befelch der Bauwheren etc. in 2 Modell gebracht etc.

[folio 3r]

Specification vnd Verzaÿchnuß.
Der Jenigen Modellen, Maschinen vnd Instrumenten, welche Johan Faulhaben See:[ligen] vff seinen Kosten hat machen lassen, vnd in seiner Kunst kam[m]er zu sehen sein etc.
Ein schön Modell einer verbesserten Rossmühlen.
Ein schön Modell einer Gewicht Mühlen.
Newe *Invention* einer Roß: hand: vnd hauß Mühlen beÿsamen in einem Modell.
Ein Mühle mit einem Tretttrad, vnd mit einem auffgnepfenden[?] Schwung.
Hand Mühle mit zween hangenden Schwenckhlen.
Hand Mühle mit einen ligenden Schwungrad.
Hand Mühle mit einer Schieb stangen.
Der Schweizer hand Mühle Abrissen[?].
Eine Newe[?] *Invention* einer leichten Mühlen.
Eine kleine hand Mühle.
Ein schön Modell einer new Inventirten Pulver Mühlen mit einen grossen Trettrad.
Dreÿ Modell einer leichten Pulver Mühlen,
Ein schöne Segemühlen. Item ein thögl einer Segemühlen.
Ein kugerl Mühle.
Visierung der Newen[?] Wassere Mühlen, welche die hollender vor herzogenbusch zu auß schöpffung deß Wassers in vertrunckhen[?] land gebraucht haben.

Ein grosses Modell eines Wasserwerkhs mit Kupfern trögen, Kupfern Rinnen, vnd einen Kupfern Rad, *repraesenti*erendt den [...] *motum perpetuum*.
Ein großes Modell eines Wasserwerkhs mit vier gevierdten Pompen.
Ein anders Rinen Wasserwerkh.

[folio 3v]

Modell wie daß gantze Werckh einer Wasser stuben nach begeren über vnd vnder sich zu schraufen.
Wie ein Wasser auß den fundament ohne andern Kosten zuerschöpfen, mit hülff eines fließenden wassers
Wasser Arch.[?] Ein *Speculation* wie in einen Casten mit Lufft Röhren vnter einen stillstehenden wasser zu bawen.
Vnderschidne wunderliche Wasser Künsten in Gläsern
Wie von einen Wuhor zum andern durch ein schlauch Wasser zu bringen.
Wie ein Schiff, welches vÿber land zu führen, in etlich stuckh mag zerlegt werden.
Jacobs Stab den Seefahrenden.
Zwaÿ Modell eines Zugs mit der Spindel ohn end, daran ein Trettrad gericht, ein grose last in die höhe zu ziehen.
Zwÿ Modell eines starckhen Zugs mit einen Schiebwerkh linckhs vnd rechts zu treiben, in Bergwerkhen Nutzlich zu gebrauchen.
dreÿ Modell eines Wunderlichen Tribs, da die Scheiben gegeneinander lauffen.
Wie ein grose Steinerne Saul vffzuwenden, vnd zu vnder fahren.
des hollendischen *Ingenieurs Simon Stevins* Wind Wagen, welche zu Delfft im zeug hauß steth, in ein klein Modell gebracht.
doppeltes Schlagwerkh, grose Pfähl schregs vnd eben ein zu zu schlagen.
dreÿ Modell eines Ziegel Offens.
Kupfer Priß
Müntzen.
Newe Invention einer doppelt Schlagbrugg
Wie die Erd vß den Graben in Trögen vff den Whal leichtlich zu hasplen[?].
Profil von holtz, wie die Werkh zu Erhöhen, vnd zu verbraitern.
Schoss Gatter

[folio 4r]

Manier einer Schlagbrugg mit kurtzen Ärmen.
Ein groses Modell eines kugelwerkhs.
Allerleÿ Seltzamer Räder, als kugelrad, schneckgenrad, handrad, windrad, Item daß aussen dem Centro hangt vnd ander dergleich.

Modell der Sailerbrugg, welche ihr fürstl.[ich] G.[naden] herzogn Bernhard von Weimar etc. oberhalb Regenspurg über die Thonau hat schlagen lassen, vmb viel verbessert.
Wunderliche Sturmbrugg, welche mann etlichmahl vß einander schieben kan.
Ein andere Sturmbrugg.
Ein Sturmbrugg, daran Sturmlaitern angemacht, welche die soldaten schieben oder ziehen könden.
Sturm laiter, welche man dreÿmahl auß Einander schieben kan.
Modell der Sturm brugg, welche die Spanier vor Ostente doch vergeblich gebraucht haben.
Verbesserung derselben Sturmbrugg.
Ein Schwem[m]ende Brugg vff Fässern über den Wasser vß dem *Uffano.*
Ein gar großes Modell einer wunderlichen Sturmbrugg.
Wunderliche *Invention* einer Wiren[?] Sturmbrugg, mit welcher durch ein anschlag ein vöstung leichtlich ein zunem[m]en welche keinem Menschen (ausserhalb Printz Moritz hochlöbl. [...] vnd heren *General Leutenant Melanter* etc.) *communicirt* worden, so Ich aber noch Meines vatters See:[ligen] ableiben zerschlagen vnd verbränth etc. Für welch kunst stuckh hern Graff Carl von Sultz den Eltern etc. Meinung vatter See:[ligen] ein tausendt Reÿchs Thaler in *specie* alhie in d[er] won in beÿßin hern hauptmann Heeluns[?] etc. baar zu Erlegen an erbatten so Ihme aber zu communicir von den heren eltern vnd Behaimen etc. nit hatt wöllen beginstigt [werden].
Ein kriegst Thurn uber sich zu schrauffen.
Ein Batteri in Eÿl über sich vnd vndernsich zu lassen, vnd uff welche seiten man will, vmb zuwenden.

[folio 4v]

New erfundene kriegsWag vff Ihren Weg.
Ein feld *Batteri* in [...] *Impresen* zu gebrauchen vff weg.
Ein Sturm wag rings vmb mit eÿsen stachlen vmbgeben.
Ein Statt Thor vßen Angel heben.
Modell wie die *Granaten* hohl zu boren.
vnderschidne Manieren die *Granaten* zu dempfen.
Ein stückhlin, welches mag leichttlich vmb wenden kan.
Ein Stückhlin uff einen Borkhenstell, welches man hinden laden kan.
Ein groß Stuckh Geschütz mit leichter Mühe vß den Schafft zu erheben, vmb zu wenden, vnd ohne gefahr zu laden, daß man außwendig vom feind nit gesehen werde.
Fünff Stückhlen vff einen schafft leichtlich, wohin man will, zu richten, vnd solche hinden beÿ der Zundt Pfannen zu lad[en].

dreÿ Stuckh Geschütz vff einen Schafft, welche man in d[er] mitte vß einander ziehen kan, darbeÿ in einen Trüchlen noch dreÿ halbe Thaÿl ligen, ahnweÿln man die 3 abschieszt, vnterdessen die andern 3 geladen werden.
Sechs Mußqueten vff einen Schiebkarren in außfällen zugebrauchen.
daß Geschütz beÿ Nacht ohne Magnet zurichten.
Pflug, daran ein *Cornet* Pferd zu spannen, ein lauffgraben damit in Eÿl auff zu werffen [?]
Wie der Petardierer im Ansetzen des *Petards* zu fangen.
Ein Brechwind, Bruggen vnd Thor zu zerreissen.
Newe Manier der *Galle*rin.
Item ein Mine.
Morgenstern, Minek*hens*, friesische Reutter, Sturm Pfähl, [...], Moßbarkhen, Schubkärch etc.

[folio 5r]

Von *Instrumenten* befinden sich zwaÿ Niederlandische *Instrumenten* von Messing zur *Fortification*
Item des Speckhlins von Straßburg, bockhs von Basel, *Zublen, Hulsÿ, Praetarÿ, Schwenteÿ, Jan Sems, Pieters Dou*, vnd anderen der besten *Authorum Instrumenta* zum abmessen vnd Grundlegen.
Ein künstlich Silbern *Instrument* zur *Fortification* vnd allerhand abmessungen dienstlich.
vnderschiene *Instrument* zur *Perspectie, Optic*, Sonnevhren etc.
Allerleÿ *Quatranten, Astrolabia* vnd dergleichen zur *Astronomj*.
Item vier schöne *Globi caelestes & terrestres*.
Schöne Quatranten vnd Maßstäb zur Büchsenmaistereÿ.
Sonderlich schöne *Proportional* zirckhel vff vnderschidene Manier.
Allerleÿ kunstliche Visier Ruthen, sonderlig d[er] harttmann Baÿers kunstreÿche Läng Ruth, darmit die gar volle Fäß gewiß zu visieren, darvon Wenig Visieren in Deütschland etwas wissen.
Viel Büschlen von geschribnen künsten, vnd von allerleÿ schön gemachten vnd getuschten abrissen, Mancherleÿ Mühlwerkh, von Menschen, Rost, Wind, vnd Wasser getriben,
Schöne vnd kunstliche Wasser werkh Zug lust vnd zur Nott *Inventirt*, lustige Fewerwerkh zu kurtz weÿl vnd ernst, Vunderschidliche schiff: floß: faß: Bisten: Sturm: vnd andere Bruggen, Schleÿder, Sturmlaitter, Straittwägen, Mühltrågern, Feld Bachoffen, allerleÿ *Stratagemata* vnd kriegs practickhen, vnd viel ander dergleichen betreffendt, so wie in des Prinzen v[on] Vranien kunst kam[m]er in haag, Item in bayden vornembsten Zeugheüssern in holland zu *Delfft* vnd *Dortrecht*

gesehen, deßgleichen was Mein vatter See:[ligen] vß andern Fürstl. Kunstkam[m]ern von dreßden, *Cassel*, Stuttgartt etc. bekom[m]en, vnd gegen andern künsten eingetauscht.

[folio 5v]

die vornembsten *Authores*, so von der *Fortification*, *Geometria*, *Astronomia*, *Arithmetica*, *Mechanica*, *Perspectiva*, Büchsenmaisterÿ vnd andern dergleichen *Scientÿs* geschriben.
Grundriß der Statt Vlm, wie diselbe disseits d[er] Thonau *fortificirt* ist, welches Ich von hern *Valckhenborchs Original Planta* in haag in seiner Behausung abgezeÿchnet etc.
Vnderschidne Bedenckhen vnd abriss anderer *Ingenieurs* über die *Fortification* der Statt Vlm, als Johann Schneiders *Ingenieurs* zu Preßlauen etc. *Ryswyckhs Ingenieurs* zu hamburg etc. heren hauptmann heren S: vnd anderer mehr etc.
Dessing vnd Abriss viler Stätt vnd Vöstungen in Deütschland, als *Hamburg*, *Augspurg*, *Dresten*, *Basel*, *Francfort*, *Manheim*, *Otenhaim*, lauging[?], Meming, Lindau etc.
Item der vornembsten vöstungen in Niderland an der *Schelt*, *Maas*, *Rhein*, *Ihre*, etc.

[folio 6r]

[folio 6v]

Specification vnd Verzaighnuß
der Jennigen Modellen, welche Johann Faulhaber See:[ligen] Uff eines Ers:[samen] Raths etc.
kosten hat machen lassen vnd Ihme
solche in seines hauß vfzubehalten
anbetrauert etc.

Item
der Jenigen Modellen, Maschinen vnd
Instrumenten, welche Er uff seinen
kosten hat machen lassen, vnd in
seiner Kunstkam[m]er zu sehen sein

Freytags den: Ersten Aprilis
ano. 1636.

7. Nicola Zabaglia's Scaffoldings for the Maintenance of Architectural Space in St. Peter's Basilica and throughout Europe in the Seventeenth to Nineteenth Centuries

Stefan M. Holzer and Nicoletta Marconi

Abstract

The scenographic architectural space of St. Peter's represents an authoritative framework for the exhibition of the Vatican's intellectual and technological potential. The creation and maintenance of St. Peter's spurred inventions in construction practices and building technology, including the development of ad hoc scaffolding systems that could be assembled in prohibitive conditions. As demonstrated in this article, St. Peter's *Fabbrica* and the Church fostered a reassuring place of experience, where rigour and tradition encouraged the realization of striking accomplishments. Notable among others were the scaffoldings designed by the master carpenter Nicola Zabaglia, to whose work the 1743 *Castelli e ponti* was dedicated. The 1824 reprint of this volume enjoyed a critical fortune in Europe, disseminating the place-specific knowledge of the Vatican *Fabbrica*.

Keywords: restoration technologies, technical treatises, history of carpentry, *Fabbrica* of St. Peter's

Introduction

The conservation of historical buildings has always depended on reliable and efficient procedures and technologies.[1] Moreover, in the early modern period as

1 This article is the result of research on construction and restoration technologies between the seventeenth and the nineteenth centuries in Europe, jointly conducted by the two authors. However, for the purposes of editorial and academic requirements, it is pertinent to note that the first part, relating to the work of Nicola Zabaglia and the restoration spaces and practices in St. Peter's *Fabbrica*, has been

Merrill, E. (ed.), *Creating Place in Early Modern European Architecture.*
Taylor & Francis Group 2022
DOI: 10.5117/9789463728027_CH07

still today, constraints on the space available for the assembly and operation of maintenance scaffolding typically entailed considerable construction challenges. A significant inventory of methods, techniques and spaces for architectural restoration was developed by the fruitful laboratory of St. Peter's *Fabbrica* in the Vatican, the papal institution in charge since 1506 for the construction and maintenance of the principal Basilica of Christianity.[2] The *Fabbrica* was one of the most influential authorities on building practice in the modern era.[3] Its extraordinary efficiency in the organization of manpower and its influence on the improvement of building techniques was not solely the product of its administrative structure or its employment of the period's best practitioners. The technical and organizational excellence of the Vatican *Fabbrica* were also connected to the development of construction and restoration scaffolding, and the working spaces to which they related.

Since its initial sixteenth-century reconstruction, the Vatican Basilica's architectural space imposed severe restrictions on the design and functionality of restoration scaffoldings. Not only did these structures have to rise great heights and accommodate large numbers of practitioners, but they also had to be assembled and used without interfering with liturgical ceremonies.[4] The innovative mobile scaffoldings developed in the first half of the eighteenth century by the illiterate St. Peter's carpenter Nicola Zabaglia (1667-1750) met these demands. They were used in Zabaglia's lifetime for the Basilica's restoration and maintenance works, and in multiple generations that followed.

Within the context of place in early modern architecture, the scaffoldings and building structures designed by Zabaglia might initially seem accessory. The place of St. Peter's Basilica is most obviously the product of its specific site: where St. Peter was martyred in the first century AD, and the location of the church of St. Peter built by Constantine. As reconstructed in the Renaissance, the basilica is most often associated with the great architects involved in its design: Bramante, Raphael, Michelangelo, Giacomo Della Porta and Bernini, among others. It is these figures who receive credited for its majestic plan, imposing domes and vaults, and the ornamentation of the façade and nave, the physical features that define the space and distinguish it as a singular place. But it is the builders who make the

written by Nicoletta Marconi. The second part of the article, concerning the critical fortune of the *Castelli e ponti* in European treatises, is by Stefan M. Holzer.

2 On the institutional and technical organization of St. Peter's *Fabbrica*, see, in particular, Renazzi, *Compendio di teorica e di pratica*; Del Re, 'La Sacra Congregazione della Reverenda Fabbrica di San Pietro'; Basso, *I privilegi e le consuetudini della Reverenda Fabbrica di San Pietro in Vaticano*; Marconi, *Edificando Roma barocca*; Lanzani, 'La Fabbrica di San Pietro'; Sabene, *La Fabbrica di San Pietro in Vaticano*.

3 McPhee, 'The Long Arm of the Fabbrica'; Marconi, 'Baupraktiken und Bautechniken in Sankt Peter vom 17. bis 18. Jahrhundert'.

4 Marconi, 'Procedure e tecnologie per il restauro tra XVIII e XIX secolo'.

structure real, and in a construction of the dimensions and scale of St. Peter's, the importance of these individuals is of crucial importance.

This contribution examines the innovations of Nicola Zabaglia as instrumental in the maintenance of St. Peter's Basilica as a place. The scaffolds he devised not only allowed the structure to retain its physical form, but were also integral to a culture of building and technical design that was unique to St. Peter's *Fabbrica*. This culture may be traced back to a physical space – the workshop that Zabaglia occupied within St. Peter's for his practical experiments – and also takes shape within the printed book of his designs, the *Castelli e ponti di mastro Nicola Zabaglia* (1743 and 1824). The inventions published here codified the building knowledge native to St. Peter's Basilica, further solidifying the identity of this exceptional place. The book also garnered an audience far beyond Rome and Italy. The inventions of Zabaglia and his colleagues represented an influential model that bridged the fields of architecture, carpentry and applied mechanics, and as exhibited in *Castelli e ponti* allowed the place of St. Peter's to extend far beyond its given site.

Building Site Technology in Early Modern Rome

In seventeenth- and eighteenth-century Rome, building site technology depended largely upon a consolidated empiricism rather than on formalized cognitive processes. Technologies inherited from Imperial Roman sources continued to prevail, renewed by the experience of the greatest Renaissance and Baroque architects. There was no precise science behind this work, but rather the implicit reference to existing constructions and to long-established practices. In this period, building scaffolding was the specific job of bricklayers and carpenters, who habitually were tasked with inventing new platforms, perfecting those already in use, and adapting each work of scaffolding to the space and place specific needs of a given construction or restoration project.

Despite the self-evident importance of scaffolding systems and restoration platforms, these structures went almost unnoticed within the principal treatises on architecture, nor were they featured in contemporary technical handbooks.[5] There are just a few exceptions within the early modern literature on artistic techniques. The construction of platforms for painters and plasterers is briefly mentioned in the *Perspectiva pictorum et architectorum* by the Jesuit Father Andrea Pozzo (1642-1709), published in Rome in 1693, as well as in *El museo pictorico* by the Spanish painter Antonio Palomino de Castro y Velasco (1655-1726), and in the *Abecedario pittorico*

5 An exception is found in Capra, *La nuova architettura famigliare*, 278-279, depicting a standard pole scaffolding as used on practically every construction site.

by the abbot Antonio Pellegrino Orlandi (1660-1727).[6] These works fit into the general context of the lavishly illustrated machine books that flourished during the sixteenth and seventeenth centuries – early exemplars of which are discussed in Elizabeth Merrill's contribution to this volume – a genre that slowly drew to an end in the early eighteenth century, due to changing attitudes towards technology.

A more empirical approach to machine development gradually started to develop in the late seventeenth century. In this period, increasing interest developed in applying scientific knowledge and reasoning to real-life problems, particularly in France. In the field of machine design, the mathematician and mechanic (*mathematicus* and *mechanicus*) Jakob Leupold (1674-1727) endeavoured to elucidate a decidedly scientific approach to machine design in his multivolume *Theatrum machinarum* (1724), an illustrated compendium of mechanical technology.[7] However, the full integration of practical and traditional knowledge, theoretical investigation and experimentation was not achieved until the advent of polytechnical education at the turn of the nineteenth century. Only then did the design of mechanical devices find a firm basis in scientific principles. Early examples of this new, scientific approach to machine design are exhibited in the textbooks of José María Lanz (1764-1839) and Augustin de Bétancourt (1758-1824), Jean Nicolas Pierre Hachette (1769-1834), the Piedmontese Giuseppe Antonio Borgnis (1781-1863), and Gérard Joseph Christian (1778-1832).[8] In these works, one also recognizes a shift in the technical value of scaffolding design. This transition is captured in the writing of the mid-nineteenth-century French architect Emmanuel Eugène Viollet-le-Duc (1814-1879). On scaffolding he noted:

> [A] well-designed scaffolding is one of the elements of the art of construction that best shows the intelligence and the good leadership of the project. One can judge the science of the builder by the manner in which he sets up the scaffolding. Well-built platforms save time and, by ensuring the workers' safety, permit them to work with greater regularity, method and care.[9]

But Viollet-le-Duc was far from first to express such beliefs on the importance of construction scaffolding. Nearly a century prior, the inventor, builder and engineer

6 Palomino de Castro y Velasco, ***El museo pictorico, y escala óptica***; Orlandi, Abecedario pittorico del M.R.P. Pellegrino Antonio Orlandi.

7 Leupold, *Theatrum machinarum hydrotechnicarum.*

8 Lanz and de Bétancourt, *Essai sur la composition des machines*; Hachette, *Traité élémentaire des machines*; Borgnis, *Traité complet de mécanique appliquée aux Arts*; Christian, *Traité de mécanique industrielle.*

9 Viollet-le-Duc, 'Échafaud', *Dictionnaire raisonné de l'architecture française du XIe au XVIe siècle*, vol. 5, 103-114.

Nicola Zabaglia had developed scaffolding systems that allowed construction to proceed more safely, efficiently and with less manpower. Moreover, the publication in two editions of the *Castelli e ponti di mastro Nicola Zabaglia* (1743 and 1824), or literally, 'scaffolds and platforms of master Nicola Zabaglia', under the auspices of the Vatican, signalled an unprecedented appreciation for these systems. What is more, the publication dates of the two editions neatly delineate a period of transition in the production of 'technical literature', from the machine model books of the sixteenth century, as epitomized in the copy volumes commonly associated with the oeuvre of Francesco di Giorgio Martini (1439-1501), Georgius Agricola (Georg Bauer, 1494-1555), Agostino Ramelli (1531-c. 1600), Jacques Besson (1540-1576), Guidobaldo Bourbon Del Monte (1545-1607), and later also Giovanni Branca (1571-1645) and Vittorio Zonca (1568-c. 1603), to the rise of a new scientific corpus of mechanical engineering.[10]

Nicola Zabaglia and the Innovation of Restoration Scaffolding

Nicola Zabaglia's inventions of scaffolding systems and restoration platforms have characteristically been described as the masterwork of his genius and his innate talents.[11] However, a more objective evaluation of his work is possible only through an in-depth analysis of his biography and an examination of the technical features of the scaffoldings he conceived. Furthermore, the reasons that motivated the *Fabbrica* of St. Peter's to produce two editions of the *Castelli e ponti* require further analysis.

Although often referenced as a humble carpenter, 'engineer', mechanic or master builder, the skills and expertise of Zabaglia are drastically misconstrued by such characterizations. Nicola was born in Rome in 1667, the son of Alessandro Zabaglia (died in 1679), who was a bricklayer in the *Fabbrica* of St. Peter's, and who, like his own father, Francesco, specialized in the construction of building machines. Nicola joined the *Fabbrica* as a labourer in 1686, at age nineteen. According to the custom of the time, however, it is probable that he started working with his father

10 On these individuals, see Fiore, *Città e macchine del '400*; Fiore, *Francesco di Giorgio architetto*; Agricola, *Opera di Giorgio Agricola de l'arte de metalli*; Ramelli, *Le diverse et artificiose macchine*; Besson, *Theatrum instrumentorum et machinarum Iacobi Bessoni Delphinatis*; Del Monte, *Mechanicorum liber* (see also edition by Pigafetta 1581); Branca, *Le Machine*; Zonca, *Novo teatro di machine et edificii*; Biral and Morachiello, *Immagini dell'ingegnere*; Rossi, *La nascita della scienza moderna in Europa*; Galluzzi, *Gli ingegneri del Rinascimento*; Scaglia, 'Drawings for Machines for Architecture from the Early Quattrocento in Italy'.

11 Among the considerable body of inaccurate information, circulating both within specialist literature and on the internet, Milizia, *Notizia sulla vita*, and Corbo, *Nicola Zabaglia*, incorrectly rely on information provided by Renazzi on Zabaglia's life and work.

a few years earlier. In 1691 he counted among seven skilled labourers working for the architects Mattia de Rossi (1637-1695) and Carlo Fontana (1634-1714). But Zabaglia's talents far superseded those of a builder or carpenter.[12] His activity is best understood in relation to a series of important interventions that were carried out during his 40-year service as carpenter in the Vatican in the first half of the eighteenth century. This was a period in which not only specific building and technical skills were established, but the diverse roles of craftsmen and designers were also increasingly delineated.[13]

If during this period an 'engineer' was defined as a person who could practice *ars* (arts) and *technè* (sciences) with ability and keen intelligence, this title could have readily been assigned to Zabaglia. His professional abilities, and the nature of his inventions, moreover, brought him closely in line with the work of contemporary architects. In the late seventeenth and early eighteenth centuries, the oral transmission of technical knowledge and operational empiricism that had long characterized building practices entered a crisis with the rapid progression of scientific methods. The inventions of Zabaglia and his successors represented an authoritative model for the cohesion of architectural theory, practical on-site experience and applied mechanics. But whereas previous generations had more readily allowed for the architect to engage in the design of machines and other utilitarian constructions, scaffolding and temporary construction equipment were increasingly considered the responsibility of bricklayers and carpenters. These individuals were entrusted with the task of planning new scaffolding and adapting these structures to the specific requirements of construction or restoration. Although supporters of the theoretical and intellectual component of the building professions were aware of the importance of scaffolding, the protagonists of this work did not achieve the privilege of being included within the intellectual scope of the *ars architectonica*.[14]

The recognition awarded to Zabaglia did not adhere to this general trend. Even with the title of '*maestro*' or '*meccanico*', Zabaglia's uncommon talents were recognized and he was openly differentiated from his peers. At the *Fabbrica*, he was exempt from the daily incumbencies on other carpenters and labourers, and given the privilege to use as own office, the so-called '*stanza delle munizioni*', or 'torch room' (Figure 7.1).[15] It was within this private workspace that Zabaglia experimented

12 Marconi, *Castelli e ponti*, 1824, 13-29.

13 Marconi, 'Tradition and Technological Innovation'.

14 Marconi, 'Know-how to Restore'.

15 The description of the study space assigned to the carpenter by the cardinals of St. Peter's *Fabbrica* is significant: 'Acciocché poi avesse egli agio di rifletter con tranquillità, e di concepire lungi da ogni strepito o distrazione, e sviluppar le sue idee, assegnolli una stanza solinga su i gran ripiani superiori della Cupola. In questa stanza, di cui ritenne l'uso finché visse, e che serve presentemente per Munizione delle fiaccole e lanternoni per illuminar la Cupola, passava Zabaglia gran parte del giorno in alto silenzio,

Fig. 7.1 Nicola Zabaglia (engraved by Girolamo Rossi after Pietro Leone Ghezzi), frontispiece. *Castelli, e ponti di maestro Niccola Zabaglia*, 1743

with mechanical prototypes, creating to-scale models of scaffolding systems and construction devices using '*legnetti*', extra scraps of wood left by the carpenters.[16] His knowledge and the insightful control of the '*contrasto e dell'equilibrio delle forze*' ('contrast and balance of forces') allowed him to conceive and improve standing and flying scaffoldings, permanent and mobile, creating inexpensive, strong, safe and suitable structures for both the routine maintenance of St. Peter's Basilica, as well as more monumental restoration procedures.

During his long career, Zabaglia successfully completed multiple technical undertakings, characterized by the use of simple wood components that could be controlled by means of a network of hoists and ropes. Through sequential modifications due to his innate and intuitive ability, Zabaglia brought these devices to perfection, improving their components, simplifying their frame and turning them into movable devices that could be quickly placed as needed. As a consequence, St. Peter's *Fabbrica* was able to reduce the time and cost required to execute major restoration works. In addition, downtime was shortened, as it was no longer necessary to dismantle and reassemble all the components of a scaffold. Thus, shoring, scaffolds and machines became more effective, and even complex interventions could be carried out in a short time, saving materials, as well as ensuring the successful completion of the work.[17]

To fully understand the reasons for Zabaglia's success, and likewise those of the ambitious editorial project that celebrated his work, it is necessary to briefly outline the works he completed in the Vatican Basilica, which are documented from 1686 to 1748. Among Zabaglia's most important inventions were the scaffolding systems used for the restoration of the stucco of the porch vault, and for the maintenance of the minor domes and pendentives of the main dome.[18] Equally important was the scaffolding he devised that was affixed to the moulding of the main dome for the restoration of the mosaics.[19] From a structural and functional standpoint, the devices he had built for the restoration of the main nave's vault and the multilevel platforms, the so-called '*Ponti Reali*' (tav. XXVIII), are of equal interest (Figure 7.2).[20]

e immerso in profonda meditazione, che faceva sembrarlo quasi estatico' (*Castelli e ponti* [1824], 3). The note included in the Zabaglia's biography by Renazzi and Gigli underlines the uniqueness of this place and the privilege granted to Zabaglia, whose creative genius is described in reverential tones.

16 A number of documents from the archives of St. Peter's relate to Zabaglia's activity as scaffolding designer. Since 1715, in addition to his ordinary work, Zabaglia attended to the design of scaffoldings for different maintenance needs. By order of the Congregation of the Cardinals of the *Fabbrica*, he also prepared a series of precious scale models of his scaffoldings, which were used for the engraved tables of the book.

17 Marconi, *Castelli e ponti*, 1824, 27-48.

18 *Castelli e ponti* (1743), pl. XXI.

19 Ibid., pl. XXVI.

20 On the restoration of the main nave's vault, see *Castelli e ponti* (1743), pl. XXV.

Fig. 7.2 Nicola Zabaglia (engraved by Giuseppe Vasi after Francesco Rostagni), scaffolding for the restoration of the nave of St. Peter's Basilica. *Castelli, e ponti di maestro Niccola Zabaglia*, 1743, pl. XXIX. National Gallery of Art, Accession Number: 1983.49.147. Mark J. Millard Architectural Collection

Comparable attention characterizes the scaffolding project Zabaglia devised to clean and maintain the 30-metre-high baldachin of Bernini.[21] Zabaglia also coordinated the installation of the 50 statues on the straight wings of St. Peter's Square. For this work, in 1703, he experimented and perfected an '*antenna*', or large wooden tower crane. Equipped with a mobile platform, the device reduced the cost and time of work, which was completed in just three months.[22] Zabaglia was also a protagonist behind the realization of the well-known consolidation of the main dome, a project that was supervised by Giovanni Poleni and Luigi Vanvitelli beginning in 1743, the same year of the first edition of *Castelli e ponti.*[23]

Zabaglia's talent for machine design and building mechanics revived an ancient operative pragmatism alongside a burgeoning wave of scientific advancement. With the publication of the volume dedicated to his work, his fame transcended to myth. The scaffoldings he designed show a constant concern for the conservation of wall surfaces, the safety of workers and the reuse of materials. They represented such remarkable progress in comparison with typical construction devices and, tellingly, were continually used through the first half of the twentieth century; they were abandoned only following the introduction of modern metal scaffoldings. Zabaglia's work as a designer and carpenter was in many respects separate from the publication of the *Castelli e ponti.* The illiterate Zabaglia did not personally oversee the publication of *Castelli e ponti.* Other individuals – building specialists and Vatican officials – selected the most interesting of Zabaglia's devices, had engravings of them made and wrote captions. This extensive and costly process was necessary to strengthen the authority of the *Fabbrica* and the Church itself. Zabaglia's work in the Vatican was specific to the context of the Basilica, but not only. As site-specific constructs, his scaffoldings responded to the immediate needs of the place. Yet, in glorifying and legitimizing Zabaglia's work, the publication of *Castelli e ponti* allowed the Vatican's technical authority, and the innovative achievements of the *Fabbrica,* to extend beyond that place.

The *Castelli e ponti*: The Construction of a Myth

Castelli e ponti di mastro Nicola Zabaglia was published under the commission of St. Peter's *Fabbrica* so as to ensure the lasting memory of Zabaglia's constructions in the Vatican, and to keep the knowledge of them alive for subsequent generations

21 Ibid., pl. XXXIV.

22 Ibid., pl. VII.

23 Marconi, 'Technicians and Master Builders'. On Poleni and Vanvitelli's restoration of St. Peter's Dome, see Dubourg Glatigny, *L'architecture morte ou vive.*

of craftsmen. In form and structure, the *Castelli e ponti* followed the model of contemporary French and German manuals. However, as printed documentation of the Vatican building authority, and of the great intellectual, technical and economic resources exerted in the construction and conservation of St. Peter's Basilica, the book also carried with it a political agenda. In transmitting generations of technical know-how from the workshop of the Vatican Basilica, it revived the centuries-old supremacy of the Church, which had been weakened by radical political and social changes. The form and composition of the book implicitly furthers this agenda. *Castelli e ponti* bears a debt to the formative model of the Italian Renaissance architectural treatise, as apparent in its dual Italian and Latin text.[24] What is more, the rich iconographic apparatus depicts with photographic sharpness the structure and elements of Zabaglia's scaffoldings, making them comparable to the most advanced scientific developments of the period and in turn, promoting the Catholic Church and the structural place that served as its foundation. But in strengthening and codifying the Vatican *Fabbrica* as a place, *Castelli e ponti* also allowed for its influence to extend beyond the confines of Rome and Italy. Due to the virtues of mechanical printing, the well-known compendium spread the fame of Zabaglia and the Vatican's *Fabbrica*, the inventions of which were recognized in carpentry treatises throughout Europe by the eighteenth century.

The *Castelli e ponti*'s *aeditio princeps* dates to August 1743. The project for the book was the initiative of the erudite Ludovico Sergardi of Siena, treasurer of St. Peter's *Fabbrica*, and of Lelio Cosatti, mathematician and mechanic, who himself composed the textual component of the book, probably with the assistance of Antonio Valeri, architect and superintendent of *Fabbrica*'s workers.[25] However, Segardi and Cosatti were not the first to conceive of the project. The idea to illustrate the Zabaglia's devices in published prints extended back to the first decade of the eighteenth century. Nevertheless, processing was postponed until 1720, when Sergardi and Cosatti instructed Baldassarre Bambucciari to make twelve medium copperplates as well as four large ones, which were executed with the collaboration of the architect and engraver Filippo Vasconi (1687-1730), who also made the plates of Giovanni Branca's *Manuale di architettura* by Paolo Giunchi (1772).[26] The plates

24 The primary precedent has been the editions of Vitruvius. Most Renaissance architectural treatises did not include both Italian and Latin text. In the late seventeenth century, an authoritative exception was the monumental compendium by Carlo Fontana (1694), in which the Latin text served as a universal language for an international audience. Fiorelli, 'Nota sul latino scientifico del '700', provides an excellent study on the use of the Latin in *Castelli e ponti*.

25 *Castelli e ponti* (1743).

26 The first of four larger engravings, printed as double-page plates, represents the scaffolding that was used to clean and provide maintenance for the Bernini baldachin; two others offer alternative views of the device, which, according to Zabaglia, had been employed for lifting the column of Antoninus Pius

for *Castelli e ponti* were completed at the end of 1722, although it would take another two decades until the book was published.

As executed, *Castelli e ponti* is composed of three sections. The first illustrates tools, machines and work utensils ordinarily used by masons and carpenters.[27] The second section explains the scaffoldings designed by Zabaglia for maintenance and restoration practices.[28] This includes scaffoldings for painters, plasterers and mosaicists, as well as those necessary for bricklayers, carpenters and stonecutters. Within the second section, attention is also given to scaffolds and platforms designed by Zabaglia for diverse interventions, including projects outside the Vatican.[29] The third and last section of *Castelli e ponti* extends beyond Zabaglia, shedding light on the greater tradition of which he was a part. The highlight here is a selection of plates representing the famous relocation of the Vatican obelisk, carried out in 1586 by Domenico Fontana (1543-1607) and then celebrated in the magnificent *Della trasportatione dell'Obelisco Vaticano*.[30] By 1743, the original plates depicting the obelisk transport were lost, but copies had been re-engraved for inclusion in Carlo Fontana's *Templum Vaticanum* (1694) in an attempt to redirect the fame of the namesake to his non-related successor. Carlo's plates were kept in the Vatican and could be reused without additional cost, and with a similar purpose, in *Castelli e ponti*. Here, however, the sequence of the plates illustrating the transportation of the Vatican obelisk, ignored or not understood in Fontana's *Templum Vaticanum*, is reproposed.[31] *Castelli e ponti* concludes with an image of scaffolding built by Tommaso Albertini, one of Zabaglia's skilful assistants, which was used to replace a similar structure previously made by Zabaglia for the restoration of the tribune of the church of Santi Simeone and Giuda.[32]

The sequential ordering of the volume and plates supports both the understanding of each of the individual devices, and the publication's general aims. The first plates are devoted to the tools for wooden works, connection devices and the knotting of ropes. These plates, in their graphic composition and framework, evoke French compendia of the previous century, such as *L'art de la charpenterie* by Mathurin Jousse (1575-1645), republished in 1702 in Paris.[33] The accuracy of the illustrations of work tools, ropes, wooden grafts and lifting

in Campo Marzio in 1704. The last engraving, derived from the Domenico Fontana's volume, shows the machines used for the raising of the Vatican Obelisk in St. Peter's Square.

27 *Castelli e ponti* (1743), pl. I-XVII.

28 Ibid., tavv. XVIII-XXXVI.

29 Ibid., pl. XXXI-XXXVI.

30 Fontana, Della Trasportatione dell'Obelisco Vaticano, pl. XXXVII-LIV.

31 The illustration of the Vatican obelisk appears in *Castelli e ponti* (1743), pl. XXXVII-LIV.

32 Ibid., pl. LV.

33 Jousse, *Le théâtre de l'art de charpentier*; see also de la Hire, *L'art de charpenterie de Mathurin Jousse*.

machines reveals a consistency and typology, underlining their origins in the traditional equipment of masons, stonecutters and carpenters. In regards to the subsequent representations of the scaffoldings, the scenographic perspective views increase the magnificence of the machines and impress the reader, as in the classical presentation books of the Renaissance age.[34] But perspective aside, the plates excel in their minute detail, enabling the reconstruction of the devices from the printed depictions. It is indeed possible to reproduce, virtually or materially, all the scaffoldings depicted in the *Castelli e ponti*'s plates, thanks to the graphic precision of the illustrations showing the individual components and connection systems.

The efficacy of the plates also stems from the concise captions, which compliment other information supplied in the book. The detailed descriptions provided in *Castelli e ponti* concern not only the great constructions and machines, but also address materials, measures and weights, with the evident aim to demonstrate the practical aspects of the devices. The ordering of devices and tools follows a criterion based on the context of their employment. In this sense, it seems that the volume was probably conceived in part to function as a real operative handbook. It not only celebrated the extraordinary work and restoration techniques carried out by master carpenters and technicians within St. Peter's *Fabbrica*, but also perpetuated these models for subsequent reference. The function of *Castelli e ponti* as a type of handbook is further supported by the fact that within his lifetime, Zabaglia became the progenitor of a valuable group of St. Peter's craftsmen. These individuals, due to their technical acumen, were often tasked with solving difficult technical issues in worksites outside the Vatican during the seventeenth, eighteenth and early nineteenth centuries.

The Legacy of Nicola Zabaglia and the Second Edition of *Castelli e ponti*

The biography of Zabaglia, which accompanied the second, 1824 edition of the *Castelli e ponti*, asserts that Zabaglia's followers formed a veritable 'school' within the *Fabbrica* of St. Peter's.[35] This text was initiated and signed by the lawyer Filippo Maria Renazzi (1745-1808) and completed by Filippo Gigli, the manager of the Vatican astronomical observatory.[36] While such a school never existed, Zabaglia's teaching

34 Jousse, *Le théâtre de l'art de charpentier*, pl. I-VI. See the essay by Wolfgang Lefèvre in this volume for the development of perpsective as the lingua franca of architectural representation in the early modern period.

35 Marconi, 'Il contributo di Filippo Maria Renazzi'.

36 Renazzi was active in St. Peter's *Fabbrica* from 1785 to 1799, and died in 1808. Gigli died in 1821, but lived long enough to complete Zabaglia's biography.

and mentorship to other labourers of the *Fabbrica* guaranteed the transmission of his valuable technical knowledge. The accomplishments of this next generation of technicians was in turn memorialized in the second edition of the *Castelli e ponti*. Renazzi's characterization of a school within the *Fabbrica* was thus not entirely erroneous, and given the political background of the time, the claim was in fact telling. During the French invasion of Rome (1798-1799), and in the ensuing period of occupation of the Church State (1808-1812), papal authority and the secular tradition advanced by the Vatican were placed under intense scrutiny. The *Fabbrica* of St. Peter's was challenged with the idea of implementing a modern system of technical education, founded on scientific principles and an openness to progress. Under French occupation, new teaching criteria were imposed on all training sectors, including those of the skilled professions and crafts. These disciplines were reorganized according to the exemplary French model of the Schools of Arts and Crafts.[37]

Renazzi's conception of a school within the *Fabbrica* (although not referable to Zabaglia himself) was undoubtedly related to the Christian School of Drawing. Founded in 1795 and administrated by the *Fabbrica*, this school allowed the workshop to continue to pursue its long-term operative tradition.[38] Regulations published in conjunction with the establishment in 1822 of the Pontifical Arts School delineated its core ideas. Composed by the architect Giuseppe Valadier, the *Regolamento per lo Studio Pontificio delle Arti* (Regulations for the Pontifical Arts Study) expressed the need to shape future generations of skilled craftsmen with the aim of keeping alive important knowledge on technical design and mechanical construction. Just five years prior, the need for scientific advancement had prompted Pope Pius VII Chiaramonti to establish the *Regolamento della Scuola degli Ingegneri Pontifici* (Regulations of the Papal School of Engineers), with the aim of training new civil engineers. The year 1817 was thus crucial for institutions engaged in the traditional Roman technical training. The Pontifical Arts Study, administrated by St. Peter's *Fabbrica*, defined the educational requirements for the candidate carpenters. These individuals were trained in theoretical notions of geometry, and practical mechanics, which could be applicable to frameworks, scaffoldings and construction machinery. The scientific conception of the curriculum was reflected in the educational apparatus that was assembled for the Papal School. This included the *Teoria e pratica di architettura civile* by Girolamo Masi, published in Rome in 1788, which 'plagiarized' some of Zabaglia's plates, as well as the French compendia

37 In early eighteenth-century France, two authoritative research institutions for the construction and mechanics of buildings were established: Corps des Ponts et Chaussées (1716) and the Ecole des Ponts et Chaussées (1747), directed by J.R. Perronet.

38 Di Sante, '"Non tutti, anzi rarissimi sono i Zabaglia"'; Di Sante, 'Apprendere le arti applicate a Roma tra '700 e '800'.

by Jean Baptiste Rondelet (*Traité théorique et pratique de l'art de bâtir*, 1802-1817) and Jean Rodolphe Perronet (*Oeuvre*, 1783-1788).[39]

The *Castelli e ponti* also reflected an increasingly scientific approach to mechanics and technical design, and the codification of these sectors of knowledge, although still rooted in the permanence of the old operative tradition. It was thus not unexpected when in July 1809 a reprint of the book was announced; it was eventually published by the printing shop of Crispino Puccinelli in 1824.[40] The second edition comprises 62 engraved copperplates and 48 pages with explanatory texts. In addition, it features a new dedication to Pope Leo XII, an introduction by the treasurer of St. Peter's *Fabbrica*, Monsignor Castruccio Castracane, and the aforementioned biography of Zabaglia by Renazzi.

Preparations for the publication of the second edition started in 1821. The development of the volume speaks to the tradition and sense of place that its authors sought to assert, and at the same time, to the need to underscore the objective nature of the technical information it espoused. The reprint was to contain only Italian captions 'because the Latin explanation is a useless expense'.[41] Despite similar comments by Filippo Gigli and Giuseppe Valadier, however, the Latin explanations remained, even if they represented an antiquated legacy. The number of plates to be included in the new edition was another subject of negotiation. Initially, the edition was to contain 59 plates plus the frontispiece. Filippo Gigli, in charge of the editing of the new edition, proposed two additional plates depicting the scaffoldings designed by Angelo Paraccini; Valadier, by contrast, suggested the inclusion of a plate depicting the mobile scaffold for the restoration of the great dome. Ultimately, eight new plates were added.[42] The printing was not completed until May 1825, but the date 1824 remained on the title page. The total expense amounted to around 1800 *scudi*, compared to the 1500 *scudi* spent on the first edition.[43] In addition, 50 separate copies of Zabaglia's biography and 57 copies of his portrait by Pier Leone Ghezzi were printed.

Among the new plates appear some of the extraordinary technical inventions of Zabaglia's most notable followers. By including the work of Tommaso Albertini, Pietro Albertini, Giovanni Corsini and Angelo Paraccini, who all contributed to

39 See the clear correspondences between *Castelli e ponti* (1743), pl. XIII, and Masi, *Teoria e pratica di architettura civile*, pl. IV.

40 *Castelli e ponti* (1824).

41 'Il testo latino fa meno onore al Branca del volgare. [...] Pare scritto da un notaio.' This statement echoes the 1772 edition of the *Manuale di Architettura di Giovanni Branca* by Leonardo de' Vegni: 'the Latin text is less honourable than the vernacular. [...] It seems written by a notary.'

42 *Castelli e ponti* (1824), pl. LV-LXII.

43 On the editorial activity of St. Peter's *Fabbrica*, see Turriziani, 'Le opere a stampa della Fabbrica di San Pietro'.

the enhancement of building practices within the *Fabbrica*, the new edition of *Castelli e ponti* reinforced the continuity of the workshop's technical tradition. Tommaso Albertini, supervisor of the *Fabbrica* from 1773 to 1787, realized scaffolding for the restoration of the secondary dome of St. Gregory's chapel and for the restoration of the barrel vaults of the main nave, which replaced Zabaglia's original solution.[44] The flying scaffolding he devised for the restoration of the inner shell of the main dome of St. Peter's, engraved by Giacomo Sangermano in 1772, is equally remarkable. Its profile is designed to match the shape of the dome through the overlapping of different working platforms. The upper part of the scaffolding is anchored to three long poles fixed to the lantern's base, which is connected with long inclined scissor braces. The scaffolding Tommaso Albertini developed for the restoration of the nave's vaults – a design that featured a great bridge with eleven platforms, lifted to the cornice with six winches – was further perfected by his son, Pietro Albertini (Figure 7.3).[45] This framework, put in place on 26 November 1773, was acknowledged for its reliability and safety, as well as its preservation of the existing masonry work, floors and ornamentation, and stands out among the most brilliant mobile scaffoldings. The plates show not only the massive and safe structure, but also the equipment needed for its installation, including iron crowbars used to assure the anchoring.

The activities of Angelo Paraccini and Giovanni Corsini are likewise documented in the 1824 edition. Angelo was involved in important projects directed by the architects Giuseppe Piermarini (1734-1808) and Giuseppe Valadier. Giovanni Corsini, called 'Campanarino', earned considerable recognition when, in 1756, he was commissioned to direct the *Fabbriceri* of the Campidoglio in the restoration of the dome of the Pantheon, a task for which he designed a rotating scaffolding, together with Tommaso Albertini.[46]

44 For the scaffolding used in St. Gregory's chapel, see *Castelli e ponti* (1824), pl. LVI. For the scaffolding used in the main nave, see ibid., pl. LV.

45 Depicted in ibid., pl. LVIII-LX.

46 Giovanni Corsini, who was superintendent of St. Peter's *Fabbrica*, was involved with Tommaso Albertini on the project of a scaffolding inspired by Zabaglia's works. But Corsini applied the scaffolding to much more complex spatial systems, such as the dome of the Pantheon. Corsini's scaffold had a width equal to one-sixteenth of the Pantheon's shutter circumference and flowed along a track fixed to its large frame. The scaffold had fixed and moving parts. Its main structure was shaped like a slice of a dome, so as to allow for the restoration of a complete row of coffers at the same time. At the top, the scaffolding was fixed to a joint that allowed it to rotate on the vertical axis. This device was depicted by Corsini himself in a drawing, which was later given to Giovanni Battista Piranesi and then engraved by his son and added to the *Raccolta de' templi antichi di Francesco Piranesi architetto romano*, published in 1790. See Pasquali, *Il Pantheon*.

Fig. 7.3 Nicola Zabaglia (engraved by Giacomo Sangermano), mobile scaffolding designed by Pietro Albertini in the nave of St. Peter's Basilica, 1773. *Castelli, e ponti di maestro Niccola Zabaglia*, second edition, 1824, pl. LIX. The Metropolitan Museum of Art, Accession Number: 69.651(1). The Elisha Whittelsey Collection, The Elisha Whittelsey Fund, 1969

Tracing the *Castelli e ponti* in Italy and Beyond

It might be expected that the lavish and immediately comprehensible illustrations of *Castelli e ponti* would ensure its direct and prompt reception, even beyond the Italian borders, given that the book was donated to many foreign visitors by Vatican authorities. However, the first edition of the book scarcely left a trace in the literature of the middle of the eighteenth century. The publication only gained popularity around the time of the printing of the second edition, probably due to the rise of new scientific approaches in mechanical engineering and machine design, and as a result, a revival of interest in the daring inventions of the *Fabbrica* of St. Peter's. And it was material from the second edition that was most frequently cited and reproduced. What is more, much of attention directed to the book focused on the two scaffolds designed by Zabaglia's pupil Albertini, rather than on devices by Zabaglia himself. Ironically, it was Albertini who was most responsible for solidifying Zabaglia's lasting fame.

The confluence in the identities of the two men stemmed in part from the solid tradition of the *Fabbrica*. It was here that young apprentices were trained in the secrets of a long-standing knowledge, and instructed according to a rigorous management system. Since the start of St. Peter's reconstruction in 1506, the inventions of architects and technicians merged with traditional building practice, enriching the knowledge and experience of its workers. Over time, every new invention developed on previous technical achievements, in perfect adherence to an authoritative and univocal operational pragmatism. Therefore, the identification of Zabaglia's work with that of his successors is not surprising, because it refers to the Vatican building tradition. The exceptional technical legacy of Zabaglia constituted a know-how of primary importance for his successors, who, forged within his 'school' and by the strict discipline of the Vatican building yard, continued to pursue his research. The addition of the scaffolding designed by Zabaglia's successors at the second edition of *Castelli e ponti* highlighted the solidity of the Vatican building tradition. The *Fabbrica*, and the Church, identified themselves as a place of experience, a place – both material and immaterial – where rigour and tradition encouraged even the humblest minds, leading them to do striking things, and never forgetting the achievements of their predecessors.

The holy space of St. Peter's – without equal in the world – spurred architects and workers to realize specific inventions both in construction practice and building technology. With the end of the construction works, at the mid-seventeenth century, new requirements came to the fore; the maintenance and restoration of the Basilica's internal space required the invention of ad hoc scaffolding, and the assembly of these systems in prohibitive conditions. The scenographic architectural space of St. Peter's thus represented the authoritative frame for the exhibition of the Vatican's intellectual and technological potential. The virtual space of political necessity obliged the diffusion of the *Fabbrica*'s technical achievements. Not by chance, in *Castelli e ponti* the architectural space is depicted in perspective, while subsequent European treatises (which also deal with the restoration of French and German monumental buildings) preferred orthogonal projections. Orthogonal renderings were better suited to the technical manual than to an architectural treatise of Renaissance derivation. Therefore, it is possible to say that *Castelli e ponti* used architectural perspective as a vehicle of authorship and technical diffusion.

From an operational point of view, the architectural space of St. Peter's was conceived and preserved over time by a group of men, who still today are referred to as '*sanpietrini*'. Within the *Fabbrica* they found an identity and sense of belonging, as well as a technical authority, universally recognized both in Rome and outside the Papal States. The most talented among these men were Zabaglia's collaborators or successors.

The first echoes of Zabaglia's work in later publications appears in the sumptuous *Traité complet de mécanique appliquée aux arts* by Giuseppe Antonio Borgnis.[47] This encyclopaedic attempt to present all kinds of machines in a uniform setting includes a volume on moving great weights. Here, Borgnis recalls the removal from the Basilica of a wall fresco of Domenichino and its transport to Santa Maria degli Angeli. 'When the order was issued, most artists considered this an impossible task; however, this did not prevent the famous Zabaglia from accepting the charge, and he completed it with full success.'[48] In the same volume, Borgnis mentions the lifting of the statues to the straight wings of St. Peter's Square.[49] However, no graphical representations of Zabaglia's machines are included in Borgnis' work.

The same holds true for the two most influential Italian textbooks on construction and technology from the first half of the nineteenth century, the *Istituzioni di architettura statica e idraulica* (1826-1827) by Nicola Cavalieri San-Bertolo and *L'architettura pratica* (1828-1839) by Giuseppe Valadier. Still, Cavalieri San-Bertolo did refer to Zabaglia in his chapter on construction machinery and architectural procedures.[50] Valadier, in turn, relied on the layout of Zabaglia's plate IV as a model for his plate LXVI, showing various Roman roof trusses. His book also includes a brief discussion on how to replace a column from a colonnade, his plate CCLXXII echoing Zabaglia's plate XXXI. However, in the text, Valadier simply refers the

47 Cigola and Ceccarelli, 'Giuseppe Antonio Borgnis'.

48 Borgnis, *Traité complet de mécanique appliquée aux Arts*, 221: 'Lorsque cet ordre fut donné, la plupart des artistes jugèrent qu'on ne pouvait l'exécuter; cela n'empêcha pas le fameux Zabaglia de se charger, et d'elfectuer l'opération avec le plus grand succès.'

49 Ibid., 324: 'Un grand nombre de statues décorent à Rome la balustrade qui surmonte l'entablement du magnifique portique environnant la place de Saint-Pierre. Ces statues, dont le poids de chacune est de sept à huit milliers, furent élevées et placées d'une manière remarquable, aussi simple qu'expéditive, sans aucun échafaud.'

50 Cavalieri San-Bertolo, *Istituzioni di architettura statica e idraulica*, vol. 2, 269, 292, 296, 306, 316, 318.

reader 'who wants to see more examples of this type', to the works of Zabaglia and Fontana, without any further discussion.[51]

Beyond these early Italian references to the first edition of Zabaglia, the work received virtually no acclaim. Notably, the *Castelli e ponti* is not cited in the widespread *Traité théorique et pratique de l'art de bâtir* (1802-1817) by Jean Baptiste Rondelet, nor was it included in one of Rondelet's major sources on carpentry, the *Plans, coupes et élévations de diverses productions de l'art de la charpente* (1805) by Jean-Charles Krafft (1764-1833).[52] Krafft, a productive carpenter, surveyor, architectural teacher and engraver, also failed to include any material borrowed from Zabaglia into his six-volume *Traité sur l'art de la charpente, théorique et pratique* (1819-1822). But this was probably due not to his ignorance of Zabaglia, but rather reflected the fact that all material referring to temporary works such as scaffolding, centres and lifting gear was excluded from his specialized *Traité des échafaudages*, which was printed only posthumously in 1856.[53]

The second edition of *Castelli e ponti*, by contrast, garnered much greater attention and was rapidly exploited in other publications; its critical fortune was conveyed by its acceptance within technical schools and its applications to the building site. The Milanese architects Felice Pizzagalli and Giulio Aluisetti, for instance, made ample use of Zabaglia's engravings to enrich their ambitious if half-hearted textbook *Dell'arte pratica del carpentiere*, which appeared in small irregular instalments of six plates each, between 1827 and 1835. Whereas by far the majority of the 30 plates contained in the first volume of this work were copied from Krafft, twelve plates from the second part were directly extracted from the Zabaglia corpus, with the majority stemming from the additional plates of the second edition. The engravings of *Dell'arte pratica del carpentiere* appear to have been directly copied from those of *Castelli e ponti*, as deduced from the absolute correspondence in the size of the figures. However, lacking the ornamental and graphic qualities of the original prints, the engravings of *Dell'arte pratica del carpentiere* appear as mere outlines.[54] Pizzagalli's and Aluisetti's work remained the only Italian treatise on timber construction until the second half of the nineteenth century, when it was replaced in this role by Luigi Mazzocchi's *Trattato su le costruzioni in legno* (1872 and 1879). Pietro Albertini's scaffolding for the nave of St. Peter's, prominently presented by Pizzagalli and Aluisetti (plate 28 and 29), even found its way into this late work (Figure 7.4).[55]

51 Valadier, *L'architettura pratica*, vol. 4, 88.

52 Rondelet, *Traité théorique et pratique de l'art de bâtir.*

53 Krafft, *Traité des échafuadages ou choix des meilleurs modeles de charpentes.*

54 Pizzagalli and Aluisetti, *L'arte pratica del carpentiere*. Specifically, in part II, pl. 10, 11, 21, 24-30, are direct copies of Zabaglia (sometimes uniting two plates of Zabaglia on a single sheet), whereas pl. 3 and pl. 9 combine details from Zabaglia with material from other sources, mostly Krafft.

55 Mazzocchi, *Trattato su le costruzioni in legno*, pl. 45.

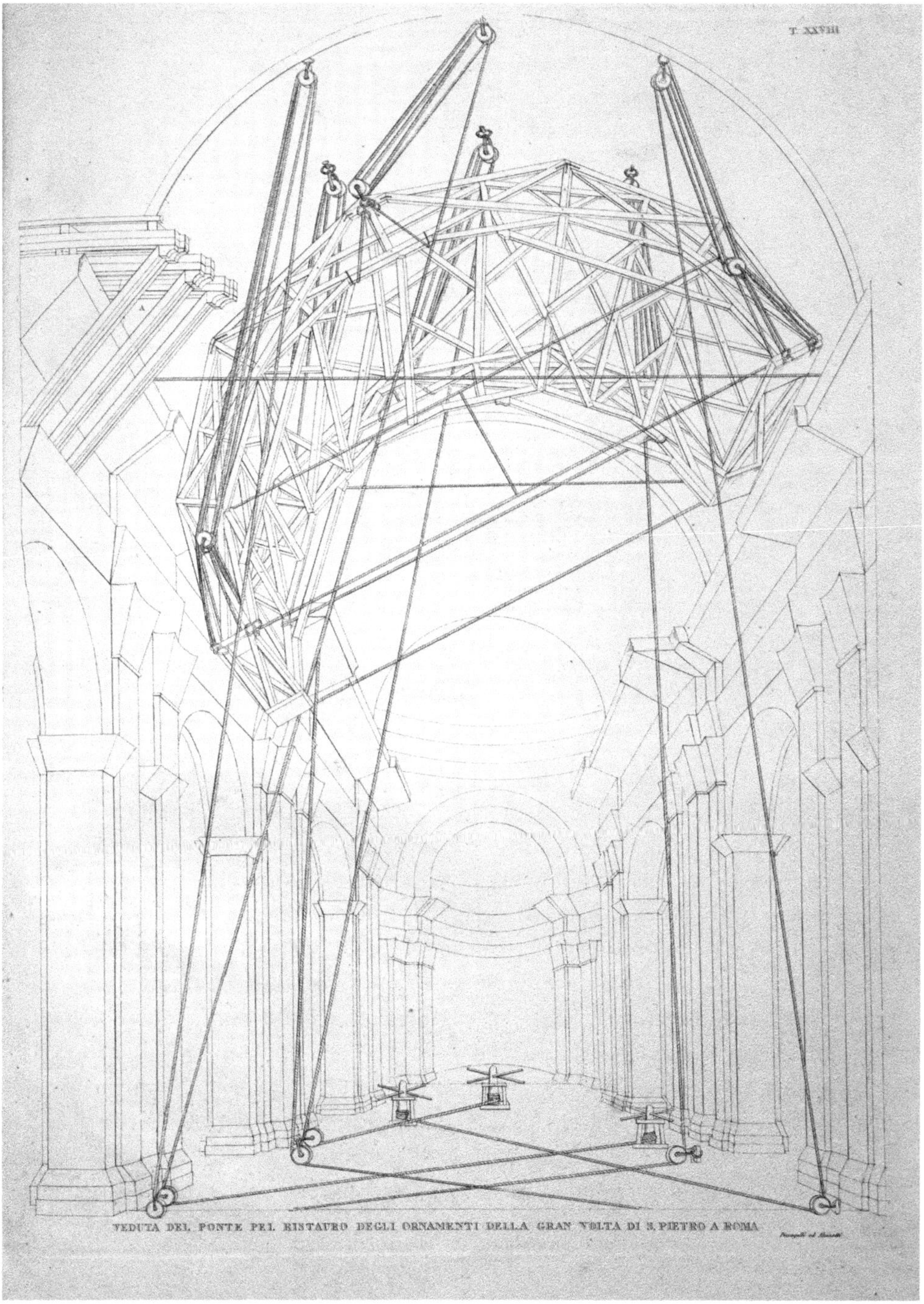

Fig. 7.4 Felice Pizzagalli and Giulio Aluisetti after Nicola Zabaglia, installation of a scaffolding in the nave of St. Peter's Basilica. *L'arte pratica del carpentiere*, II, 1827, pl. XXVIII. From private collection

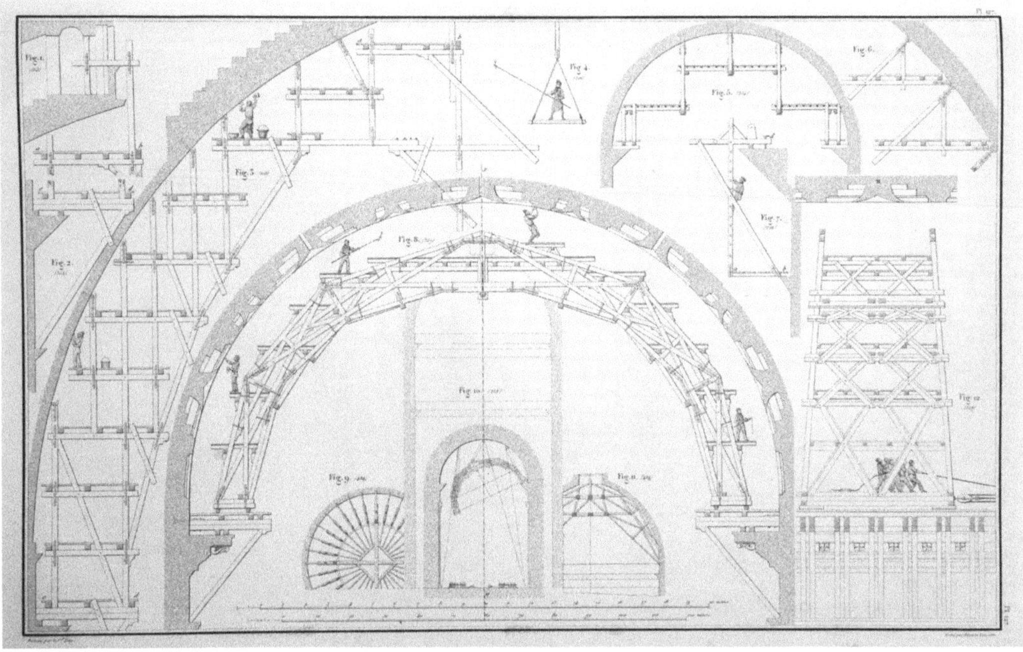

Fig. 7.5 Amand-Rose Émy after Nicola Zabaglia, scaffoldings for the restoration of the dome and the nave of St. Peter's Basilica. *Traité de l'art du charpentier*, 1837-1841, pl. 127. From private collection

The reverence for *Castelli e ponti* in Italy was also captured in the 1886 statements of Andrea Busiri Vici (1817-1911), president of the *Accademia Romana di San Luca* and architect of St. Peter's. Busiri Vici wrote that 'it was to Zabaglia's simple brilliance that we owe the invention of the most difficult combination of connections, insertions, and knotted ropes, to which are entrusted the lives of our workers'.[56] Indeed, the high degree or specialization of the Vatican technicians, the building and restoration practices they employed, and the unique set of tools, equipment and machines they made use of constituted an exceptional, *Fabbrica*-specific resources well into the twentieth century.

Outside Italy, Zabaglia's work was introduced into the scope of the principal textbooks on carpentry by the work of Amand-Rose Émy, *Traité de l'art de la charpenterie* (1837-1841), a publication that would soon become the reference text for the French-speaking world. Émy was obviously most impressed by the Albertini scaffoldings (Figure 7.5). He calls the scaffolding for the dome of St. Peter's 'the most remarkable

56 Busiri Vici, *L'Obelisco Vaticano nel terzo centenario della sua erezione*, 13: 'Questi sono i brillanti successi dei degni successori dello Zabaglia, al cui semplice ingegno sono dovute le più difficili combinazioni nei legamenti, negli innesti, nei noti dei canapi e delle funi alle quali è affidata la vita degli operai.'

flying scaffolding', depicting it along with the scaffolding for the nave.[57] The dome scaffolding, however, had already been included into the series of engravings published in 1763 in *Détails des plus intéressantes parties d'architecture de la Basilique de St. Pierre de Rome*, by Gabriel-Martin Dumont.[58] The most striking difference between the originals and the French reproductions is the reduction of perspective views and insertion of strictly orthonormal projections with precise scales. This is characteristic of the scientifically informed French approach to machine design. Similarly, the famous Piranesi engraving of Campanarino's rotating scaffolding for the restoration of the Pantheon dome (not included in Zabaglia), was taken up by Émy, who commented: 'We give its details in an orthogonal projection, drawn after a perspective view engraved by the calcographie of the Piranesi brothers'.[59] Of course, the orthonormal projection facilitated practical usage of the drawings and therefore corresponded better to the requirements of an educational treatise like Émy's.

The Albertini scaffoldings reappear in Jean-Charles Krafft's *Traité des échafaudages*, this time without any reference to the source.[60] This oeuvre includes a selection of restoration scaffoldings, among which it's possible to distinguish the Albertini's scaffold for the main vault of St. Peter's, as well as other fixed and mobile devices, complete with the anchoring systems tested by Zabaglia and his successors. A wooden truss similar to that designed by Zabaglia for the Teatro Argentina in Rome is included as well.[61] It is unclear whether the figures were copied directly from Zabaglia or from Émy, but the graphic presentation is far less crowded than in Émy's renderings, suggesting direct knowledge of Zabaglia's work. However, like Émy, Krafft transforms the original perspectives into orderly orthonormal views. Curiously, extracts from Krafft's belated published collection immediately found their way into the contemporary journal literature, notably with a series of articles in the *Allgemeine Bauzeitung*, Vienna. The 1859 volume contained a very brief anonymous note on Albertini's nave scaffolding, and the drawing borrowed from Krafft.[62] Obviously, the construction was sufficiently up to date not to arouse suspicion in contemporary readers who evidently believed that the scaffolding had recently been used in the Basilica.

57 Émy, *Traité de l'art de la charpenterie*, 353. The nave scaffolding is described on 357-358, pl. 127.

58 Dumont, *Détails des plus intéressantes parties*, pl. 48.

59 Émy, *Traité de l'art de la charpenterie*, 360: 'Échafauds tournant de la coupole du Panthéon de Rome. La forme circulaire des édifices permet de simplifier celle des échafauds mobiles, en les faisant tourner autour de l'axe vertical de la sur face de révolution qui forme les parois intérieures des couples. Le plus bel échafaud, le plus ingénieux qui ait été construit est celui qui a servi en 1756 à la restauration intérieure de l'admirable coupole du Panthéon à Rome, par Campanarino ; nous en donnons les détails pl. CXXVIII, par des projections octogonales d'après une vue perspective, gravée dans la Chalcographie des frères Piranesi, in-folio, tome VI du *Supplément aux Antiquités*.'

60 Krafft, *Traité des échafuadages ou choix des meilleurs modeles de charpentes*, pl. 32-33.

61 Ibid., pl. 31-32.

62 '*Rollendes Gerüst in der St. Peterskirche in Rom*', 100 and pl. 250.

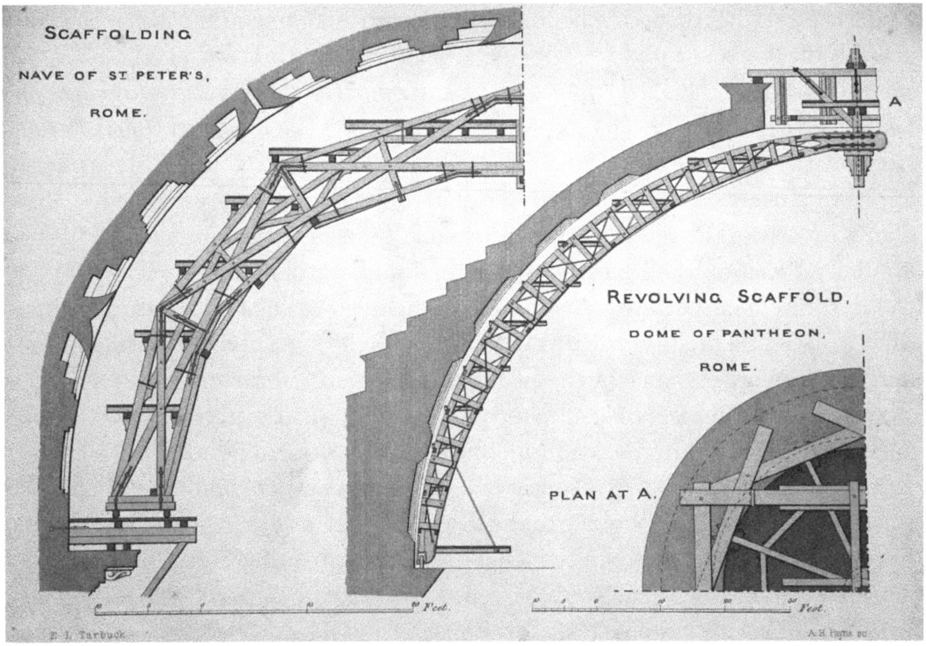

Fig. 7.6 Edward Lance Tarbuck, scaffold for the restoration of the dome of the Pantheon and the nave of St. Peter's Basilica. *Encyclopedia of Practical Carpentry and Joinery*, 1859, pl. 49. From private collection

Zabaglia's designs attracted attention even beyond the European continent. His opus was first mentioned in 1847 in the comprehensive civil engineering manual of the Englishman Edward Cresy, who wrote: 'To Nicholas Zabaglia, who was born in Rome in 1674, we are indebted for designs of some of the best scaffolds that have been erected.'[63] Like Émy, Cresy reproduced the two Albertini scaffolds and Campanarino's Pantheon scaffold, both represented in orthonormal projection. Later, the Zabaglia scaffolds were taken up again in another English carpentry manual, *The Encyclopaedia of Practical Carpentry and Joinery*, published by Edward Lance Tarbuck in London between 1857 and 1859 in 32 small instalments (Figure 7.6). Here, with explicit reference to Zabaglia, Albertini's scaffolding for the nave of St. Peter's and Campanarino's rotating scaffolding for the Pantheon are again united in a single plate, both in orthonormal projection. The adjoining text notes that their 'lightness and beauty can hardly be too much admired. The Italians, indeed, are the boldest and most skilful scaffold builders in the world, although Sir Charles Barry has designed scaffolds for the Houses of Parliament which may challenge comparison with any for security'.[64] The last trace of Zabaglia within later technical literature is included

63 Cresy, *An Encyclopaedia of Civil Engineering*, vol. 2, 1414.
64 Tarbuck, *The Encyclopaedia of Practical Carpentry and Joinery*, 195 and pl. 49.

in a comprehensive collection of loose plates, published by the Viennese contractor and carpenter Andreas Baudouin in 1908.[65] Once again, the plate shows the nave scaffold of Albertini. When Baudouin's collection was reprinted in an abridged version in 1926, this plate was omitted, and the reception of Zabaglia came to a close.

In examining the works of Zabaglia and his followers outside the confines of St. Peter's *Fabbrica* and of Italy, it is worth underscoring the fact that the first edition of *Castelli e ponti*, bound with considerable political implications, essentially failed to fulfil its prime purpose. However, in terms of restoration practices, the fortune of Zabaglia's work was extensive and widespread. The original edition of *Castelli e ponti* appeared at the end of a long epoch of spectacularly illustrated architectural treatises and presentation books. The revival of architectural and engineering volumes during the Industrial Revolution was facilitated by their exclusive content and by the relatively recent origin of this material, which found parallels with the accomplishments of the early science-based engineering. The transformation of Zabaglia's representations into more canonical orthogonal projections was an implicit precondition for the *Castelli e ponti*'s late success in Europe. For us today, Zabaglia's astonishing accomplishments prove that the modern scientific approach did not override the empirical approaches, but rather combined efficiently with established tradition.

Bibliography

Agricola, Georgius, *Opera di Giorgio Agricola de l'arte de metalli* (Basel: Hieronimo Frobenio et Nicolao Episcopio, 1563).

Basso, Michele, *I privilegi e le consuetudini della Reverenda Fabbrica di San Pietro in Vaticano (secc. XVI-XX)* (Rome: 1987).

Baudouin, Andreas, *Der Zimmerer-Meister. Ein Überblick über die gesamten Zimmerungen und ihre Vorbedingungen in vier serien* (Vienna: Author, 1908).

Besson, Jacques, *Theatrum instrumentorum et machinarum Iacobi Bessoni Delphinatis* (Genève: Barth Vincent, 1582).

Biral, Alessandro and Paolo Morachiello, *Immagini dell'ingegnere tra quattro e settecento* (Milan: Franco Angeli, 1985).

Borgnis, Giuseppe Antonio, *Traité complet de mécanique appliquée aux arts: Mouvement des Fardeaux* (Paris: Bachelier, 1818-1820).

Branca, Giovanni, *Le Machine* (Rome: Mascardi, 1629).

Busiri Vici, Andrea, *L'Obelisco Vaticano nel terzo centenario della sua erezione* (Rome: Civelli, 1886).

65 Baudouin, *Der Zimmerer-Meister*, pl. 399.

Capra, Alessandro, *La nuova architettura famigliare* (Bologna: G. Monti, 1678).
Castelli e ponti di maestro Niccola Zabaglia: con alcune ingegnose pratiche e con la descrizione del Trasporto dell'Obelisco Vaticano e di altri del Cavaliere Domenico Fontana (Rome: Pagliarini, 1743).
Castelli e ponti di maestro Niccola Zabaglia: con alcune ingegnose pratiche e con la descrizione del Trasporto dell'Obelisco Vaticano e di altri del Cavaliere Domenico Fontana, coll'aggiunta di macchine posteriori e premesse le notizie storiche della vita e delle opere dello stesso Zabaglia. Compilate dalla Ch. Me. dell'Avvocato Filippo Maria Renazzi (Rome: Puccinelli, 1824).
Cavalieri San-Bertolo, Nicola, *Istituzioni di architettura statica e idraulica*, 2 vols (Bologna: Cardinali e Frulli, 1826-1827).
Christian, Gérard Joseph, *Traité de mécanique industrielle* (Paris: Bachelier, 1822-1825).
Cigola, Michela and Marco Ceccarelli, 'Giuseppe Antonio Borgnis and Significance of His Handbooks on Representation and Terminology of Machines Systems', in Victor Petuya, Charles Pinto and Erwin-Christian Lovasz (eds), *New Advances in Mechanisms, Transmissions and Applications* (Berlin: Springer, 2014), 301-308.
Corbo, Anna M., *Nicola Zabaglia. Un geniale analfabeta* (Rome: Edilazio, 1999).
Cresy, Edward, *An Encyclopaedia of Civil Engineering*, 2 vols (London: Longman, Brown, Green, and Longmans, 1847).
de la Hire, Gabriel-Philippe (ed.), *L'art de charpenterie de Mathurin Jousse. Corrigé and augmenté de ce qu'il y a de plus curieux dans cet Art, and des machines les plus necessaires à un charpentier* (Paris: Moette, 1702).
Del Monte, Guidobaldo, *Mechanicorum liber* (Pesaro: H. Concordiam, 1577).
Del Re, Niccolò, 'La Sacra Congregazione della Reverenda Fabbrica di San Pietro', *Studi Romani* 3 (1969), 287-301.
Di Sante, Assunta, '"Non tutti, anzi rarissimi sono i Zabaglia": lo Studio Pontificio delle Arti nelle Scuole Cristiane presso San Salvatore in Lauro', in Angela Marino (ed.), *Sapere e saper fare nella Fabbrica di San Pietro* (Roma: Gangemi, 2008), 92-105.
Di Sante, Assunta, 'Apprendere le arti applicate a Roma tra '700 e '800. La Scuola del Disegno e lo Studio Pontificio delle Arti a San Salvatore in Lauro', *Rivista Lasalliana* 2 (2009), 297-308.
Dubourg Glatigny, Pascal, *L'architecture morte ou vive. Les infortunes de la coupole de Saint-Pierre de Rome au XVIII siecle* (Rome: École Française de Rome, 2017).
Dumont, Gabriel-Martin, *Détails des plus intéressantes parties d'architecture de la Basilique de St. Pierre de Rome* (Paris: Auteur and Chereau, 1763).
Émy, Amand-Rose, *Traité de l'art de la charpenterie* (Paris: Carilian-Goeury and Anselin, 1841).
Fiore, Francesco Paolo, *Città e macchine del '400 nei disegni di Francesco di Giorgio Martini* (Florence: Olschki, 1978).
Fiore, Francesco Paolo (ed.), *Francesco di Giorgio architetto* (Milan: Electa, 1993).
Fiorelli, Vanda, 'Nota sul latino scientifico del '700', in Angela Marino (ed.), *Sapere e saper fare nella Fabbrica di San Pietro in Vaticano* (Rome: Gangemi, 2008), 122-124.

Fontana, Carlo, *Templum Vaticanum et ipsius origo* (Rome: Buagni, 1694).

Fontana, Domenico, *Della trasportatione dell'Obelisco Vaticano et delle fabriche di Nostro Signore Papa Sisto V, fatte dal Cavalier Domenico Fontana, architetto di Sua Santità* (Rome: Domenico Basa, 1590).

Galluzzi, Paolo (ed.), *Gli ingegneri del Rinascimento da Brunelleschi a Leonardo da Vinci* (Florence: Giunti, 1996).

Hachette, Jean Nicolas Pierre, *Traité élémentaire des machines* (Paris and St. Petersburg: Klostermann, 1811).

Holzer, Stefan M., *Statische Beurteilung historischer Tragwerke, Band 2: Holzkonstruktionen* (Berlin: Ernst & Sohn, 2015).

Holzer, Stefan M., 'Vitruvianismus und Bautechnik', *Architecture-Seitschrift für Geschichte der Baukunst* 44 (2014-2015), 17-36.

Holzer, Stefan M. and Bernd Köck, *Meisterwerke barocker Bautechnik. Kuppeln, Gewölbe und Kirken-dachwerke in Südbayern* (Regensburg: Schnell-Steiner, 2008).

Jousse, Mathurin, *Le théâtre de l'art de charpentier* (La Flèche: G. Griveau, 1627).

Krafft, Jean-Charles, *Traité des échafuadages ou choix des meilleurs modeles de charpentes* (Paris: Librairie Encyclopédique de Roret, 1856).

Lanz, José María and Augustin de Bétancourt, *Essai sur la composition des machines* (Paris: Imprimerie Impériale, 1808).

Lanzani, Vittorio, 'La Fabbrica di San Pietro. Una secolare istituzione per la Basilica Vaticana', in Alfredo Maria Pergolizzi (ed.), *Magnificenze Vaticane. Tesori inediti dalla Fabbrica di San Pietro* (Rome: De Luca, 2008), 55-60.

Leupold, Jakob, *Theatrum machinarum hydrotechnicarum* (Leipzig: Christoph Zunkel, 1724).

Marconi, Nicoletta, 'Baupraktiken und Bautechniken in Sankt Peter vom 17. bis 18. Jahrhundert', in Martine Boiteaux et al. (eds), *Der Vatikan. Architektur, Kunst, Zeremoniell* (Stuttgart: Belser, 2014), 217-271.

Marconi, Nicoletta, *Castelli e ponti. Apparati per il restauro nell'opera di mastro Nicola Zabaglia per la Fabbrica di San Pietro in Vaticano* (Foligno: Il Formichiere, 2015).

Marconi, Nicoletta, *Edificando Roma barocca. Macchine, apparati, maestranze e cantieri tra XVI e XVIII secolo* (Città di Castello: Edimond, 2004).

Marconi, Nicolleta, 'Il contributo di Filippo Maria Renazzi alla seconda edizione di *Castelli e ponti di maestro Nicola Zabaglia* (Rome, 1824): propaganda e divulgazione tecnica nella Fabbrica di San Pietro in Vaticano', in Paolo Alvazzi del Frate, Maria Rosa Di Simone and Carla Frova (eds), *Filippo Maria Renazzi. Università e cultura a Roma tra Settecento e Ottocento* (Rome: Istituto Nazionale di Studi Romani, 2019), 91-109.

Marconi, Nicoletta, 'Know-how to Restore: Construction Techniques in Baroque Rome – Practices, Devices and "Secrets"', in Carlos Brebbia and A. Torpiano (eds), *Stremah IX: Proceedings of Ninth International Conference on Structural Studies, Repairs and Maintenance of Heritage Architecture* (Southampton: Wessex Institute of Technology, 2005), 73-82.

Marconi, Nicolleta, 'Procedure e tecnologie per il restauro tra XVIII e XIX secolo: il contributo della Fabbrica di San Pietro in Vaticano', in Claudia Conforti and Vittorio Gusella (eds), *AID Monuments. Conoscere, Progettare, ricostruire. Galeazzo Alessi architetto ingegnere* (Rome: Aracne, 2013), 473-486.

Marconi, Nicoletta, 'Technicians and Master Builders for Restoration of the Dome of St. Peter's in Vatican in the Eighteenth Century: The Contribution of Nicola Zabaglia (1664-1750)', in Karl E. Kurrer (ed.), *Proceedings of Third International Congress on Construction History*, 3 vols (Berlin: Neunplus1, 2009), vol. 2, 991-1000.

Marconi, Nicoletta, 'Tradition and Technological Innovation on Roman Building Sites from the 16th to the 18th Century: Construction Machines, Building Practice and the Diffusion of Technical Knowledge', in Hermann Schlimme (ed.), *Practice and Science in Early Modern Italian Building: Toward an Epistemic History of Architecture* (Milan: Electa, 2006), 137-152.

Marino, Angela, 'La scuola romana degli ingegneri pontifici', in *Storia dell'Ingegneria* (Naples: Cuzzolin, 2006), 235-241.

Masi, Girolamo, *Teoria e pratica di architettura civile per istruzione della gioventù specialmente romana* (Rome: Fulgioni, 1788).

Mazzocchi, Luigi, *Trattato su le costruzioni in legno*, 2nd ed. (Milan: Antonio Vallardi, 1879).

McPhee, Sarah, 'The Long Arm of the Fabbrica: St. Peter's and the City of Rome', in Georg Satzinger and Sebastian Schütze (eds), *Sankt Peter in Rom, 1506-2006: Beiträge der internationalen Tagung vom 22.-25. Februar 2006 in Bonn* (Munich: Hirmer, 2008), 353-373.

Milizia, Umberto Maria, *Notizia sulla vita e sulle opere di Nicola Zabaglia mastro muratore in Roma* (Rome: Artecom, 1999).

N.N., 'Rollendes Gerüst in der St. Peterskirche in Rom', *Allgemeine Bauzeitung* 24 (1859), 100.

Orlandi, Antonio Pellegrino, *Abecedario pittorico del M.R.P. Pellegrino Antonio Orlandi, bolognese, contenente le notizie de' professori di pittura, scoltura, ed architettura* (Venice: G. Pasquali, 1753).

Palomino de Castro y Velasco, Antonio, *El museo pictorico, y escala óptica* (Madrid: Sancha, 1795).

Pasquali, Susanna, *Il Pantheon. Architettura e antiquaria nel Settecento a Roma* (Modena: Panini, 1996).

Picon, Antoine, *Architectes et ingénieurs au Siècle des Lumière* (Marseille: Parentheses, 1988).

Pigafetta, Filippo (ed.), *Le mechaniche dell'illustrissimo signor Guido Ubaldo de' Marchesi del Monte* (Venice: F. di Franceschi, 1581).

Pizzagalli, Felice and Giulio Aluisetti, *L'arte pratica del carpentiere* (Milan: Autori, 1827).

Ramelli, Agostino, *Le diverse et artificiose macchine del capitano Agostino Ramelli* (Paris, 1588).

Renazzi, Filippo Maria, *Compendio di teorica e di pratica ricavato dalli decreti e risoluzioni originali della Sagra Congregazione della Reverenda Fabbrica di San Pietro per uso de' Commissarj ed altri uffiziali della medesima* (Rome, 1793).

Rondelet, Jean Baptiste, *Traité théorique et pratique de l'art de bâtir*, 7 vols (Paris: L'auteur, 1802-1817).

Rossi, Paolo, *La nascita della scienza moderna in Europa* (Rome and Bari: Laterza, 2000).

Sabene, Renata, *La Fabbrica di San Pietro in Vaticano: dinamiche internazionali e dimensione locale* (Rome: Gangemi, 2012).

Scaglia, Gustina, 'Drawings for Machines for Architecture from the Early Quattrocento in Italy', *Journal of the Society of Architectural Historians* 25 (1966), 90-114.

Tarbuck, Edward Lance, *The Encyclopaedia of Practical Carpentry and Joinery* (Leipzig, Dresden and London: A.H. Payne and J. Hagger, s.d. [1857-1859]).

Turriziani, Simona, 'Le opere a stampa della Fabbrica di San Pietro. Tra consacrazione storica dell'attività edilizia e trasmissione del sapere', in Giovanni Morello (ed.), *La Basilica di San Pietro. Fortuna e immagine* (Rome: Gangemi, 2012), 535-557.

Valadier, Giuseppe, *L'architettura pratica dettata nella scuola e cattedra dell'insigne Accademia di S. Luca*, 5 vols (Rome: Società Tipografica, 1828-1839).

Verdi, Orietta, 'Agrimensori, architetti ed ingegneri nello Stato Pontificio del primo Ottocento', in Carlo M. Travaglini (ed.), *Corporazioni e gruppi professionali a Roma tra XVI e XIX secolo* (Rome: Università degli studi di Roma Tre, 1998), 367-396.

Viollet-le-Duc, Eugène Emmanuel, *Dictionnaire raisonné de l'architecture française du XIe au XVIe siècle*, 10 vols (Paris: B. Bange, 1854-1875).

Zonca, Vittorio, *Novo teatro di machine et edificii: per uarie et sicure operationi; có le loro figure tagliate in Rame é la dichiaratione e dimostratione di ciascuna; opera necesaria ad Architetti, et a quelli ch di tale studio si dilettano* (Padua: Bertelli, 1607).

About the Authors

Stefan Holzer is Professor of Building Archaeology and Construction History at the ETH, Zurich. He has published extensively on building technology in the Baroque period, with a particular focus on the construction of roofs in southern Germany. His monographs include *Der Ludwig-Donau-Main-Kanal* (2018), *Statische Beurteilung historischer Tragwerke* (2013 and 2015), and *König-Ludwig-Brücke Kempten* (2012).

Nicoletta Marconi is Associate Professor of Architectural History at the University of Rome Tor Vergata. Her research focuses on the history of pre-industrial architecture, construction and building technologies, primarily within the context of Rome. In addition to dozens of articles, she is the author of *Edificando Roma barocca: Macchine, apparati, cantieri* (2004) and *Castelli e ponti. Apparati per il restauro nell'opera di Nicola Zabaglia* (2015).

Part III

Excavating Place

8. Building on 'Hollow Land': Skill and Expertise in Foundation-Laying Practices in the Low Countries in the Fifteenth to the Seventeenth Centuries

Merlijn Hurx

Abstract

Foundation-laying practices for marshy conditions have received comparatively little attention in architectural history; however, in the seventeenth century Netherlandish specialized skill and knowledge for the construction of pile foundations was recognized as being exceptional and garnered international esteem. Based on new archival material, this article provides insight into the rigorous processes of foundation design, and draws attention to its multidisciplinary nature. In addition, it sheds new light on the introduction of deep foundations, which was a major engineering innovation, providing greater stability because of the use of longer piles that reached the first solid layer deep below the surface. While Dutch expertise was directly related to the landscapes they inhabited, other factors that fostered innovation in foundation design are considered as well.

Keywords: pile foundations, deep foundations, architectural drawings, soil sampling, sluice building

In setting out to explain the etymological origin of 'Holland' in the discussion of the county in his 1567 *Descrittione dei tutti Paesi Bassi*, the Italian writer and merchant Lodovico Guicciardini considered two alternative explanations. It was generally believed that the place name derived from the Old Dutch term *Holtlandia*, meaning 'woodland', because in ancient times the land had been forested, an explanation that is still accepted in modern scholarship. However, since Holland was almost completely deforested by the sixteenth century, Guicciardini believed a second explanation to be more likely, which traced name to the contraction '*hol*'

Merrill, E. (ed.), *Creating Place in Early Modern European Architecture*.
Taylor & Francis Group 2022
DOI: 10.5117/9789463728027_CH08

and '*land*', meaning literally 'hollow land'. This explanation was substantiated by his own observations, because when travelling through the county he had himself noted how the ground quaked, giving the impression that the subsoil did not have a proper foundation, but actually rested on a bed of water.[1] Although Guicciardini did not consider the difficulties that such marshy conditions posed for building in his discussion of Holland, he did address the topic in his description of Amsterdam. Here, he described the entire city as being supported by a forest of piles, 'which had been driven into the ground with great force using hoisting devices [*argani*] and other instruments'. Then, citing an unnamed friend, he asserted that if only visible, this forest would certainly be the most beautiful in the world.[2]

Guicciardini's admiration for the great expense and effort involved in building in a marshy environment became a topos frequently repeated in early modern descriptions of Amsterdam, many of which were accompanied by discussions of the technical difficulties encountered in such construction. For instance, the earliest description of Amsterdam from around 1500, which was included in Johannes Pontanus' 1614 *Historische Beschrijvinghe der seer wijt beroemde Coop-stadt Amsterdam*, contained a detailed description of the construction of the city's pile foundations. The anonymous author explained that a wooden grid was placed in the excavated pit with a depth of 6 to 8 Amsterdam feet (1.7 to 2.3 metres), after which as many piles as possible, each 40 to 60 feet in length (11.5 to 17 metres), were driven into the ground in each of the grid's squares.[3] The skill of constructing such pile foundations garnered much contemporary esteem. For instance, in the 1612 Dutch

1 Guicciardini, *Descrittione di M. Lodovico Guicciardini*, 175. The text reads: 'altri affermano (co quali io adherisco) essere nome composto da queste due voci Teutoniche Hol & Lant, che vogliono propriamente dire paese concavo, o vacuo: perche camminando a carro, o a cavallo si vede manifestamente in molti luoghi tremare il terreno, come cosa quasi gallegiante in su l'acqua'.

2 Ibid., 184. The foundations were said to be very expensive, matching the costs of the remainder of the building. The text reads: 'E Amsterdam fondata tutta in su pilari di lungissimi & grossissimi alberi, fitti a forza d'argani, & d'altri strumenti nel fondo di quelle acque.'

3 Pontanus, *Historische Beschrijvinghe der seer wijt beroemde Coop-stadt Amsterdam*, 358. The text reads: 'Voorts soo is de Stadt Amsterdam by nae ghelijck Venetien uut morasschen met grooten costen opghehaelt / ende daerom van natuere ende gheleghentheyt seer sterck; ende heeft den gront soo weec ende modderich dat de kercken ende by na alle de huysen ende ander edificien / mitsgaders oock des stadtsmueren / niet als op afgehouwen troncken van boomen ofte houte palen inde aerde gheslaghen / en connen gefondeert worden / t' welck gheschiet in deser manieren. Eerst die aerde ses ofte acht voeten diep uutghegraven zijnde / werde daerinne gheleyt twee balcken na de lengde vande muer diemen wil fonderen van malcanderen verscheyden / na de breedde ende dicte vande selve muer / welcke balcken met eenige dweershouten vast aen malcanderen geknocht werden / waer tusschen daernae paelen innegheslaghen ende gheheyt worden van 40 / 50 oft ooc wel van 60 voeten lanck / nae den eysch ende swaerte van t'werck / t'welckmen daer op wil bouwen / dicht neffens den anderen soo veel alsser tusschen de voorsz. dweershouten moghen ingaen / waer op eyntelick de fondementen vande mueren ende t'werck voorts opghe ghemaeckt werdt.' The Amsterdam foot is 28.31 centimetres.

Fig. 8.1 Claes Jansz Visscher II, bird's-eye view of the Amsterdam Exchange. Lodovico Guicciardini, *Beschryvinghe van alle de Nederlanden*, 1612. Rijksmuseum, Object Nr. RP-P-1880-A-3841

translation of Guicciardini by Petrus Montanus and Cornelis Kiliaan, Amsterdam's exchange building, constructed after designs by Hendrick de Keyser between 1608 and 1611, received particular praise, not because of its original treatment of classical ornaments, but because of its large dimensions and strong foundations (Figure 8.1). According to Montanus and Kiliaan, the building's magnificence, equal to that of any other building in Europe, lay largely in its construction in such a challenging site. The building was supported by large barrel vault, which bridged the River Amstel and allowed ships to pass underneath. For its foundations, Montanus recounted, wooden piles of 50 to 60 feet in length (about 14 to 17 metres) had been drilled into the muddy riverbed.[4]

4 Guicciardini, *Beschryvinghe van alle de Nederlanden anderssins ghenoemt Neder-Duytslandt*, 214: 'een werck dat in grootheydt ende ghebouw gheene van de andere van Europa en wijckt. Want beneffens dat het uyt ontrent veertich colomnen bestaet, in den modderighen grondt vanden Amstel ghemaeckt, soo vertoont het in't in doen een ghewelf, door het welck de schepen uyt den Amstel in het Tye, ende insghelijcks uyt het Tye in den Amstel komen. Den grondt daer de fondamenten op zijn gheleyt, is heel van hout uyt ronde palen vijftich oft tsestich voeten lang, met heyen (het water aldaer eerst uytghemalen zijnde) seer vast in de aerde ghedreven.'

Despite early modern admiration for the skills involved in laying building foundations in the Low Countries, the topic has attracted comparatively little attention in architectural history. Although foundation-laying practices have gradually received more interest within the emerging field of construction history, there are few comprehensive studies on historical foundations, and no surveys of the topic exist for the Low Countries.[5] The literature that does exist is limited, and in regards to the Dutch Republic concentrates mainly on dwellings in Amsterdam, with research based largely on archaeological evidence.[6] With the exception of the studies by van Tussenbroek, this research gives little attention to historical records, and therefore provides limited insight into the knowledge required to lay building foundations.[7] It is generally believed that foundation-laying practices were largely guided by tradition and that expertise was locally available. While this may have been true for the construction of smaller dwellings, there is ample evidence that for heavy structures – churches, towers, and fortifications – as well as for hydraulic works, much consideration went into the planning of foundations. More significantly, for complex matters of construction, consultants from diverse backgrounds were invited to provide and assess proposals, and in several cases they came up with a range of solutions. In such circumstances the laying of foundations was not simply a matter of well-established and straightforward rules of thumb. On the contrary, by the end of the seventeenth century, Dutch expertise in construction in marshlands was considered to be exceptionally high, and engineers from all over Europe travelled to the Dutch Republic to study contemporary pile foundations.

This article investigates foundation-laying practices in the Low Countries in the early modern period, calling attention to the extensive expertise that this involved, as well as to how this knowledge was applied to individual, site-specific constructions. The discussion begins with a review of the different pile foundation techniques used in the period, and then examines the contemporary acclaim for these practices. Building on a sequence of examples, as documented in newly discovered survey reports and drawings, the article then explores the myriad processes that went into the planning of foundations. The examination of the construction of two stone sluices in Holland from the mid-sixteenth century, for

5 See Borrmann, *Historische Pfahlgründungen*; García Gamallo, 'The Evolution of Traditional Types of Building Foundation'; Geleyns and De Jonge, 'New Light'; Mendonça de Oliveira and Pousada Presa, 'Reinforcing Foundations with Wood Piles'; De Voght and De Jonge, 'Foundation Techniques in the Early Modern Low Countries'; Adam, 'Pfahlgründungen des 15. bis 18. Jahrhunderts'.

6 Den Boer, 'Van heien en heipalen en het probleem van de Amsterdamse bodem'; Zantkuijl, *Bouwen in Amsterdam*; Gawronski and Veerkamp, 'Over staal, kleef en stuit'; Gawronski and Veerkamp, 'Über staal, kleef und stuit'.

7 Van Tussenbroek, 'Was wiegt ein Haus?'; van Tussenbroek, 'The Foundations of the Nieuwe Kerk Tower in Amsterdam'.

which large sets of documentation regarding the planning of the foundations survive, offers insight into the rigorous and painstaking nature of this process, which involved numerous experts: architects, masons, carpenters and administrators. The realization of these sluices not only derived from place-specific factors, but was also formative in further distinguishing these singular places.

Pile Foundation Techniques and Technologies

For construction in marshy conditions, several alternative pile foundation techniques were available in the Low Countries. The most straightforward, and probably also the oldest technique, consisted of short stakes driven into the ground on which the footing of the wall rested directly. A second and more elaborate alternative included an intermediate layer of horizontally placed trunks or plank boards, on which bricks were more easily laid. A third technique entailed a wooden grid, which prevented the piles from drifting apart, while also facilitating the levelling of the pile heads (Figure 8.2).[8] In the Middle Ages, the stakes and piles usually had a limited length of several metres, and thus did not reach a solid bed of sand. Piles were driven into the ground at very close intervals to improve the soil's load-bearing capacity through compaction, while the frictional resistance along the length of the piles gave the foundations additional strength.[9] Several examples of foundations that supported large and heavy structures are known from excavations, such as the fourteenth-century foundations of the Oude Kerk in Amsterdam.[10]

The technique of driving piles into soggy subsoil for the purpose of buttressing building foundations was widespread in Europe, and there remains ample archaeological and historical evidence for such practices as employed in England, France, and south-west Germany, as well as of course Venice, as cited by Ludovica Galeazzo in her contribution to this volume.[11] Piledriving techniques were already known in antiquity; Vitruvius briefly described how the load-bearing capacity of the soil could be improved by driving charred stakes or piles into the ground at very close intervals. From the thirteenth century onward, the three previously given methods were applied in large parts of Europe. Piledriving techniques were also described in several sixteenth-century architectural treatises, especially in regards to fortifications,

8 Gawronski and Veerkamp, 'Über staal, kleef und stuit'. My thanks to Gabri van Tussenbroek for allowing the reproduction of these drawings.

9 De Voght and De Jonge, 'Foundation Techniques in the Early Modern Low Countries'.

10 Janse, *De Oude Kerk te Amsterdam*, 25, 38-39.

11 Harvey, *Mediaeval Craftsmen*, 102-103; Salzman, *Building in England Down to 1540*, 83-87, 328-329; Kérisel, *Down to Earth*; Borrmann, *Historische Pfahlgründungen*.

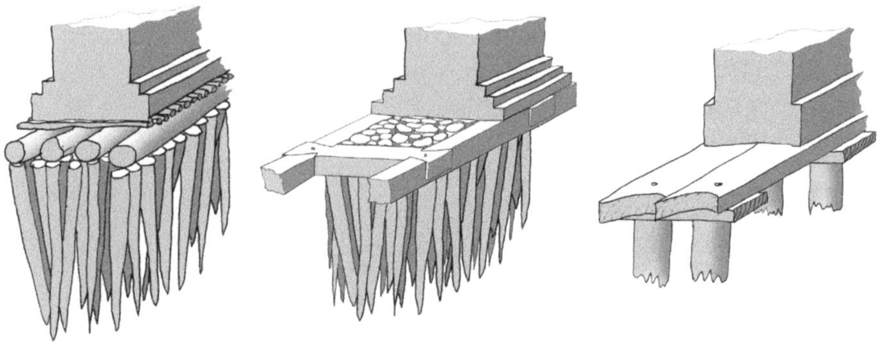

Fig. 8.2 Three different types of pile foundations: (1) stakes with an intermediate layer of horizontally placed trunks; (2) stakes with a wooden grid; and (3) the so-called 'Amsterdam foundation' with long piles that reached the first solid layer below the earth's surface. Courtesy of Dik de Roon, Monumenten en Archeologie Amsterdam

as for instance, in Giacomo Fusto Castriotto and Girolamo Maggi's *Della fortificatione delle città* (1564) (Figure 8.3) and Daniel Specklin's *Architectura von Vestungen* (1589).[12]

Although pile foundations were ubiquitous, the construction of foundations from piles that reached solid layers deep below the earth's surface was particular to the Low Countries. A survey by Bormann in the Holy Roman Empire shows that prior to the eighteenth century, piles typically had an average length of 1 to 3 metres, with the longest examples being 4 to 6 metres in length.[13] Also in Venice typically piles were no longer than 3 or 4 metres.[14] Early modern architectural treatises confirm the moderate length of most piles. Specklin considers piles of 10 to 12 feet (3-3.6 metres) sufficient for soggy soil, while in *Della fortificatione delle città*, Maggi considers foundation piles of 5 to 6 metres to be somewhat exceptional.[15]

In Holland, however, piles of more than 10 metres in length were generally employed from late sixteenth century onward. This development is well-documented for construction in Amsterdam, where the first solid sand layer is found 12 metres below the earth's surface. For Amsterdam Town Hall (1648-1665), for instance, 13,659

12 Schukking, 'Iets over het voormalige kasteel te Harlingen'.

13 Borrmann, *Historische Pfahlgründungen*, 50-51, 192. His observations are confirmed by archival records found by Adam for northern Germany (Hamburg, Hannover) where in the seventeenth- and eighteenth-century piles had an average length of 3.5 to 7 metres. Adam, 'Pfahlgründungen des 15. bis 18. Jahrhunderts'.

14 Bernabei, 'The Wooden Foundations of Rialto Bridge'; Lazzarini, 'Legno e pietra'; Lazzarini, 'Palificate di fondazione a Venezia'.

15 'pali, assai grossi, arficci alle punte, e non manco lunghi di sette, ò vero ottto [sic] braccia'. See Castriotto and Maggi, *Della fortificatione delle città*, 86; Specklin, *Architectura von Vestungen*, 9; Borrmann, *Historische Pfahlgründungen*, 55. Slightly longer piles of 6-7.5 metres were advised by Francesco di Giorgio for the construction of low head dams. Borrmann, *Historische Pfahlgründungen*, 45.

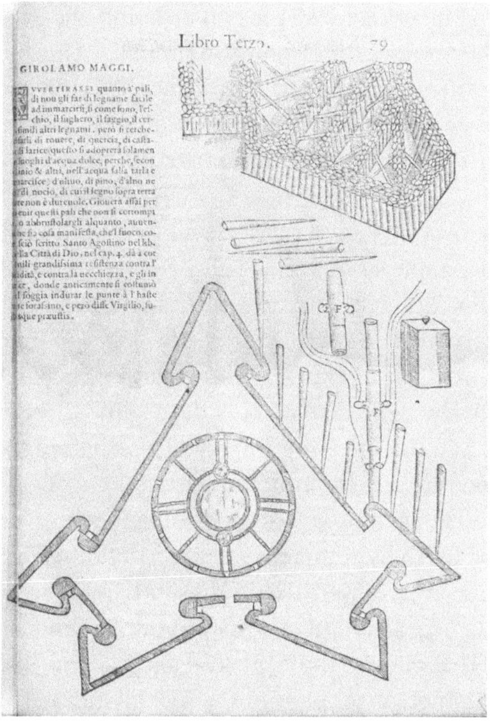

Fig. 8.3 Giacomo Fusto Castriotto and Girolamo Maggi, pile foundations. *Della fortificatione delle città*, 1564, 79r. Courtesy of The Getty Research Institute

piles with an average length of 12.5 metres were used.[16] Many more structures of the seventeenth century have similarly deep foundations. For this type of foundation, which came to be called the 'Amsterdam foundation', typically no grid was applied, but piles were paired and connected by a crossbeam, and driven into the ground at regular intervals of almost a metre (Figure 8.2).[17] On top of the crossbeams, plank boards were placed that connected each of the pairs lengthways and supported the footing of the walls. The seventeenth century also saw the advent of the 'Rotterdam foundation', which was similar to the method used in Amsterdam apart from the fact that single, as opposed to paired, piles were driven into the ground.[18]

The main advantage of such deep foundations, called '*op stuit*' (meaning 'on the bump'), was obviously their greater solidity, the result of the piles reaching the solid subterranean layer. But the deep foundations were probably also more

16 Bie Leuveling Tjeenk, 'De paalfundeering van het Koninklijk Paleis te Amsterdam'.
17 Gawronski and Veerkamp, 'Über staal, kleef und stuit'; van Tussenbroek, 'Was wiegt ein Haus?'
18 Gawronski and Veerkamp, 'Über staal, kleef und stuit', 55.

economical, due to the fact that they no longer required the construction of a grid, and fewer piles had to be driven into the ground, thus saving on timber.[19] Another reduction of costs was achieved by limiting the need to move the piledrivers at the construction site as there were fewer piles.[20] However, the additional cost of the larger piledrivers and the greater difficulty in handling longer piles may have outweighed this advantage.

It is generally believed that two factors contributed to the development of deep foundations. First, the realization of deep foundations may have been spurred by a fundamental transition in construction that occurred around 1600, from timber frame dwellings to those with solid brick walls, which due to their greater weight required stronger foundations.[21] However, it is worth noting that large and heavy structures existed before the sixteenth century, which were erected without deep foundations.[22] In addition, there is evidence that deep foundations were employed long before the turn of the century. Already around 1500 there is reference to 17-metre-long piles.[23] Although this might be an exaggerated length, excavations in the 1960s proved that for the transept of the Nieuwe Kerk in Amsterdam, constructed in the second quarter of the sixteenth century, piles of 13 metres were used.[24] In short, by 1550, the use of long piles was probably no longer an exception in Amsterdam, and indeed by this time, piledrivers were available that could handle piles up to 12 metres. The second and crucial factor for the adoption of longer piles in the second half of the sixteenth century lay in the increased availability of pinewood from Scandinavia.[25]

In addition to the increased weight of buildings and the augmented supply of wood, improved drilling methods may have also contributed to the use of longer piles in the sixteenth century. Refined drilling techniques likely provided builders with a better understanding of the subsoil composition, thus granting them with essential information for the construction of firm foundations. To determine the required length of piles, it was customary in the fifteenth century to simply drive a pile into the ground to see how deep it would extend. However, as noted by the famous mathematician and engineer Simon Stevin in the beginning of the seventeenth century, soil surveys had since become more extensive. 'For many years

19 Van Tussenbroek, 'Was wiegt ein Haus?', 220. There are few exceptions and for exceedingly challenging projects like the tower of the Nieuwe Kerk and Amsterdam Town Hall, a grid continued to be used in combination with long piles. See van Tussenbroek, 'The Foundations of the Nieuwe Kerk Tower in Amsterdam'.

20 Gawronski and Veerkamp, 'Über staal, kleef und stuit', 54.

21 Ibid., 23.

22 Van Tussenbroek, 'Was wiegt ein Haus?'

23 Pontanus, *Historische Beschrijvinghe der seer wijt beroemde Coop-stadt Amsterdam*, 358; van Tussenbroek, 'Was wiegt ein Haus?', 217.

24 Van Tussenbroek, 'Was wiegt ein Haus?', 217-218.

25 Ibid., 221.

large augers have been used to drill into the ground to examine the soil on which a dam, water mill or other massive building is to be built'.[26] The earliest documented cases of soil sampling with an earth auger or drill go back to at least the beginning of the sixteenth century. As will be discussed, such surveys could be extensive and sometimes lasted several days. Augers were usually made of wood, but iron augers also existed, which could be drilled through harder layers. At the end of the sixteenth century drills improved considerably, allowing the sampling of even deeper strata. In 1605, Pieter Pietersz Ente succeeded in drilling a 232-foot-deep well (approximately 73 metres) in an attempt to find potable groundwater. Ente's spring well attracted the attention of several scholars, including Simon Stevin, who claimed that this technique was a new Dutch invention, and was even unknown to the ancients. Ente did indeed receive an *octrooi* (patent) from the States-General for an improved iron drill in 1602.[27] His design appears to have been successful, as a similar instrument was discovered during recent archaeological excavations done for the construction of Amsterdam's North-South metro line. The seventeenth-century drill was found between wooden piles of a bridge, indicating that it was likely used for a soil survey for the laying of foundations.

In his report on Ente's drilling Stevin noted the various layers encountered. According to his record, on the first day a solid layer of sand was reached, totalling 10 feet (2.8 metres), at a depth of 51 feet (14.4 metres). This depth, he noted, was generally used as support for foundations in Amsterdam.[28] While surveys for construction did not have to go as deep as Ente's drill, Stevin's records show that at other places the first solid layer could be found at greater depths, as in Rotterdam were the muddy soil was 60 feet deep. Such a depth, according to Stevin, was too deep for the use of piles.[29]

Examining the soil for the construction of foundations was common in the rest of Europe, however the great depth at which samples were taken was probably particular to the Dutch Republic. In comparison, the German master mason Lorenz Lechler described in his 1516 treatise *Unterweisungen* how he determined the proper depth of the foundations by using a long hooked skewer with which he collected samples.[30] It seems improbable that his tool allowed him reach deep underground layers, and according to Borrmann, soil sampling outside the Dutch Republic rarely exceeded the depth of 3 metres prior to the eighteenth century.[31]

26 The full passage reads: 'For many years large augers have been used to drill into the ground to examine the soil on which a dam, water mill or other massive building is to be built, as well as to find out the depth of the peat, sludge, clay and other soils.' Translation from Van den Heuvel, *'De Huysbou'*, 237.

27 Abrahamse and Feiken, 'Driftig veen en onderaards bos', 36-37.

28 Van den Heuvel, *'De Huysbou'*, 476.

29 Ibid., 89-90.

30 Borrmann, *Historische Pfahlgründungen*, 42.

31 Ibid., 50, 177-1778.

The 'Hollandish Manner of Construction'

The admiration for deep pile foundations in Dutch building, and in Amsterdam construction in particular, became a recurrent theme in contemporary city descriptions. A laudatory poem on Amsterdam that was added to the Dutch Guicciardini edition, for instance, explicitly addresses the importance of the city's pile foundations. The poem, taken from Hadrianus Junius' *Batavia* (1588), a history of Holland commissioned by its Estates, urges the beholder of the city's buildings to admire their foundations even more than the structures that stand on them. According to the poem, the 'wooden foundations' were not to be ignored, because it was due to these structures, laid with great cost and labour, that Amsterdam's lofty churches rose high into the sky.[32] Such admiration extended far beyond the borders of the Dutch Republic. For instance, in the accounts of the visit of the German adventurer Johann Albrecht von Mandelslo to Amsterdam in 1640, the city was praised because of its adornment with numerous beautiful and richly furnished palaces. However, according to Mandelslo, the greatest expense 'is least seen' as it concerned the cost of the pile foundations. He believed it equalled the remainder of the building, and echoing Guicciardini, he praised the pile foundations as being the most noble underground forest in the world.[33] In his *Present State of the United Provinces* (1669), the English physician and art connoisseur William Aglionby likewise asserted that the entire city of Amsterdam was supported by an underground forest of piles.[34] And when recounting that Amsterdam Town Hall surpassed the Seven Wonders of the World, Aglionby did not credit its classicist style or its richly decorated interior, but was most impressed by the expense of its foundation.[35]

32 The poem reads: 'Lustich ben ick beset van't water: Poelen sacht / Doorstrijcken mijn landouw. Op palen vast sonderen / Aensietmen het ghebouw van mijn daecken gheacht: / Meer is hierom de grondt, dan 'tghetimmer van d'huysen, / Costlijcker oock vermaert: door swaren arebeyt / Op't houtich fondament, 'tis niet om te vergusen / Rysen hooch tot de locht oock mijn Kercken gheheyt.' See Guicciardini, *Beschryvinghe van alle de Nederlanden anderssins ghenoemt Neder-Duytslandt*, 214.

33 The passage reads: 'But what most speaks the cost imploy'd about them is least seen: For all the Houses being built on piles, it must be confessed, the foundations are no less precious then the rest of the Structure, and that there is not so noble a Forrest in the World as that which the City of Amsterdam hath under its houses.' The report of his travels was published in 1647 and translated into English in 1669. See Olearius, *The Voyages and Travells of the Ambassadors Sent by Frederick Duke of Holstein*, 231. My thanks to Annette Knol for bringing this source to my attention.

34 Aglionby, *Present State of the United Provinces*, 275-276.

35 On Amsterdam, Aglionby wrote: 'All this great Town is built upon pilotis, which are great Trees driven by main force into the ground, which is all moorish, to be as a foundation to build upon; and ordinarily it costs as much laying, as all the rest of the Fabrick does building up.' And on the town hall he wrote: 'The Town-house which is now a building, the foundations of which have cost many thousands of Pounds, is to be a Master-piece, and a miracle beyond the seven that Antiquity bragg'd so much of.' Aglionby based his publication on *Les délices de la Hollande* by Jean-Nicolas de Parival, who in 1651 similarly considered the

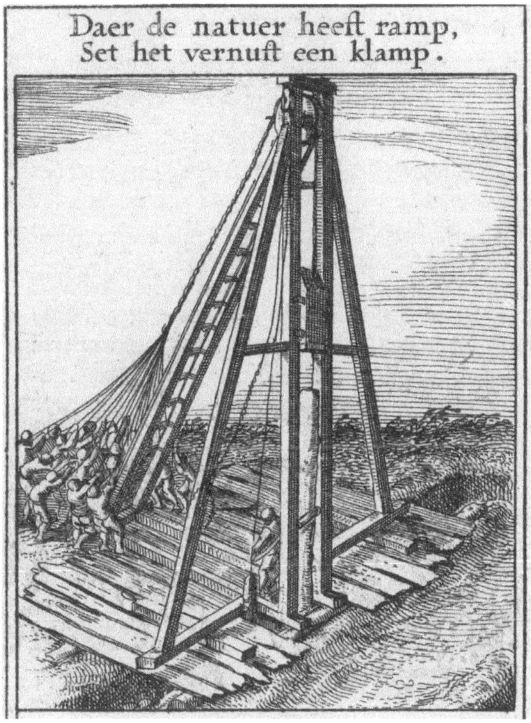

Fig. 8.4 Claes Jansz Visscher II, piledriving machine. Detail from Roemer Visscher, *Sinnepoppen*, 1614, 127. Rijksmuseum, Object Nr. BI-1893-3539-127

Whereas most descriptions of the Dutch pile foundations concentrated on their great cost, some authors also praised the skill and know-how required for their construction. For instance, the Amsterdam merchant and rhetorician Roemer Visscher devoted one of the emblems in his eblemata *Sinnepoppen* (1614) to the mechanical devices used for piledriving. The emblem shows a tall machine that is operated by a large crew, which is busy driving a massive pile into a foundation trench (Figure 8.4). The motto, 'When nature brings distress, ingenuity provides solidness', and the accompanying text clarify that the piledriver serves to illustrate human ingenuity, which allows mankind to cope with nature's troubles.[36]

pile foundations of Amsterdam, and admired the great cost of the town hall's foundations: 'L'Hostel de Ville qui se bastit aujourd'huy, & duquel les fondemens, & les maisons que l'on a abbattues, ont cousté je ne sçay combien de tonnes d'or, doit estre un chef d'oeuvre, & un autre miracle par dessus les sept merveilles du monde; l'art & l'argent conduisant cette haute entreprise, ne, peuvent rien produire que de miraculeux.' See Parival, *Les délices de la Hollande*, 79, 81. My thanks to Sander Karst for bringing this source to my attention.
36 The text states that due to the unfavourable ground conditions no building could be erected in Holland, and in Amsterdam in particular, without driving piles into the ground to provide solid foundations.

The English traveller John Evelyn also gave attention to the tools used by the Dutch in the construction of foundations. When he visited the construction site of the citadel in 's-Hertogenbosch in 1641, Evelyn wrote in his diary that the 'Hollanders' made used of all kinds of inventions, for which they were considered to be 'the most expert in Europe' at constructing large structures in marshy conditions:

> I went toward Bois-le-Duc where we arrived on the sixteenth, at the time when the new citadel was advancing, with innumerable hands, and incomparable inventions for draining the waters out of the fens and morasses about it, being by buckets, mills, cochleas, pumps and the like; in which the Hollanders are the most expert in Europe.[37]

These 'incomparable inventions' in hydraulic engineering were highly valued, as were the skills required to lay foundations, and as a result, Dutch engineers were in high demand abroad.[38] Several European powers, including Cosimo III de' Medici, Jean-Baptiste Colbert and Tsar Peter the Great, sent their own engineers and architects – the divisions between both professions were quite fluid in this period – to the Netherlands to study construction techniques.[39] A letter from Peter the Great to his agent in Holland, Johannes van der Burgh, from 1724 clearly explains the reasons why the tsar sent Russian architectural students to the Low Countries. He instructed Van der Burgh to make sure that they learned 'the Hollandish manner of construction [*manir gollanskoj arhitektury*] and especially how to make foundations, because we have the same situation because of the water level and reduced thickness of the walls'.[40] Peter held Dutch expertise to be indispensable for the building of St. Petersburg.

Significantly, drawings of Netherlandish pile foundations made their way into archives as distant as Tuscany and Lisbon. Pietro Guerrini, who went on a study tour to northern Europe in the 1680s on behalf of Cosimo III de' Medici, carefully recorded the pile foundations of the fortifications of Sas van Gent, which were

To facilitate this laborious work, the piledriving machine was invented. 'Dese Landen hier in Hollandt gheleghen, ende bysonder hier ontrent Amsterdam, hebben dat ghebreck dat men daer gheen heerlijck ghebouw maecken of timmeren mach, sonder de grondt dapper te versorghen met palen daer in te heyen; dan de mensche aensiende de ghelenghentheydt van de plaetse en haven, heeft raet ghevonden met dusdanighen Instrument de grondt vast te maecken, om alsoo daer haer nootduftighe wooninghe daer op te setten.' See Visscher, *Sinnepoppen*, 121.

37 Evelyn, *The Diary of John Evelyn*, vol. 1, 45.

38 Danner, *Polder Pioneers*; Ciriacono, *Building on Water*; Martens and Ottenheym, 'Fortifications and Waterworks'.

39 Martelli, *Il viaggio in Europa di Pietro Guerrini (1682-1686)*; Mahoney, 'Organizing Expertise'.

40 Translation in Van de Vijver, 'Epilogue', 419.

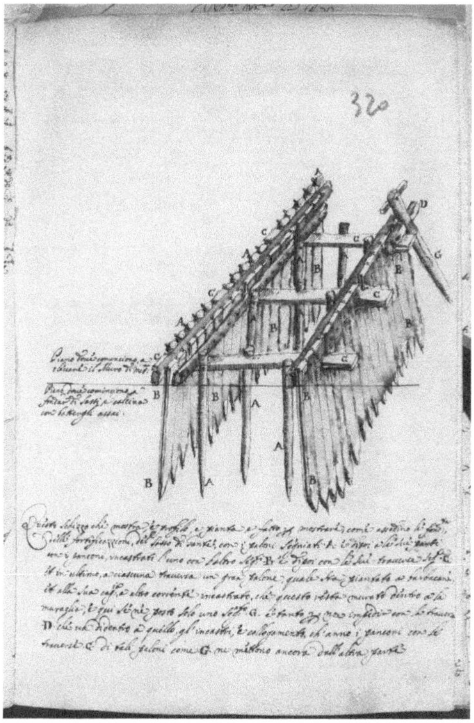

Fig. 8.5 Pietro Guerrini, drawing of the pile foundations of the fortifications at Sas van Gent, 1683. Archivio di Stato di Firenze, Mediceo del Principato, 6390, c. 320r.

erected by the Dutch after the town was seized by stadtholder Frederik Henderik in 1644.

The drawing (Figure 8.5) depicts in great detail the rows of piles, marked A, and sheet piling along the length of the foundation (B), which are held together by the transversal plank boards (C). The foundation was further reinforced by an outward sloping pile, delineated by G, which was probably to prevent the brick wall from tilting forward. Guerrini wrote that the sheet piles, joined together by tongue and groove joints, were reinforced by iron nails and bars.[41] He did not explain its function, but it is likely that it provided a barrier against water, so as to protect the soil around the piles from calving off.

The National Library of Portugal also preserves a drawing that depicts the foundations of fortifications, specifically those of the *Papenbril*, which was the nickname of the citadel of 's-Hertogenbosch (Figure 8.6). Although the Dutch

41 Martelli, *Il viaggio in Europa di Pietro Guerrini (1682-1686)*, vol. 1, 193.

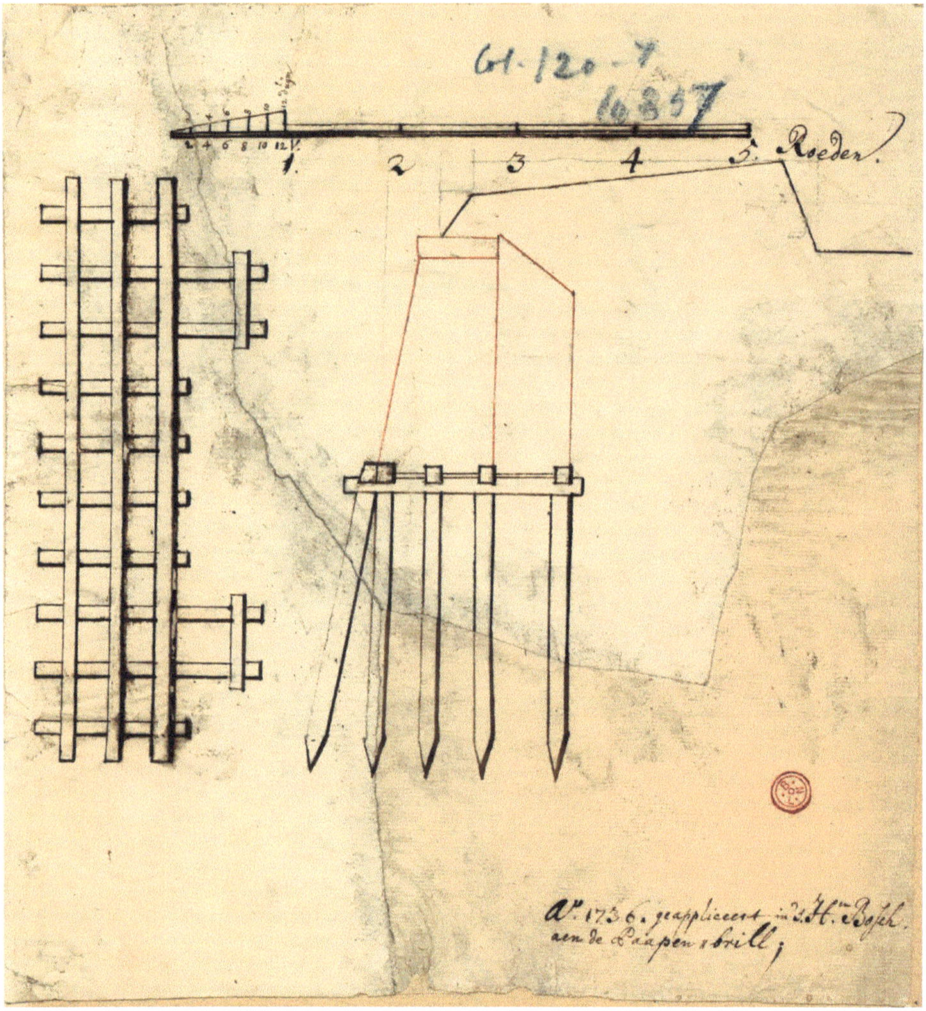

Fig. 8.6 Anonymous draughtsman, plan and section of pile foundations of the citadel in 's-Hertogenbosch, 1736. Biblioteca Nacional de Portugal, Lisbon, D. 250 P

caption dates the drawing in 1736, the citadel itself was built over a century earlier between 1637 and 1645, after the city was conquered by the Dutch troops in 1629.[42] The drawing shows a cross section of an earthen slope with its brick masonry facing (indicated by red lines), which is supported by piles. Next to the section is a plan

42 The caption reads: 'A° 1736. Geappliceert in 's H^{en} Bosch aen de Paapen, brill'. Biblioteca Nacional de Portugal, D. 250 P. (cat no. 824). The drawing was obviously made by a Dutchman, and although it is unknown how and when the drawing made its way to Portugal, it seems probable that it happened in the eighteenth century. See also Mendonça de Oliveira and Pousada Presa, 'Reinforcing Foundations with Wood Piles', 1539.

of the grid that was placed upon the heads of the piles to join them together. Like at Sas van Gent, the outward sloping pile was intended to prevent the brick wall from tilting forward, while the back of the wall was supported by buttresses that protruded into the earthworks.

That the draughtsman endeavoured to record the extraordinary foundations of the citadel of 's-Hertogenbosch, even long after its construction, underscores the degree to which the Dutch excellence in this field was recognized and valued. The Dutch ability to construct secure foundations in marshy conditions was directly related to the landscapes they inhabited and the places they sought to develop. But this place-generated knowledge could also be exported. By the end of the seventeenth century, the Dutch Republic was regarded as the best place to acquire specialized know-how in the construction of pile foundations.

The Planning of Foundations

Although Amsterdam's foundations are most often highlighted in the encomia of the seventeenth century, comparable ground conditions, and comparably impressive foundations, existed in coastal areas throughout the Low Countries. One of the earliest records that sheds light on the meticulous planning of pile foundations is a description by the monk Gaspar Ofhuys (d. 1523) of the history of Rouge-Cloître Abbey in the Sonian Forest (Zoniënwoud) near Brussels.[43] Before commencing work on the abbey, the prior of Rouge-Cloître, Johannes Rampaert, who according to Ofhuys had himself considerable knowledge of foundations, consulted with a series of experts so as to avoid any future settlement of the structure's foundation, which could damage the building or even could cause it to collapse.[44] The first to be called was Jacobus van Dinter, prior at nearby Groenendaal, who was considered 'an expert in [building] foundations for weak and floating [soil]' (*'in fundamentis mollibus et defluentibus expertus erat valde'*).

In this period, it was common for the overseer of a major building project to elicit the opinion of multiple experts. But the case of the Rouge-Cloître Abbey is somewhat exceptional, as those called to advise Johannes Rampaert had remarkably disparate backgrounds. Besides several eminent stonemasons from nearby Brussels, Rampaert invited experts who did not belong to the building trades, including the princely officer in charge of the Sonian Forest (*woudmeester*), the receiver of

43 Gaspar Ofhuys, *Originale Coenobii Rubeaevallis*, s.d. (Royal Library Brussels, Manuscripts, II 480). Printed in Johannes Gielemans, *De codicibus hagiographicis Iohannis Gielemans*.

44 Gielemans, *De codicibus hagiographicis Iohannis Gielemans*, 396.

Brabant, and a fisherman.[45] Because each counsel proposed his own solution for the laying of foundations, no agreement was reached, and Rampaert decided to wait for the advice of the eminent master mason to the court of Emperor Maximilian I in Brabant, Anthonis I Keldermans. After Keldermans inspected the site and studied the drawings of the new church, he instructed that 9-to-10-foot-long oak piles (approximately 2.5 metres) be driven into the ground in two rows at a distance of 7 feet (approximately 2 metres) from each other at intervals of one foot.[46] On top of this base, a grid was to be made of plank boards, each four thumbs thick, holding together the piles in each row. Transversal planks were placed on top of this to join the two rows together.[47] This construction differs somewhat from early-sixteenth-century techniques used in Amsterdam, as the space between the piles was much larger and the wooden plank boards were placed on top of the piles, whereas usually the squares of the grid were filled in with as many as piles as possible.

The only difficulty in Keldermans' proposal was that it proved problematic to purchase straight oak piles of sufficient length. But the brothers of the Rouge-Cloître Abbey finally succeeded in obtaining good quality piles, some of which were even 18 feet tall (approximately 5 metres). Ofhuys' chronicle shows that a mechanical device was used for pile-driving: a 25-foot-tall machine (almost seven metres), which was constructed at the site. The device contained a heavy trunk covered with iron that could be raised ten to twelve feet (approximately three metres) by a crew of eight to nine brothers pulling a rope.[48]

The knowledge necessary to drive foundation piles in soggy subsoil was so advanced in the Low Countries by the early sixteenth century that large and heavy structures, such as towers and fortifications, could even be built in marshy areas and next to deep, open water. One of the most challenging engineering feats from this period was the construction of the Blauwe Toren (Blue Tower) built in Gorinchem for Charles the Bold when he was still count of Charolais. The castle, which derived its name from the cladding of the facing wall with large blocks of blue limestone, was located south of the town at the banks of the River Merwede (Figure 8.7).

45 Hurx, *Architecture as Profession*, 233.

46 The Brussels foot is 27.56 centimetres.

47 'Ordinavit ergo quod pilae pararentur ligneae et quercinae aut alterius generis, longitudinis novem aut decem pedum, qui violenter intruderentur distantes ab invicem unius pedis spatio; ipse autem fundus hoc modo ad omne minus septem pedum latitudine pilaretur. Quo bene pilato, fortissimo tegeretur loramento, cuius asseres sive tabulae quattuor pollicibus essent spissae; quibus concatenatis et fortiter combinatis, desuper asseribus per transversum deductis invicem colligarentur.' See Gielemans, *De codicibus hagiographicis Iohannis Gielemans*, 398.

48 'Erat enim ibi quaedam machina sive instrumentum viginti.' See Gielemans, *De codicibus hagiographicis Iohannis Gielemans*, 404.

Fig. 8.7 Pieter Sluyter, map of Gorinchem showing the Blauwe Toren at the banks of the Merwede (detail), 1553. Nationaal Archief, The Hague, Kaarten Hingman, 4.VTH 2453

Although, it was entirely demolished at the end of the sixteenth century, written and topographical sources show that it was an entirely freestanding, massive circular structure with a diameter of 35 metres and surrounded by a moat.[49] Just above the water level there were vaulted cellars, while the main representative rooms were arranged around a rectangular courtyard, a full level above ground.

The few remaining records for the Blauwe Toren show that careful planning preceded construction, and that numerous experts were consulted in the

49 Hurx, '"Een alten wonderlijcken structure ende fortresse"'.

summer of 1462. Charles engaged the most prominent masters of the works (*werkmeesters*) in the northern Netherlands, including Jacob van der Borch, master of Utrecht Cathedral, master Claes of Saint John's in 's-Hertogenbosch, and Evert Spoorwater, who was master of various important churches in Brabant and Holland. The principle designer of the castle, however, was Jean Marchant, who was one of the masters of the works at Palais Rihour, Philip the Good's residence in Lille. Together with two master carpenters from the nearby towns of 's-Hertogenbosch and Heusden, the group of experts visited the building site for three days to discuss the foundations in the company of the financial supervisor of the building works, the castellan, the sheriff, and the lieutenant of the bailiff of Gorinchem, as well as 'others who were knowledgeable in such works'.[50] Prior to this meeting Marchant had travelled to the town of Dordrecht to ask master carpenters and master masons how pile foundations of heavy works were laid in the region (*'pour avoir leur adviz dela maniere quilz ont pilloter en pays pour fondemens de gros ouvraiges'*).[51] Apparently one did not dare to rely only on experts from the northern Low Countries; on the advice of Jean Marchant the master carpenter working on the ducal palace in Lille, Evrard des Mazières, was invited to come to Gorinchem. In a letter requesting permission from the Chamber of Accounts in Lille for Evrard to travel north, the financial supervisor of the works in Gorinchem stressed the importance of his visit to the construction site by pointing out that the castle would be entirely built on pile foundations, and that Evrard was highly skilled in this technique. Moreover, the supervisor wrote that the works should not be led by builders from the 'peripheral lands' where the castle was located without the design oversight of masters from the south.[52]

The fragmentary sources only give a general impression of the foundations of the castle and how they were realized. Multiple techniques were combined. The ground was compacted using great quantities of rubble stone imported from quarries around Brussels. For the pile foundations, large quantities of long oak piles called '*mairien*' (also spelled as '*mairain*' and '*merrain*'), which measured 30 feet (approximately 9 metres) in length, were purchased. Together with long oak

50 'Durant le quel terme ilz estoient journelement ensemble avec maistre Evrart Sporwatre et avec ledit Jehan Marchant en disputant et en conseillant le bien diceulx fondemens en la presence du chastellain, de lescoutette et du lieutenant de drossat dudit Gorinchem dudit Fastret et dautres se cognoissans en ouvraiges.' Archives départementales du Nord, Lille (ADN), B 2047, no. 63531. See Hurx, '"Een alten wonderlijcken structure ende fortresse"', 195-196.

51 ADN, B 2047, no. 63531. Hurx, '"Een alten wonderlijcken structure ende fortresse"', 195.

52 'a fin que cesd ouvrages ne soient point totalement conduiz par gens deces marches icy sans en avoir aucuns de pardela pour veoir e ouyez l'entendement de chacune' (ADN, B 17692). See Hurx, '"Een alten wonderlijcken structure ende fortresse"', 195.

beams called '*ontdraghers*' they were 'to be applied for the *pilotis*'.[53] Considering the difficulty the Rouge-Cloître Abbey encountered in acquiring 10-foot-long oak piles, it seems remarkable that much longer oak piles were obtained for the foundations of the Blauwe Toren. Their length would suggest that these were actually deep foundations that rested on a solid sand layer below the surface.

Comparably detailed insight into the planning of foundations in similar conditions can be derived from the 1524-1525 building accounts of the never-completed castle of Schoonhoven. Its location between the town and the River Lek was akin to the position of the Blauwe Toren. The castle was designed by Rombout Keldermans, the master of works to Charles V, who visited Schoonhoven several times to inspect the building site. However, construction near deep water proved to be difficult, and accounts show that, although the works were well-planned, execution of the project suffered several setbacks. Before works commenced in the spring of 1524, the soil of the site was meticulously investigated for four days by a carpenter who, using his 'instruments' (probably an earth auger), tried to determine its composition.[54] Soon after the workmen started excavations for the foundation, they reported that the soil was very muddy. To prevent water from filling the pits, two pumps were installed that were operated by a crew of 15 to 20 people day and night.[55] Meanwhile a piledriver was constructed in the pits, which measured 40 feet or about 11.5 metres, according to the Antwerp foot of 28.56 centimetres. The size suggests that piles of considerable length, possibly up to 8 metres, were used. However, it is unknown if they were long enough to reach the first solid layer of subsoil.

Piledriving at the castle of Schoonhoven began under the supervision of Hubrecht Frederikszn, a close assistant of Rombout Keldermans. His permanent presence at the site was required, because 'the workers had little knowledge in such matters'. He was to make sure that they followed the ground plan ('pattern') made by Rombout Keldermans, taking particular care that the exact outline of the castle was followed.[56] It is not clear whether this drawing was specifically made for the foundations, or if the plan showing the general outline of the castle, still preserved in the National Archive in The Hague, was used (Figure 8.8). However, and as will be subsequently discussed in greater detail,

53 'pour convertir esdits en pillotements desdit ouvraiges' (ADN, B 2050, nos. 63767, 63768, 63769 and 63770). See Hurx, '"Een alten wonderlijcken structure ende fortresse"', 196.

54 Hermans and Brongers, 'Het niet voltooide kasteel te Schoonhoven', 35.

55 Ibid., 37.

56 'zo int wysen ende beweghen hoe ende in wat manieren datmen die pylen slaen zoude omme dat zy buyten den voirn. patrone nyet ghaen en zoude midts dat die arbeyders daer luttel verstans aff hadden'. Nationaal Archief, The Hague (NA), Grafelijkheidsrekenkamer (GRK), 5008, 119v. Leys, 'De invloed van Anthonis I en Rombout II Keldermans', 164-165.

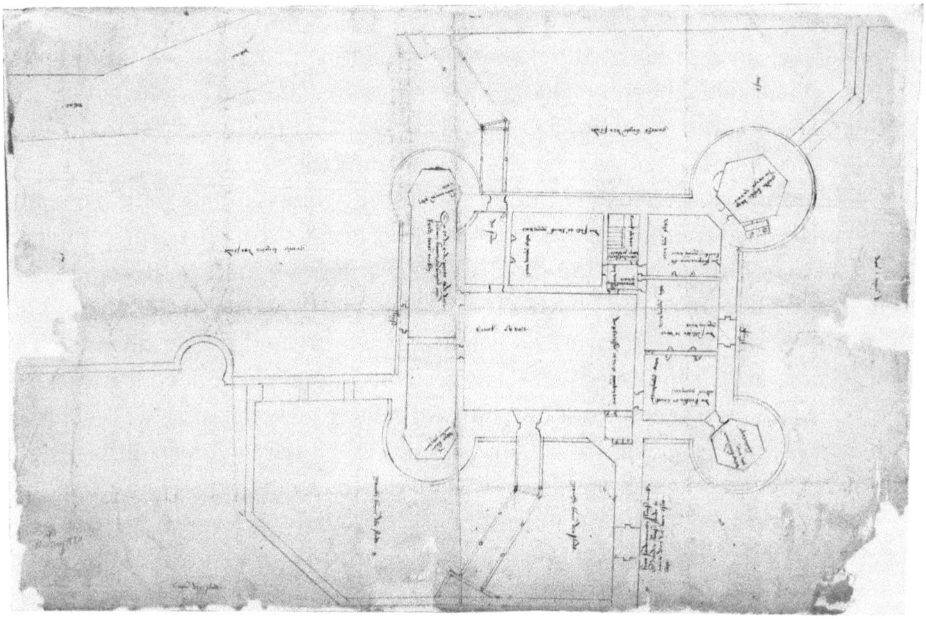

Fig. 8.8 Rombout II Keldermans, plan of Schoonhoven Castle, 1524. Nationaal Archief, The Hague, Kaarten Hingman, 4.VTH 3352

it is probable that detailed drawings of the foundations were made. These were not generic plans, but place-specific designs, which involved site surveys, detailed measures and an acute understanding of the local environment and structural engineering.

Stone Sluices for the Rijnland

Among the earliest preserved examples of detailed plans made specifically for the purpose of laying foundations are drawings for the sluices in Halfweg and Alphen aan den Rijn. These constructions belong to the earliest generation of stone sluices in Holland, and were realized on behalf of the water board (*Hoogheemraadschap*) of Rijnland, which oversaw the water management in an area stretching from Haarlem and Amsterdam in the north, to The Hague and Gouda in the south.[57] The responsibilities of this regional government body included protecting the land from flooding, but also regulating water levels in the polders, and maintaining waterways. Although the sluices no longer remain,

57 Van Dam, 'Ecological Challenges, Technological Innovations'.

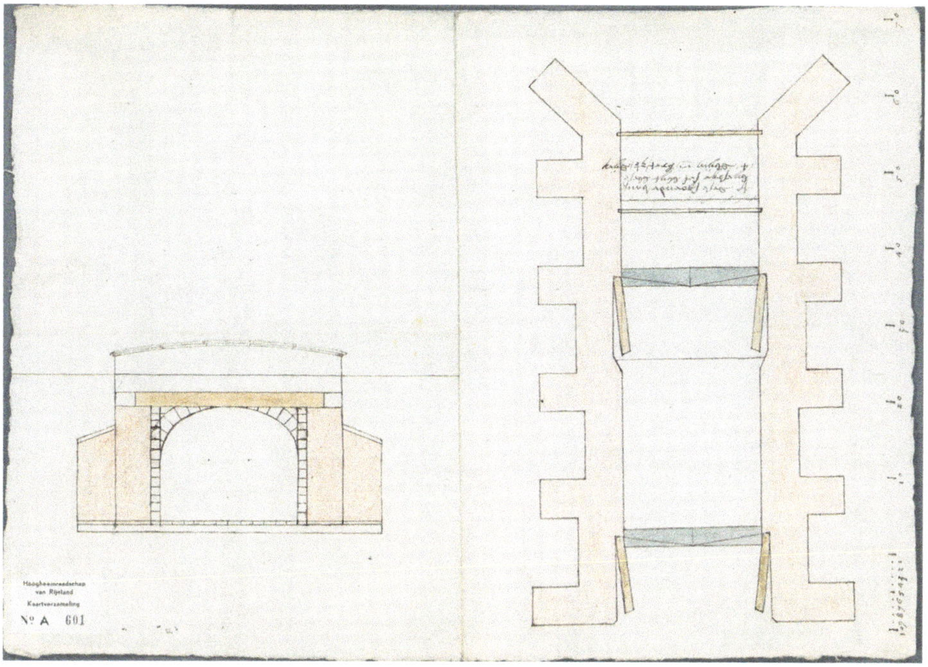

Fig. 8.9 Cornelis Fredrickszn, elevation and plan of the Westsluis at Halfweg, 1556. Oud Archief van Rijnland, Leiden, Collectie Kaarten, A 601

the survival of drawings, building specifications, accounts and letters in the archive of the water board provide detailed insight into the careful planning of their foundations.[58]

The Westsluis at Halfweg, which was used for drainage purposes, was located in the Spaarndammerdijk halfway between Amsterdam and Haarlem. It connected the Spieringmeer with the IJ, which at that time was still an extremity of the Zuiderzee. In 1556, the water board engaged Cornelis Frederickszn vander Goude, who was the master of the works of Saint John's in Gouda.[59] Cornelis is mentioned in the accounts of Schoonhoven Castle as the cousin of the aforementioned Hubrecht Frederiksz, and thus he may have obtained first-hand knowledge of the difficulties of foundation laying at Schoonhoven early in his career.[60] By the time he was working on the sluice in Halfweg, he was already a fully-fledged master with ample experience in foundation laying. He had guided the works at several churches, and had consulted

58 For the development of foundations techniques for sluices in the fifteenth century, see ibid.

59 Oud Archief van Rijnland, Leiden (OAR), 1.1.1, inv. no. 4856. See Van Amstel-Horák, 'Nieuwbouw van twee sluizen in een benarde tijd'.

60 NA, GRK, 5008, fol. 156v.

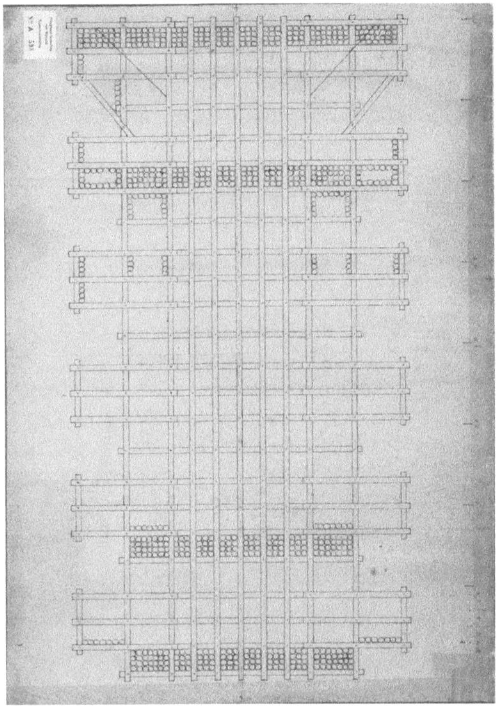

Fig. 8.10 Cornelis Frederickszn, plan of the foundations of the Westsluis, 1556. Oud Archief van Rijnland, Leiden, Collectie Kaarten, A 598

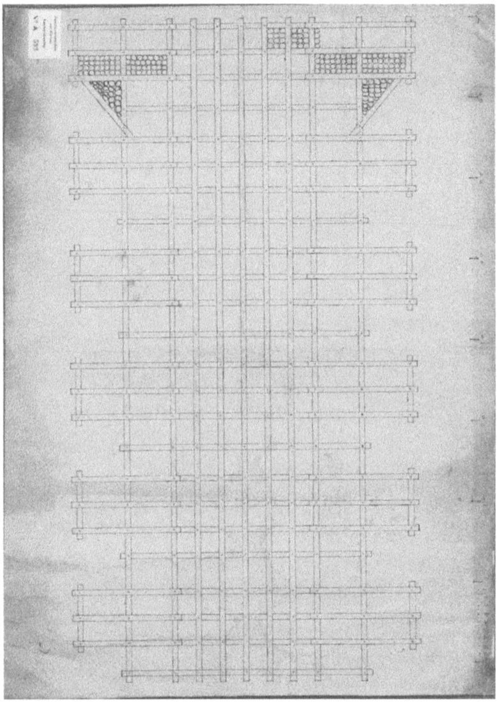

Fig. 8.11 Cornelis Frederickszn, plan of the foundations of the Westsluis, 1556. Oud Archief van Rijnland, Leiden, Collectie Kaarten, A 599

on the construction of the Maaslandersluis at Vlaardingen in 1548.[61] His expertise in foundation laying is also affirmed in the fact that in 1531 he consulted on the foundations in the reconstruction of the church tower in Culemborg.[62]

Cornelis Frederickszn provided drawings for the new sluice at Halfweg after he had inspected the ground conditions (Figures 8.9-8.11). He designed a sluice made of Bentheimer sandstone and bricks, with a vaulted sluice chamber that had two pairs of mitre-gates, measuring about 70 feet long and 20 feet wide (about 22 metres and 6.3 metres, according to the Rhineland foot of 31.4 centimetres). The preserved set of seventeen drawings includes two plans for the pile foundations, which both show a regular grid that follows the general outline of the sluice with buttresses that protrude into the main body of the dyke (Figures 8.10 and 8.11).

The plans are almost identical and are drawn to the same scale (based on units of 10 Rijnland feet). It is not clear why these two nearly identical drawings were made. The only obvious difference concerns the position of the piles. The plan given on

61 Van Amstel-Horák, 'Nieuwbouw van twee sluizen in een benarde tijd', 63.

62 Van den Berg, *De Sint-Janskerk in Gouda*, 78-80.

folio A 599 (Figure 8.11) shows only a few squares at the top that are filled in with piles, where they were to support the oblique buttresses that pointed towards the Spieringmeer in the south. By contrast, in the plan on folio A 598 (Figure 8.10), there are several squares that have piles only at their outer edges, while four strips of piles are drawn at the very extremities of the grid and at the spot where heavy blue limestone thresholds would support the mitre-gates. The building specifications that accompanied the images explain that all squares, called 'spaces or holes' (*camers oft ghaten*), were to be filled in with alder piles measuring 24 feet (about 7.5 metres) or longer. Extra care was to be given to the squares at the grid's outer edges and the squares that supported the limestone thresholds, in which the piles were to be driven extra tightly together.[63]

It is unclear if the 7.5 metre long piles used in the construction of the sluice at Halfweg reached firm ground, but it is clear that this would have been possible. Mid-sixteenth-century specifications in the water board archive, regarding the construction of camp-shedding along the Spaarndammerdijk, show that when necessary, piles of at least 36 feet (about 11 metres) could be driven into the ground.[64] Whether or not long piles were needed depended on both the weight the foundations had to carry, and on the composition of the soil. Interestingly, the contractor of a timber sluice that was built near Halfweg in exactly the same years asked the water board's officers if he could use shorter piles than those agreed upon in the contract. Because of the firmness of the soil, it was exceedingly difficult to drive piles of 12 and 16 feet long (3.8-5 metres) into the ground.[65] Possibly, the weight of the dyke in which the sluice was constructed had compacted the soil to such an extent that piledriving had become difficult.

A comparable question about the stability of the subsoil became a matter of dispute when plans were made for a new stone sluice near Alphen aan den Rijn, called the Gouwsluis. The recorded history of the design and construction of this sluice provides additional insight into the Dutch expertise in pile foundations, as well as the painstaking site-specific processes – technical and administrative – by which these were realized. Located at the junction of the Rivers Oude Rijn and Gouwe, two of the main shipping routes in Holland, the new and wider Gouwsluis was to allow vessels to pass more easily.[66] In search of a master, in April 1562 the

63 'Item men zal alle die camers oft ghaten die dan in de voorn. bodem vallen zullen vol elsen paelen heyen zo dat behoort van XXIIII voeten lanc, of langer indient van noode es, ende van vyf palmen ten minsten dicke twee voeten van tbyleynde, ende desgelyx onder dat slothout voor ende achter, ende ooc onder die deurbinden daermen die dreppels op zetten zal naer behooren wel dicht ende vast gestopt naerden oorbaer vand wercke.' See OAR, 1.1.1, inv. no. 9579d.

64 OAR, 1.1.1, inv. no. 150.

65 OAR, 1.1.1, inv. no. 9578, fols. 406v.-407r.

66 Ibelings, 'De route "binnendunen". De scheepvaartroute langs de Goudse sluis', 251-252.

water board turned to Amsterdam and approached its city master mason, Reynier Corneliszn, asking him to provide designs (*grondt, besteck, ende patroen*) for the Gouwsluis.[67]

Apart from the fact that Corneliszn had been Amsterdam's master mason since 1554, little is known about him.[68] He appears to have enjoyed a good reputation as a designer, as in his letters to the water board he styled himself 'architect', a title which was still quite uncommon in the second half of the sixteenth century in the Low Countries.[69] The duties as city master left him little opportunity to leave Amsterdam and inspect the site of the sluice. Therefore, rather than making the initial site visit himself, the water board sent him two drawings with information on the new sluice, which he received on 8 April 1562.[70] But Reynier also needed to visit the site, and asked permission of the water board to complete an inspection with Amsterdam's city carpenter, Pieter Janszn, because he was better able to analyse the subsoil. In his letter to the board, Reynier explained that the sluice likely needed pile foundations, because even at sites in Utrecht, which had far better ground conditions, it was necessary to use piles to support bridges and sluices.[71]

The two Amsterdam city masters travelled to Alphen on the first of May to inspect the site, and to examine the composition of the soil by using an earth auger. Their first survey was unsuccessful, because the auger was not long enough to reach deeper layers in the soil, and as a result, they ventured a second attempt two weeks later. The masters wrote to the water board's receiver (14 May 1562) that they would like to use the board's iron auger, as they owned only a wooden auger, and no iron auger could be purchased in Amsterdam. However, as the board's iron auger was too short, they proposed to make it twice as long using a wooden rod.[72] For their extensive survey on 18 May, the two masters were aided by several assistants, and this time gained sufficient insight into the soil's composition. The

67 OAR, 1.1.1, inv. no. 3590a.

68 Van Essen, *Het stadsfabriekambt*, 12.

69 Hurx, *Architecture as Profession*, 37-39; Ottenheym, 'The Rise of a New Profession'.

70 OAR, 1.1.1, inv. no. 9582, fol. 259r.

71 The letter from Reynier Corneliszn to the receiver of the Hoogheemraadschap of Rijnland, 18 April 1562, reads: 'overmits dat ick een weijnich voerden grondt daer de sluyse leggen sal sorge, datse sal moeten geheijt sijn want die van Utrecht die oock een seer goeden gront hebben noch sommige bruggen ende oock haer sluyse ande vaert moeten heyen, aldus om te beter desen grondt te doersijen so begeerde ick wel onsen timmerman mede te hebben' (OAR, 1.1.1, inv. no. 3590a).

72 The letter from Reynier Corneliszn to the receiver of the Hoogheemraadschap of Rijnland, 14 May 1562, reads: 'met ons brengende tselfde gereetscap van een boor als wij connen crigen, hier tot Amsteldam en sijn niet dan houten boeren waer om wij op u eerwaerdicheit wel souden begeren dat [...] dat ijseren boer twelck laest tot Alphen was, de helft langer wilde laten maken van houten boven an, op dat wij versekert syn ende wij sullen altydt noch onse houten boer met ons nemen' (OAR, 1.1.1, inv. no. 3590a).

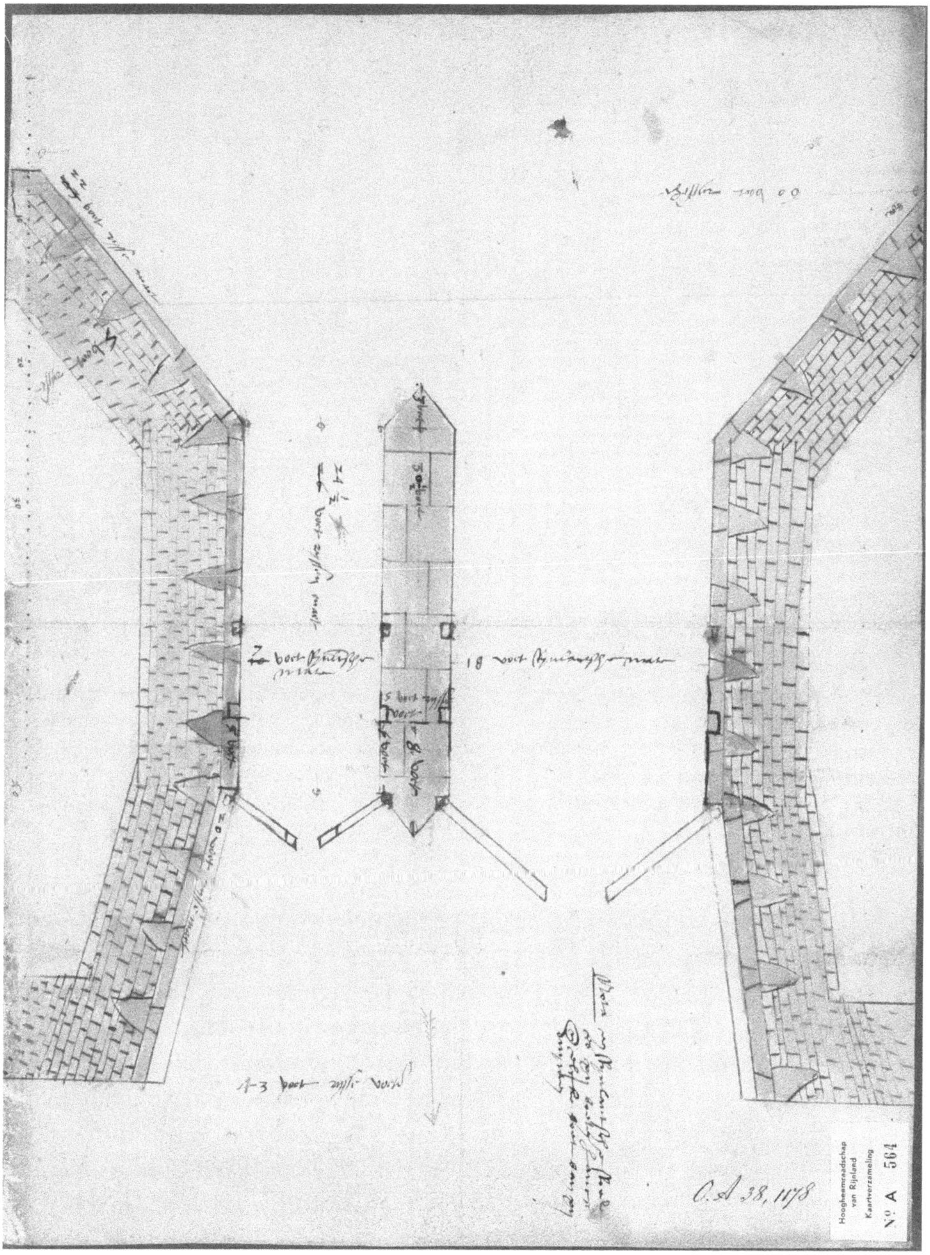

Fig. 8.12 Reynier Corneliszn, plan of the Gouwsluis at Alphen aan den Rijn, oriented to the south, 1562. The verso contains the note: 'Mr. Reyer stadsmetselaer tot Aemstelredam.' Oud Archief van Rijnland, Leiden, Collectie Kaarten, A 564

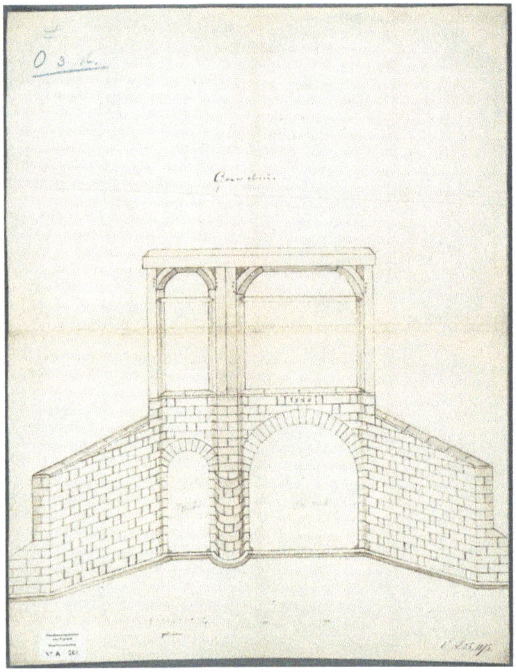

Fig. 8.13 Cornelis Fredericksz van Montfoort (attributed), elevation of the Gouwsluis seen from the Oude Rijn at the north, 1562. The verso contains the note: 'Die Orthigraphie ofte Recht opstaende bescrivinghe ende toninghe van de Sluyze tot Alphen.' Oud Archief van Rijnland, Leiden, Collectie Kaarten, A 568

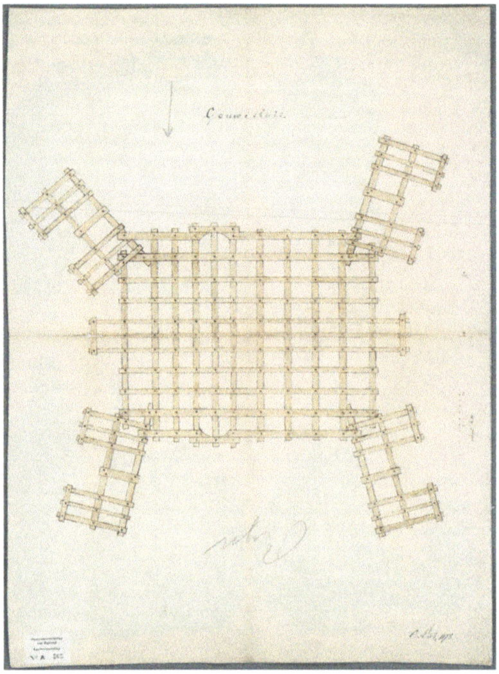

Fig. 8.14 Cornelis Fredericksz van Montfoort (attributed), plan of the foundations of the Gouwsluis, oriented to the south, 1562. The verso contains the note: 'Het Slothout of den eersten Gront van de Goutsche Zluyse leggende tot Alphen in den Rijndijck.' Oud Archief van Rijnland, Leiden, Collectie Kaarten, A 565

master craftsmen reported that the soil was reasonably well suited for construction with a clay stratum of 4.5 Rhineland feet in width (1.4 metre).[73]

Shortly after the survey, Reynier provided a design for the sluice (Figure 8.12), which was reviewed by the water board in The Hague in the summer of 1562.[74] The outcome of this discussion is unclear, but on 7 October 1562 the town of Gouda objected to the new plans, putting forward a cheaper alternative made by the master carpenter of St. John's in Gouda, Cornelis Frederickszn van Montfoort (not to be confused with the master mason Cornelis Frederickszn vander Goude).[75] Frederickszn van Montfoort's design involved substituting most of the massive and

73 OAR, 1.1.1, inv. no. 3590b.

74 OAR, 1.1.1, inv. no. 3590c.

75 Letter from the city authorities of Gouda to the Hoogheemraadschap of Rijnland, 17 October 1562: 'bevynden dat die ordonnantie by die van Amsterdam gemaect zo merckelijk groote penningen costen zouden datmen met die derde penninck min wel zal maecken. Te weten dat het heyen ende die blaeuwe steen zeven ofte acht voet onder water gemetselt te vergeefs es' (OAR, 1.1.1, inv. no. 3590a).

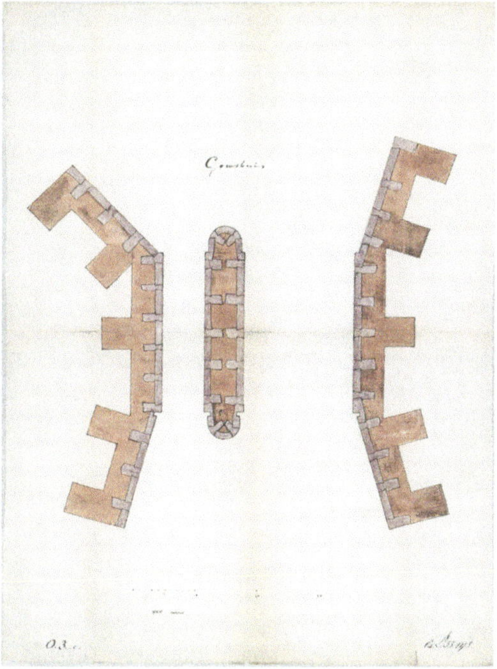

Fig. 8.15 Cornelis Fredericksz van Montfoort (attributed), Plan of the Gouwsluis, 1562. The image is oriented to the south. The verso contains the note: 'Die Ichnographie of platten grondt van de Sluyse in den Rijndijck leggende tot Alphen.' Oud Archief van Rijnland, Leiden, Collectie kaarten, A 567

heavy blue limestone blocks with a combination of bricks and hydraulic cement (Figures 8.13-8.15). These alternative building materials were not only more economical, but also considerably reduced the weight of the sluice, thus allowing for lighter foundations. Another reduction of costs was achieved by opting for sliding or guillotine gates instead of mitre-gates as shown in Reynier's drawing.[76]

Between November and the following spring, Cornelis Frederickszn van Montfoort travelled between Gouda, Leiden and Alphen to discuss his plans with the water board and to inspect the site, and on 24 April 1563 he entered into a contract for the laying of foundations. The contract stipulated that if the driving of piles

76 The solution of the drawing seems to correspond with the preserved specifications of 18 November 1562, which also provided for guillotine gates. The specifications were made after a wooden model ('after volgende dat houten bestek') and were accompanied with three drawings ('drie concepten'). OAR, 1.1.1, inv. no. 3590a.

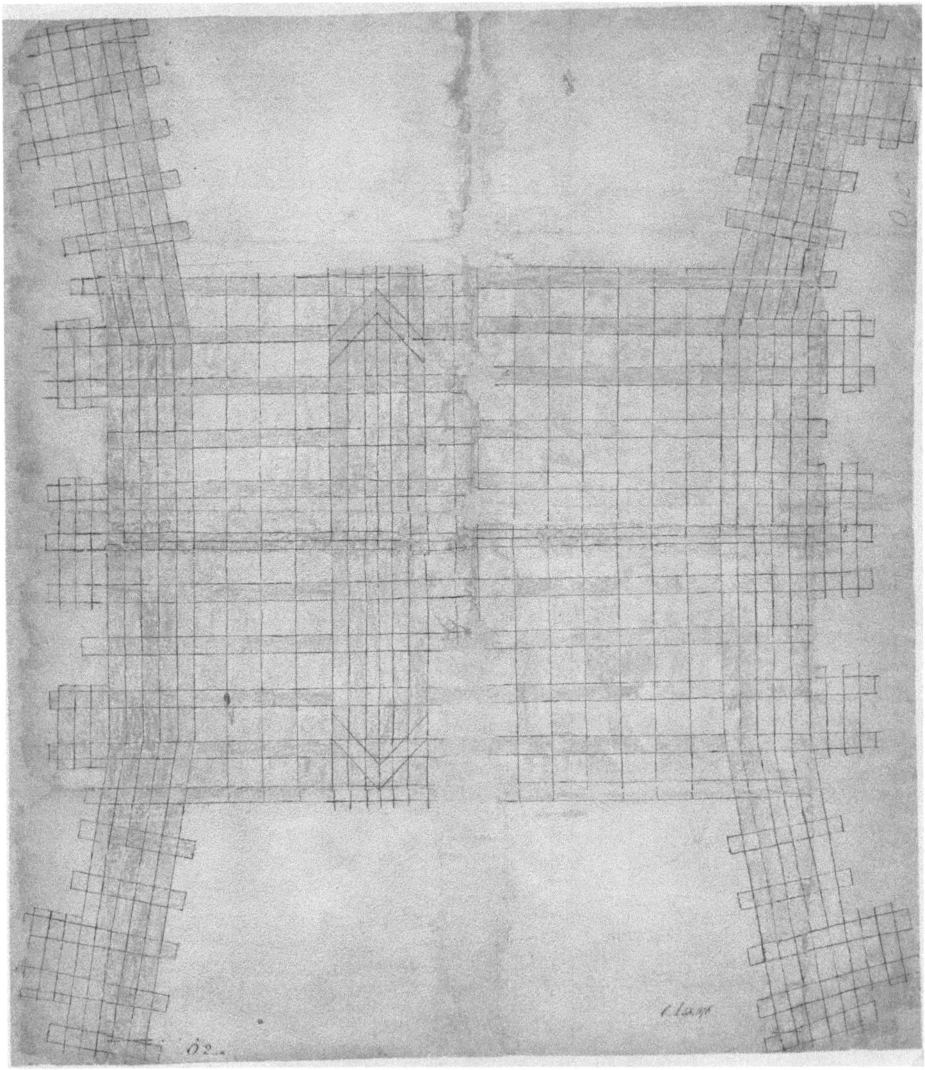

Fig. 8.16 Anonymous draughtsman, plan of the foundations of the Gouwsluis, oriented to the south, 1562-1563. Oud Archief van Rijnland, Leiden, Collectie Kaarten, A 561

was necessary, he was to bring his own piledriver. In addition he was compelled to bring a windlass to remove the existing piles of the former sluice.[77]

Even at this advanced stage there was still doubt whether the sluice could be built without the support of pile foundations. One drawing for the Gouwsluis seems to provide an alternative and cheaper solution, showing a grid on top

77 OAR, 1.1.1, inv. no. 3590b.

of which tightly joined plank boards were placed to form a platform, called a 'raft' (Figure 8.16). In keeping with the project's specifications, narrow and thick planks are used to support the walls and the pier of the sluice, while wider and thinner planks were sufficient for the floor of the sluice's chamber.[78] Such a method was common and is also described by Andries Vierlingh, receiver of the Prince of Orange in Steenbergen, in his treatise on the construction of dykes (*Tractaet van dyckagie*, c. 1576-1579).[79] According to Vierlingh, the bottom of the foundation trench should be filled with stamped *'derrie'*, a mixture of peat and clay that would form the bed for the wooden raft made of plank boards. If done properly, Vierlingh guaranteed that such foundations provided a better solution for sluices than pile foundations, because he believed that the vibrations of the water rushing through the sluice made the piles tremble, which ultimately could loosen them.[80]

Seeking to avoid any risks, Frederickszn van Montfoort and the water board made an additional survey of the subsoil at Alphen. On 8 July 1563, several masters were consulted, including Jan Jansz of Haarlem, who had been appointed master mason of the Gouwsluis on 16 March earlier that year. According to Jansz, Frederickszn van Montfoort did not want to proceed without pile foundations.[81] Three master craftsmen from the towns of Vianen, Gouda and Delft, who were specialized in the construction sluices and dams, were called in to inspect the site with earth augers. On 12 July, they reported that the soil was sufficiently stable to construct the sluice without pile foundations.[82] Finally, under the supervision of Jan Jansz, the raft was placed in the foundation trench without the driving of piles. Jansz remained at the construction site for ten days until the process of bricklaying commenced.

78 OAR, 1.1.1, inv. no. 3590b.

79 Vierlingh, *Tractaet van dyckagie*, 205-206. See also Van Dam, 'Ecological Challenges, Technological Innovations', 517.

80 Crone et al., *The Principal Works of Simon Stevin*, vol. 5, 72.

81 'meester Cornelis dat vlot soude inleggen ende wilde dat nijet doen sonder heyen' (OAR, 1.1.1, inv. no. 3590c). Jan Jansz also contracted the stone Oostsluis at Halfweg for the water board in 1566. See Josephan Amstel-Horák, 'Nieuwbouw van twee sluizen in een benarde tijd', 74.

82 'Wy Leners Wouter zoen van Vijanen, Evert Jacop zoen vand Goude, Sebastyaen pyeler zoen van Delft als warckluden ende meesters van slusen ende dammen bekennen mits desen geweest te hebben tot goutsse sluijs op de XII july anno LXIII om de suaerychheyt van de gront dije meester Cornelis met u bekondige [?] wilde de sluys op te stellen sonder de gront te heijen. Alwelke gront by ons geboort is gewest ende bevonden de selfde alsulck goet ende hart genouch om de selfde sluyse daer op te moghen stellen sonder eenich perykel ende vreese van dat warck te bederven' (OAR, 1.1.1, inv. no. 3590b).

Conclusion: Specialized Knowledge and Innovative Designs

Despite the appeal of the sixteenth-century writer Hadrianus Junius to value a building's foundations on par with the building itself, foundations, and foundation-laying practices in the Low Countries have long been neglected in architectural history. This is particularly remarkable in light of the fact that in the early modern period there was great admiration for the specialized skills needed to build in marshy conditions. From the early sixteenth century onward, no city description of Amsterdam fails to mention the difficulty and great cost of the construction of pile foundations. The ability to build in marshy conditions was directly related to the landscape the Dutch inhabited, and the places they sought to develop. Such knowledge was also exported to other regions in Europe with comparable environments, including northern Germany and the Baltic, eastern England, and south-west France. In the seventeenth century, Holland developed into an international centre of expertise for specialized foundation techniques. Dutch skills and know-how garnered international esteem, and foreign architects and engineers carefully studied foundation design and lightweight construction techniques, dubbed the 'Hollandish manner of construction' by Tsar Peter the Great in the early eighteenth century.

The laying of foundations for heavy structures on unstable soil required specialized knowledge, and prior to commencing any building project, Dutch patrons regularly consulted experts from far and wide. The backgrounds of these individuals could be surprisingly varied. The driving of piles and excavation of pits in marshy conditions was by definition an interdisciplinary endeavour, and required the expertise of architects, masons, carpenters and administrators, among others. It is interesting that many who were most expert on foundation construction were prominent master masons who also designed some of the most opulent palaces and churches. However their knowledge overlapped largely with that of master carpenters, and in the sixteenth century it seems that experts emerged who specialized in the construction of heavy hydraulic works, such as sluices, dams and dykes. Collaboration between the trades was not always on the initiative of the patron, but as the example of the Gouwsluis shows, experts themselves could also prefer to work in teams.

To reduce the risk of foundation problems, often a long planning process preceded construction. Ample documentation of these processes survives, and among the earliest preserved drawings made of pile foundations are plans of the foundations of the stone sluices at Halfweg and Alphen aan den Rijn, which date from the mid-sixteenth century. They show that straightforward solutions were not available; there was no formula by which foundations could be planned and laid. Rather, the documents show a continual process of analysis and adjustment, as the experts continually generated notably different, place-specific designs, based on their design and construction experience, and knowledge of the soil composition.

A wide variety of methods and foundation techniques were developed in the Low Countries in this period, but the principal innovation was the application of longer piles, which reached the first solid sand layer deep below the surface. The earliest examples of deep foundations in Amsterdam date from the early sixteenth century, but there is evidence that they were constructed even earlier. Documentation regarding the foundations of the Blauwe Toren in Gorinchem, for example, dates from the 1460s. Interestingly, the experts involved in the realization of this project, both masons and carpenters, came from a wide geographic area, including Brabant, Utrecht and Holland. Even expertise from Lille (Flanders) was deemed indispensable. In regards to the concept of place, an interesting tension thus exists, as both the environmental context and realization of the Blauwe Toren were inherently place-specific, but the expertise that went into the structure derived from a much broader area.

Little research has been done on the spread of Dutch foundation techniques. However, from the fact that deep foundations came to be employed in France and the Holy Roman Empire at the end of the seventeenth century, it can be surmised that Holland served as the nexus and exponent of early modern foundation design. While the Dutch employed longer piles in response to the region's ground conditions – in many towns in Holland, the first solid layer was found at depths of more than 10 metres below the surface – it was not only an accommodation to need that allowed the Dutch to excel in foundation design. Of great importance was Holland's access to an international timber market, with Dordrecht and Amsterdam being the main hubs, enabling builders to acquire piles of sufficient length. From around 1550 the increasing availability of more affordable pinewood from Scandinavia was also critical in furthering the development of deep foundations. Another factor that may have contributed to the ascendance of the Dutch in this field was the economy of their design. By the mid-sixteenth century, a wooden grid was no longer necessary for foundation construction and fewer piles had to be driven into the ground, thus saving on timber. Additional cost savings was achieved by reducing the need to move the piledrivers at the construction site, as fewer piles were needed. Finally, improvements made to drilling instruments are likely to have played an instrumental role in the realization of deep foundations. Archival records reveal that for heavy structures, extensive soil surveys were undertaken, using an earth auger that could reach deeper strata. Sampling allowed masters to learn the subsoil's composition, thus allowing them to better determine the appropriate foundation technique.

Bibliography

Manuscript Sources

Brussels, Royal Library
Manuscripts, II 480: Gaspar Ofhuys, Originale Coenobii Rubeaevallis, s.d.
The Hague, Nationaal Archief
Grafelijkheidsrekenkamer
Inv. no. 5008
Leiden, Oud Archief van Rijnland
1.1.1, inv. no. 150
1.1.1, inv. nos. 3590a, 3590b, 3590c
1.1.1, inv. no. 4856
1.1.1, inv. no. 9578
1.1.1, inv. no. 9579d
1.1.1, inv. no. 9582
Lille, Archives départementales du Nord
B 2047 (no. 63531)
B 2050 (nos. 63767, 63768, 63769, 63770)
B 17692
Lisbon, Biblioteca Nacional de Portugal
D. 250 P. (cat no. 824)

Printed Sources

Abrahamse, Jaap Evert and Rik Feiken, 'Driftig veen en onderaards bos. Nicolaas Witsen, het landschap van Amstelland en de grondbeginselen van de moderne geologie', *Bulletin KNOB* 118 (2019), 33-54.

Adam, Bernd, 'Pfahlgründungen des 15. bis 18. Jahrhunderts. Beispiele aus Norddeutschland', in Nina Hennig and Michael Schimek (eds), *Nah am Wasser, auf schwankendem Grund. Der Bauplatz und sein Haus* (Aurich: Ostfriesische Landschaft, 2016), 189-208.

Aglionby, William, *Present State of the United Provinces* (London: Printed for John Starkey, 1669).

Amstel-Horák, van, M.H.V., 'Nieuwbouw van twee sluizen in een benarde tijd: Halfweg 1556-1558', in Ludy Giebels (ed.), *Zeven eeuwen Rijnlandse uitwatering in Spaarndam en Halfweg. Van beveiliging naar beheersing* (Leiden: Uitgeverij Verloren, 1994), 47-74.

Arends, G.J., *Sluizen en stuwen. De ontwikkeling van de sluis- en stuwbouw in Nederland tot 1940* (Utrecht: Matrijs, 1994).

Berg, van den, Bianca, *De Sint-Janskerk in Gouda. Een oude stadskerk volgens een nieuw ruimtelijk plan* (Hilversum: Uitgeverij Verloren, 2008).

Bernabei, Mauro et al., 'The Wooden Foundations of Rialto Bridge (Ponte di Rialto) in Venice: Technological Characterisation and Dating', *Journal of Cultural Heritage* 36 (2019), 85-93.

Bie Leuveling Tjeenk, Jan de, 'De paalfundeering van het Koninklijk Paleis te Amsterdam', *Bouwkundig Weekblad Architectura* 60 (1939), 108-110.

Boer, den, J.F.M., 'Van heien en heipalen en het probleem van de Amsterdamse bodem', *Amstelodamum* 47 (1955), 27-47.

Borrmann, Michael, *Historische Pfahlgründungen. Untersuchung zur Geschichte einer Fundamentierungstechnik dargestellt an römischen, mittelalterlichen und neuzeitlichen Beispielen, hauptsächlich aus dem süddeutschen Raum* (Karlsruhe: Inst. für Baugeschichte der Univ. Karlsruhe, 1992).

Castriotto, Giacomo Fusto and Girolamo Maggi, *Della fortificatione delle città* (Venice: Rutilio Borgominiero, 1564).

Ciriacono, Salvatore, *Building on Water: Venice, Holland and the Construction of the European Landscape in Early Modern Times*, trans. by Jeremy Scott (New York: Berghahn Books, 2006).

Crone, Ernst et al. (eds), *The Principal Works of Simon Stevin*, 6 vols (Amsterdam: C.V. Swets & Seitlinger, 1955-1966).

Dam, van, Petra, 'Ecological Challenges, Technological Innovations: The Modernization of Sluice Building in Holland, 1300-1600', *Technology and Culture* 43 (2002), 500-520.

Dam, van, Petra, 'Spuien en heien. Innovatie en de rol van de stedelijke elite bij sluisbouw te Spaarndam in de 15de eeuw', in Ludy Giebels (ed.), *Zeven eeuwen Rijnlandse uitwatering in Spaarndam en Halfweg. Van beveiliging naar beheersing* (Leiden: Uitgeverij Verloren, 1994), 29-46.

Danner, Helga S. (ed.), *Polder Pioneers: The Influence of Dutch Engineers on Water Management in Europe, 1600-2000* (Utrecht: Royal Dutch Geography Society, 2005).

De Voght, Maud and Krista De Jonge, 'Foundation Techniques in the Early Modern Low Countries (1600-1750): A Problematic Case – St. Walburgis in Antwerp', in Robert Carvais et al. (eds), *Nuts & Bolts of Construction History: Culture, Technology and Society*, 3 vols (Paris: Picard, 2012), vol. 3, 29-36.

Essen, van, Gea, 'Het stadsfabriekambt. De organisatie van de publieke werken in de Noordelijke Nederlanden in de zeventiende eeuw', 2 vols, PhD diss., University of Utrecht, 2011.

Evelyn, John, *The Diary of John Evelyn*, ed. by Austin Dobson, 3 vols (London: Macmillan, 1906).

Gamallo, Ana Maria García, 'The Evolution of Traditional Types of Building Foundation Prior the First Industrial Revolution', in Santiago Huerta (ed.), *Proceedings of the First International Congress on Construction History*, 3 vols (Madrid: Inst. Juan de Herrera, 2003), vol. 2, 943-956.

Gawronski, Jerzy and Jørgen Veerkamp, 'Over staal, kleef en stuit. Funderingen in Amsterdam', in Jerzy Gawronski, Freek Schmidt and Marie-Thérèse van Thoor (eds), *Amsterdam: Monumenten & Archeologie* 2 (Amsterdam: Uitgeverij Bas Lubberhuizen, 2003), 11-23.

Gawronski, Jerzy and Jørgen Veerkamp, 'Über staal, kleef und stuit. Fundamente in Amsterdam', in Gabri van Tussenbroek (ed.), *Hausbau in Holland. Baugeschichte und Stadtentwicklung* (Marburg: Jonas Verlag, 2010), 45-62.

Geleyns, Piet and Krista De Jonge, 'New Light on Specialized XVIth Century Construction Techniques in the Low Countries', in Santiago Huerta (ed.), *Proceedings of the First International Congress on Construction History*, 3 vols (Madrid: Inst. Juan de Herrera, 2003), vol. 2, 987-995.

Gielemans, Johannes, *De codicibus hagiographicis Iohannis Gielemans canonici regularis in Rubea Valle prope Bruxellas. Adiectis Anecdotis* (Brussels: Gregg Associates, 1961), 391-417.

Guicciardini, Lodovico, *Beschryvinghe van alle de Nederlanden anderssins ghenoemt Neder-Duytslandt* (Amsterdam: Willem Jansz Blaeu, 1612).

Guicciardini, Lodovico, *Descrittione di M. Lodovico Guicciardini patritio fiorentino di tutti i Paesi Bassi altrimenti detti Germania inferiore* (Antwerp: Willem Silvius, 1567).

Harvey, John, *Mediaeval Craftsmen* (London: Batsford, 1975).

Hermans, Taco and Machteld Brongers, 'Het niet voltooide kasteel te Schoonhoven', *Castellogica, Mededelingen van de Nederlandse kastelenstichting* I (1983), 32-38.

Heuvel, van den, Charles, *'De Huysbou': A Reconstruction of an Unfinished Treatise on Architecture, Town Planning and Civil Engineering by Simon Stevin* (Amsterdam: Royal Netherlands Academy of Arts and Sciences, 2005).

Hurx, Merlijn, *Architecture as Profession: The Origins of Architectural Practise in the Low Countries in the Fifteenth Century* (Turnhout: Brepols, 2018).

Hurx, Merlijn, '"Een alten wonderlijcken structure ende fortresse": De Blauwe Toren van Karel de Stoute in Gorinchem', *Bulletin KNOB* 116 (2017), 184-208.

Ibelings, Bart J., 'De route "binnendunen". De scheepvaartroute langs de Goudse sluis en tol, de Wassenaerse Gouwesluis en de Spaarndammertol (13^{e} tot 16^{e} eeuw)', in Dick E.H. de Boer, Jannis W. Marsilje, and Johannes G. Smit (eds), *Vander Rekeninghe. Bijdragen aan het symposium over onderzoek en editieproblematiek van middeleeuws rekeningmateriaal, gehouden in Utrecht op 27 en 28 februari 1997* (The Hague: Instituut voor Nederlandse Geschiedenis, 1998), 221-255.

Janse, Herman, *De Oude Kerk te Amsterdam. Bouwgeschiedenis en restauratie* (Zwolle: Waanders, 2004).

Kérisel, Jean, *Down to Earth: Foundations Past and Present: The Invisible Art of the Builder* (Rotterdam: CRC Press, 1987).

Lazzarini, Antonio, 'Legno e pietra. Sottofondazione e fondamenta del Ponte di Rialto', *Archivio veneto* 149 (2018), 75-152.

Lazzarini, Antonio, 'Palificate di fondazione a Venezia. La Chiesa della Salute', *Archivio veneto* 139 (2008), 33-60.

Leys, Jolanda, 'De invloed van Anthonis I en Rombout II Keldermans op de kasteelfortificaties', in J.H. van Mosselveld (ed.), *Keldermans, een architectonisch netwerk in de Nederlanden* (The Hague: Staatsuitg., 1987), 155-171.

Mahoney, Michael S., 'Organizing Expertise: Engineering and Public Works under Jean-Baptiste Colbert, 1662-83', *Osiris* 25 (2010), 149-170.

Martelli, Francesco (ed.), *Il viaggio in Europa di Pietro Guerrini (1682-1686). Edizione della corrispondenza e dei disegni di un inviato di Cosimo III dei Medici*, 2 vols (Florence: L.S. Olschki, 2005).

Martens, Pieter and Konrad A. Ottenheym, 'Fortifications and Waterworks: Engineers on the Road', in Krista De Jonge and Konrad A. Ottenheym (eds), *The Low Countries at the Crossroads: Netherlandish Architecture as an Export Product in Early Modern Europe (1480-1680)* (Turnhout: Brepols, 2013), 361-378.

Mendonça de Oliveira, Mário and Erundio Pousada Presa, 'Reinforcing Foundations with Wood Piles: Origin and Historic Development', in Santiago Huerta (ed.), *Proceedings of the First International Congress on Construction History*, 3 vols (Madrid: Inst. Juan de Herrera, 2003), vol. 3, 1537-1545.

Olearius, Adam, *The Voyages and Travells of the Ambassadors Sent by Frederick Duke of Holstein* (London: Printed for John Starkey and Thomas Basset, 1669).

Ottenheym, Konrad A., 'The Rise of a New Profession: The Architect in 17th-Century Holland', in Guido Beltramini and Howard Burns (eds), *L'architetto: ruolo, volto, mito* (Venice: Marsilio, 2009), 199-219.

Parival, Jean-Nicolas de, *Les délices de la Hollande* (Leiden: Pierre Leffen, 1655).

Pontanus, Johannes, *Historische Beschrijvinghe der seer wijt beroemde Coop-stadt Amsterdam* (Amsterdam: Iudocum Hondium, 1614; rpt Amsterdam: Facsimile Uitagven Nederland, 1968).

Salzman, Louis Francis, *Building in England Down to 1540: A Documentary History* (Oxford: Clarendon Press, 1952).

Schukking, W.H., 'Iets over het voormalige kasteel te Harlingen en over paalfundeeringen in de 16e en het begin der 17e eeuw', *De Ingenieur* 51 (1936), 205-207.

Specklin, Daniel, *Architectura von Vestungen* (Strasbourg: Bernhart Jobin, 1589).

Tussenbroek, van, Gabri, 'The Foundations of the Nieuwe Kerk Tower in Amsterdam (1645-52)', in Ine Wouters et al. (eds), *Building Knowledge, Construction Histories*, 2 vols (Leiden: CRC Press, Taylor & Francis Group, 2018), vol. 2, 1313-1320.

Tussenbroek, van, Gabri, 'Was wiegt ein Haus? Wechselwirkungen zwischen Untergrund und Hausbau im Amsterdam des späten Mittelalters und der Frühen Neuzeit', in Nina Hennig and Michael Schimek (eds), *Nah am Wasser, auf schwankendem Grund. Der Bauplatz und sein Haus* (Aurich: Ostfriesische Landschaft, 2016), 209-228.

Van de Vijver, Dirk, 'Epilogue: Paradigm Change in the Early Eighteenth Century', in Krista De Jonge and Konrad A. Ottenheym (eds), *The Low Countries at the Crossroads: Netherlandish Architecture as an Export Product in Early Modern Europe (1480-1680)* (Turnhout: Brepols, 2013), 409-430.

Vierlingh, Andries, *Tractaet van dyckagie*, ed. by J. De Hullu and A.G. Verhoeven (The Hague: M. Nijhoff, 1920).

Visscher, Roemer, *Sinnepoppen* (Amsterdam: Willem Jansz Blaeu, 1614).
Zantkuijl, Henk J., *Bouwen in Amsterdam. Het woonhuis in de stad* (Amsterdam: Architectura & Natura, 1993).

About the Author

Merlijn Hurx is Professor of Architectural History at KU Leuven. His PhD thesis on the architect and the building industry in the Low Countries in the fifteenth and sixteenth centuries was published by Vantilt as *Architect en aannemer* (2012) and received the Karel van Mander prize for the best architectural history publication in the Netherlands for the period 2011-2015. He is author of *Architecture as Profession: The Origins of Architectural Practise in the Low Countries in the Fifteenth Century* (Brepols 2018).

9. The 'Conquest' and Construction of an Urban Place: The *Insula dei Gesuiti* in Venice in the Early Modern Period

Ludovica Galeazzo

Abstract

This article examines the production of place and its socio-economic impact in early modern Venice, reconstructing the urban dynamics in one of the lesser-known peripheries of the city, the *insula dei Gesuiti*. Building on the idea of place making as a collective enterprise, it concentrates on three stages of urban growth and its pertaining agents: the colonization process undertaken by private citizens and ecclesiastical institutions; their efforts toward a residential urban development; and the state-imposed action to determine the *insula*'s final outline. These practices were instrumental in securing significant real estate holdings, but they also initiated a profound change in the area's intended use. Urban transformations engendered a new social identity that would serve as a model for the redesigned Venetian margins.

Keywords: land reclamation, spatial maturation, urbanization processes, entrepreneurial strategies

In a volume concerned with the multiple dimensions of the construction of place, a study based on the early modern land formation of a city's peripheral area may seem prosaic. By the very nature of its meaning, place is a space constituted by one or many settlements shaped by buildings, streets or landscapes. However, the analysis of an urban place may become less obvious if the focus is shifted from the physical built fabric to the set of relations, between individuals and processes, which determined its creation. As Bruno Zevi vigorously affirmed as early as 1948, the feature distinguishing architecture from other forms of art is its three-dimensional vocabulary that includes man.[1] Urban spaces are constituted by people and neighbours who

1 Zevi, *Architecture as Space*, 22.

Merrill, E. (ed.), *Creating Place in Early Modern European Architecture*.
Taylor & Francis Group 2022
DOI: 10.5117/9789463728027_CH09

Fig. 9.1 Jacopo de' Barbari, View of Venice, 1500. Detail of the *insula dei Gesuiti*. Venice, Correr Museum, Cl. XLIV, n. 57

share relationships through social and political practices, as well as economic and work exchanges. Places are not empty vessels existing prior to the matter that fills them. On the contrary, they are the social product of people's activities and, thus, are intimately bound up with their occupants' sources of meaning and experience.[2]

Adopting this approach, this article explores the broad dynamics that led to the development and spatial organization of Venetian urban fringes by focusing on the history of the *insula dei Gesuiti*, a marginal area located at the northern limit of Venice, on the western tip of the Fondamente Nuove, the paved pedestrian walkway that solidifies the northern border of the city (Figure 9.1).[3] As its boxy shape reveals, the island is the result of seamless and long-term interventions of consolidation undertaken by diverse actors. Beginning in the early thirteenth century, patrician families, religious communities and, later on, the Venetian state, undertook extensive operations of land reclamation, at times even on the scale of

2 On the rejection of Emmanuel Kant's perception of place as a priori space, see Lefebvre, *The Production of Space*, 1-2. Lefebvre's idea of place as a social construction led by economic factors, social realities and cultural phenomena is today an integral part of urban and architectural history. See Butler, *Henri Lefebvre*, 37-54. More recently, Torre has argued that places are created by articulations of social relations and intricate human practices. See Torre, *Luoghi*.

3 For a more comprehensive history of the *insula*, see Galeazzo, *Venezia e i margini urbani*.

multiple urban blocks. These pioneering campaigns were an attempt to rectify the irregular margins of the city, as well as an endeavour to enhance urban areas still dominated by undeveloped and unremunerative spaces.

While this study focuses on a specific geographical location and the physical efforts that were made to develop it, the concept of place making is taken to extend beyond the narrow confines of labour process. Embracing the ontological implications of considering place as a social and political instrument, it is argued here that practices of urban planning hinge on synergistic cultural, social and economic dynamics. The analysis begins, therefore, with an examination of the processes by which new land was formed for living and establishing economic activities. The endless fifteenth- and sixteenth-century draining interventions and illegitimate land reclamations that occurred along the margin of the *insula* are key elements within the investigation, the result of demographic and economic pressures. These actions brought the island's urban transformation to completion, thus determining the final outline of the northern edge of the city. The second part of the article turns to examine the urbanization processes that followed land reclamations, focusing on the social use of place. The spatial practises of neighbourhood building carried out by inhabitants initiated a profound change in the area's purpose and in the intended use of its structures. Within this, a proto-capitalistic model of real estate entrepreneurship was established, which would shape the quality and the final appearance of this liminal place as well as future urban expansions in the city.

The Process of Spatial Maturation: A Collective Enterprise

The idea of Venice as a city constantly in motion has been recognized for some time, so much so that it has become a significant feature of its own image. Movement does not only concern individuals, goods and objects, but also its urban space. As high and low tides constantly shift within the urban fabric, the city itself acted – and still acts – upon its civic borders through a gradual and persistent advancement toward the lagoon. This phenomenon has always characterized the history of Venice, a settlement physically on the verge of land and water.[4] Unlike other places where urban development always corresponded to an enlargement beyond the medieval city walls, in Venice this process turned out to be much more invasive, as it inevitably involved the encroachment of its 'liquid walls'.[5] In Venice, therefore, the word

4 See Concina, 'Venezia, "tra due elementi sospesa"'.

5 The aphorism about the holy water walls of Venice occurs in countless treatises on the lagoon and is praised by the famous humanist Giovanni Battista Egnazio in his verses for the office of the *Magistrato alle acque*. See Settis, 'Premessa'.

'growth' has always carried with it the connotation of 'change'. This might pertain to the relationship between land and water, but also and equally importantly, it could involve the functional uses of space, the articulation of collective facilities and the city's appearance.

Although urban dynamism was always an innate condition of Venice, the evolution of the city became particularly intense in the fifteenth century when a series of motivations drove new leaps in expansion. The explosion in population, the necessity of investing in the land market, as well as the government's need to define a regular and permanent boundary for the urban settlement, pushed urban development.[6] Although, at the time, the concentration of residential buildings was well advanced, swamps and marshes were still largely present along the urban contours of the city. Frayed margins alternated with large empty lands, vegetable gardens, vineyards and unhealthy sand shores.[7] The actual urban portrait of the city was far distant from the literary and iconographic imagery of the capital as a compact and successful artefact, miraculously founded thanks to divine intervention, located within a safe and secure lagoon. This interpretation is regarded today as part of the great myth of the city, an evocative picture intentionally constructed in Venice, by Venice, to emphasize its uniqueness.[8] Likewise, the city itself embodied the triumph of human industry and mastery over the physical environment.

In his 1556 commentary on Vitruvius' *De architectura*, the influential Venetian humanist Daniele Barbaro claimed that architecture – and more broadly institutions – were in charge of 'violently' contrasting Nature's 'violence'.[9] This is to say, the built environment was responsible for providing the spaces, structures and shelters that would protect human civilization and allow it to thrive. Venice could not but be a living principle for him. *Technè* (technical knowledge) and *virtus* (capacity) were the building blocks that had enabled the city to construct, piece by piece, its physical presence, wresting land from the waters.[10] In Barbaro's words, the concept of place – whether natural or artificial – was the result of a series of human interventions intimately tied to the social political, and ideological conditions on which society's

6 See Concina, *Venezia nell'età moderna*, 105-125.

7 These features are portrayed in the well-known Jacopo de' Barbari's *View of Venice* of 1500. This representation constitutes an exception in the iconography of Venice at the time as it depicts the city in its real urban configuration.

8 See Crouzet-Pavan, 'Toward an Ecological Understanding'.

9 'A wonderful thing is the power for the common good to assemble coarse men, and unite them in faith and discipline, secure and tranquil in the cities and fortresses: then with greater violence done to nature, to cut the rocks, tunnel through the mountains, fill the valleys, dry the swamps, build ships, straighten rivers, supply ports, build bridges, and overcome Nature herself, which we have vanquished by lifting immense weights, and satisfying in part the desire of eternity.' Barbaro, *I dieci libri dell'architettura*, I, fol. 15.

10 D'Evelyn, *Venice and Vitruvius*, 23-26.

actors operated, both individually and collectively. Indeed, in Renaissance Venice the material construction of place was a matter – and a business – that intertwined public and private enterprise, with the Venetian state drawing up the general terms by which private initiatives were undertaken. Magistrates, architects, and master builders, as well as the clergy and private sponsors, were equally involved in the establishment of new urban settlements. The convergence of interests and needs, their multiform negotiations as well as their persistent disputes, are the coordinates for a comprehensive analysis of the dynamic, ever transforming, Venetian site.

The *insula dei Gesuiti* provides a special lens through which to examine the configuration of space in early modern Venice. As the northern offshoot of the city overlooking the mainland, the area was a multifaceted and layered hub for the functional management of the capital. Its socio-economic importance derived from its position, enclosed by two of the fundamental waterways that fed into the Grand Canal and the mainland. Moreover, its fortune was related to its proximity to the Sacca della Misericordia, the water basin in which timber coming from the mainland was stored. The island's strategically placed location made it a perfect site for major trade and economic transactions. Over the centuries it systematically developed and became equipped to host a variety of specialized activities, primarily related to lumber, as well as other marketable goods such as sugar, wax and leather.[11]

In terms of its social and cultural ownership, the island was parcelled between multiple actors. Two flourishing religious communities constituted the twin foci of the area's vitality: the Crociferi – the twelfth-century friars replaced in 1657 by the Jesuit Order – and the Augustinian nuns of Santa Caterina dei Sacchi.[12] Although supposedly bound by vows of poverty, both religious institutions were actually the principal agents of the urban transformation of the island, initiatives that altered the shape, function and identity of the area. Around their spiritual walls, patrician and wealthy families, along with upper-middle-class citizens, were engaged in the consolidation of their economic and social status through sequential real estate transactions.

The urban memory of these real estate transactions is recorded in hundreds of notarial deeds, bequests and witnesses' written descriptions meticulously preserved in the *fondo* of the *Giudici del piovego* and later in the *Savi ed esecutori alle acque* (the authority responsible for water resources), as well as in ecclesiastical archives.[13] By retracing these detailed stories, one can pinpoint commonalities and consistent

11 Concina, *Venezia nell'età moderna*, 53-71.

12 On the Venetian monastic community of the Crociferi, see Sherman, 'The Lost Venetian Church'. On the nunnery of Santa Caterina dei Sacchi, which survived until the Napoleonic suppression in 1806, see Toffolo, 'Art and the Conventual Life'.

13 The *Savi ed esecutori alle acque* was an office founded in the year 1501 to oversee the hydrological welfare of the waterways and the lagoon. See Svalduz, 'Al servizio del magistrato'.

patterns in the processes of land development. But above all, the documents highlight the panoply of different interests as well as the variety of figures – experts, government officials and engineers – mobilized in the construction of place. Punctuated moments of acceleration and stasis determine the rhythm of the site's urban development. At the same time, they are a significant litmus test for the principal events of Venetian history.

Between Land and Water: The Crociferi's Profitable Investments

The first step in the fifteenth-century expansion of the area was to create – in a physical sense – additional solid soil on which to develop new material constructions, and with these, new monetary opportunities. This involved a series of 'conquests' over the salt water that surrounded the existing landforms. The Crociferi were forerunners in converting the insalubrious marshlands encircling their complex into lucrative ventures. Between 1456 and 1463, the friars began a massive and hectic property sales campaign.[14] Through private loan agreements – called *livelli* – they conceded wide stretches of the lagoon that extended all the way along the *insula*'s northern margin, until the island of San Michele. The first of these economic transactions (6 June 1456), between the prior Giovanni Buoso and the noblemen Girolamo Barbarigo and Matteo Tiepolo, is particularly significant for a host of reasons. First, it brings us closer to the history of the Crociferi's enterprise of expansion, as well as their jurisdictional rights.[15] As usual in legal provisions, the appointed notary carefully recorded the series of events preceding the new contract. In particular, he recalled the 1357 petition of the prior Tommaso da San Severino Marche over the Crociferi's ownership of the marshland. On that occasion, the friar not only asked that the three *Giudici del piovego* survey the area, but he also took the documentation into his possession.

Thus, the notary's reference to the 1357 petition was linked to the bequest of Bonavere Gussoni in the year 1170. In his will, the patrician donated a broad marshland that extended more than 300 metres on the western side of the *insula*, on which the order erected its religious buildings.[16] The notary's interest in such a long sequence of economic transactions cannot be reduced to the concept of a preamble. On the contrary, this was a calculated and deliberate urban strategy. By placing their indelible mark on the 9 hectares of lagoon in front of their religious house, the Crociferi were claiming their long-lasting and vested legal power over

14 Notarial documents are in Archivio di Stato di Venezia (ASVe), *Archivio Gradenigo Rio Marin*, b. 237, fasc. V: 'scriture pertinente le aque driedo li Crosechieri, et Santa Catherina'.

15 See Crouzet-Pavan, 'Sviluppo e articolazione della città'.

16 In 1186, Urban III granted the Crociferi permission to build a church and a monastery dedicated to the Assumption of the Virgin on that location. ASVe, *Procuratori di San Marco, de Citra, Commissarie*, b. 233, fasc. 27, fol. 6v.

this place. In specifying their abiding agreement with the Venetian state, they were also declaring that their properties were private, and therefore exempted from any judicial provision and disciplinary procedure imposed by the *Giudici del piovego*. Moreover, this condition allowed the Crociferi to predate restrictions imposed by the Republic on water legislation in the last decades of the thirteenth century.[17] This event clearly reveals the enduring legacy of friars in the management and urban organization of their land and water assets. It also singles the construction of place in this period as a systematic process that entangled social and political stakes.

The 1357 site visit recorded by the notary is furthermore important because it offers a material picture of the traditional survey procedure. The technique was relatively simple. Namely, the three judges would access the area via boats, place wooden pilings to delimit the marshland's perimeter, and run a rope through them to define its contours.[18] As was common practice, measurements were usually annotated on technical reports and – rarely – entrusted to simple and schematic sketches showing plans for reclaimed areas.[19]

Quite extraordinarily, the survey process is visualized in a marvellous watercolour that minutely documents the main *insula*'s features (Figure 9.2). Alongside the principal churches, residential buildings and palaces, the everyday infrastructure of urban life is carefully represented in its shape and materiality, albeit in a simplified manner. The image presents empty spaces for storing boats, wooden bridges and docks, lagoon defences made of wooden piles and a stone cistern. Although the drawing is not dated, it must have been produced long after the 1357 survey, most likely between the 1490s and the first years of the sixteenth century, as some architectural elements depicted suggest.[20] The date of origin of the image aside, the fascinating document allows us to engage in the urban dynamics of the area in the early modern period. In its abundance of detail, colour and material, the most relevant element of the drawing for our purposes almost disappears from view. Barely visible in the upper part of the map, a row of seventeen pilings connects the island of San Michele with the *insula*, forming an arch shape. A sequence of numbers above the individual piles provides the distance, measured in Venetian

17 In order to stop illegal reclamation practices, urban authorities had begun to strictly oversee and limit the use of the water environment. Measures adopted pertained disciplinary regulation, estate holders' interrogation and, above all, on-site inspection. See *Codex Publicorum*, xxvii.

18 Survey data are often difficult to interpret since measurements were taken without making a clear distinction between water and land.

19 For an overview on early modern Italian topographical maps and survey techniques, see Folin, *Rappresentare la città*. The reference for the Venetian case study is Svalduz, 'Visti dall'acqua'.

20 In the drawing, both Palazzo Sceriman and the residential building on the Calle dei Volti (under construction) are represented. The first palace was built at the end of the fifteenth century for the Dolce family, while the second complex was begun in 1495.

Fig. 9.2 Watercolour map of the area between the Sacca della Misericordia and Biri, c. 1490. ASVe, *Archivio Gradenigo Rio Marin*, b. 237, fasc. V

feet, from one pole to the other, as recorded on the magistrates' notes. To some extent, the representation seems to capture the exigencies of the city's physical growth by tackling the problems of urban expansion and land reclamation. In its richness, it conveys the significance of looking simultaneously at the water environment and surrounding context.

Ultimately, this event is interesting for understanding the fine line drawn between private and public place jurisdiction in early modern Venice. On 3 March 1361, the *Giudici* unanimously established that the property should belong to the monastery, but they also specified that it '*semper esse debeat publicum, et commune, et ad utilitatem communem, et publicas debeat in perpetuum conservari*' ('must always remain public and available for the communal use and thus must be forever preserved'). This decree was recorded in their office's register. It was not simply a formulaic statement, but empowered the Republic to re-establish its right over the lagoon environment and, consequently, its administrative jurisdiction over the area.[21]

21 The subject of Venice's medieval urban expansion has been masterfully studied by Crouzet-Pavan, 'La maturazione dello spazio urbano'.

However, the attention of the ecclesiastical community was not merely directed towards the reorganization of their water patrimony. From 1455 to 1513, the friars gradually but adamantly finalized a series of loans with the Enzo, Zane, Salvazo and Zen families, which allowed them to utilize properties adjacent to their religious complex.[22] These consisted of *case da stazi* (patrician residences), as well as empty spaces stretching back towards the lagoon. Equipped with wooden defences and warehouses, these plots hosted a variety of remunerative commercial activities, primarily related to the storing of timber and wax refinement.[23] Over the course of the following decades, the concession of such property holdings became one of the order's highest sources of income.[24]

In analysing the Crociferi's multifaceted urban landholdings, one might question the reasons that lay behind the friars' intense trade programme. A *livello* dated 1 September 1463 provides an explanation.[25] As clearly stated in the lease contract, real estate transfers were motivated by marketing interests: marshlands and empty lands were not just pointless, but their maintenance was also highly expensive. In addition, the friars' actions were compelled by the urgent necessity of gaining substantial profits. These were intended to finance the restoration of their monastery, which had fallen into disrepair, as well as the construction of a new church, later initiated by the lay procurator Alvise Dardani.[26] The significance of the Crociferi's initiative cannot be overlooked. By capitalizing on unused water and land spaces, the friars achieved a twofold objective: addressing the contingencies of a degraded urban environment and transforming it into a lucrative investment. In regards to the notion of production of space, such liminal place making took on the guise of a carefully designed land management strategy.

The Micro-dynamics of Urban Expansion: Private Land Reclamation Activities

If the Crociferi were eager to set their wetland property apart, the *particulari* – the Venetian name for private citizens – were exactly the opposite as active agents of

22 Galeazzo, *Venezia e i margini urbani*, 30-40.

23 Biblioteca del Museo Correr (BMCVe), ms. P.D.c. 1004/95.

24 See the sixteenth-century *condizione* ('declaration of property') of the Crociferi preserved in ASVe, *Sopraintendenti alle decime del clero*, 1564, b. 33 n. 173.

25 ASVe, *Archivio Gradenigo rio Marin*, b. 237, fasc. V, fols. 19r-24r (1 September 1463). The *livello* again involved Mattio Tiepolo, but this time, in conjunction with the patrician Marco Michiel.

26 The church was constructed around 1490 and is visible in Jacopo de' Barbari's *View* as well as in some paintings by Jacopo Palma il Giovane in the Crociferi oratory. See Sherman, 'La collocazione originale del Martirio'.

landfill interventions. Economic, productive and social interests were motivating factors in these secular activities, which are plainly reflected in the hundreds of patents presented by individuals to the Republic for dredging and reclamation machines.[27] As is the case with the Low Countries described by Merlijn Hurx in this volume, patents granted by the Venetian state offered privileges to inventors for both craft processes and mechanical inventions. The extensive production of drawings, models and descriptions is a leading indicator of the technological expertise developed in Venice over centuries. But it also confirms that construction site activities were a collective and mutual concern.[28]

Moreover, private endeavour vividly emerges in the countless, often illegitimate, drainage interventions carried on by private subjects along the city's margins. State control was formally guaranteed through the procedure of *gratiae*, an important mechanism of negotiation between citizens and the central government introduced in the thirteenth century.[29] *Gratiae* were land permits and concessions that authorized citizens in their reclamation activities. They were granted in response to individual or collective petitions after due confirmation by the office of *Giudici del piovego* and later, the Venetian Senate and *Collegio delle acque*.[30] These invaluable records provide a snapshot of the active engagement of Venetian citizens in the establishment of place, recording their names, requests and expenses. Furthermore, records of the *gratiae* elucidate how the concession of space was deeply wedded to the socio-economic needs of a growing city. They reveal that the areas allocated to be filled were not exceptionally extensive. Traditionally, applicants' appeals for urban enlargement dealt with tiny spits of land located on the city's fringes or alongside inner canals. Indeed, these acquisitions served to fulfil explicit needs, providing new sites for residences and, more frequently, areas on which industrial and agricultural activities could be located, far away from the city centre.

From an operational standpoint, property owners were legally responsible for the entire building process, including the costs of dredging and constructing new banks. The authorization and control of a given project was instead entrusted to the authority of the Republic. The office of the *Savi ed esecutori alle acque* was also in charge of assembling all the hydraulic records derived from entry books of the *Cancelleria Ducale*. Unfortunately, this documentation survives today only as a partial copy, composed in the mid-sixteenth century and known as *Sumario*

27 On Venetian patents concerning dredging and water-raising machines, see Berveglieri, *Le vie di Venezia*.

28 See Pavanini, 'Venezia verso la pianificazione?', 485-488.

29 BMCVe, ms. Cicogna 2562 (=3834), *Codice del piovego* (thirteenth century).

30 In 1463, the Venetian government forbade any land reclamation not directly authorized by the Senate or the *Collegio alle Acque*. ASVe, *Savi ed esecutori alle acque*, reg. 330, fol. 62r-v (14 September 1463).

delle gratie. The register reports land concessions granted between 1338 and 1503, distinguished by the six districts.[31]

These recorded land permits allow us to closely analyse the social status of petitioners, shedding light on the breadth and diversity of place making in early modern Venice. Applicants mostly belonged to the middle class and, more narrowly, to artisanal professions. Zorzi della Stella was a renowned glazier, Bortolamio Marcadelli a member of an important family of jewellers, and Matteo d'Oro a famous dry cleaner.[32] Within this list, many also came from the upper echelons, such as the Grimani da Santa Caterina, Pesaro da San Giovanni Decollato, and Priuli da San Felice families, as well as men of letters and statesmen, including, among others, Febo Capella, secretary of the Venetian Republic. It is therefore reasonable to assume that state concessions were not a discretionary instrument entirely in the hands of patrician families, but rather an integral part of Venetian political and social life.[33] Yet they marked a real opportunity for anyone who might want to invest in real estate. In addition, the documents highlight the importance of neighbourhood as a social form. Traditionally engaged in long-term disputes, neighbours were brought together within the system to make claims for a common interest.

Administratively, *gratiae* represented an early step in the Venetian political management of public space. However, they failed as an effective control programme. The alarming rise in the number and proportion of illegal reclamations forced the Venetian authorities to introduce a series of systematic and global surveys, which were conducted in 1485, 1503 and 1556. In these inspections, every square foot of unauthorized reclaimed land was assigned a standard value according to the area's location.[34] Despite the increased efforts and the strict surveillance over this kind of infringement, the government proved unable to impose obedience, and urban regulations were brazenly contravened.[35] The landowner Francesco della Torre, the patrician Zaccaria Grimani, and the two *cittadini* (citizens by birth) Alvise Rosso and Piero Bon lead the list of names regularly registered on the magistrates' books.[36] The accounts also record how new

31 ASVe, *Savi ed esecutori alle acque*, reg. 219, 'sumario delle gratie, che son nell'Offitio dei Pioveghi tratto dai libri dell'Offitio dei Pioveghi per mi pre' Marin Rusco nodaro del detto Offitio' (mid-sixteenth century).

32 ASVe, *Savi ed esecutori alle acque*, reg. 219, fol. 70r.

33 Romano, '"Quod sibi fiat gratia"'.

34 Pecuniary penalties ranged from half a ducat (twelve *grossi*) for valuable sites in the heart of the city, to eight *grossi* in the islands of San Giorgio and Giudecca, to six *grossi* in Murano and for areas belonging to religious complexes located outside the city centre. Significantly, this governmental approach reveals a clear urban geography within the city.

35 Piasentini documents severe punishments, including whippings, in St. Mark's Square, six months' imprisonment or ten years' banishment. Piasentini, 'Aspetti della Venezia d'acqua', 42-43.

36 Every possible witness was called to testify about these private *atterrazioni* (reclamations). Depositions from neighbours, fishermen or *barcaruoli* (boatmen) create a colourful image of the dynamic space.

lands were used, serving for example as vegetable gardens or spaces for boat shelters (*cavane*), as well as housing proto-industrial buildings, as is the case of the Grimanis' structure for the glass paste production.[37] While the urban impact of such private citizens' actions did not strongly affect the *insula*'s development, the reiteration of these abuses underscores the perpetual failure of authorities' control as a means of reform.

Beyond Monastic Walls: The Augustinian Nuns of Santa Caterina's March

In the drive towards the lagoon, the convent of Santa Caterina was ahead of the game. Powered by noble blood and entrepreneurship, the Augustinian nuns managed to elevate their small peripheral community to become one of the wealthiest Venetian religious complexes.[38] Thanks to inheritances and bequests, along with a strategically calculated financial policy, the nuns, beginning in the thirteenth century, gradually gained control of all the properties around their convent. As the *insula*'s unbuilt space began to diminish, they rapidly turned their attention to extending their real estate assets over the marshlands surrounding the religious walls.

In the management of their convent, the Augustinian sisters wielded truly exceptional skills. Among the robust 39 *buste* that constitute their archive, almost every document is purely related to property: records of the sale or acquisition of land, contracts for building works, rental agreements and endless accounts of land reclamation processes. One *fascicolo*, or small register, vividly illustrates the force of the nuns' strategy.[39] The folder neatly gathers the complete documentation on the 'water business' carried on by several abbesses between 1502 and 1595. It includes extracted copies of technical reports, land measurements, as well as ordinances compiled by the *Savi ed esecutori alle acque*. Appended to this dossier are three drawings recalling interventions made just north of the convent. Although apparently quite similar, the images were made by different authors, in different years, and for distinct purposes.

The first two sketches both bear the label 'draft'. Most likely, they served as the basis for the last drawing, an ink and watercolour map on parchment. The first

37 ASVe, *Savi ed esecutori alle acque*, reg. 219, fol. 28v (30 July 1503).

38 Due to the practice of coerced monachization, nuns almost exclusively belonged to the Venetian patriciate. As the Patriarch Francesco Vendramin remarked in his letter to the Senate in 1619, noblewomen numbered 99 among the 100 nuns at Santa Caterina. See Archivio Storico del Patriarcato di Venezia (ASPVe), *Curia, Archivio segreto, Visite pastorali a monasteri femminili*, Vendramin (21 May 1616). On this topic, see Galeazzo, 'Entrepreneurship beyond Convent Walls'.

39 The *fascicolo* is in ASVe, *Santa Caterina dei Sacchi* (hereafter *SCdS*), b. 20, proc. 7, 'Acquisti delle monache di Terreni e Palludi Contrà di Santa Soffia, San Felice, e Santi Apostoli vendutisi dal Magistrato alle Acque.'

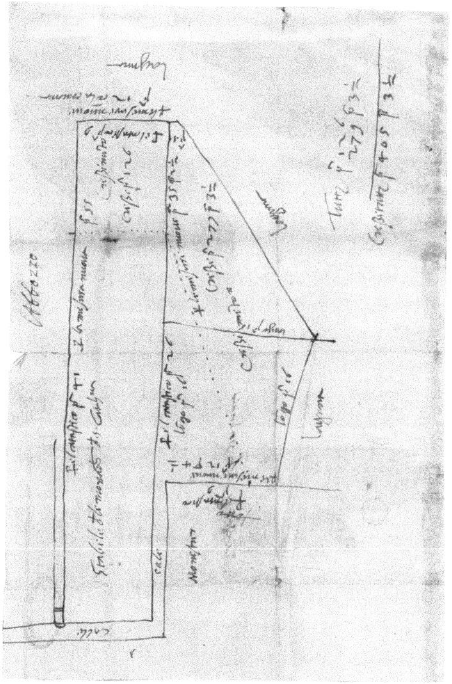

Fig. 9.3 Cristoforo Sabbadino, survey of the reclaimed plots located behind the convent of Santa Caterina, 8 March 1556. Archivio di Stato di Venezia, *SCdS*, b. 20, proc. 7, fol. 20r

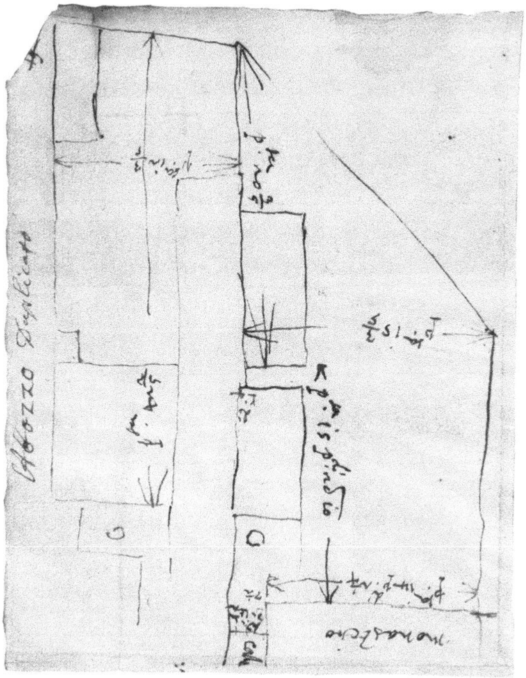

Fig. 9.4 Design for the urban development of the plots located behind the convent of Santa Caterina, post-1556. Archivio di Stato di Venezia, *SCdS*, b. 20, proc. 7, fol. 20r

plan, dated 8 March 1556, might be considered a visualization of the growth of the Augustinian land property (Figure 9.3). While simple sketched lines delineate the urban contours of the area, a few dotted lines along with measurements and annotations give life to the gradual maturation of the urban space. For further insight into this representation, one must examine it in relation to pertinent written documents. Moving in tandem between these sources, it is possible to reconstruct the chronology of the events as well as to localize buildings and spaces depicted in the sketch. The first drainage intervention began on 30 June 1503.[40] It consisted of 126 square feet of illegally reclaimed land (more than 200 square metres), which are represented as a square box in the upper part of the paper. Precisely a month later, a second reclamation completely filled the triangular space on the right side of the convent. A third intervention – recorded in the plan drawing – took place over 50 years later, in March 1556. The notorious Venetian engineer Cristoforo Sabbadino (1487-1560) was in charge of the measurements, and on the basis of the

40 ASVe, *Savi ed esecutori alle acque*, reg. 219, fol. 28v (30 June 1503).

compositional design of the survey, its calligraphy and explanatory notes, he may also be considered the author of this document.[41] According to the calculations of the *proto* (master builder), the nuns had expanded their real estate holdings by 405 Venetian square feet (roughly 700 square metres). This area was assessed at 101 ducats and ten *grossi*, a quite small amount compared to future government land sales.[42]

If the 1556 drawing constitutes a schematic map that traces the perimeter of the Augustinian nuns' acquisitions, the second plan, executed sometime shortly later, has an utterly different nature (Figure 9.4). Here, reclaimed land is no longer the subject of the author's investigation. Buildings, public infrastructure and urban facilities (such as the two cisterns appearing at the bottom part of the sketch that were to be built) come into view and constitute the study's main subjects. This observation suggests that at this time, the act of unlawful reclamation was slowly turning into a more systematic process of urban development. According to subsequent fiscal sources, the buildings constructed here a few years later were used as oil warehouses, granaries and houses to rent.[43] In looking at these initial and, to some extent, still hesitant real estate activities, one might find the seed of that proto-capitalist strategy that would be extensively developed by the Augustinian nuns in the following decades.

Returning to the sisters' unabated march toward the lagoon, not even the government's fiscal amnesty stopped their cunning plan. On 26 June 1594, the *viceproto* of the *Officio delle Acque*, Giovanni Alvise Galesi, surveyed a small reclamation (about sixteen square feet) at the far north end of the convent. Confiscated for a year, the site was then sold to the sisters for 2 ducats per square foot, according to their pre-emptive rights.[44] This land acquisition may appear as one of the numerous achievements accomplished by the female community. Its dating, moreover, is historically significant as it coincides with the construction of the Fondamente Nuove (1590-1603), which came to define – as will be further explained – the northern extremity of the city.

This final intervention also helps in understanding the last drawing preserved in the register. The map is signed by Giovanni Alvise Galesi himself, but this time in his capacity of member of the *provveditori sopra beni inculti* (superintendents of uncultivated resources).[45] The fact that the map was composed on parchment, along with the notable quality of the design and colour variation, suggest its function as a presentation piece (Figure 9.5). The inscription '*ad istantia delle Reverende Madre*

41 ASVe, *SCdS*, b. 20, proc. 7, fols. 7r-8r (8 March 1556).

42 ASVe, *SCdS*, b. 20, proc. 7, fol. 10r (19 August 1556).

43 ASVe, *Dieci savi alle decime in Rialto*, 1661, b. 421.

44 ASVe, *SCdS*, b. 20, proc. 7, fol. 22r (15 November 1594).

45 ASVe, *SCdS*, b. 20, proc. 7, fol. 21r. The office of the *Provveditori sopra beni inculti* was charged with supervising the reclamation of uncultivated land, irrigation and drainage.

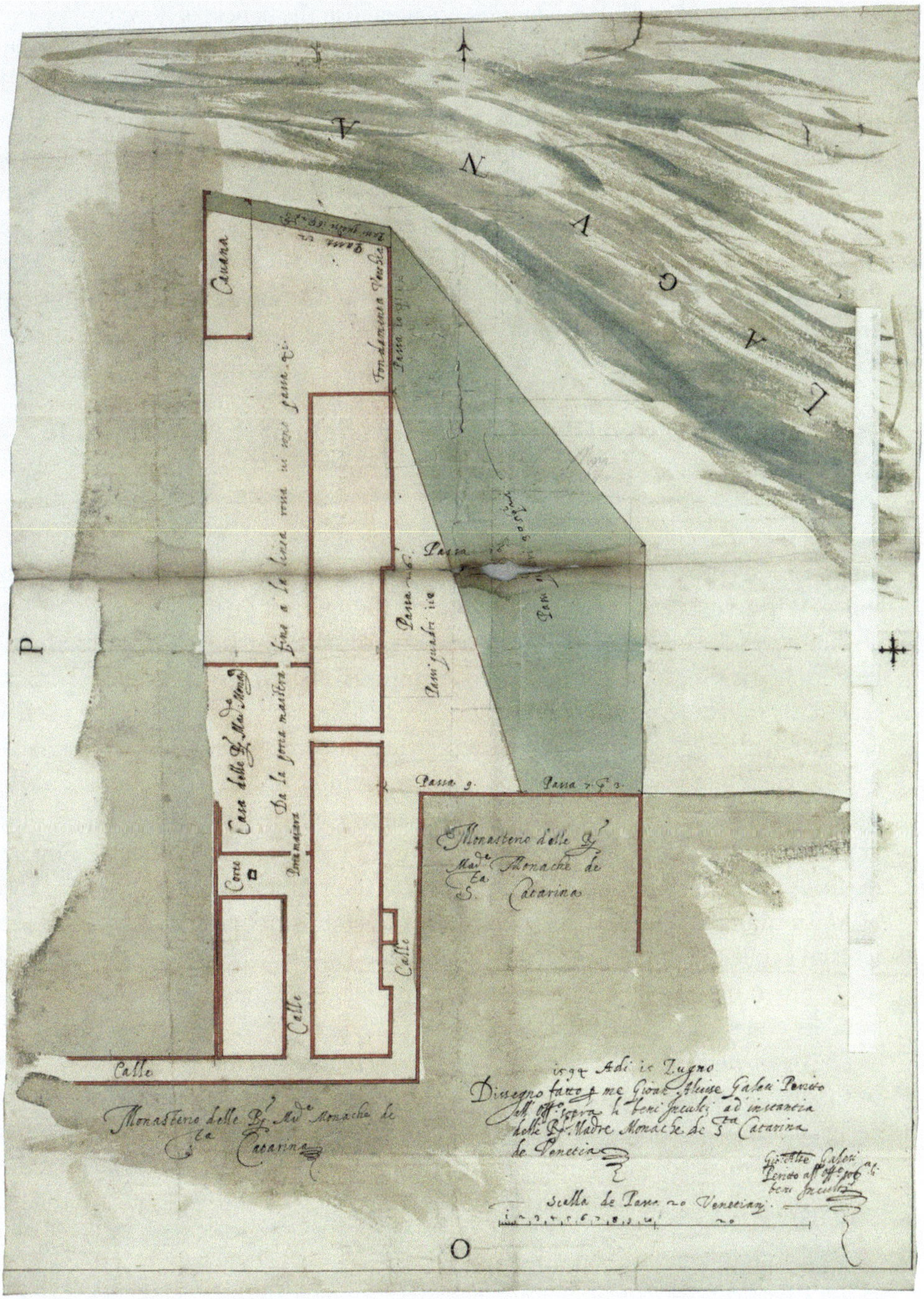

Fig. 9.5 Alvise Galesi, reconstruction of the land reclamation interventions carried on by the nuns of Santa Caterina, 15 June 1594. Archivio di Stato di Venezia, *SCdS*, b. 20, proc. 7, fol. 21r

Monache de Santa Catarina di Venezia' ('conducted at the behest of Reverend Mother Nuns') corroborates this interpretation. The drawing was likely commissioned by the nuns and was intended as a graphic history – a kind of visual inventory – of their real estate achievements. The direct involvement of such a group of entrepreneurial nuns in the production and development of a new settlement is apparent. They did not limit themselves to the oversight and administration of their land patrimony, but were effective promoters of the construction of the place itself. This notion clearly shows how, in common with their relatives who sat in the councils of the Venetian state, the nuns were direct spokespeople and initiators in the massive programme of urban redevelopment.

Towards a Completed City: The Construction of the Fondamente Nuove (1590-1603)

Against repeated abuses and contraventions, the state's empirical and fragmentary interventions proved inefficient in containing personal individuals' hunger for space. While severe control and regulation did not put an end to the countless disputes over the urban space, these measures did disclose how legislation should proceed in creating a comprehensive plan applied on both an urban and territorial scale.[46] By the mid-sixteenth century, office holders became aware of the need to embrace hydrological problems with political and socio-economic concerns. It became clear that water management, urban planning and health policy should be considered as an entwined endeavour. The delineation of these related dimensions of place – the physical and the lived – involved many other European countries in the early modern period, and in particular the Dutch Republic. As in the case of Amsterdam, this understanding led to the establishment of a specialized and fruitful exchange of knowledge among diverse figures who were engaged in the urban programme in various ways, such as architects, engineers, naturalists, master builders and state officers.[47]

The renowned *Plan of Venice*, the urban and economic planning scheme proposed by Cristoforo Sabbadino (1557), might be considered as the first relevant attempt to design a comprehensive project for the Venetian capital (Figure 9.6).[48] Considered as a manifesto for the global rethinking of Venice's urban and hydrological welfare, it became a model for future state actions. Three plans, with slight differences,

46 Selmi, 'Politica lagunare'.

47 For a comparison between Venetian and Dutch policy measures with regard to hydrological issues, see Ciriacono, *Building on Water*, 157-193, as well as the essay by Merlijn Hurx in this volume and, in particular, the description of the case of Amsterdam.

48 On this and for a complete bibliography, see Svalduz, 'Venice 1557.'

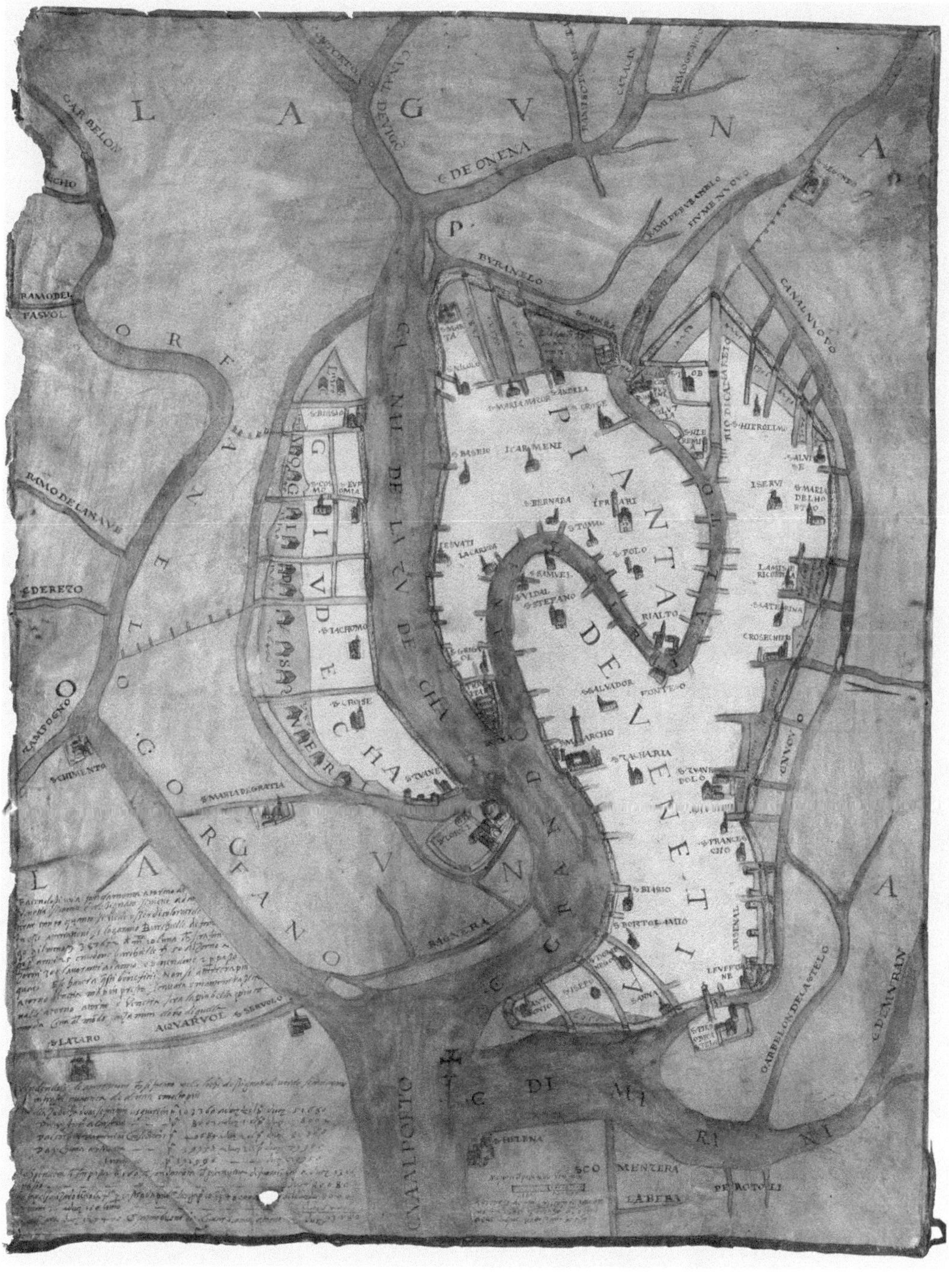

Fig. 9.6 Cristoforo Sabbadino, *Pianta de Venetia*, 1557. Archivio di Stato di Venezia, *Savi ed esecutori alle acque*, Disegni, Diversi, 128/10

tackle the problems that compromised the equilibrium of the lagoon, the siltation of waterways, and population growth. Sabbadino's proposal consisted of a long stone embankment – about 17 metres wide – which would have solidified the whole perimeter of the city, as well as two peripheral canals that would direct the flow of internal waterways towards the lagoon. In addition, the project entailed the construction of 36 new bridges and a series of plots, which would have been filled with the mud resulting from the excavations of canals. Along the northern fringe of the city, three new basins would have served as ports for the arrival and distribution of goods from the mainland. Everything was to be self-financed: reclaimed lands would have been sold at auction and the revenues would have entirely covered the urban infrastructure.[49]

Despite Sabbadino's forward-thinking proposal, public debates over the plan of Venice continued for decades and the Republic's intervention did not begin until the end of the sixteenth century. In the process of negotiations, moreover, Sabbadino's comprehensive project was reduced to nothing more than a fragment of the peripheral belt envisioned.[50] The construction of the Fondamente Nuove was limited to just the paved pedestrian walkway that links the northern border of the city from Santa Giustina to the Sacca della Misericordia, which was kept as a unique water basin for storing goods. Despite this, the addition of the Fondamente Nuove proved to be a crucial state decision as it constituted the last substantial urban transformation of the early modern period, helping the city to obtain its dolphin-shaped contours.

But what motivated the drastic curtailment of Sabbadino's initial plan? About a hundred years after other important public reclamation initiatives, such as those developed in Santa Maria Mazor and Sant'Antonio di Castello, the economic and sociopolitical structure in Venice had profoundly changed.[51] By the time the project of the Fondamente Nuove materialized, the Most Serene Republic faced a delicate juncture, which had originated with the agricultural crises of the 1560s and 1570s and the Arsenal fire in 1569, and then continued with the Turkish invasion of Cyprus in 1570, and the devastating plague epidemic of 1575-1577. The explosion in population and the building boom of the first half of the century were no longer driving growth.[52] On the contrary, economic circumstances seem to have guided the state's initiatives, namely the need to promptly reactivate the economy. At the end of the sixteenth century, the Republic entered a comprehensive recovery phase, enacting a series of stimulative monetary

49 Svalduz, 'Visti dall'acqua', 76-80 and 87-96.

50 See Tafuri, *Venice and the Renaissance*, 187.

51 On these enterprises developed by the State, see Pavanini, 'Venezia verso la pianificazione?'

52 Lanaro, 'Reinterpreting Venetian Economic History'.

and investment policies, which included the construction of the Fondamente Nuove.[53] So, more than an outlet for demographic and building pressures, the implementation of Sabbadino's revised plan constituted an effort to provide new revenue for the state coffers.

As Manfredo Tafuri argued, the building site likely began in the year 1590 and it moved from Santa Giustina to the western tip of the walkway.[54] As in the decision-making stage, the construction proceeded slowly with numerous setbacks. Moreover, a sort of empirical procedure signalled the organization of new infrastructure. It seems as though the Republic adopted a stepped approach that enabled it to push forward the work as soon as eastern sections were completed. This would explain why, in the year 1594, the *proto* Galesi was again asked to inspect all the urban fringes of the *insula*, including the convent of Santa Caterina's small land abuse of 16 square feet.

The flexible construction strategy proved to be highly efficient, as it permitted magistrates to sort out all kinds of variations, contingencies and unexpected disputes. Therefore, it was later adopted even for the urbanization process that followed the land reclamation activity.[55] Once partially filled, new lands were divided into lots (*prese*) and gradually sold at auctions (*instrumenti*) by the state even before their completion. The reference to Sabbadino's proposal is self-evident. On the one hand, this staged resolution avoided bidding that would have inflated the market; on the other, it allowed the Venetian Republic to obtain necessary revenue to carry out public interventions. While this solution had been previously used, in this instance it seems to have accommodated the need to constantly assess market demand.

The sales process could take several calls to ensure a buyer, but it also required the *Collegio*'s final authorization. In addition, the *Savi ed esecutori alle acque* was responsible for the planning design of the future urban development. As Elena Svalduz has extensively demonstrated, this was no more than a simplified scheme of the principal system of pathways. Urban infrastructure and facilities became the sole responsibility of private citizens.[56] This practice followed a long tradition, both in Venice and on the mainland, as it permitted the government to minimize its costs, welcome settlement distributions, and encourage private initiatives, in particular those from members of the patriciate. But, in the development of the Fondamente Nuove, the final results differed significantly from the Republic's expectations.

53 Pezzolo, *L'oro dello Stato*, 201-204.

54 Tafuri, 'Documenti sulle Fondamenta Nuove'.

55 On this operative urban strategy developed by the Serenissima, see Svalduz, 'Procedure materiali', in particular, 561-585.

56 Svalduz, '"Nella fine della città"'.

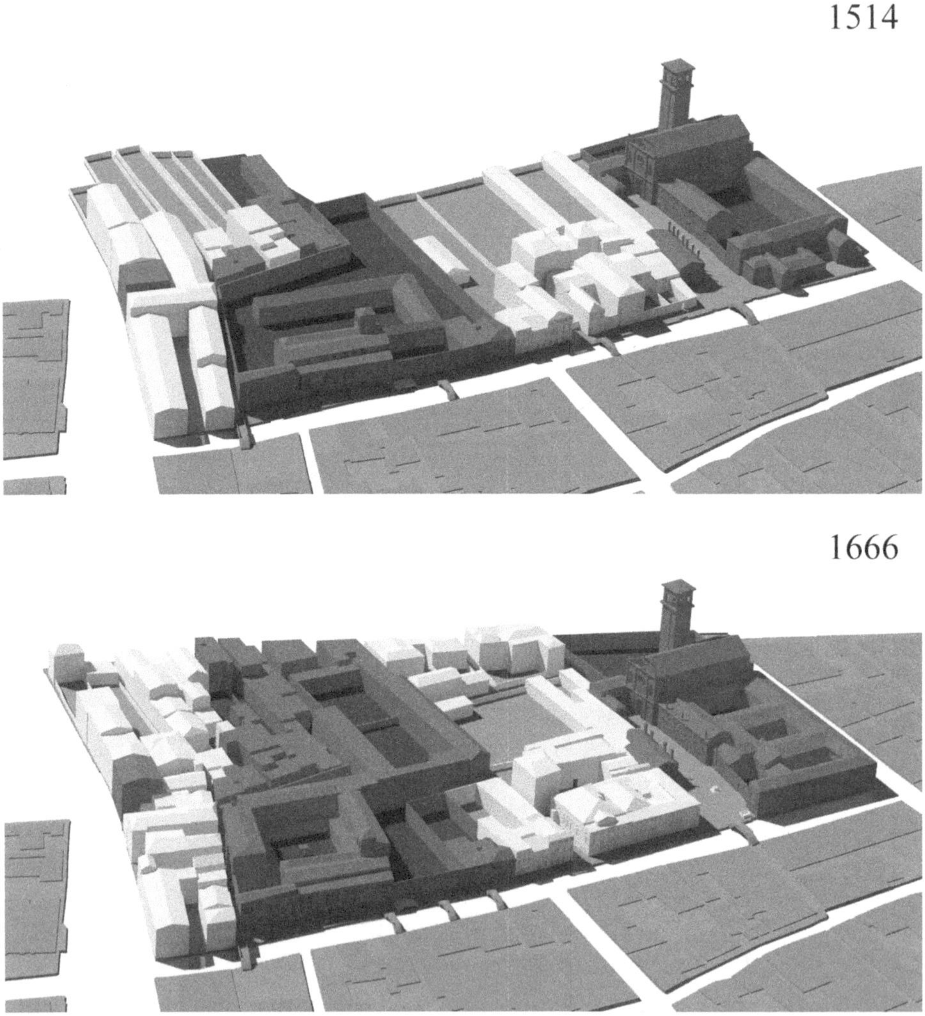

Fig. 9.7 Digital reconstruction of the *insula*'s land use (ecclesiastical and private). © Ludovica Galeazzo
a) 1514
b) 1661

The Construction of the Urban Space

A close look at the documentation regarding the urbanization processes in Venice yields positive evidence for understanding the physical procedure of place making (Figure 9.7). Even more, it helps to shed light on the evolution of the interests at

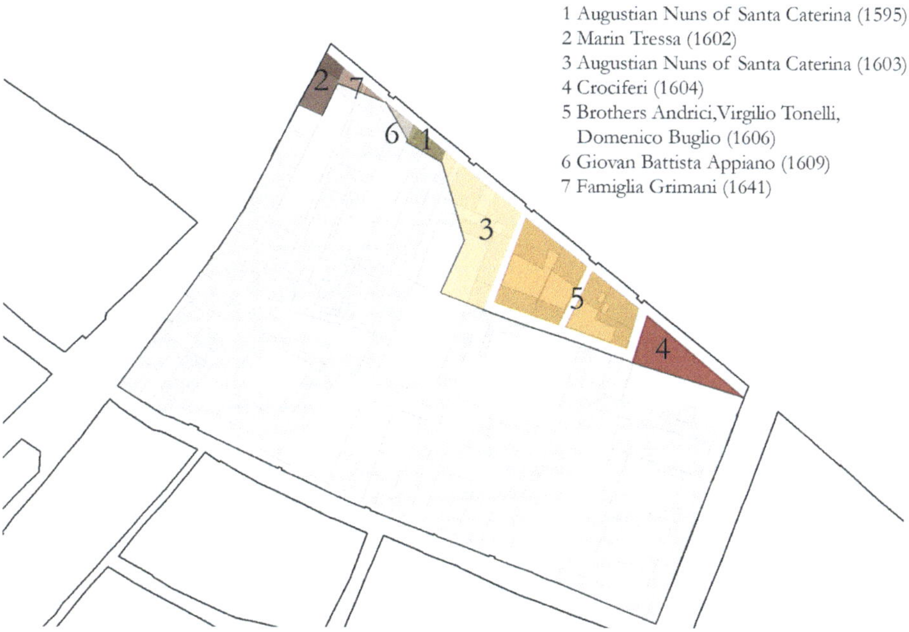

Fig. 9.8 Reconstruction of the purchase agreements following the land reclamations. © Ludovica Galeazzo

stake and on the social dynamics that determined the final definition of place.[57] The comparison between the purchase agreements of specific parcels sold at auction by the magistrate and by private ecclesiastical sources enables us to evaluate dates, procedures, and especially the consumers of the new land market (Figure 9.8). Following the 16 square-foot acquisition of 1595, six different land sales were arranged in nearly fifteen years. As the *instrumenti* reveal, a significant 60 per cent of the 8700 square metres of land sold went to ecclesiastical communities. 80 per cent of these lands were acquired by the Augustinian nuns, while the remaining 40 per cent was transferred to private owners, primarily merchants, rather than patrician citizens.[58]

Marin Tressa, a dealer famous for his spice trade between the Greek islands and England, bought the western tip of the *insula*, while the brothers Andrici, together with Virginio Tonelli, Domenico Buglio and the salt merchant Giacomo Bonsegno, acquired the wide space adjacent to the Augustinian convent. Apart from those involving religious communities, transactions tended to be extremely slow and

57 Unlike the first two *prese*, which extend from Santa Giustina to the rio dei Crociferi, the third *tranche* of the addition has received little scholarly attention.

58 This gradient reduces when we do not consider preceding illegal reclamations. In fact, the whole reclamation intervention carried on by the state consisted of a little more than 5500 square metres, 2600 of which were acquired by religious bodies and 2900 went to private owners.

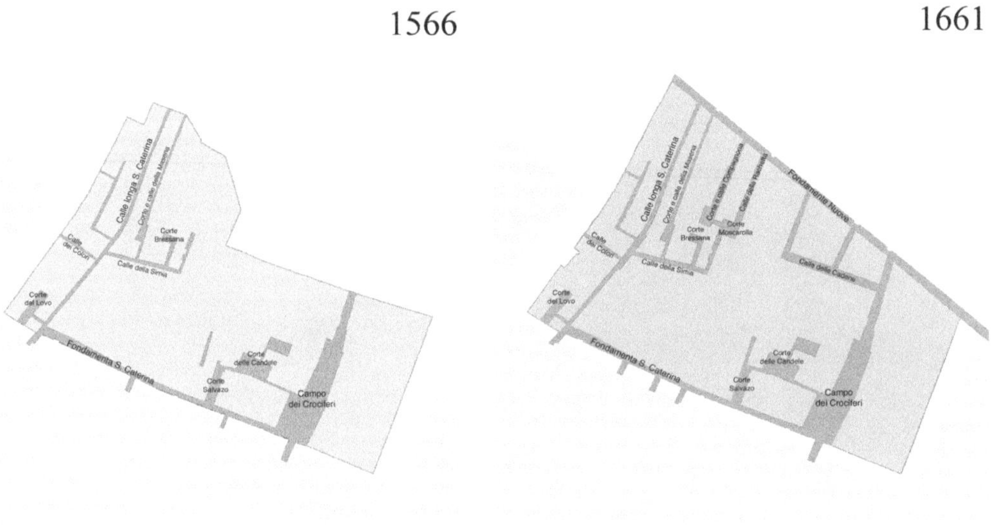

Fig. 9.9 Reconstruction of the system of public walkways. © Ludovica Galeazzo
a) 1566
b) 1661

not highly profitable for the Republic. It generally took about four or five calls to complete negotiations and the average price of the purchased lots decreased to just 2 ducats and 12 *grossi*, approximately a third of the lot price in peripheral areas at the beginning of the century.[59]

A hypothetical reconstruction of the area over time provides further insights. From an urban perspective, the enlargement of the *insula* did not lead to a strong transformation to the physical settlement. In fact, the sequence of parallel and straight spits of land that extend towards the lagoon persisted, and new lands were developed as a natural continuation of the medieval urban design. Nevertheless, as for the whole embankment, state officers paid close attention to provide a system of public walkways directed straight toward the water (Figure 9.9).

The concern about the easy access to the lagoon has always been a matter of great importance and it has been consistently regulated over time.[60] This contingency was also intimately connected with the Crociferi purchase of 257 square feet of land adjacent to their church. Repeatedly exhorted by magistrates, in 1604 the friars granted the Republic the plot (circa 33 feet wide) extending from across their

59 ASVe, *Savi ed esecutori alle acque*, reg. 323.

60 A recurring expression in archival documents is 'dar strada in fine della detta sacca', which means to create a pedestrian walkway at the end of a reclaimed area.

Fig. 9.10 Digital reconstruction of the *insula*'s land use (residential and commercial) in 1514, 1661, and 1712. © Ludovica Galeazzo

Fig. 9.11 Digital reconstruction of the *insula*'s land use (buildings for rent and private buildings) in 1514, 1661 and 1712. © Ludovica Galeazzo

church to the lagoon, so that it might be used as a public space.[61] The substantial donation was immediately rewarded by the state, which conceded the Crociferi the remaining 224 square feet of land at the sole cost of 350 ducats (approximately half a ducat per foot) and exempted them from the auction process.[62]

However, from an economic point of view, the expansion profoundly altered the site's purpose as well as the functions of its structures. As a result of recent acquisitions, both citizens and religious communities began speculative operations in order to

61 The access to the lagoon was guaranteed by a passageway (*sottoportego*) running under the building used by the furriers' guild (now lost). Thanks to this covered walkway, the public *campo* could seamlessly extend 'from water to water', namely from the rio di Santa Caterina to the lagoon. This peculiar feature still characterizes the current configuration of the *insula*.

62 ASVe, *Savi ed esecutori alle acque*, reg. 347, fol. 92v.

realize substantial profits. Their intervention aimed to fully condense the urban fabric, reserving a limited space for public areas (such as *calli* and *campielli*) or for those activities that needed empty plots. Unlike their predecessors, such as Francesco della Torre or the powerful merchants Giacomo Ragazzoni and Benetto Tiepolo, new buyers did not engage in agricultural or industrial activities.[63] Rather, they intensified their investment exclusively in real estate. As an in-depth analysis of the tax records from 1564 to 1712 shows, warehouses, simple residential buildings and low-cost houses built on two or three stories were standard developments (Figures 9.10 and 9.11).

Likewise, the Augustinian nuns' orientation followed the general economic trend as well the intensive exploitation of the new urban space. What is striking, however, is the extension of their investment programme. Of the 3000 square metres of acquired land, none was converted into spaces for the convent. All of these new properties were transformed into houses, warehouses and workshops to be rented out to members of the upper-middle class. Textual and iconographic sources confirm the speculative nature of such expansions. In one map preserved in the Archivio Patriarcale in Venice, the nuns' properties are shown in wireframe visualization. The new buildings are significantly indicated as 'chase fatte da novo dale monache da fitar' ('new houses constructed by the nuns to be rented') and 'locho da far magazine da fitar' ('place to rent as a warehouse') (Figure 9.12).[64]

The overlapping entrepreneurial strategies of ecclesiastical communities and individuals reveal how urban space was prioritized as an economic opportunity, rather than being considered a basic need. Indeed, against the Republic's desires repeatedly stated in the magistrates' reports, the expansion did not bring far-reaching residential investments or innovative architectural projects. On the contrary, the construction of place resulted in a series of autonomous and diversified acquisitions, which later led to self-determining proto-capitalist interventions. To identify the reasons that lay behind this calculated expansion, it is necessary to consider the economic and political framework of seventeenth-century Venice. In fact, the ecclesiastical entrepreneurial strategy, akin to the property owners' general approach, appears strictly tied to the gradual decline of Venice as a major international centre of trade as well as to its conversion towards a real estate-based economy.[65] The minor but repeated efforts carried on by both the nuns and private citizens were instrumental in securing a large and significant patrimony, which, as

63 The first was one of the richest and most talented merchants that the Republic could boast. In the aftermath of a long career spent between England and the Levant, he initiated numerous manufacturing activities in the area in front of his house in Santa Caterina. Benetto was the son of the renowned statesman Stefano Tiepolo and was one of the wealthiest Venetian traders of timber and iron. He constructed a series of wooden warehouses on the Augustinian nuns' land.

64 ASPVe, *Parrocchia di San Felice, Santa Sofia*, Atti generali, b. 4, fasc. 4.

65 Chauvard, *La circulation des biens*, 127-136 and 491-516.

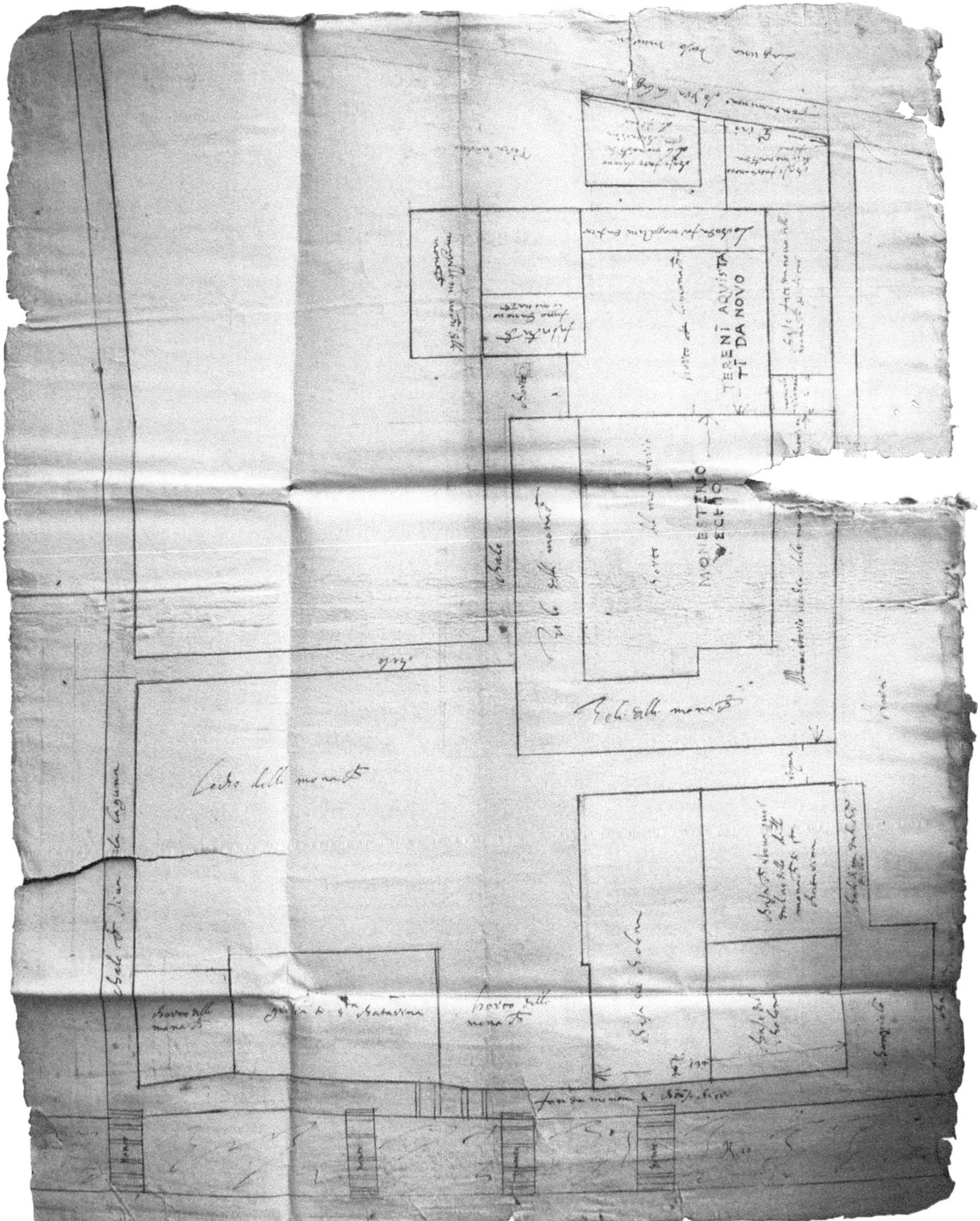

Fig. 9.12 Survey of the convent of Santa Caterina and design for the new buildings to be constructed, first half of the seventeenth century. Archivio Storico del Patriarcato di Venezia, *Parrocchia di San Felice, Santa Sofia*, Atti generali, fasc. 4

invested in the real estate market, withdrew capital from manufacturing activity and commercial trade. Thus, the growing profitability of land in the sixteenth century was almost exclusively directed toward an extensive construction of buildings and infrastructure. This decision would not only turn out to be a highly efficient and safe choice for investors, but also opened the market to a new segment of citizens and subjects prepared to take risks to improve their economic condition.[66]

Place as a New Stage Setting

To some extent, the so-called *great addition* of the Fondamente Nuove did not include prominent architecture nor any relevant large-scale building programme. Excluding the well-studied cases of Palazzo Donà and San Lazzaro dei Mendicanti, the area extending from the Sacca della Misericordia to the Arsenal does not boast other outstanding buildings.[67] Moreover, the sixteenth-century enlargement did not result in a concrete opportunity to define a new skyline for the northern margin of the city. None of the religious houses standing on this area, which were restored and reconstructed in the following centuries, had its monumental façade reoriented towards the water lagoon – as happened with the church of Spirito Santo on the Fondamenta delle Zattere in the southern fringe of Venice.[68] On the contrary, architectural and urban decisions appear to have been marked by a sort of social and political resolution in which the notion of *mediocritas* ruled supreme. Austere, mainly residential, and middle class, the architecture of the northern periphery became a prototype that would inform the future planning of outlying settlements.

Nevertheless, part of the city had been irrevocably altered with physical, psychological, cognitive and social consequences. Following the expansion, the representation of the urban enlargement became a distinguishing feature of Venice, broadly etched on the city's descriptive and visual memory. In his *Discorsi morali* [...] *contra il dispiacer di morire* (1596), the physician and philosopher Fabio Glissenti praised the beauty of walking along the new outline of the city, a place where the air was fresh and the view to Burano and Torcello amazing. It is in this location that the humanist dreamed of constructing his residence, a pleasant refuge for intellectuals and friends.[69] In his words, the grim picture of unhealthy and insalubrious lands seems far away. New concepts related to aesthetics, usefulness and health characterize the recently established place, in a strong counterpoint to the winding and narrow *calli* of the city centre.

66 Fusaro, *Political Economies of Empire*, 174-201.

67 On Palazzo Donà, see Ceriani Sebregondi, 'Un doge e il suo manifesto'. For the religious complex of San Lazzaro, see Bamji, Borean and Moretti, *La chiesa e l'Ospedale di san Lazzaro dei Mendicanti*.

68 Huse, *The Art of Renaissance Venice*, 80-81.

69 Glissenti, *Discorsi morali*, fol. 236v. On this, see Svalduz, '"Contra il dispiacere del morire"', 111-115.

Fig. 9.13 Vincenzo Maria Coronelli, *The Freezing of the Venetian Lagoon*, 1708. Venice, Biblioteca Nazionale Marciana, 150.d.5

Over centuries, many artists strengthened the recent appearance of the new place. Engravings by Vincenzo Maria Coronelli and Domenico Lovisa, and later views by Gabriel Bella and Francesco Guardi represented – although sometimes idealising it – the new urban waterfront (Figure 9.13). As Cesare de Seta has argued, iconographic views of a city are not only the most direct and faithful interpretation of that city's image, but also provide important clues for understanding culture and mentalities it promoted.[70] More than an ornamental frame or a neutral space between Venice and the mainland, the new margins of Venice were gradually perceived as connective hubs within a network of distribution of resources and places of public interest. Once merely reserved for the city's main urban sites and buildings, such as St. Mark's Square or the Ducal Palace, the new outline was taken as an iconic and moral symbol of the grandeur of Venice.

70 De Seta, 'Prefazione', vi.

Bibliography

Manuscript Sources

Venice, Biblioteca del Museo Correr

Ms. P.D.c. 1004/95, second half of fifteenth century-first half of sixteenth century

Ms. Cicogna 2562 (=3834)

Codice del piovego, thirteenth century

Venice, Archivio Storico del Patriarcato di Venezia

Curia, Archivio segreto, Visite pastorali a monasteri femminili

b. 4: *Visite Patriarca Francesco Vendramin*, 1609-1618

Parrocchia di San Felice, Santa Sofia, Atti generali

b. 4 (Fasc. 4): *Alcuni antichi Dissegni dell'antico sistema delle Case dietro il Monastero di S. Cattarina*

[...], early seventeenth century

Venice, Archivio di Stato di Venezia

Archivio Gradenigo Rio Marin

b. 237 (Fasc. V): *Scriture pertinente le aque driedo li Crosechieri, et Santa Catherina*, second half fifteenth century

Dieci savi alle decime in Rialto

b. 421 (1661)

Procuratori di San Marco, de Citra, Commissarie

b. 233 (Fasc. 27): *Privilegia Ordinis Cruciferorum*, fourteenth-sixteenth centuries

Santa Caterina dei Sacchi

b. 20 (Proc. 7): *Acquisti delle monache di Terreni e Palludi Contrà di Santa Soffia, San Felice, e Santi Apostoli vendutisi dal Magistrato alle Acque*, sixteenth century

Savi ed esecutori alle acque

reg. 219: *Sumario delle gratie* [...], sixteenth century

reg. 323: *Instrumenti rilasciati dal magistrato*, 1593-1642

reg. 330: *Parti prese nel Maggior Consiglio e nel Pregadi*, 1413-1453

reg. 347: *Capitolari*, late sixteenth century

Sopraintendenti alle decime del clero

b. 33 (1564)

Printed Sources

Bamji, Alexandra, Linda Borean and Laura Moretti (eds), *La chiesa e l'Ospedale di San Lazzaro dei Mendicanti. Arte, beneficenza, cura, devozione, educazione* (Venice: Marcianum Press, 2015).

Barbaro, Daniele, *I dieci libri dell'architettura* (Venice: per Francesco Marcolini, 1556).

Berveglieri, Roberto, *Le vie di Venezia. Canali lagunari e rii a Venezia: inventori, brevetti, tecnologia e legislazione nei secoli XIII-XVIII* (Sommacampagna: Cierre, 1999).

Butler, Chris, *Henri Lefebvre: Spatial Politics, Everyday Life and the Right to the City* (New York: Routledge, 2012).

Ceriani Sebregondi, Giuliana, 'Un doge e il suo manifesto: il palazzo di Leonardo Donà (1536-1612) alle Fondamenta Nuove a Venezia', *Annali di Architettura* 14 (2002), 231-250.

Chauvard, Jean-François, *La circulation des biens à Venise. Stratégies patrimoniales et marché immobilier, 1600-1750* (Rome: École française de Rome, 2005).

Ciriacono, Salvatore, *Building on Water: Venice, Holland and the Construction of the European Landscape in Early Modern Times*, trans. by Jeremy Scott (New York: Berghahn Books, 2006).

Codex Publicorum (*Codice del Piovego*), *Vol. 1*, ed. by Bianca Lanfranchi Strina (Venice: Stamperia di Venezia, 1985).

Concina, Ennio, *Venezia nell'età moderna. Struttura e funzioni* (Venice: Marsilio, 1989).

Concina, Ennio, 'Venezia, "tra due elementi sospesa"', in *'Tra due elementi sospesa'. Venezia, costruzione di un paesaggio urbano* (Venice: Insula-Marsilio, 2000), 15-51.

Crouzet-Pavan, Élisabeth, 'La maturazione dello spazio urbano', in Alberto Tenenti and Ugo Tucci (eds), *Storia di Venezia dalle origini alla caduta della Serenissima, V: Il Rinascimento. Società ed economia* (Rome: Istituto della Enciclopedia italiana Treccani, 1996), 3-100.

Crouzet-Pavan, Élisabeth, 'Sviluppo e articolazione della città', in Girolamo Arnaldi, Giorgio Cracco and Alberto Tenenti (eds), *Storia di Venezia dalle origini alla caduta della Serenissima, III: La formazione dello Stato patrizio* (Rome: Istituto della Enciclopedia italiana Treccani, 1997), 729-781.

Crouzet-Pavan, Élisabeth, 'Toward an Ecological Understanding of the Myth of Venice', in John Martin and Dennis Romano (eds), *Venice Reconsidered: The History and Civilization of an Italian City State, 1297-1797* (Baltimore: Johns Hopkins University Press, 2000), 39-67.

de Seta, Cesare, 'Prefazione', in *Palermo*, ed. by Cesare de Seta and Leonardo di Mauro (Bari and Rome: Laterza, 1980).

D'Evelyn, Margaret Muther, *Venice and Vitruvius: Reading Venice with Daniele Barbaro and Andrea Palladio* (New Haven: Yale University Press, 2012).

Folin, Marco (ed.), *Rappresentare la città. Topografie urbane nell'Italia di antico regime* (Reggio Emilia: Diabasis, 2010).

Fusaro, Maria, *Political Economies of Empire in the Early Modern Mediterranean: The Decline of Venice and the Rise of England, 1450-1700* (Cambridge: Cambridge University Press, 2015).

Galeazzo, Ludovica, 'Entrepreneurship beyond Convent Walls: The Augustinian Nuns of Santa Caterina dei Sacchi in Venice', in Marilyn Dunn and Saundra Weddle (eds), *Convent Networks in Early Modern Italy* (Turnhout: Brepols, 2020), 193-230.

Galeazzo, Ludovica, *Venezia e i margini urbani. L'insula dei Gesuiti in età moderna* (Venice: Istituto Veneto di Scienze, Lettere ed Arti, 2018).

Glissenti, Fabio, *Discorsi morali dell'eccellente Signor Fabio Glissenti contra il dispiacer del morire* (Venice: appresso Domenico Farri, 1596).

Huse, Norbert and Wolfgang Wolters, *The Art of Renaissance Venice: Architecture, Sculpture, and Painting, 1460-1590* (Chicago and London: University of Chicago Press, 1990).

Lanaro, Paola, 'Reinterpreting Venetian Economic History', in Paola Lanaro (eds), *At the Centre of the Old World: Trade and Manufacturing in Venice and the Venetian Mainland (1400-1800)* (Toronto: CRRS, 2006), 19-69.

Lefebvre, Henri, *The Production of Space*, trans. by Donald Nicholson Smith (Oxford: Blackwell, 1991).

Pavanini, Paola, 'Venezia verso la pianificazione? Bonifiche urbane nel XVI secolo a Venezia', in Jean-Claude Maire Vigueur (ed.), *D'une ville à l'autre. Structure matérielles et organisation de l'espace dans les villes européennes, XIIIe-XVIe siécles* (Rome: École Française de Rome, 1989), 485-507.

Pezzolo, Luciano, *L'oro dello Stato. Società, finanza e fisco nella Repubblica veneta del secondo '500* (Venice: Il cardo, 1990).

Piasentini, Stefano, 'Aspetti della Venezia d'acqua dalla fine del XIV secolo alla fine del XV secolo', in Giovanni Caniato (ed.), *Venezia la città dei rii* (Sommacampagna: Cierre, 1999), 41-67.

Romano, Denis, '"Quod sibi fiat gratia": Adjustment of Penalties and the Exercise of Influence in Early Renaissance Venice', *Journal of Medieval and Renaissance Studies* 13 (1983), 251-268.

Selmi, Paolo, 'Politica lagunare della veneta Repubblica dal secolo XIV al secolo XVIII', in *Mostra storica della laguna veneta* (Venice: Stamperia di Venezia, 1970), 105-118.

Settis, Salvatore, 'Premessa', in Donatella Calabi and Ludovica Galeazzo (eds), *Acqua e cibo a Venezia. Storie della laguna e della città* (Venice: Marsilio, 2015), 19-23.

Sherman, Allison, 'The Lost Venetian Church of Santa Maria Assunta dei Crociferi: Form, Decoration, and Patronage', PhD diss., University of St. Andrews, 2009/2010.

Sherman, Allison, 'La collocazione originale del Martirio di San Lorenzo di Tiziano: la chiesa scomparsa di Santa Maria Assunta dei Crociferi', in Lionello Puppi and Letizia Lonzi (eds), *La Notte di San Lorenzo. Genesi, contesti, peripezie di un capolavoro di Tiziano* (Crocetta del Montello: Terra Ferma, 2013), 16-43.

Svalduz, Elena, 'Al servizio del magistrato. I proti alle acque nel corso del primo secolo d'attività', in Giuliana Mazzi and Stefano Zaggia (eds), *'Architetto sia l'ingegniero che discorre'. Ingegneri, architetti e proti nell'età della Repubblica* (Venice: Marsilio, 2004), 233-268.

Svalduz, Elena, '"Contra il dispiacere del morire": i Mendicanti, le larghe paludi e il nuovo ampliamento urbano', in Alexandra Bamji, Linda Borean and Laura Moretti (eds), *La chiesa e l'Ospedale di San Lazzaro dei Mendicanti. Arte, beneficenza, cura, devozione, educazione* (Venice: Marcianum Press, 2015), 111-138.

Svalduz, Elena, '"Nella fine della città": ampliamenti e margini urbani a Venezia in età moderna', in Marco Folin (ed.), *Sistole/diastole. Episodi di trasformazione urbana nell'Italia delle città* (Venice: Istituto Veneto di Scienze, Lettere ed Arti, 2006), 207-270.

Svalduz, Elena, 'Procedure materiali, decisioni tecniche e operative nella realizzazione delle Fondamente Nuove', in Simonetta Cavaciocchi (ed.), *L'edilizia prima della rivoluzione industriale secc. XIII-XVIII* (Prato: Istituto Internazionale di Storia Economica F. Datini-Le Monnier, 2004), 555-585.

Svalduz, Elena, 'Venice 1557: Sabbadino's City Plan', in Nebahat Avcioğlu and Emma Jones (eds), *Architecture, Art and Identity in Venice and Its Territories, 1450-1750* (Farnham: Ashgate, 2013), 71-86.

Svalduz, Elena, 'Visti dall'acqua: i disegni del "far la città" e la manutenzione urbana', in Stefano Zaggia (ed.), *Fare la città. Salvaguardia e manutenzione urbana a Venezia in età moderna* (Venice: Bruno Mondadori, 2006), 71-96.

Tafuri, Manfredo, 'Documenti sulle Fondamenta Nuove', *Architettura, storia e documenti* 1 (1985), 79-95.

Tafuri, Manfredo, *Venice and the Renaissance*, trans. by Jessica Levine (Cambridge, MA: The MIT Press, 1989).

Toffolo, Francesca, 'Art and the Conventual Life in Renaissance Venice: The Monastery Church of Santa Caterina de' Sacchi', PhD diss., Princeton University, 2004/2005.

Torre, Angelo, *Luoghi. La produzione di località in età moderna e contemporanea* (Rome: Donzelli, 2011).

Zevi, Bruno, *Architecture as Space: How to Look at Architecture*, trans. by Milton Gendel, ed. by Joseph A. Barry (New York: Horizon Press, 1957).

About the Author

Ludovica Galeazzo is an architectural and urban historian whose research focuses on early modern Italian architecture. She is currently a Digital Humanities Research Associate at the Villa I Tatti, Florence. She has authored several articles about the urban and architectural history of Venice, as well as a book, *Venezia e i margini urbani. L'insula dei Gesuiti in età moderna* (2018).

10. Exploring the *Book of Fortresses*

Edward Triplett

Abstract
Duarte de Armas' *Livro das fortalezas* or *Book of Fortresses* illustrates 55 border fortresses in over 180 meticulous measured and annotated renderings. The book is even more impressive given that de Armas completed his on-site survey in a single year (1509) and finished annotating the book the following year. The book's drawings, alluring in their combination of finite time and enormous space, are difficult to link together at an intra-site or inter-site scale. Consequently, while mapping the 55 border fortresses in the book provides a greater apprehension of a historical, liminal space, this alone does not solve the greater problem of reconstructing de Armas' methods for rendering place on the Portuguese-Castilian border, nor does it acknowledge the historical moment in which it was produced. This article reconstructs the world of the *Book of Fortresses* through a novel, digital approach that acknowledges Duarte de Armas' malleable sense of space rather than 'rectifying' his work to match modern geography.

Keywords: Duarte de Armas, Manuel I, Portugal, Spain, mapping

Introduction

In 1509 Manuel I of Portugal sent a squire named Duarte de Armas on a journey to the fortified border between the Kingdoms of Portugal and Spain. The product of this mission (popularly known as the *Book of Fortresses*) is a compelling snapshot of late medieval and early modern military architecture that contains 120 perspective drawings and 51 plan drawings of 55 castles and fortified towns. The book was executed with a rare degree of completeness, geographic spread and complexity. It has most commonly been used by archaeologists looking at individual sites, or architectural historians attempting to create a typology of fortress forms from the plan drawings. Similarly, images of 'daily life' in the landscapes, and of distant ships

Merrill, E. (ed.), *Creating Place in Early Modern European Architecture*.
Taylor & Francis Group 2022
DOI: 10.5117/9789463728027_CH010

in the backgrounds of some of the perspective drawings have excited social and naval historians, who treat these elements in isolation from the rest of the codex. In most of these studies, the book is mined for information rather than considered as a holistic product representing multiple scales of space. This encyclopaedic rather than analytical approach is in no way antithetical to the original purpose of the book, but there is a larger story about the visual communication of places in the *Book of Fortresses* that still needs to be addressed. This article will outline why the *Book of Fortresses* remains easy to become lost in, but difficult to explore as a spatial source. It will also explain how the book can be better understood through the application of digital methods that acknowledge the book's historiography and spatial complexity.

The impetus for this article and the digital project associated with it was defined by historian Alfredo Pimenta in 1940:

> Rich in architectural, topographical, ethnographic, historical and linguistic information, a work of pictorial art and a work of positive science, the *Book of Fortresses* is a world that has not yet been properly explored.[1]

This idea – that the *Book of Fortresses* continues to simultaneously invite and reject spatial exploration – can be attributed to several factors. Duarte de Armas' book is not an atlas; readers cannot rely on Cartesian geometry or linear perspective to help orient themselves in the book, even when more than one place is depicted on a page. Nor is there a prefaced map in the original work showing 55 fortress icons strung across Portugal's northern and eastern borders with Spain as there is in a seventeenth-century watercolour copy of the book (Figure 10.1).[2] The plan drawings for the fortresses are also assembled after the perspective drawings, which at least partially undermines their ability to contribute to a three-dimensional impression of each fortification. Apart from a few written annotations on the drawings, the only textual section in the book is Duarte de Armas' itinerary, and this is more of a list than a narrative. It simply states where the author and his servant began each leg of their travels, where they ended up at each stage, how many streams they crossed, and the length and condition of the roads. Despite, or perhaps *because* of all of this information, as a reader it is difficult not to be left with a desire to see *between* the pages of the book: to assess how the perspective views and the plans relate to each other and to comprehend a narrative of Duarte de Armas' travels and decision-making process. Put simply, how did Duarte de Armas define Portugal's border with Castile as a series of places?

1 Pimenta, *Duarte darmas e o seu* Livro das fortalezas, 8.

2 On this copy, see Cortesão, *Cartografia e cartógrafos portugueses dos seculos XV e XVI.*

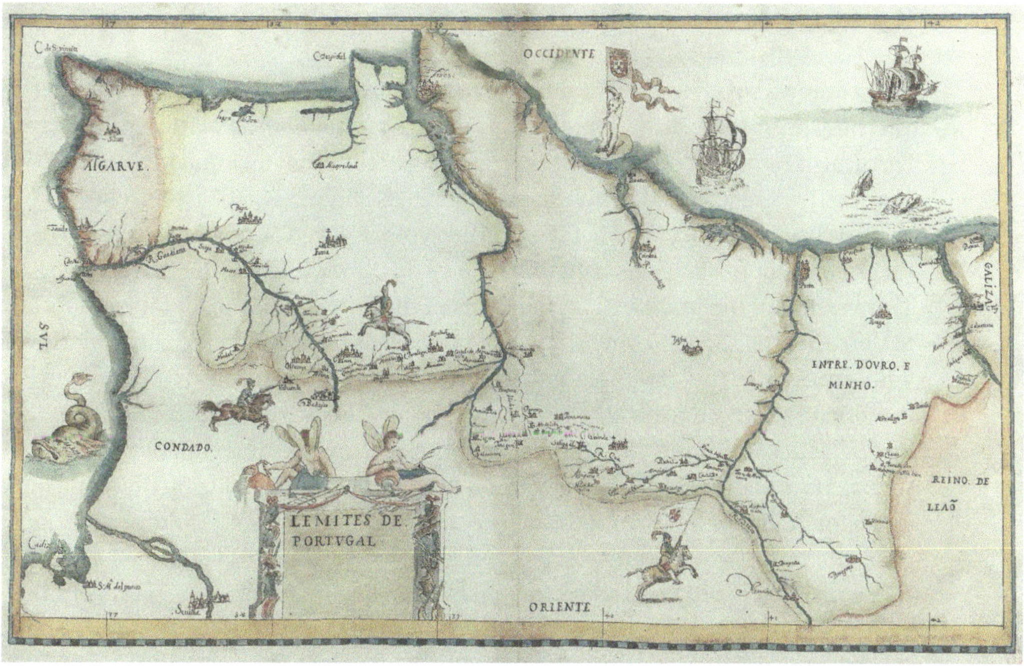

Fig. 10.1 Brás Pereira, *Fronteira de Portugal fortificada pellos reys deste Reyno*, 1642. Biblioteca Nacional de Portugal, Ms. IL 192, c. 1

The unexplored world between the pages of the *Book of Fortresses* can also be expressed through a more specific set of research questions. For instance, where was Duarte de Armas standing when he framed each perspective drawing? Similarly, what might have influenced his choices for vantage points? Also, where does the book fit within other platial image types that were emerging in the early modern period such as plans, views and chorographies? As a draughtsman, how did de Armas communicate the relationship between individual fortifications and the larger national border? Finally, are there patterns in Duarte de Armas' images that only emerge when they are structured outside of the codex form? Given these questions, it was determined early on in the process that digital methods – in particular 3D modelling and geographic information systems (GIS) – offered the best opportunity to perform a deep, source-specific study of the book at multiple spatial scales. These interventions are often referred to as reconstructions, but I will demonstrate below that *translation* is a more appropriate term for these methods. After a short summary of the form of the *Book of Fortresses* and its brief historiography, this article will explain how landscape and place theories, when applied through digital methods, are particularly useful for an interpretation of this book.

Duarte de Armas and the Form of the *Book of Fortresses*

There are two surviving original copies of the *Book of Fortresses*. The most complete, and best-preserved codex (known as codex A) is held at the National Archive of Portugal in Lisbon.[3] Codex A contains 120 perspective drawings and 51 plan drawings of 55 castles and fortified towns on the Portuguese border with Castile, followed by a short written itinerary. Most of the frontier sites received two perspective drawings drawn from opposite sides, and one plan of the inner ward of the castle or citadel. This version of the book will be the focus of the current article, but it is important to note that the second copy, known as Codex B, is not identical to the first.[4] It was 'rediscovered' in the national library in Madrid in 1910, is on flax paper rather than the parchment of Codex A, and is slightly smaller. Codex B is in worse condition than its Portuguese counterpart, and its perspective drawings are generally annotated with text rather than with images, but it was undoubtedly made by the same hand as Codex A. It can be assumed that the artist produced a series of drawings from each site in the field, then selected and transferred them to vellum (Codex A) or flax paper (Codex B) upon his return to Lisbon. Fortunately, two separate, faithful facsimiles of Codex A have been produced in recent years, and a full scan of Codex B is available for download from the National Archive in Madrid. The GIS and spatial visualizations described below are indebted to these excellent reproductions.

There is very little agreement about Duarte de Armas as an artist, or even if it is appropriate to call his work 'art'. Recent scholarship has made a point of emphasizing Duarte de Armas' role as a surveyor, 'helpful bureaucrat' and 'traveller-ethnographer' to draw attention to the practical, political purpose of the *Book of Fortresses*.[5] Conversely, Manuel da Silva Castelo Branco is quick to point out in his introduction to the 1997 facsimile of the book that Duarte de Armas was given the commission because he was trained as a surveyor and cartographer, and because his work demonstrated 'simple but well-trained technique, and [...] Art!'[6] His cartographic training is especially relevant for a spatial/platial study of the book, but it is also problematic because de Armas chose several multidimensional visualizations that do not resemble the kinds of metric chorographic views and plans that emerged later in the sixteenth century. The first terrestrial map of Portugal is still thought to have been made by Fernando Alvares Seco in 1561 (more than 50 years after Duarte de Armas' book); yet the *Book of Fortresses* coincides with the explosion of cartography associated with Portuguese

3 Arquivo Nacional Torre do Tombo, Lisbon (ANTT), Ms. 159. A fascimile of the manuscript exists, see de Armas, *Livro das fortalezas. Facsimile*.

4 'Codex B' (Ms. 9241) is preserved in the Biblioteca Nacional de Espana.

5 Cruxen, 'O viajante Duarte de Armas e sua obra imagética sobre a fronteira', 83-84.

6 De Armas, *Livro das fortalezas. Facsimile*, 1.

exploration under the reign of Manuel I.[7] It is very likely that Duarte de Armas was capable of making meticulous, near-orthographic drawings of coastlines, and there is supposition that he was employed to do this in North Africa, but this skill does not translate to the kind of survey that would have been necessary to map the terrestrial border with Castile.[8] Nonetheless, as with all attempts to categorize the *Book of Fortresses*, it is difficult to dismiss the idea that Duarte de Armas was attempting to 'map' the Portuguese border with Castile, despite the apparent anachronism of this term.[9]

Rather than reduce Duarte de Armas' work to a single spatial formula – a 'map' – it is more appropriate to describe his work as a discursive, multiscale visualization. His primary purpose was to capture and describe the individual places he travelled to, but he also sought to create a holistic impression of the entire border. In practical terms, Duarte de Armas' mission, as prescribed by his patron, Manuel I, was motivated by three factors: (1) to report on the progress of fortification repairs and expansions already begun by Manuel I, (2) to identify additional sites that needed repair, and (3) to *inscribe* the territory, that is, to make claims of sovereignty on Portugal's border by virtue of drawing its limits. If we accept that Duarte de Armas' name reflected a second aspect of his occupation – that of military engineer – it seems likely that he would have had his own side interests in documenting the state of the border. He may have seen future contracts for new fortifications among the partially ruined walls of the border fortresses, but there is no surviving reference to him being employed in this way after the completion of the book.[10] Consequently, we can speculate that he may have been motivated to exaggerate the appearance of ruined walls, but the historical evidence is slight. In the end, an effective analysis of the *Book of Fortresses'* purpose requires a deep dive into its formal characteristics; but more importantly, I argue that it needs to be freed from the codex form and translated spatially in order to perceive patterns between its pages.

Historical Context

Any effort to describe the motivations behind the creation of the *Book of Fortresses* should begin with the rivalry between the kingdoms of Castile and Portugal. Rather than summarize this long and complex history here, I will sketch three main causes that might explain why Manuel I sent Duarte de Armas to gather detailed

7 Cortesão, *Cartografia e cartógrafos portugueses dos seculos XV e XVI*, 110-113.

8 On the theory of Duarte de Armas' work in Africa, see de Armas, *Livro das fortalezas. Facsimile*, 8.

9 For a detailed narrative of the history of Portuguese cartography with special attention to the sixteenth century, see Algeria et al., 'Portuguese Cartography in the Renaissance'.

10 For a description of the occupation of 'draughtsman engineer' from a contemporary Spanish perspective, see Sánchez, 'Keeping Secrets and Mapping Frontiers'.

information about his border fortresses. In short, these reasons include Portugal's new wealth, its uncertain independence in the years prior to 1509, and Manuel's instinct to centralize his kingdom.

From a distant, satellite-scale perspective, the border between Spain and Portugal has been remarkably long-lasting and stable compared with others in Europe. With the exception of periods of dynastic war and invasion from Spain, the spatial definition of Portugal has remained roughly the same shape since the Treaty of Alcañices between Denis I of Portugal and Fernando IV of Castile in 1297.[11] The continued importance of this treaty is well illustrated by the appearance of three fortresses in Duarte de Armas' book that were also directly named in the treaty itself. In 1297 Olivença (now in Spain) was gained by Denis I, and Moura and Serpa (now in Portugal) were gained by Fernando IV. By 1509 all three of these fortified villages were held by Portuguese castellans who were named in the *Book of Fortresses*.

Like all of the other Iberian kingdoms, Portugal was defined by castles and fortified towns over the course of the Christian 'reconquest' of Muslim Iberia during the tenth through fifteenth centuries. Over time, the borders between the Christian kingdoms developed settlement patterns that were dependent on military garrisons and architectural signalling of sovereign space. On one level, Duarte de Armas' goal was to provide a transferable set of images that could create a mental image of this architectural signalling, while accounting for the military strength of each fortress. On another level, the *Book of Fortresses* could be described as an insurance document, an attempt to assess the places at greatest risk of allowing a change in the limits of the kingdom through their state of disrepair.

In 1509, Portugal had a lot more to insure than it had in previous decades. On 10 July 1499, the return of Vasco da Gama's ship the *Berrio* confirmed that the Portuguese had successfully navigated around Africa and landed at the source of the spice trade. In 1505, the sixth armada to India returned, demonstrating regular control of the spice trade. Between nine and thirteen caravels and carracks returned each summer over these years with profits that transformed Portugal from a largely ignored backwater into the richest kingdom in Europe. A Venetian in Lisbon named Girolamo Priuli was quick to note the potential impact of the return of the second Armada to India when he wrote:

> This news made the whole Venetian city dead with fear, that is, the merchants and others who considered the future and what damage this would be to the city, to have lost the [spice trade], [...] which thing was more important to the Venetian state than the Turkish war, and than any other war that might occur.[12]

11 Ackerlind, *King Denis of Portugal*, 10.

12 As quoted by Dursteler, 'Reverberations of the Voyages of Discovery in Venice', 45-46.

Manuel I was well aware of the consequences of what appeared to be a yearly influx of wealth in the early sixteenth century, especially when compared to his immediate neighbour to the east and north. The unified kingdoms of Castile and Aragon remained aggressive in the Americas, but the kingdom would not reap financial rewards until the return of the first 'treasure ship' of Aztec gold in 1521. Being the object of Castile's envy placed greater importance on the border as a possible deterrent to invasion.

Portugal had been swept up in the War of the Castilian Succession in 1475-1479, and while the border between Portugal and Castile had generally moved back to the limits established in 1297, war over Iberian unification was prevented as much through marriage as it was through fortification. Manuel I was married to Ferdinand and Isabella of Spain's first daughter, Isabella, but she died in childbirth. He then married their third daughter, Maria, all with the hope that the heir of either of these unions would be heir of the combined kingdoms, thus preventing future wars between Portugal and Spain. By 1506, the future Charles V of Spain (son of Joanna, second daughter of Ferdinand and Isabella), had survived his infancy. Consequently, despite the efforts of Manuel I and Ferdinand and Isabella to prevent future Iberian wars through dynastic alliances, the fact that Charles I was a Hapsburg, and ahead of any heir of Manuel I for the Castilian crown, meant that Portugal would have a rival to the east and north in the immediate future. The Habsburg connection brought to Spain wealth and an expansionist record that must have influenced Manuel's decision to assess his fortifications.

The *Book of Fortresses* also aligns with Manuel I's other efforts to centralize monarchical power in Portugal through new laws and standards. For example, at the end of the sixteenth century, Manuel I fixed the kingdom's measurement standards. This initative involved sending bronze weights to the towns of his kingdom, and fixing length measurements based on the *vara*, a yard that was roughly 1.1 metres long. Duarte de Armas meticulously noted these *varas* and their 1/5 division (the *palmo*) in his fortress plans (Figure 10.2(a-b)). Moreover, it is likely that Duarte de Armas drew himself and his servant holding long measuring poles nineteen times in the perspective drawings to bring attention to the fact that he was using these new measurements in his survey (Figure 10.3). By meticulously measuring the border fortifications using Manuel's *varas* and *palmo*s, Duarte de Armas articulated a connection between the periphery and the centre of the kingdom in a spatial language that was inextricably associated with the king.

At a wider scale, the *Book of Fortresses* is a quintessential example of 'inscribed space' – a mode of claiming territory by virtue of drawing its limits. Unlike the closely guarded coastline maps of the African and Asian coasts that were commissioned by Manuel I throughout his reign, the *Book of Fortresses* was likely a less secretive document. It had similarities with coastline maps through its use of a linear itinerary

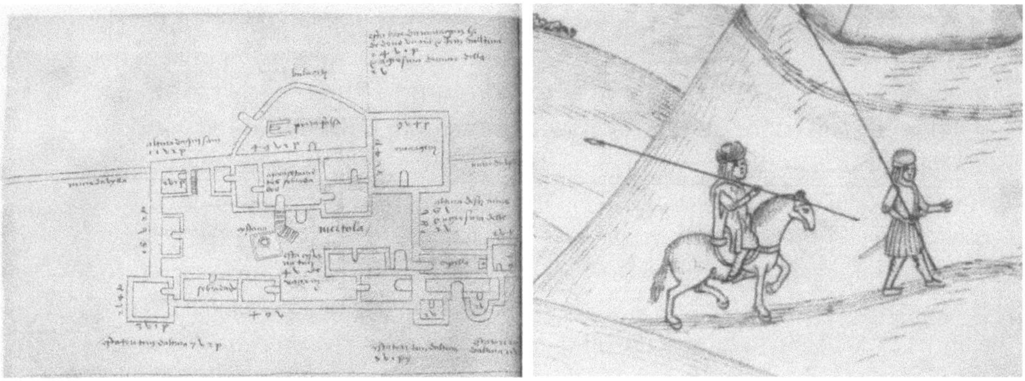

Fig. 10.2 Duarte de Armas, *Book of Fortresses*. Arquivo Nacional Torre do Tombo, Lisbon, Ms. 159
a) Plan for Mertola Castle (c. 122). Note the identification of lengths and heights in *varas* (v) and *palmos* (p)
b) Detail of Duarte de Armas and his servant at the fortress of Ouguela (c. 30)

Fig. 10.3 Duarte de Armas, south-facing view of Almeida castle, bearing the personal standard of Manuel I and the customary flag of the kingdom of Portugal. *Book of Fortresses*, Arquivo Nacional Torre do Tombo, Lisbon, Ms. 159, c. 74.

of roughly equidistant stops to aid navigation, but it is more appropriate to think of the *Book of Fortresses* as an argument than as a tool. Duarte de Armas could not have chosen a blunter symbolic assertion of Portuguese sovereignty than his enormously exaggerated and meticulously drawn flags at the top of each fortification (Figure 10.3).[13] Similarly blunt statements of authority can be seen in the common appearance of gallows or pillories in 29 of the book's perspective drawings. In a similar vein, Duarte de Armas was careful to record the name of the local governor of each fortress (above the flag) at a time when Manuel I was also issuing 596 new charters in the kingdom. Doubtless there is more that a deeper dive into the political context of early-sixteenth-century Portugal can tell us about the motivations for the *Book of Fortresses*, but in most cases, these influences appear to fall into the categories of new wealth, uncertain independence and centralized standardization.

A 'Transitional' Understanding of the *Book of Fortresses*

The term used to characterize the *Book of Fortresses* most frequently in recent scholarship is 'transitional'. In his 2015 dissertation, Edison Cruxen pointed to transition as the common denominator linking visual, architectural, geographic and historical analyses of the book.[14] Beginning with the book as a source of architectural history, Cruxen successfully argued that the best way to describe the fortresses and towns in the book is to attribute them to a period between the end of medieval castle building and the beginning of early modern fortress construction. The choice of 'transitional' rather than 'hybrid' is important in this case because Duarte de Armas' drew castles that were mostly built during the twelfth, thirteenth and (especially) fourteenth centuries. He was careful to note the appearance of round embrasures (in 35 of the fortresses) and other human-scale modernizations of the buildings, but only one out of the 55 border fortresses (Miranda do Douro) had even a prototype bastion that would become the hallmark of modern fortress building in the early modern period (Figure 10.4(a)).[15] The castles still had exterior curtain walls that were thin and tall in comparison to later sixteenth-century standards, and keeps still appeared to be the symbolic and practical centres of defence. In terms of massing and plan, these castles belonged to the period of King Denis (ruled 1279-1325) far more than Manuel I (ruled 1495-1521). Cruxen usefully noted that the depiction of rounded embrasures in Duarte de Armas' drawings was only

13 Manuel I ordered the substantial enlargement of Almeida castle just a year prior, in 1508.

14 Cruxen, 'A (re) construção de representações de uma paisagem fronteiriça fortificada em transição', 16.

15 Ibid., 160.

Fig. 10.4 Duarte de Armas, Book of Fortresses, Arquivo Nacional Torre do Tombo, Lisbon, Ms. 159
a) North-facing view of 'prototype' bastion at the fortress of Miranda do Douro, detail (c. 84)
b) North view of Vinhais, showing foundations dug for new gunner towers (c. 92)

the most exaggerated and clearly symbolized example of transitional military architecture in the book.[16] Other features, like the unbuilt foundations of evenly spaced, rounded gunner towers at Vinhais show that de Armas was careful to note larger scale transitions that were built to address the increased availability of gunpowder and artillery (Figure 10.4(b)).

Problematically, the round tower foundations at Vinhais are some of the only examples of *additive* architectural transitions in the book. De Armas' most common depiction of the fortresses shows them in a static state of disrepair or actively falling apart. The state of vulnerability is shown literally with broken walls, and sometimes more creatively with birds nesting near broken towers (Figure 10.5(a)), grass growing from the tops of low walls (Figure 10.5(b)), abandoned farmhouses (Figure 10.5(c)), and church buildings with trees growing immediately adjacent to the castle (Figure 10.5(d)).

Of the 110 perspective drawings of border fortifications in the book, 71 depicted ruined walls, towers or keeps (Figures 10.6(a-b)). The percentage is higher at the site level, as 41 out of 55 of the border fortresses had ruined walls in at least one drawing. As a viewer, the effect of so many detailed renderings of ruined walls alongside meticulous, sharply defined and crenellated walls and towers is an overall sense that the border fortresses have vulnerabilities, but they are worthy and deserving of repair. Taken further, the largely medieval-era fortifications are 'ready' for a transition into structures capable of enabling and defending against firearms.

'Transitional' has also been employed to characterise Duarte de Armas' modes of representing places and spaces visually. In comparison to the architectural transitions in the *Book of Fortresses*, the binary of 'medieval' and 'early modern' is less

16 Ibid., 128.

Fig. 10.5 Duarte de Armas, Book of Fortresses, Arquivo Nacional Torre do Tombo, Lisbon, Ms. 159
a) South-facing view of the Fortress of Nisa, with detail of Albatross nesting near a partially ruined tower (c. 48)
b) East-facing view of Montalvão castle, with detail showing grass growing from the ruined foundations (c. 51)
c) Detail of an abandoned farmhouse near the fortress of Portelo (c. 100)
d) North-facing view of the fortress of Idanha-a-Nova, with detail of growing trees (c. 54)

Fig. 10.6 Duarte de Armas, *Book of Fortresses*, Arquivo Nacional Torre do Tombo, Lisbon, Ms. 159
a) South-facing view of Castelo Mendo with a detail of crumbling towers (c. 69)
b) North-facing view of Castelo Mendo with detail of crumbling walls (c. 70)

useful when looking at the pictorial aspect of the book as a composite of plans and views. The movement from symbolic, discursive depictions of spaces and places to mathematical perspective and empirical drawing was extremely uneven in Europe in the fifteenth and sixteenth centuries, and the field of cartography was caught in its own equally fluid state of transition. Nonetheless, the temptation to define Duarte de Armas' 'idiosyncrasies' as a form of lingering medievalism in a country that was geographically distant from the humanistic centres elsewhere in Europe can be difficult for viewers to overcome. For example, Duarte de Armas clearly does not use single-point perspective in his views; he always exaggerates the heights of towers and keeps, and his plans contain precise measurements, but they are not scaled drawings. De Armas' fortress plans are geometrically simplified diagrams of the overall shape of the inner wards of each castle with precise annotations containing their dimensions. Partially because historians still perceive the medieval and early modern eras as paradigms in conflict, de Armas' pictorial decisions are seen as caught between the rationality of the modern state on one hand and the amalgamated ideal/real world of the middle ages on the other. Through this lens, it is understandable that Duarte de Armas' multi-viewpoint perspective drawings, the lack of a planimetric map of the sites in the book, and his highly personal sense of proportion seem to lack the logic and systemization of his patron, Manuel I, which in turn (mistakenly) leads to the conclusion that the *Book of Fortresses* is *almost* early modern, or struggling with a paradigm shift.[17]

The *Book of Fortresses* could certainly be described as transitional in the geographic sense, but in this case the term should be applied more metaphorically than literally. All borders are transitional, and Duarte de Armas' manner of describing the Castilian-Portuguese border emphasized the role of fortifications in defining where the transitions took place. There is not a more obvious example of border signalling in the book than the aforementioned flags that Duarte de Armas drew at the tops of each fortification (Figures 10.3 and 10.8). Again, like the meticulous drawings of broken walls, there is a clear hierarchy of effort in the natural folding curves and tight patterns of de Armas' flags, which draw the viewer's eye and underscore the importance of identifying each castle's ownership. Additional, and no less blunt assertions of sovereignty include the drawings of gallows on distant hilltops and pillories raised up unnaturally high inside many of the towns (Figures 10.7(a-b)). The placement of the gallows at the highest points in the landscape was potentially both observational on de Armas' part, as well as symbolic. These structures were symbols of swift, threatening punishment, and acted as highly

17 John Pickles summarizes the connection between periodization, representation and world view in his *A History of Spaces*.

Fig. 10.7 Duarte de Armas, *Book of Fortresses*, Arquivo Nacional Torre do Tombo, Lisbon, Ms. 159
a) South-facing view of the fortress of Penha Garcia (c. 60). Note the appearance of the gallows on hilltop to the right of the fortress; b) North-east view of town of Mogadouro, with detail of pillory (c. 79).

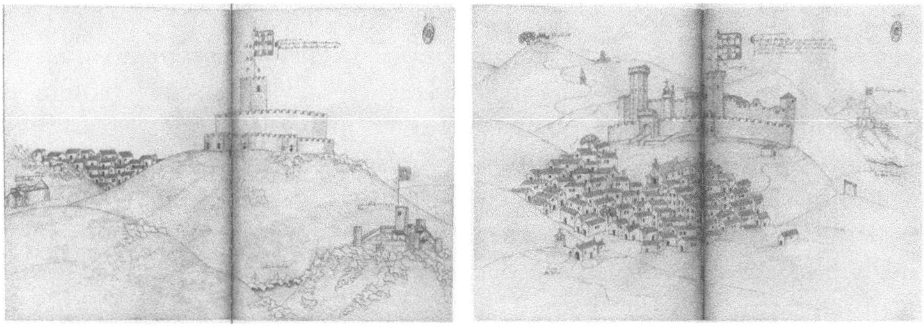

Fig. 10.8 Duarte de Armas, *Book of Fortresses*, Arquivo Nacional Torre do Tombo, Lisbon, Ms. 159
a) North-west-facing view of the fortress of Salvaterra do Extremo (c. 57). Note the subtle identification of the river that separates Salvaterra from the nearby Castilian fortress of Penafiel. This is one of the only fortresses that was likely drawn by Duarte de Armas while he stood (or projected himself) into Castilian territory; b) North-east-facing view of the fortress and town of Freixo de Espada a Cinta (c. 77). Note the depiction of Duarte de Armas and his servant travelling in the middle-distant hills.

visible statements that the associated castle was capable of executing the king's laws in an otherwise permeable space.

De Armas also used the natural environment to express a sense of transitional sovereignty – especially through his rendering of rivers and bridges (Figure 10.8(a)). These natural, linear markers allowed de Armas to depict Portuguese and Castilian castles and towns on either side of the border at almost the same scale. The width of the border was visualized as being especially thin in these images, and they effectively captured the chess match of castle and counter castle that often governed settlement patterns on the border. Conversely, the distant hilltops that either do or do not include a rival castle with a miniature Castilian flag were nearly always drawn at a very small scale, with larger, trail-covered hills in the middle ground. This middle ground of rolling hills represents the overlapping, transitional space of the border where Duarte de Armas and his servant are shown travelling over in several of the drawings (Figure 10.8(b)). In summary, Duarte de Armas was tasked with capturing a border whose permeability and rigidity was as varied as the landscapes surrounding each castle. By making sure to capture the sense of place in each of the fortress drawings, he sought to visualize a highly qualitative concept – the ways that a traveller might know when they transitioned from Castilian to Portuguese territory.[18]

Architectural Typology

The theme of transition is only one of the ways that scholars have attempted to treat the *Book of Fortresses* as a holistic source. Another popular approach to the book has been to break each of the fortresses into plan types. This practice has been particularly attractive for archaeologists, whose purposes are to mine the *Book of Fortresses* for information about Portuguese and Iberian castle building in general, and the more poorly preserved fortresses in the book, in particular. These typologies create rules based on different forms and features such as the general shape of each fortress plan, the number of wards, the appearance of round, square or polygonal towers, or whether the outer walls conformed to the terrain. What holds these sets of rules together is that they are based more on Duarte de Armas' plan drawings than his perspective views.

The most exhaustive morphological categorizations of de Armas' fortresses belong to João Gouveia Monteiro and Luis Miguel Maldonado de Vasconcelos Correia.[19] According to Monteiro's survey, the *Book of Fortresses* represents the end of the medieval period, and thus makes a perfect source for a morphological analysis of the most common configurations of medieval castle plans, keep types, door shapes, and other distinguishing features. Conversely, for Correia, de Armas' book represents a proto-modern or perhaps transitional moment of fortress building that just begins to account for gunpowder and artillery. Consequently, for Correia, Monteiro's categorization of plan types and irregular features in the *Book of Fortresses*, while 'tedious', helps to make the case that the next (late sixteenth century) phase of fortress building (represented by regularized, star-shaped plans) was a particularly dramatic rupture.[20]

These typological works bear little resemblance to the place-based, virtual and experiential approach proposed by this article, but the instinct to extract and

18 For an account of the phenomenological and social effects of living near and passing through 'thick' and 'thin' borders, see Haselsberger, 'Decoding Borders'.

19 Monteiro, *Os castelos portugueses dos finais da idade média*; de Vasconcelos Correia, 'Castelos em Portugal retrato do seu perfil arquitectónico (1509-1949)'.

20 De Vasconcelos Correia, 'Castelos em Portugal retrato do seu perfil arquitectónico (1509-1949)', 114.

structure features of the book has been inspirational for the geographic information system (GIS) portion of the digital project.[21] In other words, the statistics describing how many round, oval, rectilinear or irregularly planned fortresses appear in the *Book of Fortresses* have been less useful to this study than knowledge of *where* these plans appeared.[22] Further, the current study has generally avoided wading into the debate over specific fortress plan types due to the high number of sites whose plans were primarily affected by the natural topography. More importantly, the narrow focus on de Armas' plans actually exacerbates the spatial disconnect that already exists between the perspective views and plans in the book, and between the sites themselves. Consequently, the GIS uses a schema that tags individual features in the entire book – in landscape views, plans, and the itinerary – to detect spatial patterns regardless of where they appear in the book.

Border Visualization

The instinct to create a Cartesian map from the sites in the *Book of Fortresses* was first acted upon in 1642, when Brás Pereira began his watercolour facsimile of the book with a similarly styled map of Portugal (Figure 10.1).[23] The inclusion of knights on horseback, and the iconographic depiction of the castles in this colourful map were clearly inspired by the 'medieval' form of de Armas' drawings, but the fact that de Armas did not include (and would not have included) a planimetric map in his book cannot be overstated. Even before J.B. Harley recommended that historians of cartography 'deconstruct the map', we have known to be wary of teleological interpretations of early modern maps and views, especially for examples that may appear less 'scientific' or 'objective' in comparison to modern cartography.[24] Duarte de Armas' views would not be 'improved' by single-point perspective, and his plan drawings would not retain the same meaning if they were translated into scaled floor plans. Nonetheless, the lack of a map in the original book is what began the feeling of spatial discomfort that inspired the current study. Put simply, it may seem paradoxical to argue that the *Book of Fortresses* should be read on its own

21 For an up-to-date account of the concept of 'spatial humanities' and the argument for place-based analyses that acknowledge advances in computational methods, see Dunn, 'Spatial Humanities in the Digital Age'.

22 For another example of the meticulous work devoted to the 'peculiarities' of castle architecture on the border between Spain and Portugal, see Villena, 'Elementos peculiares en los castillos medievales de la Raya Portugal-España'.

23 Pereira, *Fronteira de Portugal fortificada pellos reys deste Reyno*, Biblioteca Nacional de Portugal (Inv. Nr. 1690359).

24 Harley, 'Deconstructing the Map', 2.

terms while also seeking to 'translate' Duarte de Armas' image of the border, but that is the approach proposed in this article.

Viewers do not need to look much further than the dotted line separating Spain from Portugal in Pereira's map to see how much the concept of a political border had changed in the century and a half between de Armas' original, first-hand survey, and Pereira's copy of it. The idea that the *Book of Fortresses* was primarily a visualization of a political border has deep roots, and it continues to be one of the three most common lenses through which the book is still viewed. Despite the ubiquity of this approach, any connection between de Armas' book and the history of late medieval borders still requires additional grounding in theories of sovereign space.

Castle historian Ronnie Ellenblum cut to the core of the problem succinctly with the title of his 2002 article 'Were There Borders and Borderlines in the Middle Ages?'[25] His subject was the Latin Kingdom of Jerusalem, but his conclusions regarding the relationship between castles and border formation are clearly applicable to the *Book of Fortresses*. Ellenblum claimed that most descriptions of medieval borders have been anachronistic, subconsciously shaped by a modern, deeply inscribed image of political boundary lines, and the laws governing political space.[26] A state without a defined boundary line is difficult for us to imagine, and despite a wealth of research on the permeability and non-linearity of pre-modern European frontiers, images of Hadrian's Wall, or the Roman *limes* loom larger in our historical memory than they should. Ellenblum and others have convincingly argued that medieval (and early modern) borders, such as the political, economic and religious ones on the periphery of the Christian Kingdom of Jerusalem in the twelfth and thirteenth centuries, were defined by centres rather than lines, and that these centres were primarily created through castles and their garrisons. While the phenomenon of castellation on medieval frontiers has been largely accepted, many historians are also eager to replace political borderlines with 'chains' of castles or 'networks' of centres, thereby perpetuating the idea of a linear border. A less anachronistic way to view these castles is to consider them as radiating centres whose power waxed and waned, overlapped and became isolated over time. The projection of a castle's influence was not measurable in the modern sense, but there are means of analysing how, and more importantly *where*, a series of castles might have projected their influence over the landscape, and how well connected these centres were.

In previous work on the formation of Iberia's medieval frontiers during the long Christian 'Reconquest' I have argued for the use of viewshed analysis as a means to comprehend how the mostly hilltop-sited castles of military-religious orders

25 Ellenblum, 'Were There Borders and Borderlines in the Middle Ages?'

26 Ibid., 105-106.

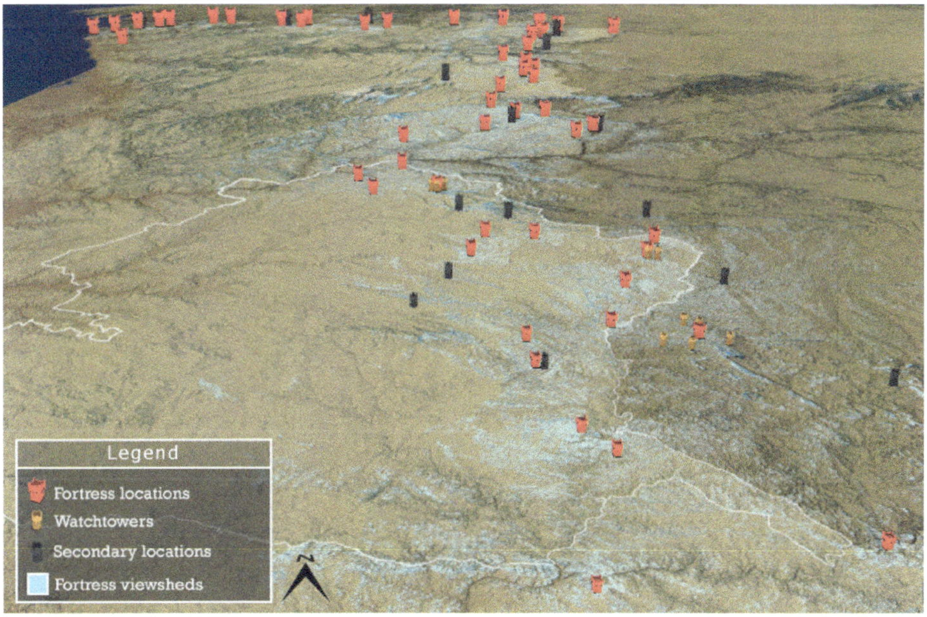

Fig. 10.9 Perspectival map showing in blue the viewsheds cast from observer locations at the top of each fortress location in the *Book of Fortresses*. This region of Alentejo Alto reveals very widely spread viewsheds. © Edward Triplett

managed to create frontier spaces between the Christian and Islamic kingdoms.[27] With similar goals of understanding Duarte de Armas' choices of vantage points in his perspective drawings and the extent to which the castles in the book formed an observable border with Spain, I ran viewshed analyses at an early stage of the GIS project. This process takes a set of point-based viewer locations (in this case the height of a person standing at the top of the keep at each castle measured by Duarte de Armas) and asks if each pixel of a 15-square-metre resolution digital elevation model (DEM) could be seen by a person standing at one of the viewer locations. Given that there is almost no reliable data to account for the vegetation in the region in the sixteenth century, I chose to use a DEM that represented a 'bare earth' version of the landscape. Ambiguities abound in this kind of study, but the process is still able to strongly suggest the shape and reach of each castle's field of view.

The viewshed analysis data are spread over a large area and it would be cumbersome to describe the results for all 55 sites, so I will summarize them by describing two patterns that emerged from these analyses. The first pattern concerns the 'raw' viewshed patterns around the border sites; the second pattern reveals the level of visible connectivity (sometimes called 'intervisibility')

27 Triplett, 'Mapping Spheres of Influence'.

Fig. 10.10 Duarte de Armas, views of Ouguela, with the Castilian castle/town of Albuquerque in the background. *Book of Fortresses*, Arquivo Nacional Torre do Tombo, Lisbon, Ms. 159, cc. 29-30

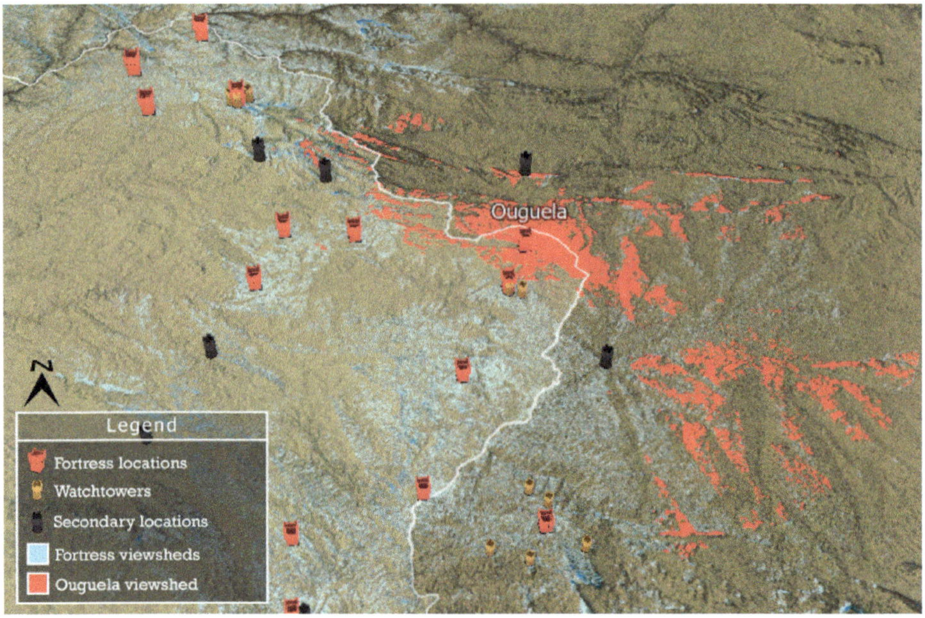

Fig. 10.11 Viewshed analysis from an observer location 10 metres above the site of Ouguela. © Edward Triplett

between the sites depicted in the book. For example, the viewsheds (in shades of blue) show that the path to Lisbon through Alentejo Alto (which had historically been used in previous invasions from Spain) was highly surveilled from multiple sites in the book (Figure 10.9). Simple heat maps can tell us that there was a higher concentration of castles in this region as well, but this two dimensional pattern does not account for the siting of these castles. The viewsheds also call attention to sites that may appear minor in the book (such as Ouguela,

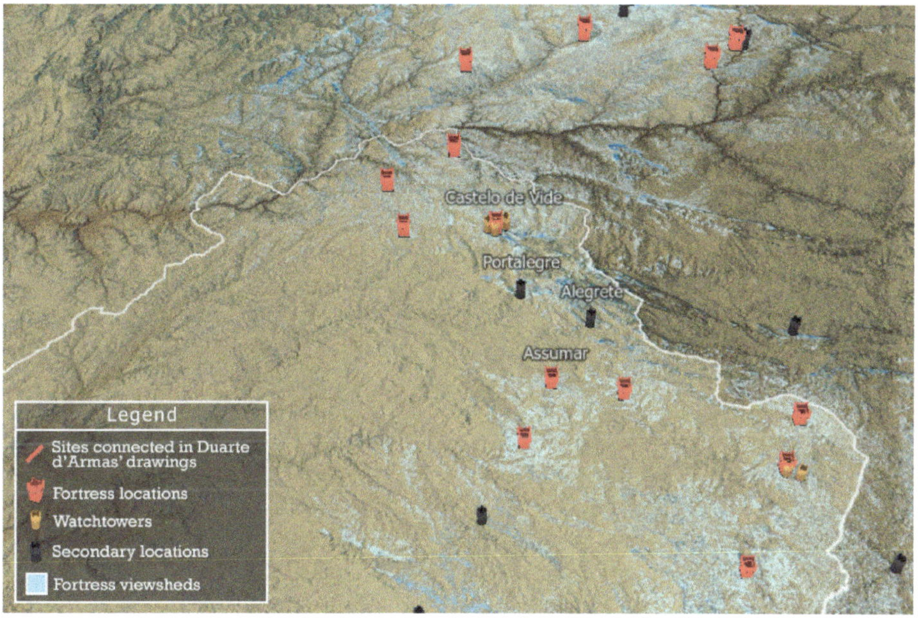

Fig. 10.12 Viewshed gap between the sites of Assumar and Castelo de Vide. Viewsheds of Portalegre and Alegrete (labelled) have been turned off to highlight the gap in visibility in the region. © Edward Triplett

Figure 10.10) but seem essential to the surveillance of the border when viewed in the GIS (Figure 10.11). The viewshed analyses only revealed one significant gap in the visible 'coverage' of the Alentejo region, between the castles of Assumar and Castelo de Vide.

Interestingly, Duarte de Armas chose to leave blank pages in the book between these sites, presumably because he intended to insert drawings of additional castles that were geographically north of Assumar and south of Castelo de Vide. The sites that historians most often speculate *should* have been drawn into these blank pages, Portalegre and Alegrete, were not included in de Armas' itinerary, nor is there any evidence that their plans were surveyed.[28] Nonetheless, given that the space between Assumar and Castelo de Vide appears to be relatively 'invisible' from de Armas' set of castles, it seems Portalegre and Alegrete may have been acknowledged silences (Figure 10.12). Consequently, it should not be assumed that this region represented a vulnerability in Portugal's border defences; rather, it appears that Duarte de Armas was justifiably aware of this gap in his book.

The GIS also reveals a great deal about the level of connectedness between the 55 border sites and between primary and secondary sites that are often drawn in the background of the perspective drawings. In total, de Armas drew sites in the

28 Cortesão, *Cartografia e cartógrafos portugueses dos seculos XV e XVI*, 3.

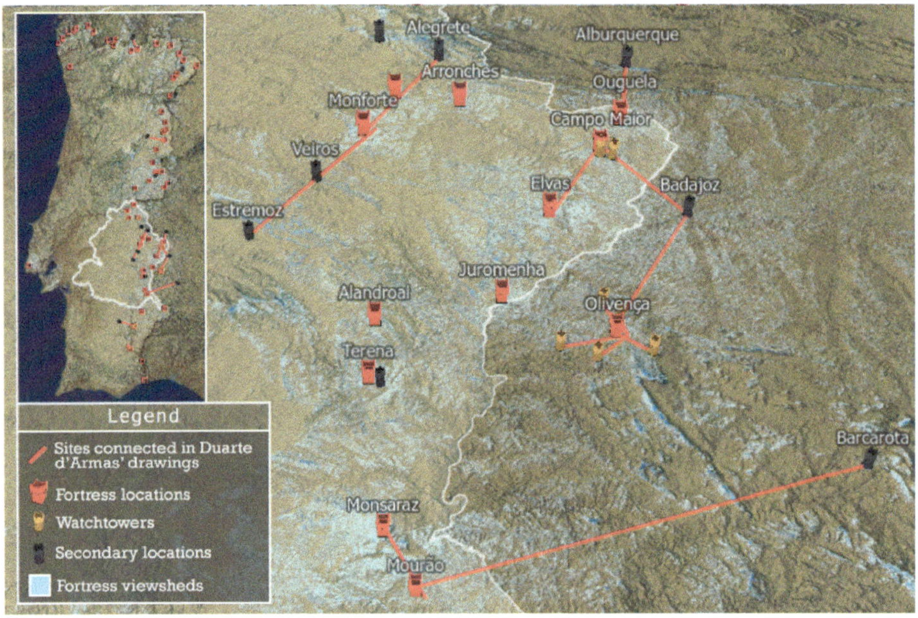

Fig. 10.13 Sites depicted in Duarte de Armas' *Book of Fortresses*. © Edward Triplett
a) With locations connected using red lines
b) Detail of clustered sites connected by Duarte de Armas in his perspective drawings

background (and occasionally in the foreground) of 28 of his perspective drawings at 25 different sites. There can be little doubt that de Armas wished to emphasize the proximity of the border in his drawings, especially in the 13 drawings containing (either iconographic or observational) images of Castilian fortresses and towns. Nonetheless, the red lines in Figure 10.13 (which connect main sites to distant Castilian and Portuguese sites if they are drawn as fortress icons in the background of one of the perspective drawings) reveal only a very subtle spatial pattern. It does not appear that de Armas was especially concerned with creating the impression of an unbroken chain of fortresses along the border (Figure 10.13(a)).

Similarly, if the viewsheds for all of the fortresses are used to create sightline analyses, it appears that Duarte de Armas does not always note these visual connections between sites in his drawings. There are fewer examples of intervisibility between castles than one would expect for a border that is described as a chain or network. Conversely, there is one area where the sites appear to be most interconnected (both by Duarte de Armas' depiction of castles in the background and via viewshed analysis): the Alentejo Alto region between the castles of Mourao and Arronches (Figure 10.13(b)). Consequently the evidence supports previous arguments that the path to Lisbon from Extremadura was denser with castles than other parts

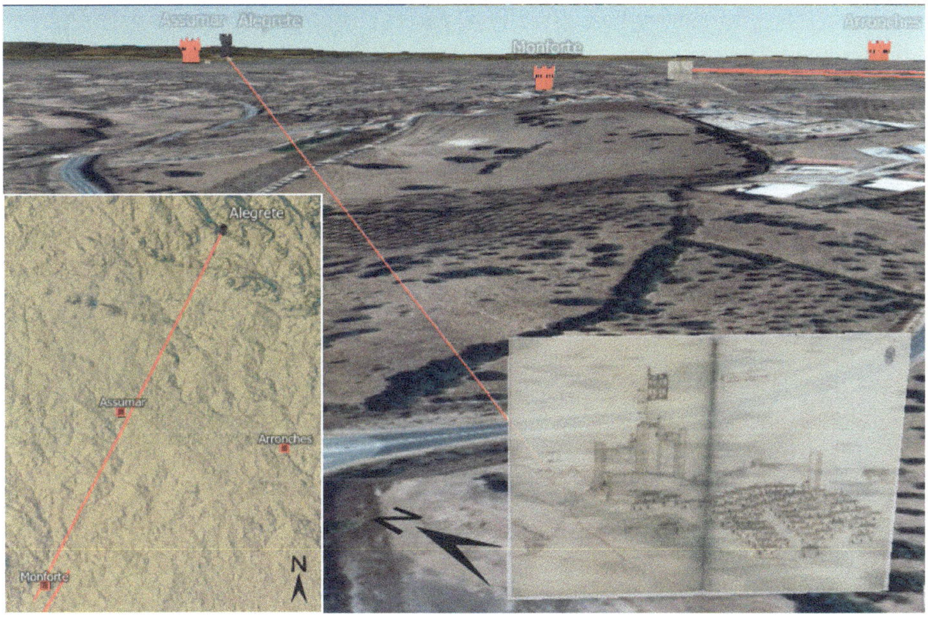

Fig. 10.14 Detail of 'billboard' north-facing view of Monforte linked to Alegrete, passing right by Assumar, which is roughly half the distance away and in the same direction as Assumar. © Edward Triplett

of the border, and that this relatively small area is the only region that Duarte de Armas appears to have purposely signalled as a 'network'.

In addition to offering further insight into de Armas' decision-making process when selecting which castles to visit and record, the GIS has introduced new questions. For instance, the lines marking distant sites in the perspective drawings reveal a peculiar pattern where Duarte de Armas occasionally decided to ignore nearby sites that are/were intervisible with the primary site, while depicting a connection with a site that is further away, and in the same direction as a site which is 'skipped over'. This 'skipping' pattern appears to the north of the previously mentioned cluster of fortresses in Alentejo Alto. In the north view of Monforte, de Armas identifies the fortress of Alegrete in the background plane (Figure 10.14). The choice to depict this castle in the background supports the idea that it was one of the castles that de Armas intended to visit and record but did not. Yet what is more surprising is that the castle of Assumar was closer, and in the same direction as Alegrete, but it was not drawn in this view. There are a few possible reasons for this, but it seems likely that if Alegrete was pointed out to Duarte de Armas in the far distance (around 24 kilometres) he was not aware that the more modest castle of Assumar was in his line of sight at about half the distance away. Alternatively, de Armas may have made a deliberate decision based on a very basic strategic and architectural hierarchy: De Armas' drawings of Assumar show that it was one of the smallest sites on his itinerary. It was also one of only a few castles that were sited in valleys, and it lacked a keep that might have stood out in the landscape. Linking Assumar to another site on the border would have elevated its apparent strategic value more than it appears to have possessed.

Single-point viewsheds have received some attention from geographers in recent years, with most agreeing that they can be too binary in their analysis of the landscape – with units of space being labelled as either visible or invisible for an entire structure. From the perspective of border castles, the location of the keep is the most logical place to set an observer point, but of course there would also have been different viewsheds for observers standing on the tops of other towers on the curtain walls. More significantly, medieval border castles often included a subnetwork of strategically sited watchtowers or *atalayas*. Duarte de Armas identified atalayas at five sites in the *Book of Fortresses*: Serpa, Mertola, Olivença, Campo Maior and Castelo de Vide. The fortress town of Olivença contained by far the most watchtowers in de Armas' drawings with five (Figure 10.15). This is hardly surprising given that Olivença was exchanged several times in treaties between Castile and Portugal, and was sited in a low valley on the opposite side of the Guadiana River from the rest of Portuguese territory. It is also the only site on Duarte de Armas' itinerary that is in modern-day Spain.

It would take an archaeological survey to find the precise locations of most of the *atalayas*, which is beyond the scope of the current project. But with the assistance of 3D GIS software and de Armas' drawings, it is possible to locate the hills that would have likely supported the towers. Given four hypothetical observation points at the tops of these hills, Olivença's apparently shallow (and therefore less assertive, or vulnerable) viewshed transforms into an important beacon of surveillance on the border (Figure 10.16).[29] More importantly, across the entire border, and especially at Castelo de Vide, the watchtowers create intervisible relationships with additional sites in the *Book of Fortresses*. It is not until these additional sightlines are added that the border begins to truly resemble a network, with most of it still concentrated around Alentejo Alto (Figure 10.17(a-b)).

29 Duarte de Armas was certain to note the towers at Olivença because they were originally commissioned by his patron Manuel I in 1500. Cruxen explains that Olivença was only the first instance of Manuel I strengthening the border with additions onto his border fortresses. In 1502 the king requested contributions from his court to build 'walls, towers and barriers' at the castles of Mourao, Arronches, Assumar, Marvao, Salvaterra, Sabugal, Alfaiates, Chaves, Melgaco, Mertola, Monsanto, Braganca and Sintra. All but two of these sites (Marvao and Alfaiates) appeared in the *Book of Fortresses*, which offers some clarity to Duarte de Armas choices on the border. See Cruxen, 'A (re) construção de representações de uma paisagem fronteiriça fortificada em transição', 96.

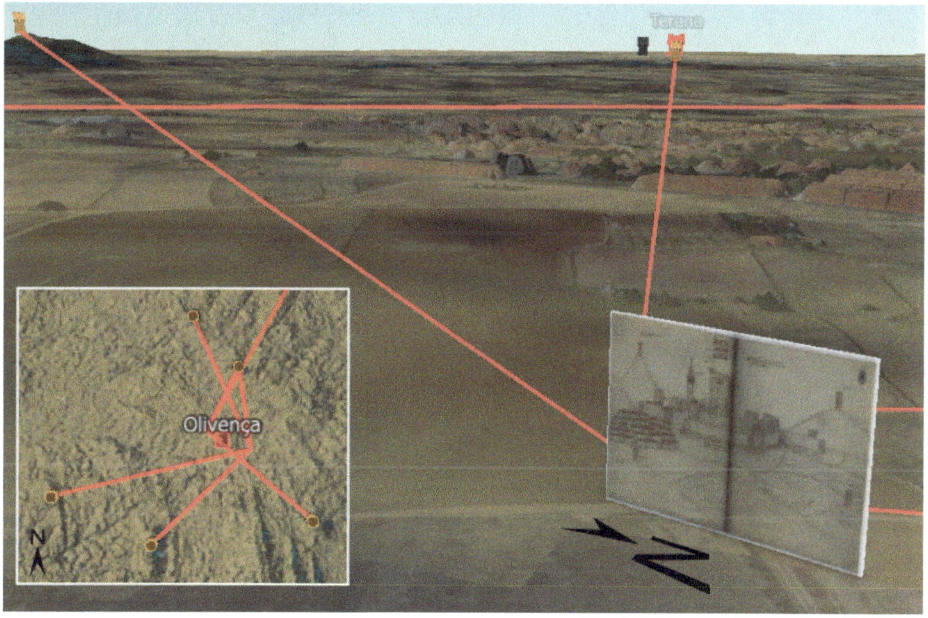

Fig. 10.15 An illustration of the use of Duarte de Armas' perspective drawings to locate watchtowers around the city of Olivença. © Edward Triplett

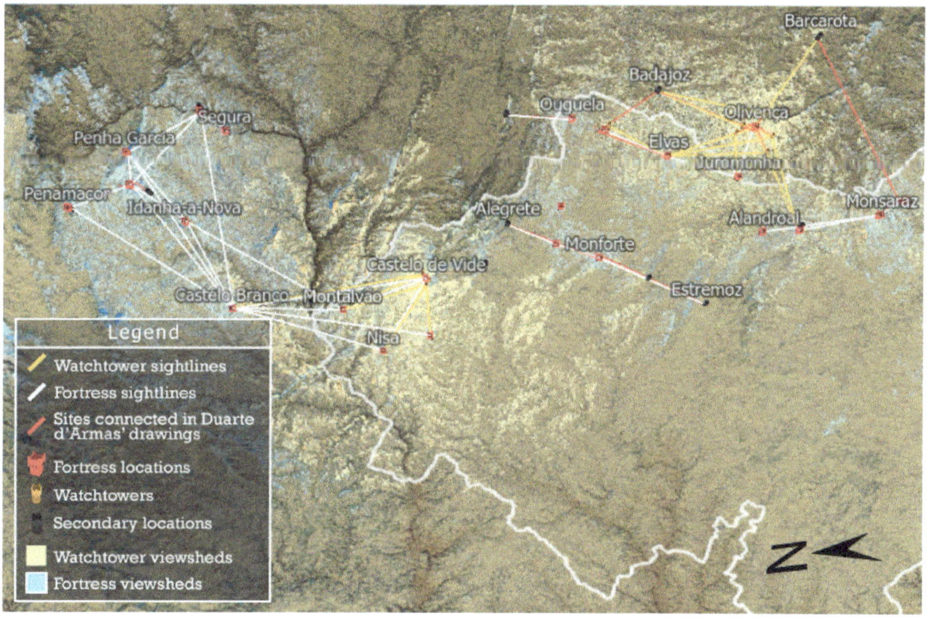

Fig. 10.16 Viewsheds after adding observers on the proposed locations of the watchtowers around Olivença and Castelo de Vide. © Edward Triplett

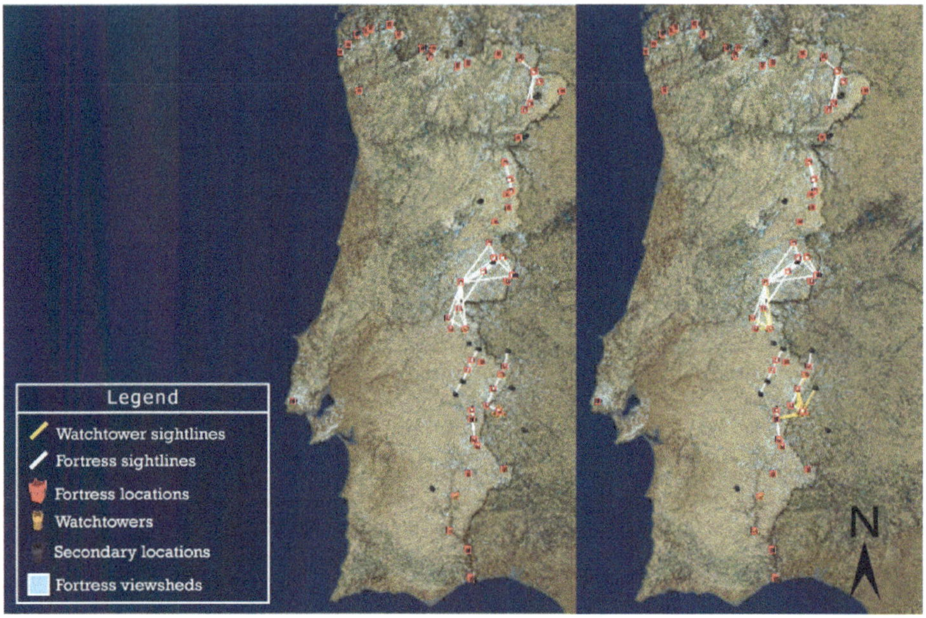

Fig. 10.17 Sightlines between fortresses drawn by Duarte de Armas. Positive intervisibility based on analysis of a 15-metre digital elevation model as previous viewshed analysis. © Edward Triplett
a) Fortress sightlines shown in white
b) Fortress sightlines shown in white with sightlines between watchtowers and fortresses shown in orange

Experiencing the *Book of Fortresses*

In addition to mapping the castle sites, which has been done before, the *Book of Fortresses* GIS project has sought to find new ways to provide spatial context for Duarte de Armas' perspectival views. The 3D GIS work below was prompted by this article's original research questions: Which hill(s) did the artist climb in order to gain particular vantage points to create his perspectival drawings? How important was it to draw the site from an elevated position versus drawing it from a more 'narrative' position, like the first view of the site from a common approach on the road? How 'panoramic' do the drawings appear to be when billboard-like digital versions of each are lined up with architectural and topographical formations in a 3D terrain (Figure 10.18)? In essence, what can be learned by 'geo-referencing' Duarte de Armas' views in the X-Z or Y-Z, as opposed to the 'top-down' X-Y plane?

The 'billboard' orientation process has helped to confirm one suspicion about Duarte de Armas' use of perspective: that he combined information from multiple vantage points into each image. At the second site on de Armas' itinerary, the view of the south-facing wall (looking north) of Alcoutim castle immediately

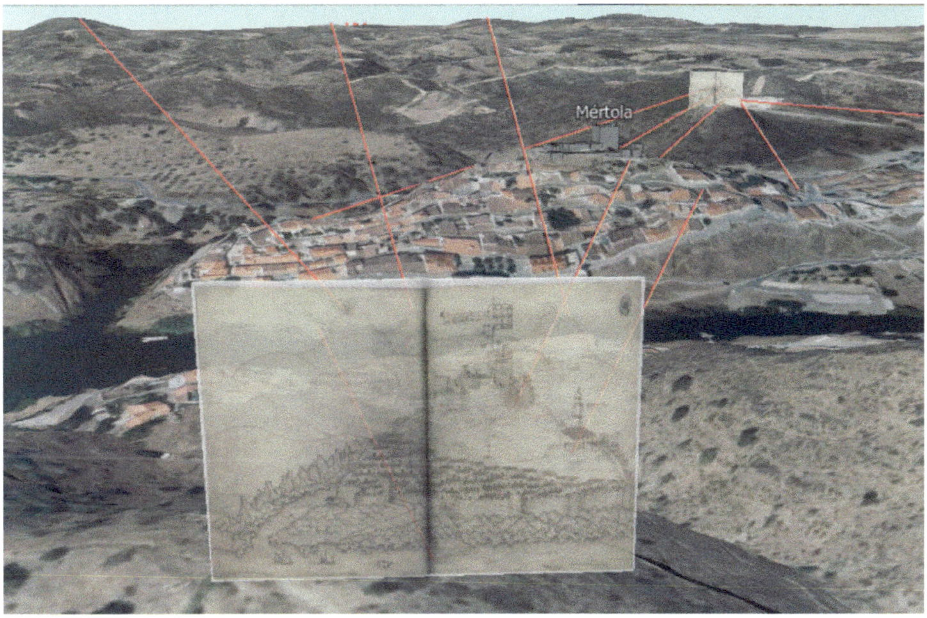

Fig. 10.18 West-facing 'billboard' image of Mertola castle in ArcGIS Pro. This is one of a select number of drawings that appears to have a single primary vantage point. © Edward Triplett

stands out as having a mysteriously incomplete, confusing sense of perspective (Figure 10.19). On the left side and centre of the drawing, the artist seems to follow standard rules of observational drawing. His vantage point was even with the top of the castle's south wall, a position that was easy to achieve thanks to a natural hill south of the castle. On the right side of drawing, de Armas offers an aerial view of the river but he depicts the houses on the opposite bank as though he were even with them in altitude. Even more strangely, he draws the ruined site of the old, 'Moorish' castle of Alcoutim on a hilltop in the distance, but he elevates this hill far above the site of the current castle. This site is 60 metres in elevation, compared to the 30 metres elevation at the newer, Portuguese castle, but the position of the 'Moorish' ruins in Duarte de Armas' drawing appears to have been forced by the more aerial perspective of the river. The hill needed to be very high to prevent the river from terminating somewhere in the sky. Especially in comparison to the other 119 perspective drawings in the book, this view of Alcoutim reveals that de Armas was willing to distort his perspective in order to deliver more useful information. Taking multiple viewpoints and reprojecting that spatial knowledge into a pseudo-perspective drawing of the river and the Castilian town on the opposite bank fits with Duarte de Armas' training as a cartographer who was tasked with drawing coastlines and the entrances of rivers. Alcoutim castle itself is also exaggerated vertically, but it is still faithful to the

Fig. 10.19 North-facing view of the Fortress of Alcoutim in ArcGIS Pro. The view presented by Duarte de Armas is placed in one of several vantage points that he likely combined in his drawing. © Edward Triplett

simple rectangular form and siting. This drawing also reveals that Duarte de Armas was capable of virtually shifting viewpoints in space, even if it is clear that he had a primary vantage point.

The task of 'lining up' Duarte de Armas' composite images must be done cautiously, with an awareness of their spatial ambiguity, and with the aid of on-site observation and data gathering. For instance, it was not until visiting Alcoutim and struggling to estimate the artist's vantage point that it became clear that de Armas' usually placed his primary vantage point in the centre of his drawings, and drew the hills that appear in the foreground by looking over his right and left shoulder. Had the artist been standing on the top of the centre hill south of Alcoutim, he would have been looking down into the castle rather than straight at its walls. It also appears that in most cases, the castles were drawn from close up, and the landscape drawn later, after de Armas backed up to take in a more panoramic view. The physical act of moving through the landscape greatly affected de Armas' processes, although most attribute his 'idiosyncratic' way of rendering places to more discursive, cartographic influences. Again, there is nothing especially unique about Duarte de Armas' technique for capturing the siting of fortresses and towns, especially given the popularity of chorographic city views in the sixteenth through the nineteenth centuries, but it does appear that the *Book of Fortresses* was a very early example of this type of place-based image making. It also appears that Duarte de Armas placed greater stock in the value of direct observation than most of the chorographers that followed him.

The 'bare earth' 3D landscape in ArcGIS Pro software is useful for finding large topographical features that can be used to search for evidence of de Armas' vantage points and movements, but this data must be considered as an exploratory, rather than an analytical environment. On-site research also has challenges when attempting to simulate an artist's point of view. Modern urban changes at a site like Serpa also make it nearly impossible to photograph parts of Duarte de Armas' views in situ. In response to this problem, the final aspect of the digital project has implemented what Karl Kullman has referred to as the 'transformative agency of the drone's-eye view'. In his article 'The Satellites' Progeny: Digital Chorography in the Age of Drone Vision', Kullman explains how images of ourselves at scale within urban places can be captured with the aid of a drone, and that these views come closer to simulating the priorities of early modern chorography than any Cartesian map can.[30] Chorography can be loosely defined as the creation of landscape-scale, rather than geographic-scale, low-altitude aerial images of places from multiple vantage points without actually leaving the ground for direct observation.[31] Early modern chorographies were far more interested in the representation of place than space, and their simulated aerial perspectives made them closer to portraits than 'maps'. Kullman's more modern, metaphorical definition states that 'chorography is analogous to a highly malleable camera lens that continuously changes viewpoints'.[32] He also cites a recent resurgence in popularity of aerial perspectives that dissolve the 'immersive horizontal eye-level view and zenithal satellite's gaze' as being a return to a human interest in representing places that orthographic maps fail to capture.[33] Put simply, Duarte de Armas' process reveals that his interests were similar to those of drone photographers: he sought to alleviate a loss of perceptual orientation in urban and natural spaces, he often situated himself within the space being mapped, and he applied a continuously varying viewpoint to form a more cohesive mental image of each place. All of these interests are hallmarks of what is often called 'virtual landscape' or an experiential approach to mapping.[34]

The drone's-eye view is not unlike the elevated perspective that we get in a 3D GIS. Drones also gain a similar perspective, but it is their ability to capture images

30 Kullman, 'The Satellite's Progeny', 4.

31 For a discussion and definition of chorography, see Shanks and Witmore, 'Echoes across the Past'.

32 Kullman, 'The Satellite's Progeny', 2.

33 Ibid.

34 For examples of these theories see, Johnson, 'Phenomenological Approaches in Landscape Archaeology'; de Boer et al., 'Virtual Historical Landscapes'; Freundschuh and Egenhofer, 'Human Conceptions of Spaces'; Dunn, 'Spatial Humanities in the Digital Age'.

Fig. 10.20 3D scene containing georeferenced photogrammetric point cloud data. This data has been invaluable for discovering vantage points used by Duarte de Armas for his perspective drawings. The fortress of Mourao, pictured here, is a typical example. The fortress of Monsaraz, which Duarte de Armas drew in the back-left of this view of Mourao, was also captured by drone and the point cloud data can be seen in the top-right corner of the figure. © Edward Triplett

with fewer occlusions that has made them especially useful for this project. In Figure 10.20 the georeferenced point-cloud data at the castle of Mourao was captured through a combination of 'terrestrial' and drone photogrammetry (Figure 10.20). The short definition of this technology is as follows: photogrammetry is similar to a reversal of the photographic process. In photography, the 3D world is captured in two dimensions. In photogrammetry, many overlapping 2D images are combined and their perspectives are calibrated against each other to rediscover where each photo was taken. This process thus uses 2D images to produce a representation of the 3D world. What is most useful about photogrammetry for the current study is that it makes it possible to simulate unobstructed views of de Armas' fortresses, and thereby test his sense of perspective against real-world data. Most importantly, it has been hugely beneficial for finding some of the multiple vantage points that were combined in his views. Finally, this data makes it possible to compare surviving masonry with 3D models that are based on de Armas' plan drawings and elevations. The results of these comparisons show that he straightened walls, simplified curves, and always exaggerated the size of towers and keeps, both vertically and in plan (Figures 10.20, 10.21, 10.22).

Fig. 10.21 CAD model of Alandroal castle, based on a tracing of Duarte de Armas' plan with extruded towers and walls according to his height measurements. This is compared to dense 3D photogrammetric data of the same site. © Edward Triplett

Fig. 10.22 Simple CAD model of Castro Marim castle based on Duarte de Armas' plans and height measurements. This is compared to dense 3D photogrammetric data of the same site. © Edward Triplett

Conclusion: Multiscale, Discursive, Malleable

The *Book of Fortresses* is an extremely complex historical source. Any discussion of the book must begin with its historical context because it offers such a remarkable image of a volatile moment in Iberia in 1509-1510. Most of this context successfully answers the question of *why* the *Book of Fortresses* was commissioned – the border was permeable, castles defined sovereign space, and Manuel I was concerned that his new wealth would make him a target for his expansionist neighbour. Nonetheless, this does not explain *how* the *Book of Fortresses* was conceived and produced. Turning its pages continues to feel like clicking through bookmarks in Google Earth, but without even the partially orienting sensation of 'jumping' between places. The codex creates a world that begs to be explored but resists modern concepts of space in favour of a more place-based, chorographic approach. In the end, the biggest hurdles to comprehension (or perhaps apprehension) of the book are its multiple, disconnected spatial scales. The plans are measured at sub-metre scale, the views are drawn at landscape-scale from two composite positions with little to no overlap between them, and all of the sites together are combined in an extremely simple written itinerary that covers the entire border with Castile.

The processes outlined in this article argue for an embrace of 3D GIS techniques to create an elastic-scale reconstruction of the book that can combine its various parts into a single system. This system cannot force or 'rectify' the book into Cartesian space without creating ahistorical and antithetical abstractions, but it is possible to use the 3D environment as a place to conduct qualitative spatial experiments. Taken further, the use of quasi-perspectival, malleable and variable viewpoints, and the creativity employed by chorographers in the early modern period share an ethos with Duarte de Armas that is echoed in the process of drone mapping. Finally, this article has emphasized the 'experiential' aspect of the book as a reaction to Duarte de Armas' own attempts to immerse himself in his subject: the 'author' or 'draughtsman' depicted himself travelling between sites nineteen times in the *Book of Fortresses* (Figure 10.23).[35] These portraits of de Armas and his servant always depict them carrying the spears or measuring sticks that were the practical and symbolic tools of their mission. By visualizing his moment of arrival or leaving, de Armas also sought to describe space through time travelled, not just through measured distances. These attempts to bring the viewer into the image should not be dismissed as merely boastful gestures; they orient the viewer between the pages of the book, and they acknowledge that connections between pages require a guide.

35 'Experiential' and 'imaginative' geographies are often described as running counter to the intentions of the developers of GIS software, yet over the past decade, geographers have begun to reassess the ability of GIS to capture these 'non-real' places and spaces through careful attention to the affordances of the medium. The tension is summarized by Aitken and Craine, 'Into the Image and beyond', 141.

Fig. 10.23 Mosaic of self-portraits of Duarte de Armas in the *Book of Fortresses*. © Edward Triplett

Bibliography

Manuscript Sources

Lisbon, Arquivo Nacional Torre do Tombo, Lisbon

Ms. 159: Duarte de Armas, *Livro das fortalezas*, 1495-1521, https://digitarq.arquivos.pt/viewer?id=3909707.

Lisbon, Biblioteca Nacional de Portugal

Ms. IL. 192: Pereira, Brás, *Fronteira de Portugal fortificada pellos reys deste Reyno*, 1642, http://purl.pt/24908.

Madrid, Biblioteca Nacional de España

Ms. 9241: Duarte de Armas, *Livro das fortalezas*, sixteenth century, http://bdh.bne.es/bnesearch/detalle/bdh0000096106.

Printed Sources

Ackerlind, Sheila R., *King Denis of Portugal and the Alfonsine Heritage* (New York: Peter Lang, 1990).

Aitken, Stuart C. and James Craine, 'Into the Image and beyond: Affective Visual Geographies and GIScience', in Meghan Cope and Sarah Elwood (eds), *Qualitative GIS: A Mixed Methods Approach* (London: Sage, 2009), 139-155, DOI:10.4135/9780857024541.n8.

Algeria, Maria Fernanda et al., 'Portuguese Cartography in the Renaissance', in David Woodward (ed.), *The History of Cartography, Vol. 3: Cartography in the European Renaissance, Part 1* (Chicago: University of Chicago Press, 2007), 975-1068.

Cortesão, Armando, *Cartografia e cartógrafos portugueses dos seculos XV e XVI. Contribuïcão para um estudo completo* (Lisbon: Edição da 'seara nova', 1935).

Cruxen, Edison Bisso, 'A (re) construção de representações de uma paisagem fronteiriça fortificada em transição: o *Livro das fortalezas* de Duarte de Armas (1509 – Portugal/ Castela)', PhD diss., Pontifícia Universidade Católica do Rio Grande do Sul, 2015.

Cruxen, Edison Bisso, 'O viajante Duarte de Armas e sua obra imagética sobre a fronteira Luso-Castelhana (1509) = The Traveler Duarte de Armas and His Imagery Work about the Portuguese-Spanish Border (1509)', *Oficina do Historiador* 5 (2012), 82-100.

de Armas, Duarte, *Livro das fortalezas* (Casal de Cambra: Caleidoscópio, 2016).

de Armas, Duarte, *Livro das fortalezas. Facsimile do Ms. da Casa Forte do Arquivo Nacional da Torre do Tombo*, ed. by Manuel da Silva Castelo Branco (Lisbon: Ediçôes Inapa, 1997).

de Boer, Arnoud et al., 'Virtual Historical Landscapes', *Research in Urbanism Series* 2 (2011), 185-203, https://doi.org/10.7480/rius.2.212.

de Vasconcelos Correia, Luís Miguel Maldonado, 'Castelos em Portugal retrato do seu perfil arquitectónico (1509-1949)', PhD diss., Universidade de Coimbra, 2011.

Dunn, Stuart E. 'Spatial Humanities in the Digital Age: The Key Debates', in *A History of Place in the Digital Age* (London: Routledge, 2019), 2-45.

Dursteler, Eric, 'Reverberations of the Voyages of Discovery in Venice, ca. 1501: The Trevisan Manuscript in the Library of Congress', *Mediterranean Studies* 9 (2000), 43-64.

Ellenblum, Ronnie, 'Were There Borders and Borderlines in the Middle Ages? The Example of the Latin Kingdom of Jerusalem', in David Abulafia and Nora Berend (eds), *Medieval Frontiers: Concepts and Practices* (London: Routledge, 2002), 105-119.

Freundschuh, Scott M. and Max J. Egenhofer, 'Human Conceptions of Spaces: Implications for Geographic Information Systems', *Transactions in GIS* 2 (1997), 361-375, doi:10.1111/j.1467-9671.1997.tb00063.x.

Harley, J.B, 'Deconstructing the Map', *Cartographica* 26 (1989), 1-20.

Haselsberger, Beatrix, 'Decoding Borders: Appreciating Border Impacts on Space and People', *Planning Theory & Practice* 15 (2014), 505-526, DOI:10.1080/14649357.2014.963652.

Johnson, Matthew H., 'Phenomenological Approaches in Landscape Archaeology', *Annual Review of Anthropology* 41 (2012), 269-284, DOI:10.1146/annurev-anthro-092611-145840.

Kullman, Karl, 'The Satellites' Progeny: Digital Chorography in the Age of Drone Vision', *Forty-Five: A Journal of Outside Research* 157 (2017), https://forty-five.com/papers/the-satellites-progeny-digital-chorography-in-the-age-of-drone-vision.

Monteiro, João Gouveia, *Os castelos portugueses dos finais da idade média: presença, perfil, conservação, vigilância e comando*, Lisboa: Edições Colibri/Faculdade de Letras de Coimbra, 1999.

Pickles, John, *A History of Spaces: Cartographic Reason, Mapping and the Geo-Coded World* (London: Routledge, 2006).

Pimenta, Alfredo, *Duarte darmas e o seu* Livro das fortalezas (Lisbon: Edição do Autor, 1944).

Sánchez, Carlos José Hernando, 'Keeping Secrets and Mapping Frontiers: Government and Image in the Spanish Monarchy', trans. by Margaret Clark, in Alicia Cámara Muñoz (ed.), *Draughtsman Engineers Serving the Spanish Monarchy in the Sixteenth to Eighteenth Centuries* (Spain: Fundación Juanelo Turriano, 2016), 143-166.

Shanks, Michael and Christopher Witmore, 'Echoes across the Past: Chorography and Topography in Antiquarian Engagements with Place', *Performance Research* 15 (2010), 97-106, DOI:10.1080/13528165.2010.539888.

Triplett, Edward, 'Mapping Spheres of Influence on Medieval Iberia's Religious Frontier via Viewshed Analysis and Cost-Distance Analysis', *Historical Geography* 45 (2017), 66-91.

Villena, L., 'Elementos peculiares en los castillos medievales de la Raya Portugal-España', *Actas del I Simpósio sobre Castillos de la Raya entre Portugal e España* (Madrid: Asociación Española de Amigos de los Castillos, 1984), 173-184.

About the Author

Edward Triplett is a Lecturing Fellow in Art, Art History and Visual Studies at Duke University. He received his PhD at the University of Virginia and also holds degrees in medieval history and 3D animation. His research interests include the history of medieval Iberia, medieval Spanish architecture, 3D visualization, GIS and photogrammetry.

Index of Names

Index of Subjects and Places

For Product Safety Concerns and Information please contact our EU representative GPSR@taylorandfrancis.com Taylor & Francis Verlag GmbH, Kaufingerstraße 24, 80331 München, Germany

* 9 7 8 1 0 4 1 1 7 7 6 9 2 *

T - #0185 - 191125 - C95 - 246/174/18 - PB - 9781041177692 - Gloss Lamination